Withdrawn

NORTHEAST
pages 24–51

ASIA
Arctic
Ocean
EUROPE
NORTH
AMERICA
AFRICA
UNITED
STATES
Atlantic
Ocean
Alaska
Hawai'i
Pacific
Ocean
SOUTH
AMERICA

Maine

Vt.

N.H.

New
York

Mass.

Conn. R.I.

Minn.

Wis.

Michigan

Pa.

N.J.

Iowa

MIDWEST
pages 82–111

Ohio

Md.

Del.

Ind.

W. Va.

Illinois

Virginia

Missouri

Kentucky

North
Carolina

Tennessee

SOUTHEAST
pages 52–81

Arkansas

South
Carolina

Georgia

Miss.

Alabama

Louisiana

Florida

Hawai'i

It's *your* country. Learn it. Love it. Explore it.

NATIONAL GEOGRAPHIC KiDS

UNITED STATES ATLAS

SIXTH EDITION

NATIONAL GEOGRAPHIC
WASHINGTON, D.C.

TABLE OF CONTENTS

FRONT OF THE BOOK

GETTING STARTED
How to Use This Atlas   6

THE PHYSICAL UNITED STATES   8
Climate   10
Natural Hazards   12

THE POLITICAL UNITED STATES   14
Population   16
People on the Move   18
Energy   20
The National Capital   22

THE NORTHEAST 24

PHYSICAL & POLITICAL MAPS   26
About the Northeast   28
Connecticut   30
Delaware   32
Maine   34
Maryland   36
Massachusetts   38
New Hampshire   40
New Jersey   42
New York   44
Pennsylvania   46
Rhode Island   48
Vermont   50

THE SOUTHEAST 52

PHYSICAL & POLITICAL MAPS   54
About the Southeast   56
Alabama   58
Arkansas   60
Florida   62
Georgia   64
Kentucky   66
Louisiana   68
Mississippi   70
North Carolina   72
South Carolina   74
Tennessee   76
Virginia   78
West Virginia   80

THE MIDWEST 82

PHYSICAL & POLITICAL MAPS   84
About the Midwest   86
Illinois   88
Indiana   90
Iowa   92
Kansas   94
Michigan   96
Minnesota   98
Missouri   100
Nebraska   102
North Dakota   104
Ohio   106
South Dakota   108
Wisconsin   110

Northeast: Maine lighthouse, p. 34

Southeast: Manatee in Florida waters, p. 62

Title page: Mountain lion; Chocorua Lake, New Hampshire; John F. Kennedy Space Center, Florida; Gateway Arch, Missouri; Zuni woman, Arizona; Statue of Liberty, New York Harbor; brown tree snake, Guam; sunflowers, North Dakota.

THE SOUTHWEST 112

PHYSICAL & POLITICAL MAPS	114
About the Southwest	116
Arizona	118
New Mexico	120
Oklahoma	122
Texas	124

THE WEST 126

PHYSICAL & POLITICAL MAPS	128
About the West	130
Alaska	132
California	134
Colorado	136
Hawai'i	138
Idaho	140
Montana	142
Nevada	144
Oregon	146
Utah	148
Washington	150
Wyoming	152

U.S. TERRITORIES 154

POLITICAL MAP & FACT BOXES	154
U.S. Caribbean Territories	154
Puerto Rico,	
U.S. Virgin Islands	
U.S. Pacific Territories	154
American Samoa	
Guam	
Northern Mariana Islands	
Other U.S. Territories	154
Baker I., Howland I.,	
Jarvis I., Johnston Atoll,	
Kingman Reef, Midway	
Islands, Navassa I.,	
Palmyra Atoll, Wake I.	
About the Territories	156

BACK OF THE BOOK

U.S. FACTS & FIGURES	158
GLOSSARY	159
POSTAL ABBREVIATIONS	159
MAP ABBREVIATIONS	160
OUTSIDE WEBSITES	160
PLACE-NAME INDEX	161
CREDITS	176

U.S. Territories: Festival dancers, American Samoa, pp. 156–157

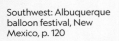

Southwest: Albuquerque balloon festival, New Mexico, p. 120

Midwest: Illinois hay field with tractor, pp. 88–89

West: Wyoming ranch, p. 152

How to Use This Atlas

This atlas is much more than just another book of maps about the United States. Of course you will find plenty of maps—country, regional, state, and territory—that have been designed to help you learn about the people and places that make up our country. But there's much more. There are essays filled with history and current facts about each state, and photos that provide an up close view of natural and cultural features. In addition, you will discover state flags and nicknames, state flowers and birds, statistics and fun facts, and even graphs and charts. Follow the captions below and to the right to discover all the special features that are waiting for you in this atlas. Turn to page 160 to find outside websites that will lead you to additional sources of information on topics of interest to you.

COLOR BARS
Each section of the atlas has its own color. Look for the color in the Table of Contents and across the top of the pages in the atlas. The name of the section and the title for each topic or map is in the color bar.

THE NORTHEAST
THE SOUTHEAST
THE MIDWEST
THE SOUTHWEST
THE WEST
U.S. TERRITORIES

STATE FACT BOX
The fact box is full of key information you need at a glance about a state: its flag, statehood, statistics about land and population*, racial and ethnic makeup** and other population characteristics, plus some Geo Whiz facts and the state bird and flower.

*Population figures are estimates from the U.S. Census Bureau: state, city (city proper unless otherwise specified), and metropolitan area, 2018; racial/ethnic groups, 2017; foreign born, 2013–2017; urban population, 2010; population density, 2018.
** Racial percentages total less than 100 percent because very small racial groups are not included. Hispanics are an ethnic group and can be included in any racial group.

44 THE NORTHEAST

THE EMPIRE STATE
NEW YORK

New York

When Englishman Henry Hudson explored New York's Hudson River Valley in 1609, the territory was already inhabited by large tribes of Native Americans, including the powerful Iroquois. In 1624 a Dutch trading company established the New Netherland colony, but after just 40 years the colony was taken over by the English and renamed for England's Duke of York. In 1788 New York became the 11th state. The powerful port city of New York, center of trade and commerce and a gateway to immigrants, is the largest city in the United States. Its metropolitan area, which extends into the surrounding states of Connecticut, New Jersey, and Pennsylvania, has more than 20 million people. Cities such as Buffalo and Rochester are industrial centers, and Ithaca and Syracuse boast major universities. Agriculture is also important, and the state is a leading producer of dairy products, fruits, and vegetables.

THE BASICS
Statehood
July 26, 1788; 11th state
Total area (land and water)
54,555 sq mi (141,297 sq km)
Land area
47,126 sq mi (122,057 sq km)
Population
19,542,209
Capital
Albany
Population 97,279
Largest city
New York City
Population 8,398,748
Racial/ethnic groups
69.6% white; 17.7% African American; 9.1% Asian; 1.0% Native American; 19.2% Hispanic origin (any race)
Foreign born
22.7%
Urban population
87.9%
Population density
414.7 per sq mi (160.1 per sq km)

GEO WHIZ
The National Baseball Hall of Fame, established in 1939 in Cooperstown, includes a museum that houses more than 40,000 artifacts of the game, including bats, balls, gloves, and uniforms.

The Erie Canal, built in the 1820s between Albany and Buffalo, opened the Midwest to development by linking the Hudson River and the Great Lakes.

EASTERN BLUEBIRD
ROSE

⚐ LADY LIBERTY. Standing in New York Harbor, the Statue of Liberty is a symbol of freedom and democracy.

URBAN GIANT
Population of city proper, 2018 data

8,398,748 — New York
3,990,456 — Los Angeles
2,705,994 — Chicago
2,325,502 — Houston
1,660,272 — Phoenix

With more than twice the population of the next largest city, New York—known as the Big Apple—is the country's largest city.

◑ NATURAL WONDER. Each year more than eight million tourists visit Niagara Falls on the U.S.-Canada border. Visitors in rain slickers trek through the mists below Bridal Veil Falls on the American side.

130 THE WEST
ABOUT THE WEST
West

THE WEST **131**
ABOUT THE WEST
WEST

The West
THE HIGH FRONTIER

The western states, which make up almost half of the country's land area, have diverse landscapes and climates, ranging from the frozen heights of Denali, in Alaska, to the desolation of Death Valley, in California, and the lush, tropical islands of Hawai'i. More than half the region's population lives in California, and the Los Angeles metropolitan area is second in population only to that of New York City. Yet many parts of the region are sparsely populated, and much of the land is set aside as parkland and military bases. The region also faces many natural hazards—earthquakes, landslides, wildfires, and even volcanic eruptions.

◑ OLD AND NEW. A cable car carries passengers in San Francisco. In the background, modern buildings rise above older neighborhoods in this earthquake-prone city.

◑ NORTHERN GIANT. Denali, a name meaning "High One" in the Athabascan language, rises more than 20,000 feet (6,100 m) in the Alaska Range. Also known as Mount McKinley, it is North America's highest peak. The same tectonic forces that trigger earthquakes in Alaska are slowly pushing this huge block of granite even higher.

◑ ELUSIVE PREDATOR. Known by many names, including cougar and mountain lion, these big cats are found mainly in remote mountainous areas of the West, where they hunt deer and smaller animals.

◑ STEAMY BATH. A mineral-rich hot spring is a colorful feature of Yellowstone National Park. Runoff from rain and snowmelt seeps into cracks in the ground, sinking to a depth of 10,000 feet (3,050 m), where it is heated by molten rock before rising back to the surface.

◑ BALANCING ACT. For many years rivers have been used to move logs from forest to market, taking advantage of the buoyancy of logs and the power of moving water. A logger stands on a floating log raft in Coos Bay, Oregon.

◑ TRADITIONAL SAILING CRAFT. A Hawaiian outrigger canoe on Waikiki Beach promises fun in the surf for visitors to the 50th state. An important part of Polynesian culture, the canoes were once used to travel from island to island.

WHERE ARE THE PICTURES?

WHERE ARE THE PICTURES?
If you want to know where a picture in any of the regional sections in the atlas was taken, check the map in the regional photo essay. Find the label that describes the photograph you are curious about, and follow the line to its location.

CHARTS AND GRAPHS
The photo essay for each state includes a chart or graph that highlights economic, physical, cultural, or some other type of information related to the state.

YOU ARE HERE
This and other locator maps show you where each region or state within the region is in relation to the rest of the United States. Each region is shown in its regional color; featured states are in yellow.

BAR SCALE
Each map has a bar scale in miles and kilometers to help you find out how far on Earth's surface it is from one place to another on the map.

MAP SYMBOLS

Maps use symbols to represent many physical, political, and economic features. Below is a complete list of the map symbols that appear in map keys in this atlas.

- • Aspen.....................town of under 25,000 residents
- • Frankfort...................town of 25,000 to 99,999
- • San Jose.................city of 100,000 to 999,999
- ⦿ New York........city of 1,000,000 and over
- ⊛ National capital
- ⊛ State capital
- ⊙ Territory capital
- ▣ Point of interest
- + Mountain peak with elevation above sea level
- ▼ Low point with elevation below sea level
- —— River
- – – Intermittent river
- ┴┴┴ Canal
- —— Interstate or selected other highway
- •—•—• Pipeline
- – – – Trail
- •••••• State or national boundary
- •••••• Continental divide
- Lake and dam
- Intermittent lake
- Dry lake
- Swamp
- Glacier
- National Wild & Scenic River, N.W.&S.R.
- Area below sea level

- ☐ Indian Reservation, I.R. *(All Indian Reservations are not shown due to map scale and the size of the I.R.)*
- ☐ **State Park unit**
  State Park, **S.P.**
  State Historical Park, S.H.P.
  State Historic Site, S.H.S.
- ☐ **National Park Service unit**
  National Battlefield, N.B.
  National Battlefield Park, N.B.P.
  National Battlefield Site, N.B.S.
  National Historic Site, N.H.S.
  National Historic Area, N.H.A.
  National Historical Park, N.H.P.
  National Lakeshore
  National Military Park, N.M.P.
  National Memorial, NAT. MEM.
  National Monument, NAT. MON.
  National Park, N.P.
  National Parkway
  National Preserve
  National Recreation Area, N.R.A.
  National River
  National Riverway
  National Scenic Area
  National Seashore
  National Volcanic Monument
- ☐ National Forest, N.F.
- ☐ National Grassland, N.G.
- ☐ National Wildlife Refuge, N.W.R.
- ☐ National Marine Sanctuary, N.M.S.

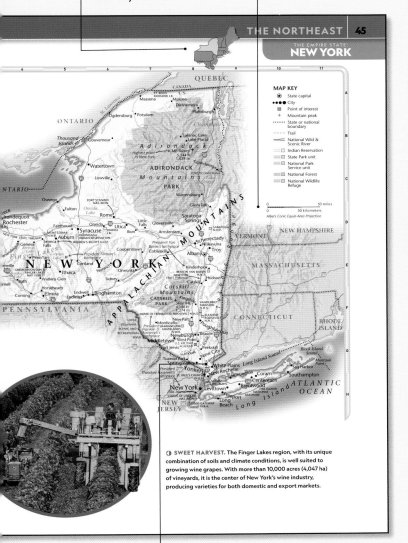

SWEET HARVEST. The Finger Lakes region, with its unique combination of soils and climate conditions, is well suited to growing wine grapes. With more than 10,000 acres (4,047 ha) of vineyards, it is the center of New York's wine industry, producing varieties for both domestic and export markets.

Tarrytown, NY **45** G8
Ta'ū (island), AS **155** I5
Ta'ū, AS **154** I4
Taum Sauk Mountain, MO **101** E6
Taunton, MA **39** D7
Taunton (river), MA **39** E7
Tawas City, MI **97** F7
Taylors, SC **75** B3
Taylorville, IL **89** E4

INDEX AND GRID
A grid system makes it easy to find places listed in the index. For example, the listing for Tarrytown, NY, is followed by **45** G8. The bold type is the page number; G8 tells you the city is near the point where imaginary lines drawn from G and 8 on the grid bars meet.

METRIC CONVERSIONS

CONVERSIONS TO METRIC MEASUREMENTS

WHEN YOU KNOW	MULTIPLY BY	TO FIND
INCHES (IN)	2.54	CENTIMETERS (CM)
FEET (FT)	0.30	METERS (M)
MILES (MI)	1.61	KILOMETERS (KM)
ACRES	0.40	HECTARES (HA)
SQUARE MILES (SQ MI)	2.59	SQUARE KILOMETERS (SQ KM)
POUNDS (LB)	0.45	KILOGRAMS (KG)
GALLONS (GAL)	3.79	LITERS (L)

CONVERSIONS FROM METRIC MEASUREMENTS

WHEN YOU KNOW	MULTIPLY BY	TO FIND
CENTIMETERS (CM)	0.39	INCHES (IN)
METERS (M)	3.28	FEET (FT)
KILOMETERS (KM)	0.62	MILES (MI)
HECTARES (HA)	2.47	ACRES
SQUARE KILOMETERS (SQ KM)	0.39	SQUARE MILES (SQ MI)
KILOGRAMS (KG)	2.20	POUNDS (LB)
LITERS (L)	0.26	GALLONS (GAL)

The Physical United States

The United States is the world's third largest country in area. It stretches from the Atlantic Ocean in the east to the Pacific Ocean and Hawai'i in the west, with Alaska, its largest state, bordering the Arctic Ocean. Physical features range from mountains to fertile plains, tropical forests, and deserts. Shading on the map indicates changes in elevation. Colors suggest vegetation patterns.

🔵 **ALASKA AND HAWAI'I.**
These two states are not directly connected to the other 48 states. If their correct relative sizes and locations were shown, the map would not fit on this page. The locator globe shows the correct relative size and location of each.

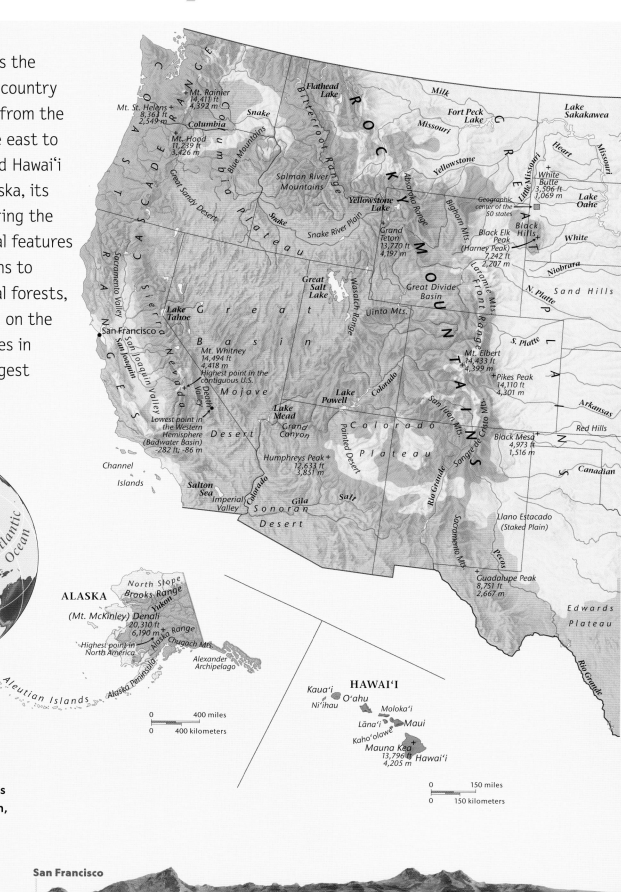

PHYSICAL MAP

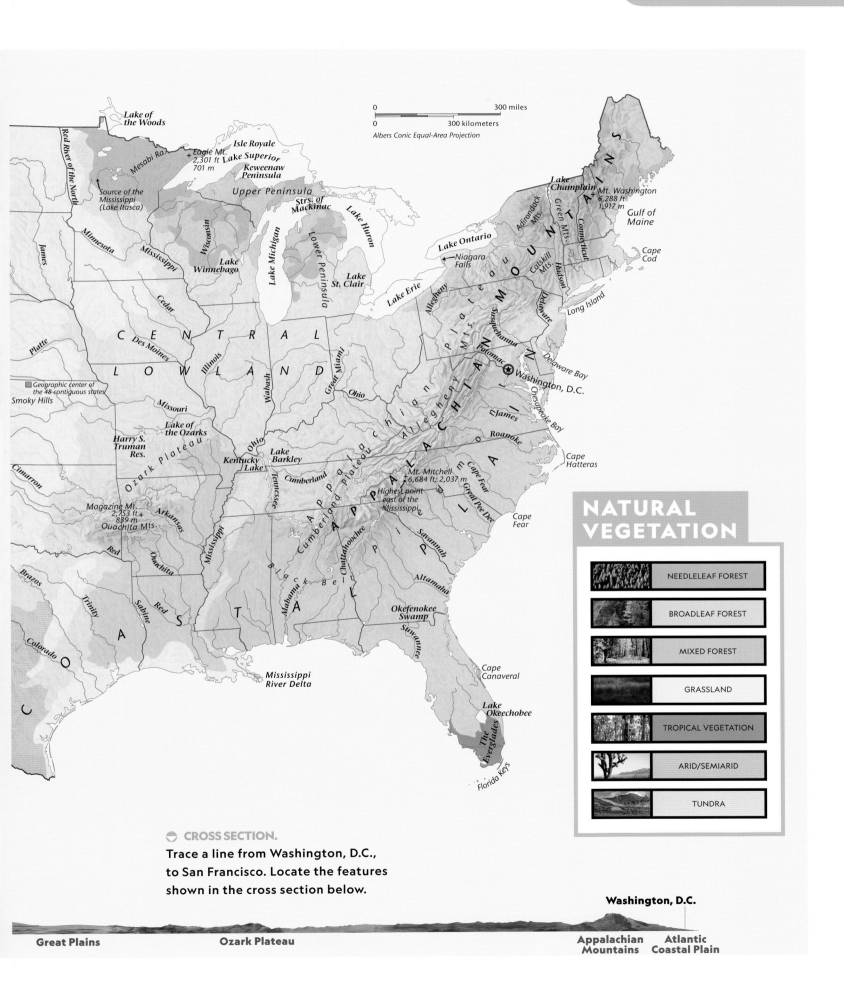

0   300 miles

0   300 kilometers

Albers Conic Equal-Area Projection

Lake of the Woods

Red River of the North

Isle Royale

+ Eagle Mt.
2,301 ft
701 m

Lake Superior

Keweenaw Peninsula

Mesabi Ra.

Source of the Mississippi (Lake Itasca)

Upper Peninsula

Strs. of Mackinac

Minnesota

Wisconsin

Lake Winnebago

Lake Michigan

Lower Peninsula

Lake Huron

Lake St. Clair

James

Mississippi

Cedar

Platte

Des Moines

Illinois

Wabash

Great Miami

Ohio

Lake Ontario

← Niagara Falls

Lake Erie

Lake Champlain

Adirondack Mts.

Green Mts.

Connecticut

Mt. Washington
6,288 ft
1,917 m

Gulf of Maine

Cape Cod

Catskill Mts.

Hudson

Allegheny

Plateau

Susquehanna

Delaware

Long Island

C E N T R A L

L O W L A N D

Smoky Hills

Geographic center of the 48 contiguous states

Missouri

Lake of the Ozarks

Harry S. Truman Res.

Ozark Plateau

Kentucky Lake

Lake Barkley

Ohio

Tennessee

Cumberland

Appalachian Plateau

Cumberland Plateau

Potomac

⊛ Washington, D.C.

James

Roanoke

Delaware Bay

Chesapeake Bay

Cape Hatteras

M O U N T A I N S

A P P A L A C H I A N

Mt. Mitchell
+ 6,684 ft; 2,037 m

Highest point east of the Mississippi

Cape Fear

Cape Fear

Great Pee Dee

Cimarron

Magazine Mt.
2,753 ft +
839 m
Ouachita Mts.

Arkansas

Red

Ouachita

Mississippi

Black Belt

Chattahoochee

Alabama

Savannah

Altamaha

C O A S T A L

P L A I N

Brazos

Trinity

Sabine

Red

Colorado

Okefenokee Swamp

Suwannee

Mississippi River Delta

Cape Canaveral

Lake Okeechobee

The Everglades

Florida Keys

NATURAL VEGETATION

	NEEDLELEAF FOREST
	BROADLEAF FOREST
	MIXED FOREST
	GRASSLAND
	TROPICAL VEGETATION
	ARID/SEMIARID
	TUNDRA

⊙ CROSS SECTION.

Trace a line from Washington, D.C., to San Francisco. Locate the features shown in the cross section below.

Washington, D.C.

Great Plains   **Ozark Plateau**   **Appalachian Mountains**   **Atlantic Coastal Plain**

CLIMATE

Climate

A big part of the natural environment of the United States is the climate. With humid areas near the coasts, dry interior regions far from any major water body, and land areas that extend from frigid northern Alaska to tropical Hawai'i and southern Florida, the country experiences great variation in climate. Location is the key to the country's climate patterns. Distance from the Equator, nearness to water, wind patterns, temperature of nearby water bodies, and elevation are things that influence temperature and precipitation. Climate affects the types of vegetation that grow in a particular place and plays a part in soil formation.

CHANGING CLIMATE

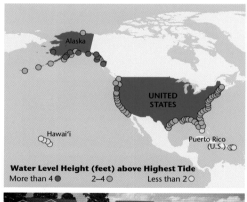

Water Level Height (feet) above Highest Tide
More than 4 ●   2–4 ◐   Less than 2 ○

Scientists generally agree that human activity has played an important role in recent changes in Earth's climate. The years 2014–2018 are the five warmest years ever recorded. Increases in average temperatures are likely to contribute to more severe storms, changes in precipitation patterns, and the spread of desert conditions. Rising temperatures also contribute to higher ocean levels and coastal flooding as glaciers melt and warmer ocean waters expand. Average sea level has risen nearly eight inches (20 cm) since 1900. Almost 40 percent of the U.S. population lives in coastal areas at risk of severe flooding. Above, floodwaters caused by Hurricane Florence in 2018 trap a car in Longs, South Carolina.

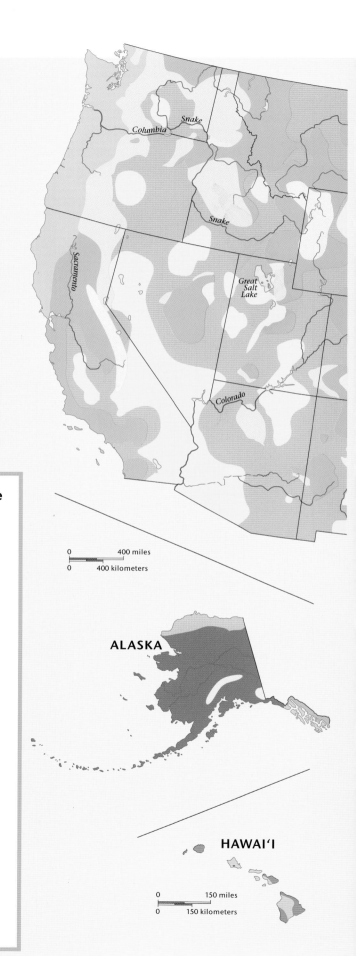

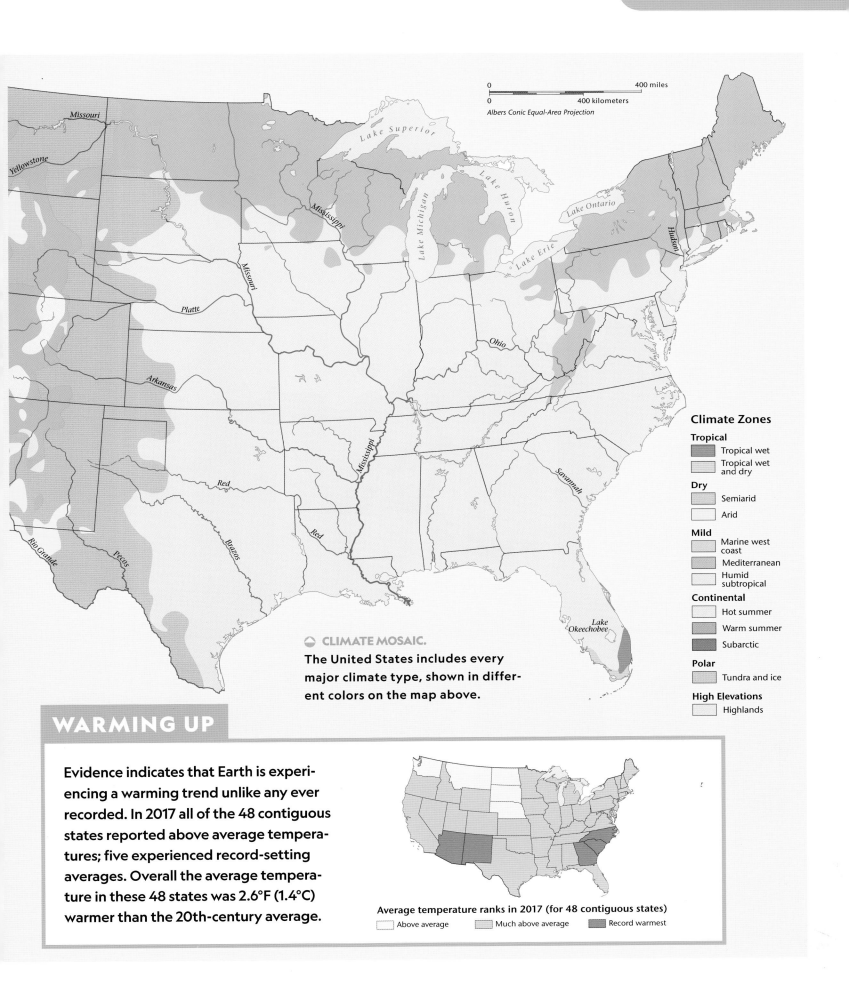

400 miles

400 kilometers

Albers Conic Equal-Area Projection

Climate Zones

Tropical
- Tropical wet
- Tropical wet and dry

Dry
- Semiarid
- Arid

Mild
- Marine west coast
- Mediterranean
- Humid subtropical

Continental
- Hot summer
- Warm summer
- Subarctic

Polar
- Tundra and ice

High Elevations
- Highlands

⬭ **CLIMATE MOSAIC.**

The United States includes every major climate type, shown in different colors on the map above.

WARMING UP

Evidence indicates that Earth is experiencing a warming trend unlike any ever recorded. In 2017 all of the 48 contiguous states reported above average temperatures; five experienced record-setting averages. Overall the average temperature in these 48 states was 2.6°F (1.4°C) warmer than the 20th-century average.

Average temperature ranks in 2017 (for 48 contiguous states)

- Above average
- Much above average
- Record warmest

NATURAL HAZARDS

Natural Hazards

The natural environment of the United States provides much diversity, but it also poses many dangers, especially when people locate homes and businesses in places at risk of natural disasters. Tornadoes bring destructive winds, and hurricanes bring strong winds, rain, the possibility of dangerous storm surges in coastal areas, and more. The shifting of Earth's crust along fault lines rattles buildings; floodwaters and wildfires threaten lives and property. More than one-third of the U.S. population lives in hazard-prone areas. Compare this map to the population map on pages 16–17.

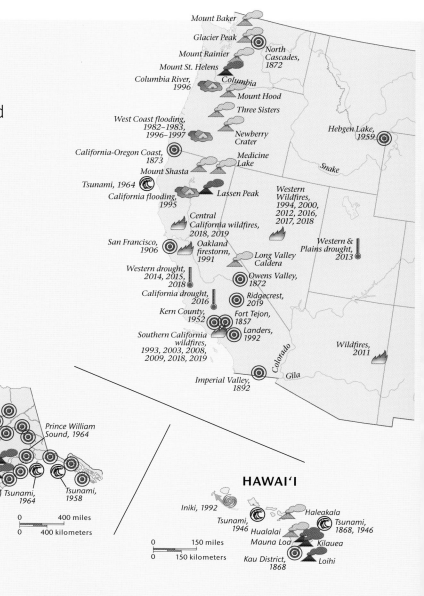

NATURAL HAZARDS

BLIZZARD. Severe storm with bitter cold temperatures and wind-whipped snow and ice particles that reduce visibility to less than 650 feet (198 m), paralyzing transportation systems

FLOOD. Inundation of buildings or roadways caused by overflow of a river or stream swollen by heavy rainfall or rapid snowmelt; may involve displacement of people

DROUGHT. Long and continuous period of abnormally low precipitation, resulting in water shortages that negatively affect people, animals, and plant life; may result in crop loss

HURRICANE. Tropical storm in the Atlantic, Caribbean, Gulf of Mexico, or eastern Pacific with a minimum sustained wind speed of 74 miles an hour (119 km/h)

ICE STORM. Damaging accumulations of ice associated with freezing rain; may pull down trees or utility lines, causing extensive damage and creating dangerous travel conditions

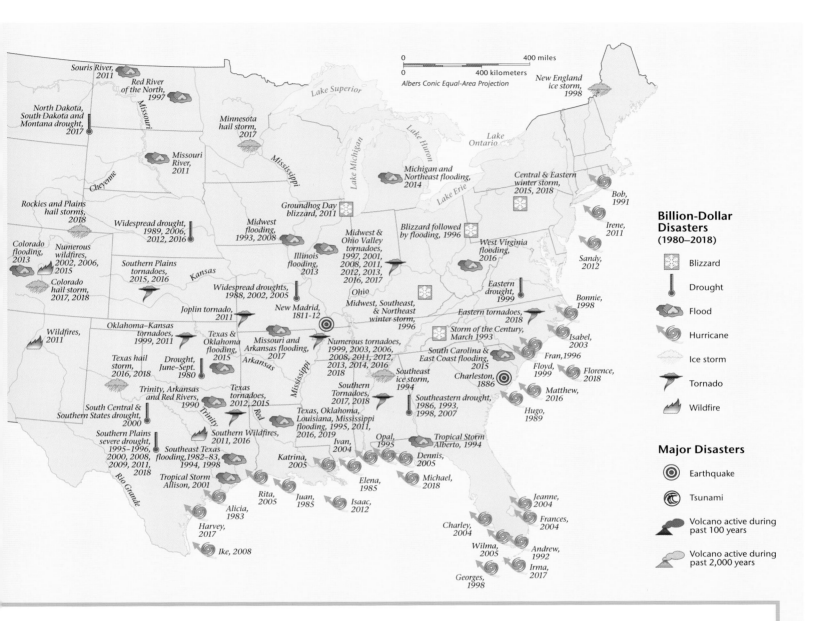

0 _____ 400 miles
0 _____ 400 kilometers
Albers Conic Equal-Area Projection

Map labels:

Souris River, 2011
Red River of the North, 1997
North Dakota, South Dakota and Montana drought, 2017
Minnesota hail storm, 2017
Lake Superior
New England ice storm, 1998
Missouri
Missouri River, 2011
Lake Michigan
Lake Huron
Lake Ontario
Lake Erie
Michigan and Northeast flooding, 2014
Central & Eastern winter storm, 2015, 2018
Cheyenne
Rockies and Plains hail storms, 2018
Widespread drought, 1989, 2006, 2012, 2016
Midwest flooding, 1993, 2008
Groundhog Day blizzard, 2011
Blizzard followed by flooding, 1996
West Virginia flooding, 2016
Bob, 1991
Irene, 2011
Colorado flooding, 2013
Numerous wildfires, 2002, 2006, 2015
Colorado hail storm, 2017, 2018
Southern Plains tornadoes, 2015, 2016
Illinois flooding, 2013
Midwest & Ohio Valley tornadoes, 1997, 2001, 2008, 2011, 2012, 2013, 2016, 2017
Kansas
Widespread droughts, 1988, 2002, 2005
Ohio
Eastern drought, 1999
Sandy, 2012
Bonnie, 1998
Wildfires, 2011
Joplin tornado, 2011
New Madrid, 1811-12
Midwest, Southeast, & Northeast winter storm, 1996
Eastern tornadoes, 2018
Storm of the Century, March 1993
Isabel, 2003
Oklahoma–Kansas tornadoes, 1999, 2011
Texas & Oklahoma flooding, 2015
Missouri and Arkansas flooding, 2017
Numerous tornadoes, 1999, 2003, 2006, 2008, 2011, 2012, 2013, 2014, 2016, 2018
South Carolina & East Coast flooding, 2015
Fran, 1996
Texas hail storm, 2016, 2018
Drought, June–Sept. 1980
Arkansas
Southeast ice storm, 1994
Charleston, 1886
Floyd, 1999
Florence, 2018
Trinity, Arkansas and Red Rivers, 1990
Texas tornadoes, 2012, 2015
Southern Tornadoes, 2017, 2018
Matthew, 2016
South Central & Southern States drought, 2000
Trinity
Red
Mississippi
Texas, Oklahoma, Louisiana, Mississippi flooding, 1995, 2011, 2016, 2019
Southeastern drought, 1986, 1993, 1998, 2007
Hugo, 1989
Southern Plains severe drought, 1995–1996, 2000, 2008, 2009, 2011, 2018
Southern Wildfires, 2011, 2016
Southeast Texas flooding, 1982–83, 1994, 1998
Ivan, 2004
Opal, 1995
Tropical Storm Alberto, 1994
Rio Grande
Tropical Storm Allison, 2001
Katrina, 2005
Elena, 1985
Dennis, 2005
Michael, 2018
Rita, 2005
Juan, 1985
Isaac, 2012
Alicia, 1983
Charley, 2004
Jeanne, 2004
Harvey, 2017
Frances, 2004
Ike, 2008
Wilma, 2005
Andrew, 1992
Irma, 2017
Georges, 1998

Billion-Dollar Disasters (1980–2018)

- ❄ Blizzard
- 🌡 Drought
- Flood
- Hurricane
- Ice storm
- Tornado
- Wildfire

Major Disasters

- ◎ Earthquake
- Tsunami
- Volcano active during past 100 years
- Volcano active during past 2,000 years

TORNADO. Violently rotating column of air that, when it reaches the ground, is the most damaging of all atmospheric phenomena; most common in the central region of the country

WILDFIRE. Free-burning fire in a forest or grassland; may result from lightning strikes or accidental or deliberate human activity in areas where conditions are dry

EARTHQUAKE. Shaking or vibration created by energy released by movement of Earth's crust along tectonic plate boundaries; can cause structural damage and loss of life

TSUNAMI. Series of unusually large ocean waves caused by an underwater earthquake, landslide, or volcanic eruption; very destructive in coastal areas

VOLCANO. Vent or opening in Earth's surface through which lava (molten rock), ash, and gases are released; often associated with tectonic plate boundaries

The Political United States

Like a giant patchwork quilt, the United States is made up of 50 states. Each is uniquely different, but collectively these units create a national fabric that is held together by a Constitution and a federal government. State boundaries, outlined in various colors on the map, set apart internal political units within the country. The national capital—Washington, D.C.—is marked by a star in a double circle. Each state capital is marked by a star in a single circle.

TIME ZONES. Earth is divided into 24 time zones, each about 15 degrees of longitude wide, reflecting the distance Earth turns from west to east each hour. The U.S. is divided into six time zones, indicated by red dotted lines on these maps. When it is noon in Boston, what is the time in Seattle?

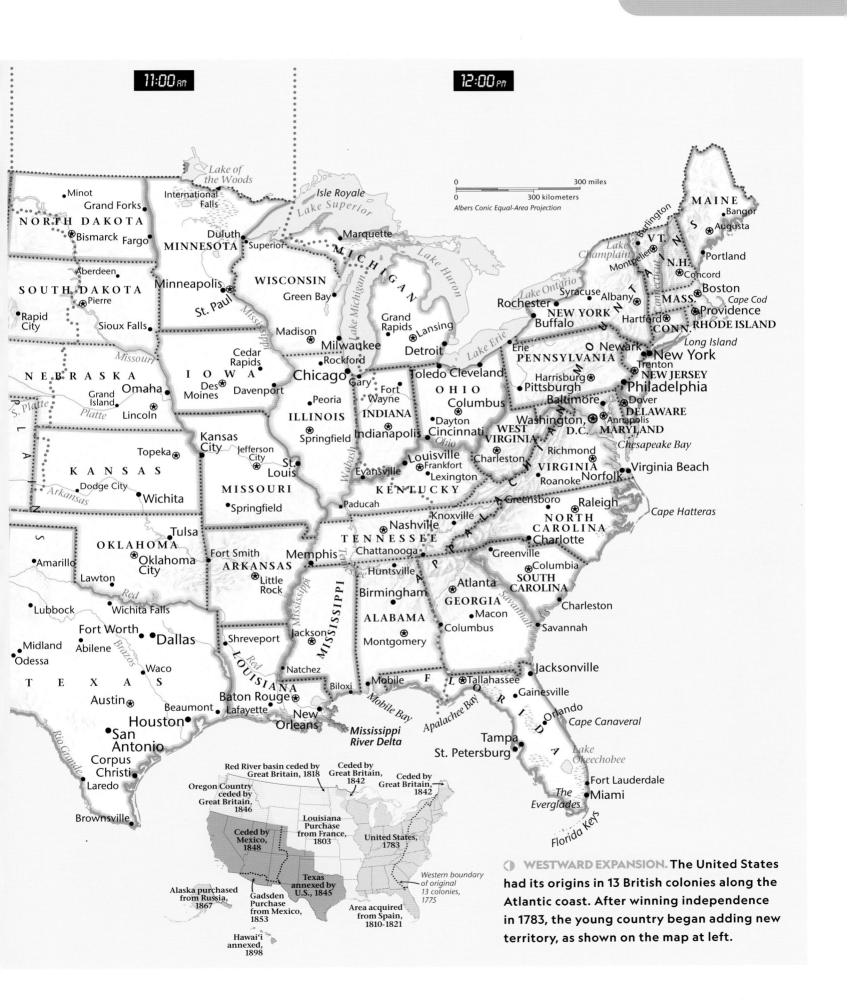

11:00 AM   12:00 PM

0   300 miles
0   300 kilometers
Albers Conic Equal-Area Projection

WESTWARD EXPANSION. The United States had its origins in 13 British colonies along the Atlantic coast. After winning independence in 1783, the young country began adding new territory, as shown on the map at left.

Red River basin ceded by Great Britain, 1818
Ceded by Great Britain, 1842
Ceded by Great Britain, 1842
Oregon Country ceded by Great Britain, 1846
Louisiana Purchase from France, 1803
United States, 1783
Ceded by Mexico, 1848
Western boundary of original 13 colonies, 1775
Alaska purchased from Russia, 1867
Gadsden Purchase from Mexico, 1853
Texas annexed by U.S., 1845
Area acquired from Spain, 1810-1821
Hawai'i annexed, 1898

Population

More than 327 million* and growing! The population of the United States topped the 300 million mark in 2006, and it continues to grow by more than two million people each year. Before the arrival of European settlers, the population consisted of Native Americans living in tribal groups scattered across the country. In the 17th century, Europeans began settling along the eastern seaboard. By the early 18th century, the population was increasing and included African slaves brought as unpaid labor for the growing plantation economy. By 1790 when the first U.S. census was taken, the country's population was almost four million people. Today, New York City alone has a population more than double that number. The country's population is unevenly distributed. The greatest densities are in the East and along the West Coast, especially around major cities. The most rapid growth is occurring in the South and the West—an area referred to as the Sunbelt—as well as in suburban areas around cities.

*July 2018 figure

COMMUTER RUSH HOUR. Crowds of people press toward trains in New York City's Grand Central Station. With more than three-quarters of the population living in urban areas, commuter transportation poses a major challenge to cities in the United States.

WHERE WE LIVE. In 1790 only 5 percent of Americans lived in towns. Today most people live in urban places (blue) and surrounding suburbs (orange), rather than in rural areas (green).

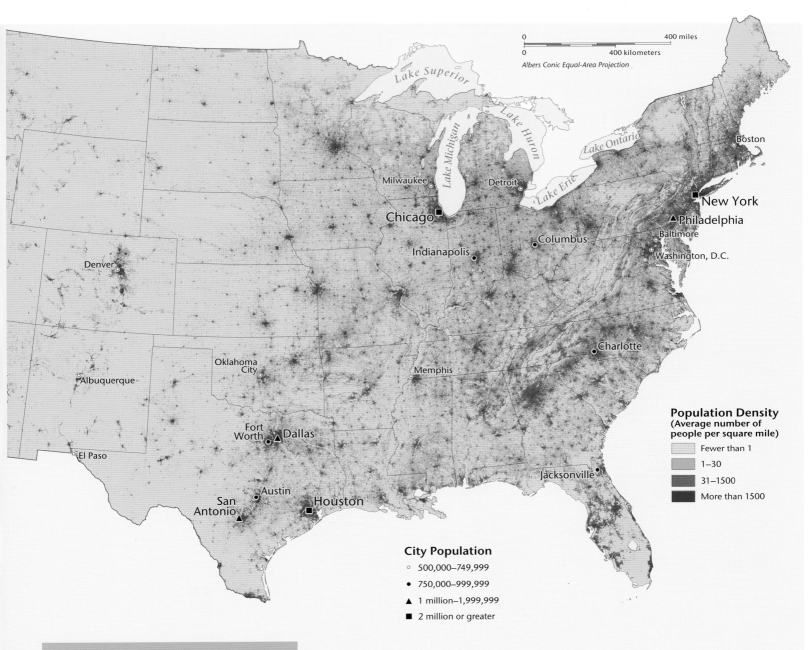

Population Density
(Average number of
people per square mile)

	Fewer than 1
	1–30
	31–1500
	More than 1500

City Population

○ 500,000–749,999

● 750,000–999,999

▲ 1 million–1,999,999

■ 2 million or greater

HOW OLD ARE WE?

Population pyramids show distribution of population by sex and age groups. In 1960 the largest group, born after World War II and called Baby Boomers (highlighted in the graphs), were under 15 years of age. By 2040 they will reach the top of the pyramid.

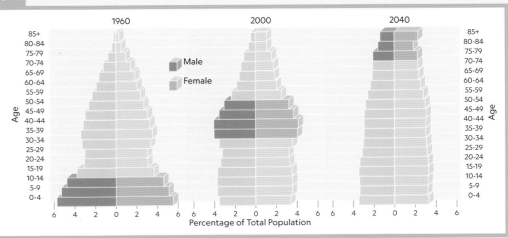

People on the Move

From earliest human history, the land of the United States has been a focus of migration. Ancestors of today's Native Americans arrived thousands of years ago. The first European settlers came in the 16th and 17th centuries, and slave ships brought Africans by way of the West Indies. Today, people are still on the move. Since the mid-1900s, most immigrants have come from Latin America, especially Mexico and Central America; and Asia, particularly China, the Philippines, and India. Although most of the population is still of European descent, certain regions have large minority concentrations (see main map) that influence the local cultural landscape.

ALASKA

| 0 | 400 miles |
| 0 | 400 kilometers |

HAWAI'I

| 0 | 150 miles |
| 0 | 150 kilometers |

⬤ **BRIDGE OF HOPE.** Many Mexicans enter the U.S. (foreground) daily for work or commerce by bridges across the Rio Grande, such as this one between Nuevo Laredo, Mexico, and Laredo, Texas.

⬤ **IMMIGRANT INFLUENCE.** A dual-language street sign in San Francisco's Chinatown shows how immigrants have contributed to the cultural landscape.

⬤ **SUNBELT SPRAWL.** Spreading suburbs are becoming a common feature of the desert Southwest as people flock to the Sunbelt.

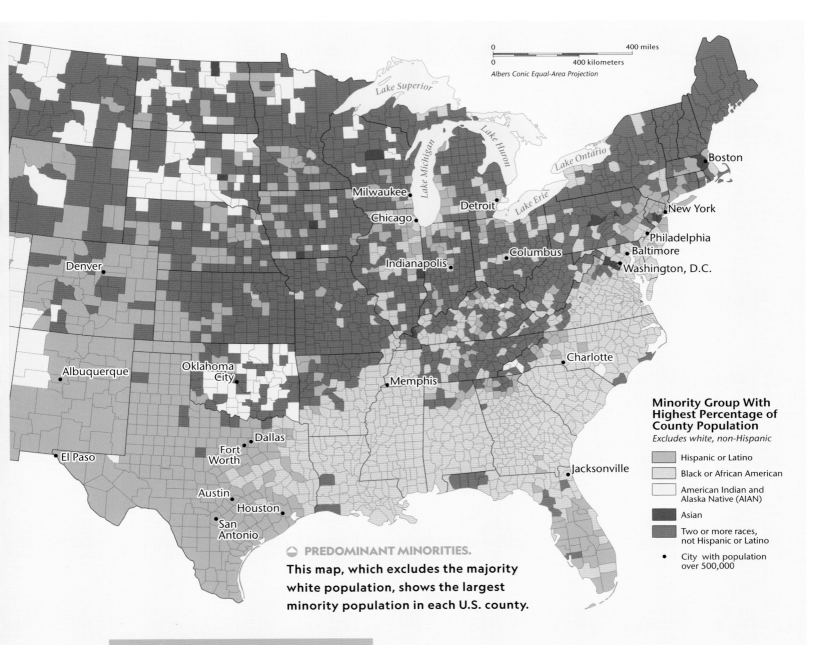

0   400 miles
0   400 kilometers
Albers Conic Equal-Area Projection

Lake Superior

Lake Michigan

Lake Huron

Lake Ontario

Lake Erie

Boston

Milwaukee

Detroit

New York

Chicago

Philadelphia

Columbus

Baltimore

Indianapolis

Washington, D.C.

Denver

Charlotte

Albuquerque

Oklahoma
City

Memphis

Dallas

Jacksonville

El Paso

Fort
Worth

Austin

Houston

San
Antonio

**Minority Group With
Highest Percentage of
County Population**
Excludes white, non-Hispanic

Hispanic or Latino

Black or African American

American Indian and
Alaska Native (AIAN)

Asian

Two or more races,
not Hispanic or Latino

• City with population
over 500,000

◯ PREDOMINANT MINORITIES.
This map, which excludes the majority
white population, shows the largest
minority population in each U.S. county.

POPULATION SHIFT

In the late 1900s, people began
moving from the industrial and
agricultural regions of the Northeast
and Midwest toward the South and
West, attracted by the promise of
jobs and generally lower living costs.
This trend is reflected in the wide
variations in state population
changes in the map at right.

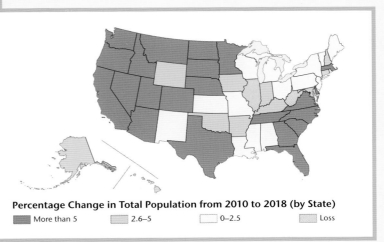

Percentage Change in Total Population from 2010 to 2018 (by State)

More than 5   2.6–5   0–2.5   Loss

Energy

People use energy every day in almost everything they do—from turning on a lamp to using a computer and riding a bus to school or work. Almost 40 percent of all energy is used to create electricity; another 27 percent is consumed by transportation. Energy sources fall into two main categories: nonrenewable and renewable. Nonrenewable energy resources, including fossil fuels (petroleum, natural gas, and coal) and uranium (nuclear power), are in limited supply and are not quickly replenished. Renewable energy sources (wind, water, solar, geothermal, and biomass materials) have an abundant supply that is constantly replenished. Most energy used in the United States comes from nonrenewable sources.

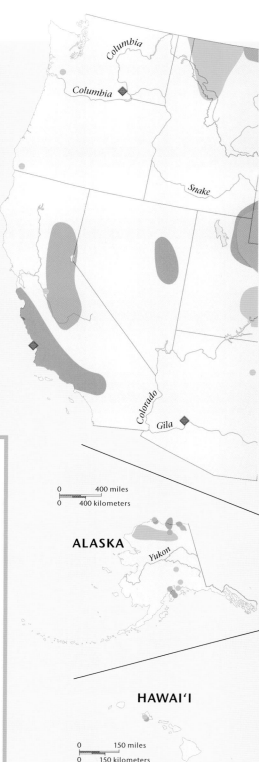

EARTHQUAKES & OIL PRODUCTION

Earthquake activity in the central U.S. increased dramatically after 2009. Geophysicists (scientists who study forces at work within Earth, including earthquakes) concluded that earthquake activity increased as a result of drilling companies pumping toxic wastewater that occurs naturally in oil and gas deposits back into the ground.

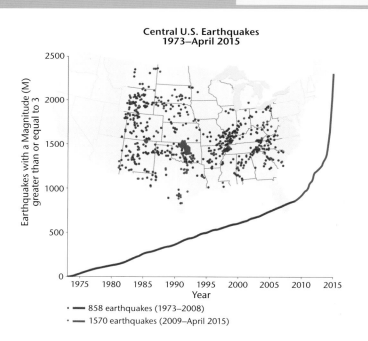

Central U.S. Earthquakes
1973–April 2015

Earthquakes with a Magnitude (M) greater than or equal to 3

Year

• ── 858 earthquakes (1973–2008)
• ── 1570 earthquakes (2009–April 2015)

From 2009 to early 2016 there were 2,310 earthquakes of magnitude 3 or greater, with most concentrated in central Oklahoma. During this time toxic wastewater pumped back into the ground doubled. In 2015 the state of Oklahoma limited the amount of wastewater that could be pumped back into the ground. Since 2016 the number of earthquakes of magnitude 3 or greater has declined steadily.

ALASKA

HAWAI'I

ENERGY

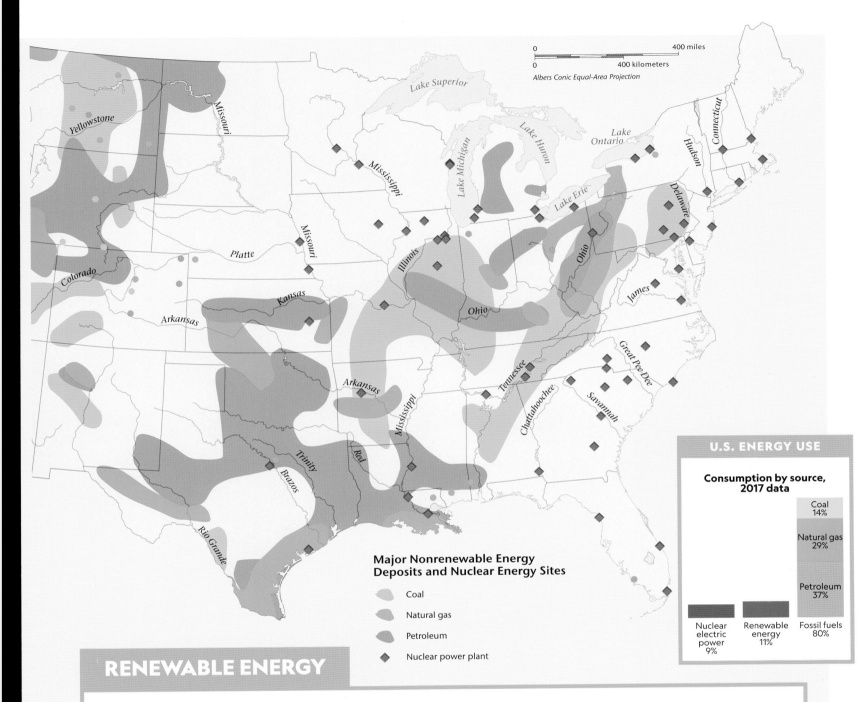

Albers Conic Equal-Area Projection

Major Nonrenewable Energy Deposits and Nuclear Energy Sites

- Coal
- Natural gas
- Petroleum
- ◆ Nuclear power plant

U.S. ENERGY USE

Consumption by source, 2017 data

Coal 14%	
Natural gas 29%	
Petroleum 37%	Fossil fuels 80%

| Nuclear electric power 9% | Renewable energy 11% | Fossil fuels 80% |

RENEWABLE ENERGY

Renewable energy comes from sources that are readily available and naturally replenished. In the United States, 11 percent of all energy consumed comes from renewable sources, including hydroelectric energy from moving water; geothermal energy from heat within Earth's core; solar energy from the sun; wind energy (left) from moving air; and biomass energy from burning organic matter such as wood, plant material, and garbage.

Renewable energy consumption by source, 2017 data*

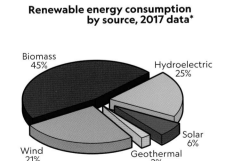

- Biomass 45%
- Hydroelectric 25%
- Solar 6%
- Geothermal 2%
- Wind 21%

*Figures do not total 100 percent due to rounding.

THE NATIONAL CAPITAL

The National Capital

THE BASICS

Founding
July 16, 1790

Total area (land and water)
68 sq mi (177 sq km)

Land area
61 sq mi (158 sq km)

Population
702,455

Racial/ethnic groups
45.1% white; 47.1% African American; 4.3% Asian; 0.6% Native American; 11.0% Hispanic (any race)

Foreign born
14.0%

Urban population
100.0%

Population density
11,515.7 per sq mi (4,445.9 per sq km)

GEO WHIZ

License plates in the District of Columbia bear the slogan "End Taxation Without Representation," reflecting the fact that residents have no voting representative in either house of the U.S. Congress.

The flag of the District of Columbia, with its three red stars and two red stripes, is based on the shield in George Washington's family coat of arms.

Chosen as a compromise location between Northern and Southern interests and built on land ceded by Maryland and Virginia in the late 1700s, Washington, D.C., is the seat of the U.S. government and symbol of the country's history. The city's design, as laid out by French architect Pierre L'Enfant, is distinguished by a grid pattern cut by diagonal avenues. At its core is the National Mall, a broad park lined by monuments, museums, and stately government buildings.

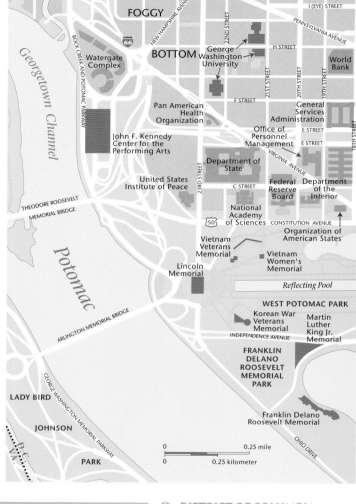

AMERICAN BEAUTY ROSE

WOOD THRUSH

DISTRICT OF COLUMBIA. Originally on both sides of the Potomac River, the city returned land to Virginia in 1846.

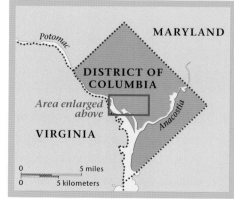

GREAT LEADER. Abraham Lincoln, who was president during the Civil War and a strong opponent of slavery, is remembered in a monument that houses this seated statue at the west end of the National Mall.

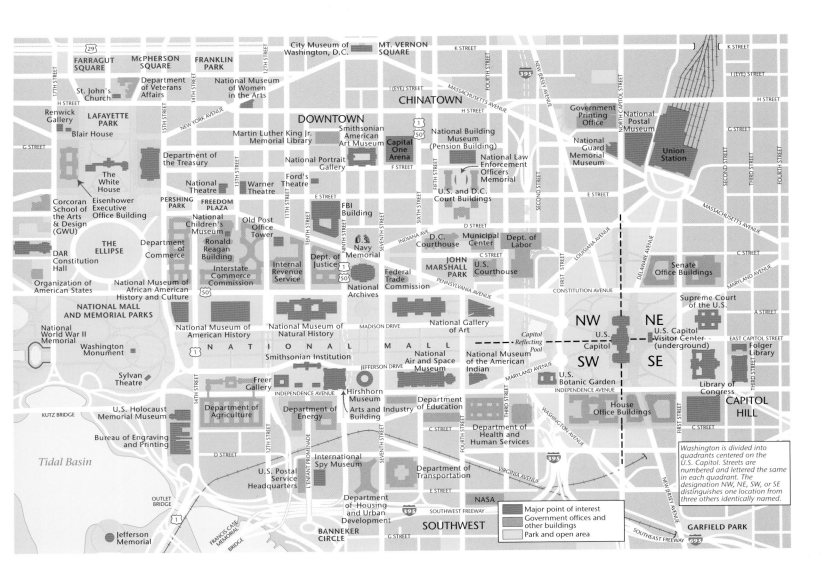

Washington is divided into quadrants centered on the U.S. Capitol. Streets are numbered and lettered the same in each quadrant. The designation NW, NE, SW, or SE distinguishes one location from three others identically named.

Major point of interest
Government offices and other buildings
Park and open area

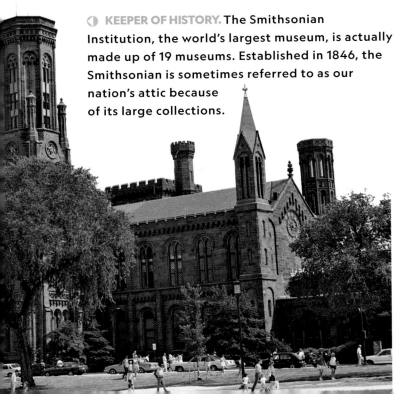

KEEPER OF HISTORY. The Smithsonian Institution, the world's largest museum, is actually made up of 19 museums. Established in 1846, the Smithsonian is sometimes referred to as our nation's attic because of its large collections.

NATIONAL ICON. The gleaming dome of the U.S. Capitol, home to the House of Representatives and the Senate, is a familiar symbol of Washington's main business—the running of the country's government.

THE REGION

PHYSICAL

Total area (land and water)
196,214 sq mi (508,192 sq km)

Highest point
Mount Washington, NH 6,288 ft (1,917 m)

Lowest point
Sea level, shores of the Atlantic Ocean

Longest rivers
St. Lawrence, Susquehanna, Connecticut, Hudson

Largest lakes
Erie, Ontario, Champlain

Vegetation
Needleleaf, broadleaf, and mixed forest

Climate
Continental to mild, with cool to warm summers, cold winters, and moderate precipitation throughout the year

POLITICAL

Total population
63,120,968

States (11):
Connecticut, Delaware, Maine, Maryland, Massachusetts, New Hampshire, New Jersey, New York, Pennsylvania, Rhode Island, Vermont

Largest state
New York: 54,555 sq mi (141,297 sq km)

Smallest state
Rhode Island: 1,545 sq mi (4,001 sq km)

Most populous state
New York: 19,542,209

Least populous state
Vermont: 626,299

Largest city proper
New York, NY: 8,398,748

THE NORTHEAST

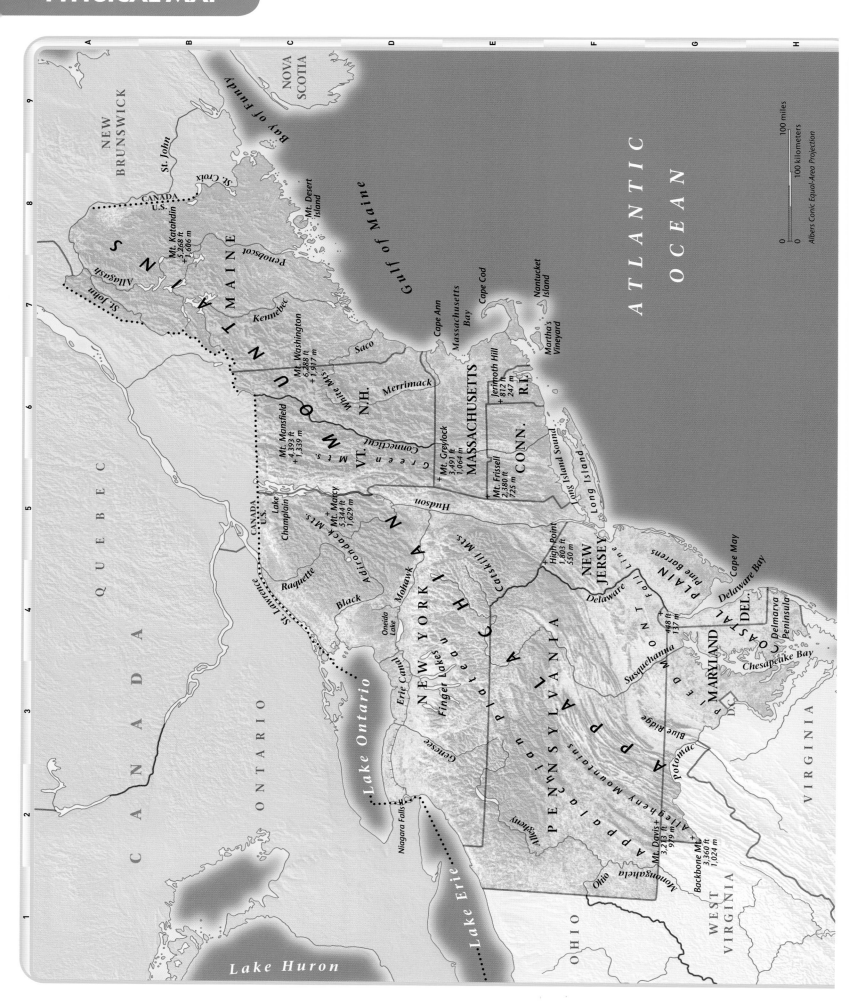

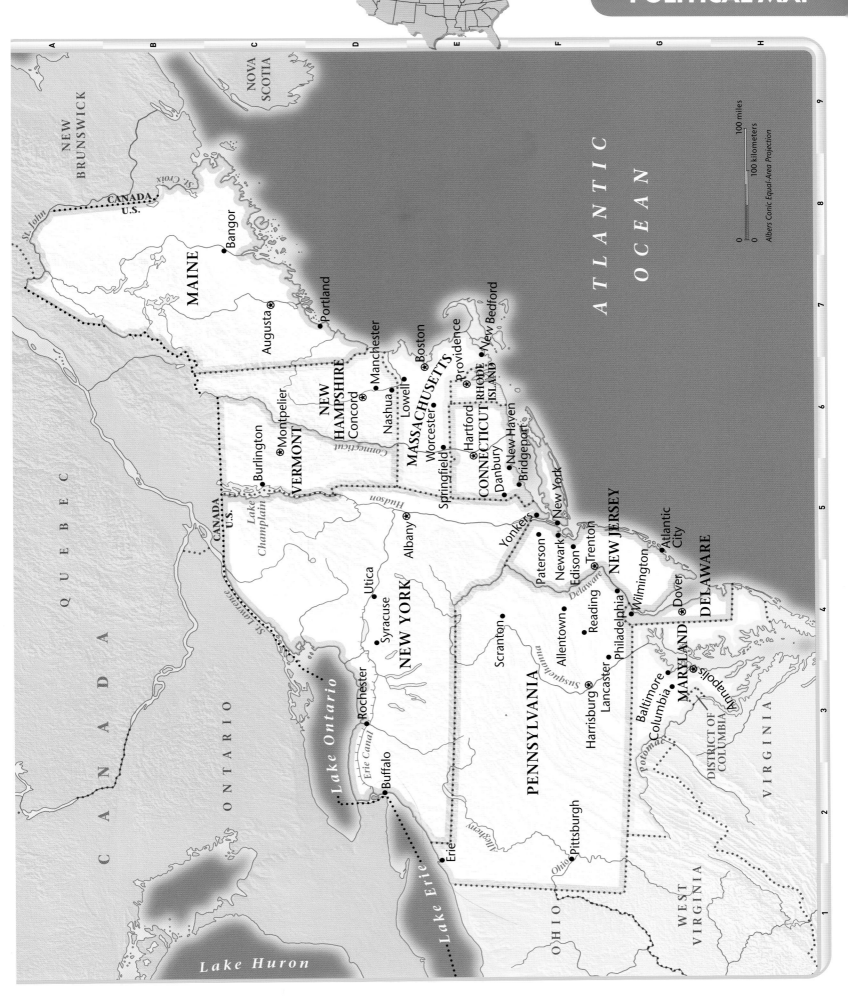

NEW BRUNSWICK

NOVA SCOTIA

ATLANTIC OCEAN

100 miles
100 kilometers

Albers Conic Equal-Area Projection

CANADA
U.S.

St. Croix

St. John

MAINE

Bangor

Portland

Augusta

QUEBEC

CANADA

Montpelier

Burlington

VERMONT

NEW HAMPSHIRE

Concord

Manchester

Nashua

Lowell

Connecticut

Boston

MASSACHUSETTS

Worcester

Springfield

Providence

New Bedford

RHODE ISLAND

Hartford

CONNECTICUT

Danbury

New Haven

Bridgeport

Lake Champlain

CANADA
U.S.

Hudson

Albany

New York

Yonkers

Paterson

Newark

Edison

Trenton

NEW JERSEY

Atlantic City

Utica

Syracuse

NEW YORK

Rochester

Erie Canal

Buffalo

ONTARIO

Lake Ontario

Lake Erie

Erie

Scranton

Susquehanna

Allentown

Reading

PENNSYLVANIA

Harrisburg

Lancaster

Philadelphia

Delaware

Wilmington

DELAWARE

Dover

Baltimore

Columbia

MARYLAND

Annapolis

DISTRICT OF COLUMBIA

Potomac

Allegheny

Pittsburgh

Ohio

OHIO

WEST VIRGINIA

VIRGINIA

Lake Huron

The Northeast

BIRTHPLACE OF A NATION

Long before the arrival of Europeans, the Northeast was inhabited by various Native American tribes who were mainly hunter-gatherers and farmers. European adventurers, traders, and settlers took over much of their land and began establishing colonies in the 17th century. Immigrants from around the globe soon followed, creating a very diverse population. Today, the Northeast includes the nation's financial center (New York City) and its political capital (Washington, D.C.). Although the region boasts tranquil mountains, lakes, and rivers, its teeming cities have always been the heart of the Northeast.

◑ DINNER DELICACY. Lobsters turn bright red when cooked. These tasty crustaceans live in the cold waters of the Atlantic Ocean. Fishermen catch them using baited traps.

◐ CHANGING FACES. The Northeast has been a gateway for immigration since colonial times. These young people, performing in traditional clothing in an India Cultural Festival in New Jersey, reflect the rich diversity of the region.

◑ DEFENDER OF FREEDOM. Rising 548 feet (167 m) above Penn Square, Philadelphia's City Hall, with its statue of William Penn, is the country's largest municipal building. Penn was the founder of the Pennsylvania colony and a defender of equal rights for men and women.

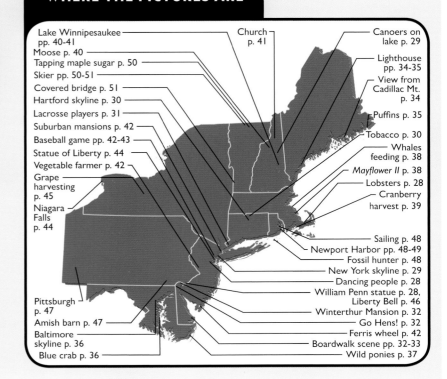

⬤ **SPARKLING LIGHTS.** The lights of New York City's skyline sparkle in the dark. The tall buildings of Lower Manhattan, reflected in the dark waters of the East River, are home to companies with influence that reaches around the world.

⬤ **STILL WATERS.** A father and son enjoy a quiet day of fishing on the smooth-as-glass waters of Chocorua Lake in New Hampshire's White Mountains. Deciduous trees turning red and gold will soon shed their leaves, and the hillsides will turn white with winter's snow, attracting skiers to the valley.

WHERE THE PICTURES ARE

Lake Winnipesaukee pp. 40-41
Moose p. 40
Tapping maple sugar p. 50
Skier pp. 50-51
Covered bridge p. 51
Hartford skyline p. 30
Lacrosse players p. 31
Suburban mansions p. 42
Baseball game pp. 42-43
Statue of Liberty p. 44
Vegetable farmer p. 42
Grape harvesting p. 45
Niagara Falls p. 44

Church p. 41

Canoers on lake p. 29
Lighthouse pp. 34-35
View from Cadillac Mt. p. 34
Puffins p. 35
Tobacco p. 30
Whales feeding p. 38
Mayflower II p. 38
Lobsters p. 28
Cranberry harvest p. 39
Sailing p. 48
Newport Harbor pp. 48-49
Fossil hunter p. 48
New York skyline p. 29
Dancing people p. 28
William Penn statue p. 28, Liberty Bell p. 46
Winterthur Mansion p. 32
Go Hens! p. 32
Ferris wheel p. 42
Boardwalk scene pp. 32-33
Wild ponies p. 37

Pittsburgh p. 47
Amish barn p. 47
Baltimore skyline p. 36
Blue crab p. 36

Connecticut

As early as 1614, Dutch explorers founded trading posts along the coast of Connecticut, but the first permanent European settlements were established in 1635 by English Puritans from nearby Massachusetts. The laws established by the colony were an important model for the writing of the U.S. Constitution in 1787, earning the state its nickname: the Constitution State. Even in colonial times Connecticut was an important industrial center, producing goods that competed with factories in England. Today, Connecticut industries make jet aircraft engines, helicopters, and nuclear submarines. The state is home to many international corporations. With headquarters of more than 100 insurance companies, Connecticut is often called the "insurance state."

LEAFY HARVEST. Tents protect shade tobacco. Leaves from the plants, which are grown on two farms in the Connecticut River Valley, are used for premium cigar wrappers.

BRIGHT CITY LIGHTS. Established as a fort in the early 1600s, Hartford was one of the earliest cities of colonial America. Today, this modern state capital is a center of economic growth and cultural diversity.

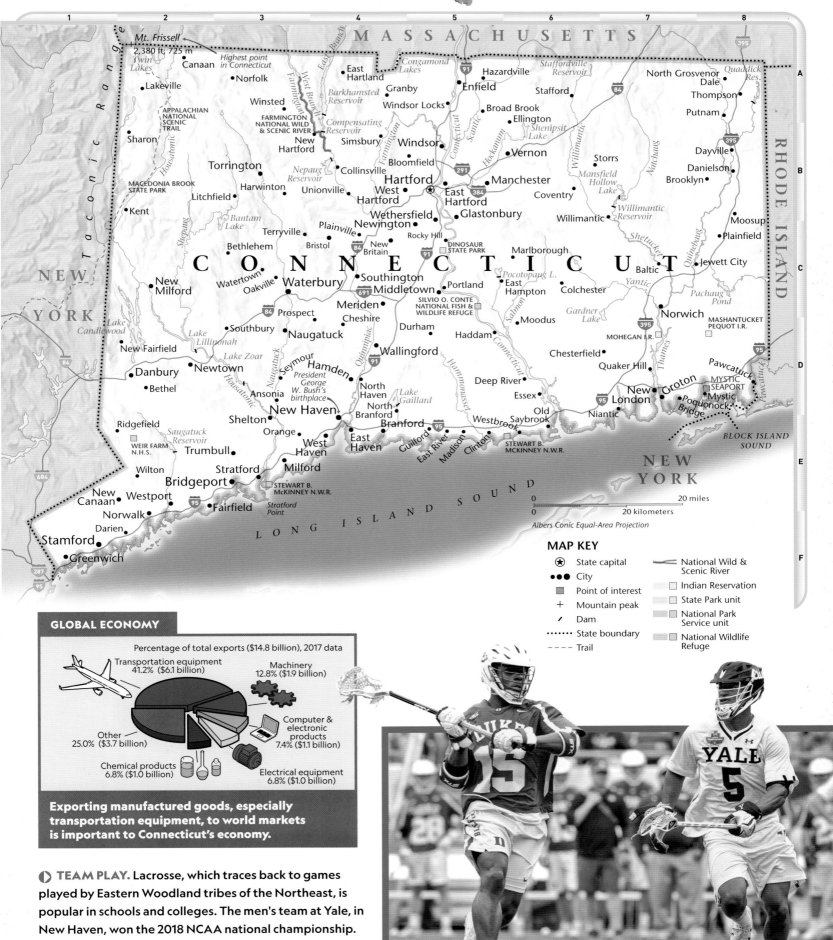

MASSACHUSETTS

Mt. Frissell
2,380 ft; 725 m
Highest point in Connecticut

Twin Lakes

Canaan

Lakeville

Norfolk

East Hartland

Congamond Lakes

Hazardville

Staffordville Reservoir

North Grosvenor Dale

Quaddick Res.

Winsted

Granby

Enfield

Stafford

Thompson

Putnam

APPALACHIAN NATIONAL SCENIC TRAIL

West Branch Farmington

Windsor Locks

Broad Brook

Ellington

Shenipsit Lake

Sharon

FARMINGTON NATIONAL WILD & SCENIC RIVER

Compensating Reservoir

New Hartford

Simsbury

Windsor

Vernon

Storrs

Dayville

Danielson

Torrington

Nepaug Reservoir

Collinsville

Bloomfield

Hartford

Manchester

Coventry

Mansfield Hollow Lake

Brooklyn

MACEDONIA BROOK STATE PARK

Harwinton

Unionville

West Hartford

East Hartford

Willimantic Reservoir

Litchfield

Bethlehem

Plainville

Wethersfield

Newington

Glastonbury

Willimantic

Moosup

Kent

Bantam Lake

Terryville

Bristol

Rocky Hill

DINOSAUR STATE PARK

Marlborough

Baltic

Jewett City

Plainfield

C O N N E C T I C U T

New Milford

Watertown

Oakville

Waterbury

Southington

New Britain

Portland

East Hampton

Colchester

Norwich

Pocotopaug L.

Prospect

Meriden

Cheshire

SILVIO O. CONTE NATIONAL FISH & WILDLIFE REFUGE

Durham

Haddam

Moodus

Gardner Lake

Chesterfield

MASHANTUCKET PEQUOT I.R.

Southbury

Naugatuck

Wallingford

MOHEGAN I.R.

New Fairfield

Lake Zoar

Seymour

Hamden

North Haven

Lake Gaillard

Deep River

Quaker Hill

Pawcatuck

Danbury

Newtown

President George W. Bush's birthplace

Ansonia

North Branford

Essex

New London

Groton

MYSTIC SEAPORT

Bethel

New Haven

Branford

Westbrook

Old Saybrook

Niantic

Mystic

Poquonock Bridge

Ridgefield

Saugatuck Reservoir

Shelton

Orange

East Haven

Guilford

East River

Madison

Clinton

STEWART B. McKINNEY N.W.R.

BLOCK ISLAND SOUND

WEIR FARM N.H.S.

Trumbull

West Haven

Milford

Wilton

Stratford

STEWART B. McKINNEY N.W.R.

NEW YORK

Bridgeport

New Canaan

Westport

Fairfield

Stratford Point

20 miles
20 kilometers

Albers Conic Equal-Area Projection

Norwalk

Darien

Stamford

Greenwich

LONG ISLAND SOUND

NEW YORK

RHODE ISLAND

MAP KEY

- ⊛ State capital
- ●●● City
- ◼ Point of interest
- + Mountain peak
- ∕ Dam
- ⋯⋯ State boundary
- --- Trail
- ～ National Wild & Scenic River
- ◻ Indian Reservation
- ◻ State Park unit
- ◻ National Park Service unit
- ◻ National Wildlife Refuge

GLOBAL ECONOMY

Percentage of total exports ($14.8 billion), 2017 data

Transportation equipment
41.2% ($6.1 billion)

Machinery
12.8% ($1.9 billion)

Computer & electronic products
7.4% ($1.1 billion)

Other
25.0% ($3.7 billion)

Chemical products
6.8% ($1.0 billion)

Electrical equipment
6.8% ($1.0 billion)

Exporting manufactured goods, especially transportation equipment, to world markets is important to Connecticut's economy.

▶ **TEAM PLAY.** Lacrosse, which traces back to games played by Eastern Woodland tribes of the Northeast, is popular in schools and colleges. The men's team at Yale, in New Haven, won the 2018 NCAA national championship.

THE BASICS

Statehood
December 7, 1787; 1st state

Total area (land and water)
2,489 sq mi (6,446 sq km)

Land area
1,949 sq mi (5,047 sq km)

Population
967,171

Capital
Dover
Population 38,079

Largest city
Wilmington
Population 70,635

Racial/ethnic groups
69.7% white; 22.8% African American; 4.1% Asian; 0.6% Native American; 9.3% Hispanic origin (any race)

Foreign born
9.1%

Urban population
83.3%

Population density
496.2 per sq mi
(191.6 per sq km)

GEO WHIZ

Each year contestants bring their pumpkins and launching machines to the World Championship Punkin Chunkin in Bridgeville to see who can catapult their big orange squash the farthest.

The Delaware Estuary is one of the most important shorebird migration sites in the Western Hemisphere.

Delaware

Second smallest among the states in area, Delaware has played a big role in the history of the United States. The Delaware River Valley was explored at various times by the Spanish, Portuguese, and Dutch, but the Swedes established the first permanent European settlement in 1638. In 1655 the colony fell under Dutch authority, but in 1682 the land was annexed by William Penn and the Pennsylvania colony. In 1787 Delaware was the first state to ratify the new U.S. Constitution. Delaware's Atlantic coast beaches are popular with tourists. Its fertile farmland, mainly in the south, produces soybeans, corn, dairy products, and poultry. But the state's real economic power is located in the north, around Wilmington, where factories employ thousands of workers to process food products and produce machinery and chemicals. Industry has been a source of wealth, but it also poses a danger to the environment. Protecting the environment is a high priority for Delaware.

PEACH BLOSSOM

BLUE HEN CHICKEN

⬡ **TEAM SPIRIT.** Enthusiastic fans and the University of Delaware band support the "Fightin' Blue Hens." Located in Newark, the university traces its roots to 1743.

⬡ **PAST GRANDEUR.** Built in 1837 in the fashion of a British country house, Winterthur was expanded from 12 to 196 rooms by the du Ponts, chemical industry tycoons. In 1951 the house was opened to the public as a museum for the family's extensive collection of antiques and Americana.

SEASIDE RETREAT.

Originally established in 1873 as a church campground, Rehoboth Beach is still a popular getaway destination on Delaware's Atlantic coastline. A concrete dolphin overlooks the town's boardwalk, a popular promenade that separates shops and restaurants from the beach. The boardwalk has been destroyed on several occasions by storms.

CHEMICAL GIANT

Manufacturing sectors in million $, 2016 data

- $986 — Chemical products
- $889 — Food, beverage, & tobacco products
- $595 — Petroleum & coal products
- $567 — Computer & electronic products
- $230 — Plastics & rubber products

A gunpowder mill founded by the du Pont family in 1802 gave rise to the production of chemicals that is now the state's leading industry.

PENNSYLVANIA

Highest point in Delaware
448 ft
137 m

Delaware and Pennsylvania are the only states that have a boundary shaped like part of a circle.

Brandywine
FIRST STATE NAT. MON.
Talleyville
Winterthur Museum and Gardens
Claymont
Hockessin
Greenville
Bellefonte
Wilmington
Elsmere
Marshallton
Newport
Newark
Brookside
New Castle
DELAWARE MEMORIAL BRIDGE
Bear
Glasgow
Delaware City
Pea Patch Island
St. Georges
Chesapeake and Delaware Canal
Port Penn
Reedy Island
Odessa
Middletown
Liston Pt.
Noxontown Pond
Townsend

NEW JERSEY

MARYLAND

Clayton
Smyrna
BOMBAY HOOK NATIONAL WILDLIFE REFUGE
Goose Point
Leipsic
Deepwater Point
Cheswold
St. Jones
Dover
Camden
Kitts Hummock
Marydel
Bowers Beach

DELAWARE

Delaware Bay

Felton
Frederica
Harrington
Houston
Milford
Slaughter Beach
Lincoln
PRIME HOOK NATIONAL WILDLIFE REFUGE
Broadkill Beach
Greenwood
Ellendale
Cape Henlopen
Milton
Lewes
Lewes & Rehoboth Canal
ATLANTIC
Bridgeville
Harbeson
Rehoboth Beach
Midway
Georgetown
Dewey Beach
Rehoboth Bay
OCEAN
Seaford
Blades
Oak Orchard
Indian River Bay
Indian River Inlet
Millsboro
Laurel
Ocean View
Bethany Beach
Dagsboro
Assawoman Canal
Frankford
Cypress Swamp
Delmar
Selbyville
Fenwick Island

MAP KEY

- ⊛ State capital
- •• City
- ▪ Point of interest
- + Mountain peak
- ⋯ State boundary
- Swamp
- National Park Service unit
- National Wildlife Refuge

0 — 10 miles
0 — 10 kilometers
Albers Conic Equal-Area Projection

THE BASICS

Statehood
March 15, 1820; 23rd state

Total area (land and water)
35,380 sq mi (91,633 sq km)

Land area
30,843 sq mi (79.883 sq km)

Population
1,338,404

Capital
Augusta
Population 18,681

Largest city
Portland
Population 66,417

Racial/ethnic groups
94.7% white; 1.6% African American; 1.2% Asian; 0.7% Native American; 1.6% Hispanic origin (any race)

Foreign born
3.6%

Urban population
38.7%

Population density
43.4 per sq mi (16.8 per sq km)

GEO WHIZ

With world shark populations declining, some conservation-minded deep-sea fishermen in Maine have turned the idea of a shark tournament upside down. They still compete to see who can catch the biggest fish, but they tag and release the sharks.

Glaciers formed during the last ice age carved hundreds of inlets out of Maine's shoreline and created some 2,000 islands.

Maine

Maine's story begins long before the arrival of European settlers in the 1600s. Evidence of ancestors of today's Native Americans dates to at least 3000 B.C., and Leif Erikson and his Viking sailors may have explored Maine's coastline as early as A.D. 1000. English settlements were established along the southern coast in the 1620s, and in 1677 the territory of Maine came under the control of Massachusetts. After the Revolutionary War, the people of Maine pressed for separation from Massachusetts, and in 1820 Maine became a state. Most of Maine's population is concentrated in towns along the coast. Famous for its rugged beauty, the coast is the focus of the tourist industry. Cold offshore waters contribute to a lively fishing industry, and timber from the state's mountainous interior supports wood product and paper businesses. Maine, a leader in environmental awareness, seeks a balance between economic growth and environmental protection.

WHITE PINE CONE AND TASSEL

CHICKADEE

⬤ **EASTERN LOOKOUT.** Acadia National Park, established in 1929, attracts thousands of tourists each year. The park includes Cadillac Mountain, the highest point along the North Atlantic coast and the site from which the earliest sunrises in the continental United States can be viewed from October 7 through March 6.

BLUEBERRY LEADER

Production in million lb (million kg)

Year	Production
2012	91.1 (41.3)
2013	87.1 (39.5)
2014	104.4 (47.4)
2015	101.1 (45.9)
2016	101.8 (46.2)
2017	67.8 (30.8)

Blueberries thrive in Maine's poor, acidic soil. Annual production fluctuates depending on weather and the availability of workers to harvest the crop.

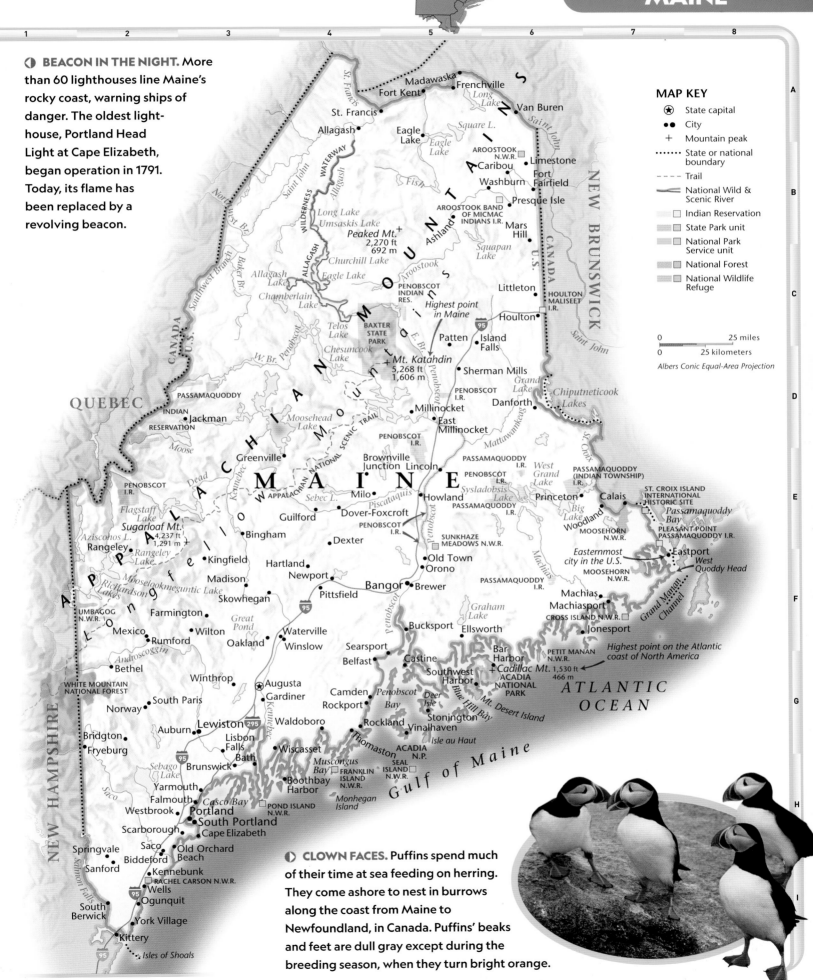

◑ **BEACON IN THE NIGHT.** More than 60 lighthouses line Maine's rocky coast, warning ships of danger. The oldest lighthouse, Portland Head Light at Cape Elizabeth, began operation in 1791. Today, its flame has been replaced by a revolving beacon.

MAP KEY

⊛ State capital
•• City
+ Mountain peak
••••• State or national boundary
- - - Trail
⌇ National Wild & Scenic River
☐ Indian Reservation
☐ State Park unit
☐ National Park Service unit
☐ National Forest
☐ National Wildlife Refuge

0 — 25 miles
0 — 25 kilometers
Albers Conic Equal-Area Projection

◑ **CLOWN FACES.** Puffins spend much of their time at sea feeding on herring. They come ashore to nest in burrows along the coast from Maine to Newfoundland, in Canada. Puffins' beaks and feet are dull gray except during the breeding season, when they turn bright orange.

THE OLD LINE STATE:
MARYLAND

THE BASICS

Statehood
April 28, 1788; 7th state

Total area (land and water)
12,406 sq mi (32,131 sq km)

Land area
9,707 sq mi (25,142 sq km)

Population
6,042,718

Capital
Annapolis
Population 39,174

Largest city
Baltimore
Population 602,495

Racial/ethnic groups
59.0% white; 30.8% African American; 6.7% Asian; 0.6% Native American; 10.1% Hispanic origin (any race)

Foreign born
14.9 %

Urban population
87.2%

Population density
622.5 per sq mi
(240.3 per sq km)

GEO WHIZ

The Naval Support Facility Thurmont, better known as Camp David, is the mountain retreat of American presidents. It is part of Catoctin Mountain Park in north-central Maryland.

Residents on Smith Island, in the lower Chesapeake Bay, face loss of their land and their traditional livelihood due to rising sea levels and dwindling blue crab harvests.

The name of Baltimore's professional football team—the Ravens—was inspired by the title of a poem by Edgar Allan Poe, who lived in Baltimore in the mid-1800s.

Maryland

Native Americans who raised crops and harvested oysters from the nearby waters of Chesapeake Bay lived on the land that would become Maryland long before early European settlers arrived. In 1608 Captain John Smith explored the waters of the bay, and in 1634 English settlers established the colony of Maryland. In 1788 Maryland became the seventh state to ratify the new U.S. Constitution. Chesapeake Bay, the largest estuary in the United States, almost splits Maryland into two parts. East of the bay lies the flat coastal plain, and to the west the land rises through the hills and mountains of the panhandle. Chesapeake Bay, the state's economic and environmental focal point, supports a busy seafood industry. It is also a major transportation artery, linking Baltimore and other Maryland ports to the Atlantic Ocean. Most of the people of Maryland live in an urban corridor between Baltimore and Washington, D.C., where jobs in government, research, and high-tech businesses provide employment.

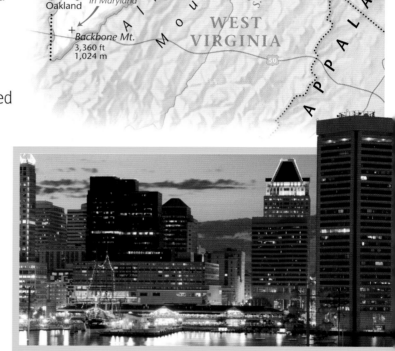

GATEWAY CITY. Since the early 1700s, Baltimore has been a major seaport and focus of trade, industry, and immigration. Today, the Inner Harbor is not only a modern working port but also the city's vibrant cultural center.

BLACK-EYED SUSAN

NORTHERN (BALTIMORE) ORIOLE

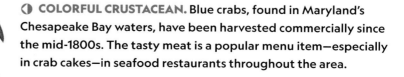

COLORFUL CRUSTACEAN. Blue crabs, found in Maryland's Chesapeake Bay waters, have been harvested commercially since the mid-1800s. The tasty meat is a popular menu item—especially in crab cakes—in seafood restaurants throughout the area.

THE OLD LINE STATE:
MARYLAND

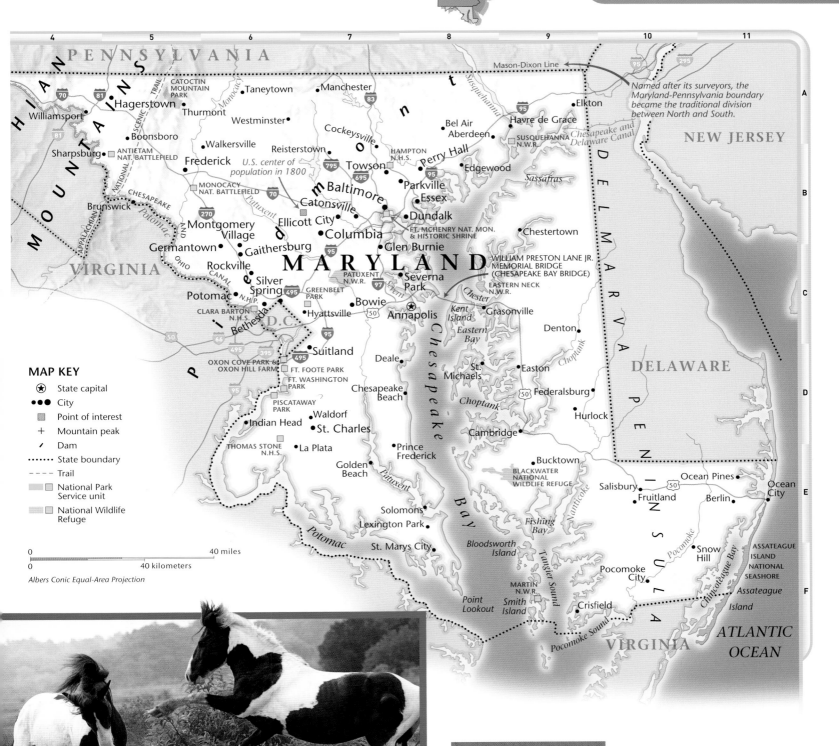

PENNSYLVANIA

Mason-Dixon Line ←

Named after its surveyors, the Maryland-Pennsylvania boundary became the traditional division between North and South.

NEW JERSEY

Williamsport
Hagerstown
Thurmont
Taneytown
Manchester
Boonsboro
Westminster
Cockeysville
Bel Air
Aberdeen
Havre de Grace
Elkton
Sharpsburg
ANTIETAM NAT. BATTLEFIELD
Walkersville
Reisterstown
HAMPTON N.H.S.
Perry Hall
SUSQUEHANNA N.W.R.
Chesapeake and Delaware Canal
Frederick
U.S. center of population in 1800
Towson
695
Edgewood
Sassafras
Brunswick
CHESAPEAKE
MONOCACY NAT. BATTLEFIELD
Catonsville
Baltimore
Parkville
Essex
Montgomery Village
Ellicott City
Dundalk
Chestertown
Germantown
Columbia
FT. McHENRY NAT. MON. & HISTORIC SHRINE
Glen Burnie
Gaithersburg
VIRGINIA
Rockville
MARYLAND
WILLIAM PRESTON LANE JR. MEMORIAL BRIDGE (CHESAPEAKE BAY BRIDGE)
Silver Spring
Potomac
PATUXENT N.W.R.
Severna Park
EASTERN NECK N.W.R.
CLARA BARTON N.H.S.
GREENBELT PARK
Chester
Bethesda
D.C.
Bowie
Hyattsville
Annapolis
Kent Island
Grasonville
Eastern Bay
Denton
Choptank
DELAWARE
Suitland
Deale
St. Michaels
Easton
OXON COVE PARK & OXON HILL FARM
FT. FOOTE PARK
FT. WASHINGTON PARK
Chesapeake Beach
Choptank
Federalsburg
PISCATAWAY PARK
Waldorf
Hurlock
Indian Head
St. Charles
Cambridge
THOMAS STONE N.H.S.
La Plata
Prince Frederick
Bucktown
Golden Beach
BLACKWATER NATIONAL WILDLIFE REFUGE
Ocean Pines
Salisbury
Ocean City
Patuxent
Fruitland
Berlin
Solomons
Fishing Bay
Lexington Park
Nanticoke
Snow Hill
ASSATEAGUE ISLAND NATIONAL SEASHORE
St. Marys City
Bloodsworth Island
Pocomoke City
Assateague Island
Potomac
Tangier Sound
MARTIN N.W.R.
Point Lookout
Smith Island
Crisfield
Pocomoke Sound
VIRGINIA
ATLANTIC OCEAN

Chesapeake Bay

Susquehanna

Monocacy

Patuxent

Potomac

APPALACHIAN

MOUNTAINS

CATOCTIN MOUNTAIN PARK

DELMARVA PENINSULA

Chincoteague Bay

MAP KEY

- ⍟ State capital
- ●●● City
- ▪ Point of interest
- + Mountain peak
- ⟋ Dam
- ········ State boundary
- - - - - Trail
- National Park Service unit
- National Wildlife Refuge

```
0                    40 miles
0              40 kilometers
```
Albers Conic Equal-Area Projection

HORSEPLAY. Wild ponies have lived on Assateague Island since the 1600s. Some believe the original ponies were survivors from a Spanish galleon that sank offshore. Today, more than 300 ponies live on this Atlantic barrier island shared by Maryland and Virginia.

CHESAPEAKE HARVEST

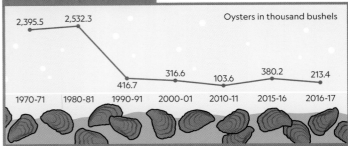

Oysters in thousand bushels

1970-71	1980-81	1990-91	2000-01	2010-11	2015-16	2016-17
2,395.5	2,532.3	416.7	316.6	103.6	380.2	213.4

Maryland's oyster harvest fell dramatically due to over-harvesting, pollution, and disease. It has since struggled to make a comeback.

Massachusetts

The earliest human inhabitants of Massachusetts were ancestors of today's Native Americans who arrived more than 10,000 years ago. The first Europeans to visit Massachusetts may have been Norsemen around A.D. 1000, and later fishermen came from France and Spain. But the first permanent European settlement was established in 1620, when people aboard the sailing ship *Mayflower* landed near Plymouth on the coast of Massachusetts. The Puritans arrived soon after, and by 1630 they had established settlements at Salem and Boston.

By 1640 more than 16,000 people, most seeking religious freedom, had settled in Massachusetts. The early economy of Massachusetts was based on shipping, fishing, and whaling. By the 19th century, industry, taking advantage of abundant water power, had a firm foothold. Factory jobs attracted thousands of immigrants, mainly from Europe. In the late 20th century, Massachusetts experienced a boom in high-tech jobs, drawing on the state's skilled labor force and its more than 100 colleges and universities.

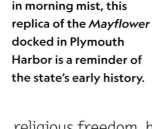

⬤ **REMINDER OF TIMES PAST. Shrouded in morning mist, this replica of the *Mayflower* docked in Plymouth Harbor is a reminder of the state's early history.**

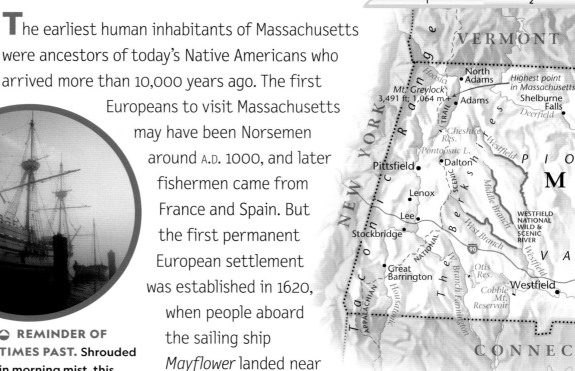

THE BASICS

Statehood
February 6, 1788; 6th state

Total area
(land and water)
10,554 sq mi
(27,336 sq km)

Land area
7,800 sq mi
(20,202 sq km)

Population
6,902,149

Capital
Boston
Population 694,583

Largest city
Boston
Population 694,583

Racial/ethnic groups
81.3% white; 8.8% African American; 6.9% Asian; 0.5% Native American; 11.9% Hispanic origin (any race)

Foreign born
16.2%

Urban population
92.0%

Population density
884.9 per sq mi
(341.7 per sq km)

GEO WHIZ

Massachusetts is the birthplace of several inventors, including Eli Whitney, Samuel Morse, and Benjamin Franklin.

The country's first lighthouse was built on Little Brewster Island in Boston Harbor in 1716.

CHICKADEE

MAYFLOWER

◗ **LEVIATHANS OF THE DEEP. In the 1800s** Massachusetts was a major center for the whaling industry, with more than 300 registered whaling ships. Today, humpback whales swim in the protected waters of a marine sanctuary in Massachusetts Bay.

NEW HAMPSHIRE

ATLANTIC OCEAN

Amesbury
Haverhill
Newburyport
Methuen
Lawrence
Ipswich
PARKER RIVER N.W.R.
Winchendon
Turners Falls
Orange
Athol
Gardner
Fitchburg
LOWELL N.H.P.
Lowell
Dracut
Chelmsford
Wilmington
Danvers
Gloucester
Cape Ann
SALEM MARITIME N.H.S.
Beverly
Salem
Peabody
Marblehead

One of the ten most populous cities in the U.S. in 1790

Greenfield
Deerfield
Leominster
Quabbin Reservoir
OXBOW N.W.R.
SUDBURY, ASSABET & CONCORD NATIONAL WILD & SCENIC RIVER
MINUTE MAN N.H.P.
Concord
Lexington
Woburn
SAUGUS IRON WORKS N.H.S.
Lynn

MASSACHUSETTS

STELLWAGEN BANK NATIONAL MARINE SANCTUARY

Massachusetts Bay

Silvio O. Conte N.W.R.
NEER
VALLEY
Amherst
Northampton
Wachusett Res.
ASSABET N.W.R.
GREAT MEADOWS N.W.R.
Medford
Malden
Cambridge
BOSTON N.H.P.
Boston
Marlborough
Shrewsbury
Sudbury Res.
Wellesley
Brookline
BOSTON HARBOR ISLANDS N.R.A.
Quincy
Weymouth
Birthplace of Presidents John Adams and John Quincy Adams

South Hadley
Easthampton
Holyoke
Ludlow
Chicopee
Springfield
Agawam
SPRINGFIELD ARMORY N.H.S.
Ware
Spencer
Auburn
Worcester
Framingham
Milton
President Kennedy's birthplace
President George H.W. Bush's birthplace
Norwood
Randolph
Rockland
Whitman

CONNECTICUT

Sturbridge
Southbridge
Webster
Oxford
Bellingham
Milford
Franklin
Stoughton
Brockton

Lake Quinsigamond

Blackstone

Charles

TICUT
RHODE ISLAND
North Attleboro
Attleboro
Taunton
TAUNTON NATIONAL WILD & SCENIC RIVER
Bridgewater
Middleboro
Assawompset Pond
Silver Lake
Cape Cod Canal

Provincetown
CAPE COD NATIONAL SEASHORE
Plimoth Plantation
Truro
Plymouth
MASSASOIT N.W.R.
Wellfleet

Cape Cod Bay

Seekonk
Somerset
Long Pond
Great Quittacus Pond
Buzzards Bay
Sandwich
Dennis
Orleans

Fall River
NEW BEDFORD WHALING N.H.P.
New Bedford
Fairhaven
Barnstable
Hyannis
Chatham
S. Yarmouth
MASHPEE N.W.R.
CAPE COD
Monomoy Island
MONOMOY N.W.R.

Rhode Island Sound

Woods Hole
East Falmouth
Falmouth
Vineyard Haven
Oak Bluffs
Nantucket Sound
NANTUCKET N.W.R.

Elizabeth Islands
Buzzards Bay
Vineyard Sound
Edgartown
Chappaquiddick Island
NANTUCKET

Gay Head
WAMPANOAG I.R.
Martha's Vineyard

Nomans Land
NOMANS LAND ISLAND N.W.R.
Nantucket Island
Nantucket

0   15 miles
0   15 kilometers
Albers Conic Equal-Area Projection

MAP KEY

⭐ State capital
●●● City
+ Mountain peak
⟋ Dam
⋯⋯ State boundary
---- Trail
National Wild & Scenic River

☐ Indian Reservation
☐ National Park Service unit
☐ National Wildlife Refuge
☐ National Marine Sanctuary

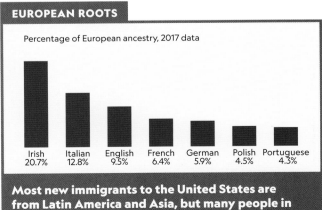

BIG BUSINESS. Cranberries, grown in fields called bogs, are one of the state's main crops. These tiny berries, one of only a few fruits native to North America, are consumed mainly as juice or as a tasty accompaniment to holiday dishes. Workers harvest floating berries in flooded fields.

EUROPEAN ROOTS

Percentage of European ancestry, 2017 data

| Irish 20.7% | Italian 12.8% | English 9.5% | French 6.4% | German 5.9% | Polish 4.5% | Portuguese 4.3% |

Most new immigrants to the United States are from Latin America and Asia, but many people in Massachusetts trace their ancestry to Europe.

New Hampshire

The territory that would become the state of New Hampshire, the ninth state to approve the U.S. Constitution in 1788, began as a fishing colony established along the short 18-mile (29-km)-long coastline in 1623. New Hampshire was named a royal colony in 1679, but as the Revolutionary War approached, it was the first colony to declare its independence from English rule. In the early 19th century, life in New Hampshire followed two very different paths. Near the coast, villages and towns grew up around sawmills, shipyards, and warehouses. But in the forested, mountainous interior, people lived on small, isolated farms, and towns provided only basic services. Today, modern industries such as computer and electronic component manufacturing and other high-tech companies, together with biotech and medical research, have brought prosperity to the state. In addition, the state's natural beauty attracts tourists year-round to hike on forest trails, swim in pristine lakes, and ski on snow-covered mountain slopes.

THE BASICS

Statehood
June 21, 1788; 9th state

Total area (land and water)
9,349 sq mi (24,214 sq km)

Land area
8,953 sq mi (23,187 sq km)

Population
1,356,458

Capital
Concord
Population 43,412

Largest city
Manchester
Population 112,525

Racial/ethnic groups
93.6% white; 1.6% African American; 2.8% Asian; 0.3% Native American; 3.7% Hispanic origin (any race)

Foreign born
5.9%

Urban population
60.3%

Population density
151.5 per sq mi
(58.5 per sq km)

GEO WHIZ

The Granite State boasts more than 200 different kinds of rocks and minerals, making it a great destination for collectors.

The first potato grown in the United States was planted in 1719 in Londonderry.

⬤ **LUMBERING GIANT.**
Averaging six feet (2 m) tall at the shoulders, moose are the largest of North America's deer. Moose are found throughout New Hampshire.

PURPLE FINCH
PURPLE LILAC

⬤ **SUMMER FUN.** Children play in the cool waters of Lake Winnipesaukee, a popular New Hampshire vacation spot. The lake's name is derived from an Abenaki word meaning "Smile of the Great Spirit."

ROARING WINDS

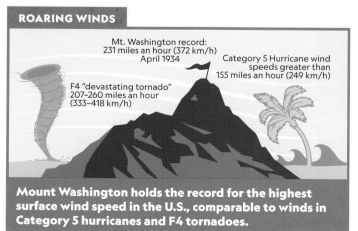

Mt. Washington record:
231 miles an hour (372 km/h)
April 1934

Category 5 Hurricane wind speeds greater than 155 miles an hour (249 km/h)

F4 "devastating tornado"
207–260 miles an hour
(333–418 km/h)

Mount Washington holds the record for the highest surface wind speed in the U.S., comparable to winds in Category 5 hurricanes and F4 tornadoes.

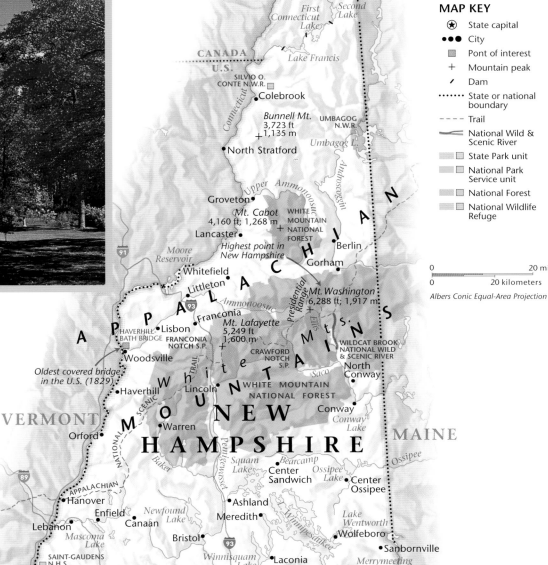

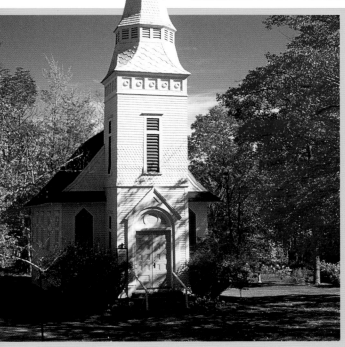

AUTUMN PEACE. A white steepled church sits nestled among trees in a village near the White Mountains. Such traditional churches, common in the New England landscape, are a reminder of early settlers' search for religious freedom.

MAP KEY

⊛ State capital
●●● City
■ Pont of interest
+ Mountain peak
↗ Dam
••••• State or national boundary
– – – Trail
〜 National Wild & Scenic River
□ State Park unit
□ National Park Service unit
□ National Forest
□ National Wildlife Refuge

0 ——— 20 miles
0 ——— 20 kilometers
Albers Conic Equal-Area Projection

QUEBEC

Third L.

First Connecticut Lake

Second Lake

Lake Francis

CANADA
U.S.

SILVIO O. CONTE N.W.R.

● Colebrook

Bunnell Mt. 3,723 ft +1,135 m

UMBAGOG N.W.R.

Umbagog L.

● North Stratford

Upper Ammonoosuc

Groveton ●

Mt. Cabot 4,160 ft; 1,268 m +

WHITE MOUNTAIN NATIONAL FOREST

Lancaster ●

● Berlin

Highest point in New Hampshire

Moore Reservoir

Whitefield ●

Gorham ●

Littleton ●

Presidential Range

Mt. Washington 6,288 ft; 1,917 m +

Ammonoosuc

Franconia ●

HAVERHILL BATH BRIDGE

Lisbon ●

Mt. Lafayette 5,249 ft +1,600 m

FRANCONIA NOTCH S.P.

WILDCAT BROOK NATIONAL WILD & SCENIC RIVER

Woodsville ●

CRAWFORD NOTCH S.P.

Saco

North Conway ●

Oldest covered bridge in the U.S. (1829)

Haverhill ●

Lincoln ●

WHITE MOUNTAIN NATIONAL FOREST

VERMONT

Orford ●

● Warren

NEW HAMPSHIRE

Conway ●

Conway Lake

MAINE

Baker

Pemigewasset

Squam Lake

Bearcamp

Ossipee

Ossipee Lake

Center Sandwich ●

● Center Ossipee

Hanover ●

APPALACHIAN

Newfound Lake

● Ashland

Meredith ●

Lake Wentworth

Enfield ●

Canaan ●

Lebanon ●

Bristol ●

Winnipesaukee

Wolfeboro ●

● Sanbornville

Mascoma Lake

SAINT-GAUDENS N.H.S.

Winnisquam Lake

● Laconia

Merrymeeting Lake

Franklin ●

Tilton ●

Crystal Lake

● Alton Bay

Farmington ●

● Milton

New London ●

Northfield ●

Cochecho

Sunapee Lake

Suncook Lakes

Claremont ●

Sugar

Newport ●

JOHN HAY N.W.R.

MT. SUNAPEE S.P.

Mt. Sunapee 2,726 ft +831 m

Merrimack

Canterbury ●

Rochester ●

Somersworth ●

Pittsfield ●

Salmon Falls

Charlestown ●

Contoocook ●

Concord ⊛

Bow Lake

Dover ●

President Pierce's birthplace

Henniker ●

Durham ●

GREAT BAY N.W.R.

North Walpole ●

Hillsboro ●

Suncook ●

LAMPREY NATIONAL WILD & SCENIC RIVER

Newmarket ●

Great Bay

Portsmouth ●

Highland Lake

Walpole ●

Contoocook

Raymond ●

Lamprey

Antrim ●

Surry Mt. Lake

Nubanusit Lake

Manchester ●

Massabesic Lake

Exeter ●

Rye ●

Isles of Shoals

Keene ●

Monadnock Mt. 3,165 ft +965 m

Kingston ●

Peterborough ●

East Derry ●

Londonderry ●

Derry ●

Plaistow ●

Hampton ●

ATLANTIC OCEAN

PISGAH S.P.

WAPACK N.W.R.

Wilton ●

Merrimack ●

Atkinson ●

Salem ●

Hinsdale ●

Troy ●

Jaffrey ●

Milford ●

Greenville ●

Winchester ●

New Ipswich ●

Nashua ●

Merrimack

MASSACHUSETTS

THE BASICS

Statehood
December 18, 1787; 3rd state

Total area (land and water)
8,723 sq mi (22,591 sq km)

Land area
7,354 sq mi (19,047 sq km)

Population
8,908,520

Capital
Trenton
Population 83,974

Largest city
Newark
Population 282,090

Racial/ethnic groups
72.1% white; 15.0% African American; 10.1% Asian; 0.6% Native American; 20.4% Hispanic origin (any race)

Foreign born
22.1%

Urban population
94.7%

Population density
1,211.4 per sq mi
(467.7 per sq km)

GEO WHIZ

Site of a one-time trash heap, the Meadowlands, a swampy lowland along the Hackensack River, is now home to a major sports complex.

In 1930 New Jerseyite Charles Darrow developed the game Monopoly. He named Boardwalk and other streets in the game after those in Atlantic City.

AMERICAN GOLDFINCH

VIOLET

New Jersey

Long before Europeans settled in New Jersey, the region was home to hunting and farming communities of Delaware Indians. The Dutch set up a trading post in northern New Jersey in 1618, calling it New Netherland, but yielded the land in 1664 to the English, who named it New Jersey after the English Channel Isle of Jersey. New Jersey saw more than 90 battles during the Revolutionary War. It became the third U.S. state in 1787 and the first to sign the Bill of Rights. In the 19th century, southern New Jersey remained largely agricultural, while the northern part of the state rapidly industrialized. Today, highways and railroads link the state to urban centers along the Atlantic seaboard. New Jersey farms grow fruits and vegetables for nearby urban markets. Industries as well as services and trade are thriving. Beaches along the Atlantic coast attract thousands of tourists each year.

⚬ **HOLD ON!** New Jersey's Atlantic coast is lined with sandy beaches that attract vacationers from near and far. Amusement parks, such as this one in Wildwood, add to the fun.

⚬ **SUBURBAN SPRAWL.** With almost 95 percent of the state's population living in urban areas, housing developments with close-set, look-alike houses are a common characteristic of the suburban landscape. Residents commute to city jobs.

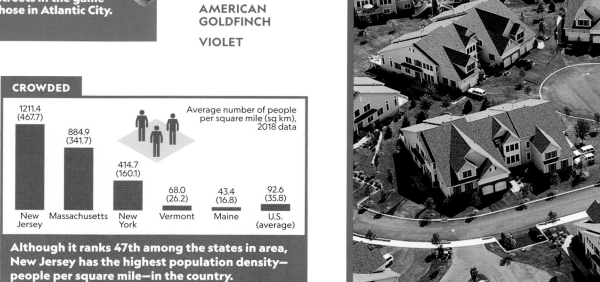

CROWDED

Average number of people per square mile (sq km), 2018 data

New Jersey	1211.4 (467.7)
Massachusetts	884.9 (341.7)
New York	414.7 (160.1)
Vermont	68.0 (26.2)
Maine	43.4 (16.8)
U.S. (average)	92.6 (35.8)

Although it ranks 47th among the states in area, New Jersey has the highest population density—people per square mile—in the country.

SHINE BRIGHT. Designated a National Historic Landmark, the Sandy Hook Lighthouse has been in service since 1764, making it the oldest operating lighthouse in the United States.

HEADED TO MARKET. New Jersey is a leading producer of fresh fruits and vegetables. These vegetables are headed for urban markets in the Northeast.

MAP KEY

- ⭐ State capital
- ●●● City
- ＋ Mountain peak
- Dam
- ⋯⋯ State boundary
- --- Trail
- Swamp
- National Wild & Scenic River
- State Park unit
- National Park Service unit
- National Wildlife Refuge
- National Reserve boundary

0 — 10 miles
0 — 10 kilometers

Albers Conic Equal-Area Projection

NEW YORK

High Point 1,803 ft 550 m — Highest point in New Jersey

Highland Lakes
WALLKILL RIVER N.W.R.
West Milford — Ringwood
Franklin
Newton — Ramsey
Sparta — Wanaque
President Cleveland's birthplace — Ridgewood — Paramus
Wayne
Hopatcong — Paterson — Clifton — Hackensack
Dover — Caldwell — Passaic — Fort Lee
Budd Lake
Hackettstown — Parsippany
Morristown — EDISON N.H.S. — Union City
MORRISTOWN N.H.P. — Newark
Washington — Bernardsville — GREAT SWAMP N.W.R. — Irvington — Jersey City
Phillipsburg — High Bridge — Berkeley Heights — Elizabeth — Bayonne
Plainfield — Ellis Island
Round Valley Res.
Somerville — Menlo Park — Rahway — Lower Bay
Flemington — Piscataway — Edison — Perth Amboy
Electric light invented by Thomas Edison, 1879 — New Brunswick — Sandy Hook Bay — Sandy Hook GATEWAY N.R.A.
Sayreville — Keansburg
Kendall Park — East Brunswick — Cheesequake — Red Bank
Lambertville
Princeton — Eatontown
WASHINGTON CROSSING S.P. — Hightstown — Tinton Falls — Long Branch
Ewing — Mercerville — Freehold — Neptune — Asbury Park
Trenton — Belmar
PENNSYLVANIA — White Horse — NEW JERSEY — Manasquan — Point Pleasant
Burlington — Lakewood — Lakehurst
Willingboro — JERSEY
Cinnaminson — Mount Holly — Crestwood Village — Toms River — Gilford Park
Pennsauken — Browns Mills — Double Trouble — Seaside Heights
Camden — Cherry Hill — Haddonfield
First dinosaur skeleton discovered in North America, 1858 — PINELANDS NATIONAL RESERVE BOUNDARY — Barnegat Bay
Paulsboro — Woodbury — Lindenwold — Long Beach Island
Penns Grove — Pine Hill — PINE BARRENS
Glassboro — Surf City — Ship Bottom
Williamstown — Hammonton — E. B. FORSYTHE N.W.R. — Little Egg Harbor — Beach Haven
Salem — Woodstown — Egg Harbor City — Mystic Island
SUPAWNA MEADOWS N.W.R. — GREAT EGG HARBOR NAT. WILD & SCENIC RIVER — Great Bay
Salem — Vineland — Absecon — Pleasantville — Brigantine
Bridgeton — Mays Landing — Atlantic City
Cohansey — Millville — Ventnor City — Somers Point — Ocean City
MAURICE NAT. WILD & SCENIC RIVER — Tuckahoe — ATLANTIC OCEAN
Woodbine
DELAWARE — Sea Isle City
CAPE MAY N.W.R.
Delaware Bay — Cape May Court House
Villas — CAPE MAY — North Wildwood
Wildwood
Cape May
Cape May Canal

THE EMPIRE STATE: NEW YORK

New York

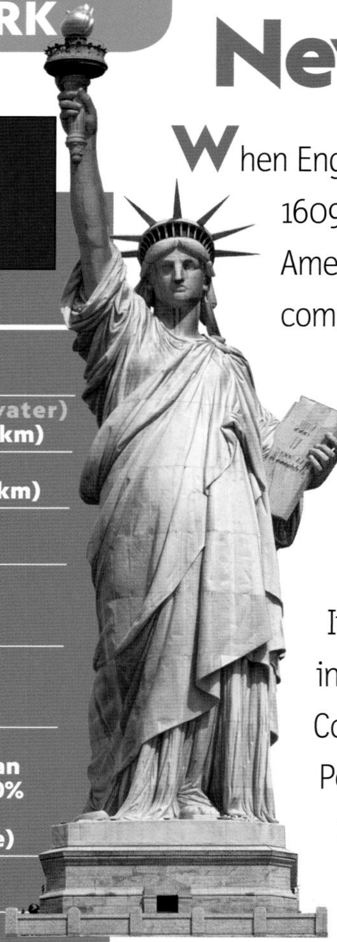

1   2   3

When Englishman Henry Hudson explored New York's Hudson River Valley in 1609, the territory was already inhabited by large tribes of Native Americans, including the powerful Iroquois. In 1624 a Dutch trading company established the New Netherland colony, but after just 40 years the colony was taken over by the English and renamed for England's Duke of York. In 1788 New York became the 11th state. The powerful port city of New York, center of trade and commerce and a gateway to immigrants, is the largest city in the United States. Its metropolitan area, which extends into the surrounding states of Connecticut, New Jersey, and Pennsylvania, has more than 20 million people. Cities such as Buffalo and Rochester are industrial centers, and Ithaca and Syracuse boast major universities. Agriculture is also important, and the state is a leading producer of dairy products, fruits, and vegetables.

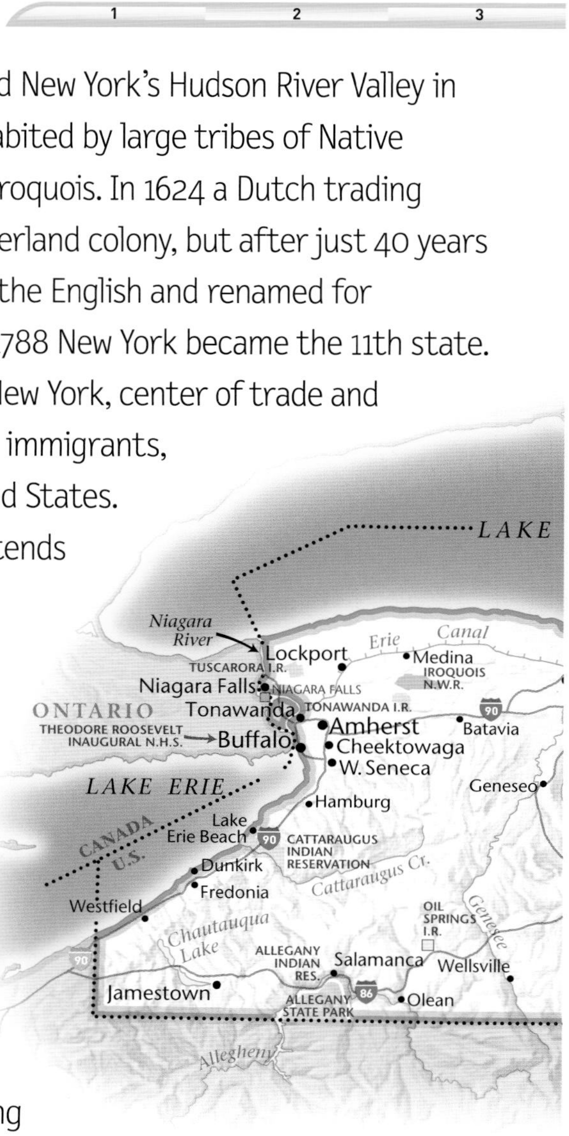

THE BASICS

Statehood
July 26, 1788; 11th state

Total area (land and water)
54,555 sq mi (141,297 sq km)

Land area
47,126 sq mi (122,057 sq km)

Population
19,542,209

Capital
Albany
Population 97,279

Largest city
New York City
Population 8,398,748

Racial/ethnic groups
69.6% white; 17.7% African American; 9.1% Asian; 1.0% Native American; 19.2% Hispanic origin (any race)

Foreign born
22.7%

Urban population
87.9%

Population density
414.7 per sq mi
(160.1 per sq km)

GEO WHIZ

The National Baseball Hall of Fame, established in 1939 in Cooperstown, includes a museum that houses more than 40,000 artifacts of the game, including bats, balls, gloves, and uniforms.

The Erie Canal, built in the 1820s between Albany and Buffalo, opened the Midwest to development by linking the Hudson River and the Great Lakes.

⬤ **LADY LIBERTY.**
Standing in New York Harbor, the Statue of Liberty is a symbol of freedom and democracy.

EASTERN BLUEBIRD

ROSE

Map labels: LAKE; Niagara River; Lockport; Erie Canal; Medina; TUSCARORA I.R.; IROQUOIS N.W.R.; Niagara Falls; NIAGARA FALLS; ONTARIO; Tonawanda; TONAWANDA I.R.; 90; THEODORE ROOSEVELT INAUGURAL N.H.S.; Buffalo; Amherst; Batavia; Cheektowaga; W. Seneca; LAKE ERIE; Geneseo; Hamburg; CANADA U.S.; Lake Erie Beach; 90; CATTARAUGUS INDIAN RESERVATION; Dunkirk; Cattaraugus Cr.; Westfield; Fredonia; OIL SPRINGS I.R.; Genesee; Chautauqua Lake; 90; ALLEGANY INDIAN RES.; Salamanca; Wellsville; Jamestown; ALLEGANY STATE PARK; 86; Olean; Allegheny

URBAN GIANT

Population of city proper, 2018 data

City	Population
New York	8,398,748
Los Angeles	3,990,456
Chicago	2,705,994
Houston	2,325,502
Phoenix	1,660,272

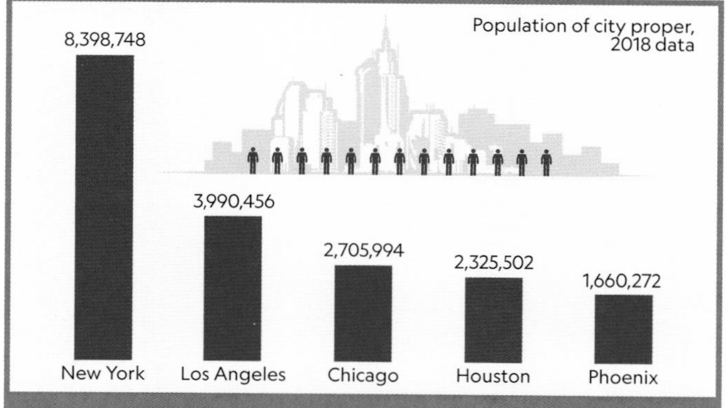

With more than twice the population of the next largest city, New York—known as the Big Apple—is the country's largest city.

◐ **NATURAL WONDER.** Each year more than eight million tourists visit Niagara Falls on the U.S.-Canada border. Visitors in rain slickers trek through the mists below Bridal Veil Falls on the American side.

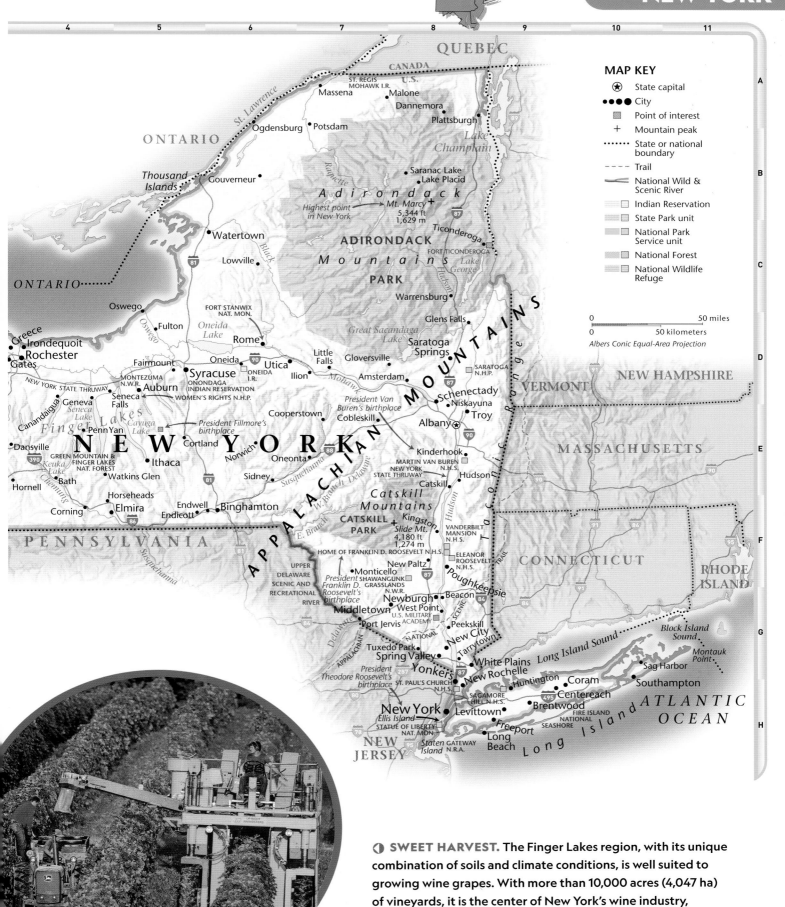

4 5 6 7 8 9 10 11

QUEBEC
CANADA
U.S.

ST. REGIS MOHAWK I.R.

Massena
Malone
Dannemora
Plattsburgh

Ogdensburg
Potsdam

ONTARIO

Lake Champlain

Thousand Islands
Gouverneur

Saranac Lake
Lake Placid

A d i r o n d a c k

Highest point in New York
Mt. Marcy
5,344 ft
1,629 m

87

Watertown

81

Black

Lowville

ADIRONDACK

M o u n t a i n s

Ticonderoga
FORT TICONDEROGA

Lake George

ONTARIO

PARK

Hudson

Oswego

Oswego

Fulton

Oneida Lake

Rome

FORT STANWIX NAT. MON.

Warrensburg

Greece
Irondequoit
Rochester
Gates

Oneida

90

Utica

Little Falls

Gloversville

Saratoga Springs

Glens Falls

Great Sacandaga Lake

SARATOGA N.H.P.

VERMONT

91

NEW HAMPSHIRE

Fairmount

MONTEZUMA N.W.R.

Syracuse

Auburn

ONONDAGA INDIAN RESERVATION

WOMEN'S RIGHTS N.H.P.

ONEIDA I.R.

Ilion

Mohawk

Amsterdam

Schenectady
Niskayuna
Troy

Taconic Range

50 miles
0
50 kilometers
Albers Conic Equal-Area Projection

Geneva
Seneca Falls

Canandaigua

Seneca Lake

F i n g e r

Penn Yan

Cayuga Lake

President Fillmore's birthplace

Cooperstown

President Van Buren's birthplace
Cobleskill

Albany

90

MASSACHUSETTS

90

N E W   Y O R K

Dansville

Cortland

Norwich

Oneonta

Kinderhook

MARTIN VAN BUREN N.H.S.

Ithaca

GREEN MOUNTAIN & FINGER LAKES NAT. FOREST

Keuka Lake

390

L a k e s

Watkins Glen

Sidney

Susquehanna

MARTIN VAN BUREN NEW YORK STATE THRUWAY

Hudson

E

Hornell
Bath

Chemung

Horseheads

Endwell

Binghamton

Catskill
M o u n t a i n s

Catskill

Elmira
Corning

Endicott

86

W. Branch Delaware

CATSKILL PARK

Kingston
Slide Mt.
4,180 ft
1,274 m

Hudson

VANDERBILT MANSION N.H.S.

Scenic Trail

CONNECTICUT

84

86

F

PENNSYLVANIA

Susquehanna

E. Branch

HOME OF FRANKLIN D. ROOSEVELT N.H.S.

ELEANOR ROOSEVELT N.H.S.

RHODE ISLAND

95

UPPER DELAWARE SCENIC AND RECREATIONAL RIVER

President Franklin D. Roosevelt's birthplace

Monticello

SHAWANGUNK GRASSLANDS N.W.R.

New Paltz

87

Poughkeepsie

91

84

86

Newburgh
West Point
Middletown

Beacon

G

Port Jervis

U.S. MILITARY ACADEMY

Peekskill

95

Block Island Sound

Delaware

NATIONAL

APPALACHIAN

New City

Tarrytown

Long Island Sound

Montauk Point

Tuxedo Park
Spring Valley

Yonkers

White Plains
New Rochelle

Sag Harbor

80

President Theodore Roosevelt's birthplace

ST. PAUL'S CHURCH N.H.S.

87

Huntington
Coram

Southampton

287

SAGAMORE HILL N.H.S.

495

Centereach

New York

Levittown

Brentwood

FIRE ISLAND NATIONAL SEASHORE

ATLANTIC OCEAN

Ellis Island

Freeport

STATUE OF LIBERTY NAT. MON.

NEW JERSEY

95

Staten Island

Long Beach

GATEWAY N.R.A.

L o n g   I s l a n d

H

MAP KEY
⭐ State capital
●●● City
▪ Point of interest
+ Mountain peak
⋯ State or national boundary
--- Trail
〰 National Wild & Scenic River
▫ Indian Reservation
▨ State Park unit
▨ National Park Service unit
▨ National Forest
▨ National Wildlife Refuge

🌀 **SWEET HARVEST.** The Finger Lakes region, with its unique combination of soils and climate conditions, is well suited to growing wine grapes. With more than 10,000 acres (4,047 ha) of vineyards, it is the center of New York's wine industry, producing varieties for both domestic and export markets.

Pennsylvania

Pennsylvania, the 12th of England's 13 American colonies, was established in 1682 by Quaker William Penn and 360 settlers seeking religious freedom and fair government. The colony enjoyed abundant natural resources—dense woodlands, fertile soils, industrial minerals, and water power—that soon attracted Germans, Scotch-Irish, and other immigrants. Pennsylvania played a central role in the move for independence from Britain, and Philadelphia served as the new country's capital from 1790 to 1800. In the 19th century, Philadelphia, in the east, and Pittsburgh, in the west, became booming centers of industrial growth. Philadelphia produced ships, locomotives, and textiles, while the iron and steel industry fueled Pittsburgh's growth. Jobs in industry as well as agriculture attracted immigrants from around the world. Today, Pennsylvania's economy has shifted toward information technology, health care, financial services, and tourism, but coal and steel production continue to play a role in the state's economy.

◔ **LET FREEDOM RING. The Liberty Bell, cast in 1753 by Pennsylvania craftsmen, hangs in Philadelphia. Because of a crack, it is no longer rung.**

THE BASICS

Statehood
December 12, 1787; 2nd state

Total area (land and water)
46,054 sq mi (119,280 sq km)

Land area
44,743 sq mi (115,883 sq km)

Population
12,807,060

Capital
Harrisburg
Population 49,229

Largest city
Philadelphia
Population 1,584,138

Racial/ethnic groups
82.1% white; 11.9% African American; 3.6% Asian; 0.4% Native American; 7.3% Hispanic origin (any race)

Foreign born
6.6%

Urban population
78.7%

Population density
286.2 per sq mi
(110.5 per sq km)

GEO WHIZ

The Martin Guitar Company in Nazareth has been handcrafting guitars for musicians all over the world since 1833.

For more than a century, streets in Philadelphia have been transformed on New Year's Day for the annual Mummers Parade.

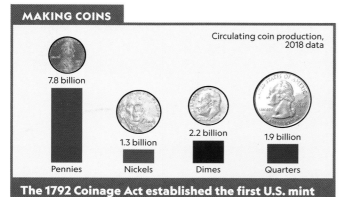

MOUNTAIN LAUREL
RUFFED GROUSE

1 2

LAKE ERIE

Erie
Millcreek
Corry
90
79
Meadville
ERIE NATIONAL WILDLIFE REFUGE
Pymatuning Reservoir
Titusville
OHIO
Greenville
Oil City
Sharon
80
Grove City
Beaver
New Castle
376
76
Butler
79
Beaver Falls
OHIO RIVER N.W.R.
Ohio
McCandless
Aliquippa
76
Plum
279
Pittsburgh
376
Penn Hills
McKeesport
79
Jeannette
Washington
70
Monessen
70
70
79
Connellsville
Waynesburg
Uniontown
FRIENDSHIP HILL N.H.S.
FT. NECESSITY NATIONAL BATTLEFIELD
Monongahela
Cheat
WEST VIRGINIA

MAKING COINS

Circulating coin production, 2018 data

7.8 billion
Pennies

1.3 billion
Nickels

2.2 billion
Dimes

1.9 billion
Quarters

The 1792 Coinage Act established the first U.S. mint in Philadelphia. It is still one of the country's main coin-producing facilities.

◑ **RIVER TOWN. Pittsburgh, one of the largest inland ports in the United States, was established in 1758 where the Monongahela and Allegheny Rivers meet to form the Ohio River. Once a booming steel town, Pittsburgh is now a center of finance, medicine, and education.**

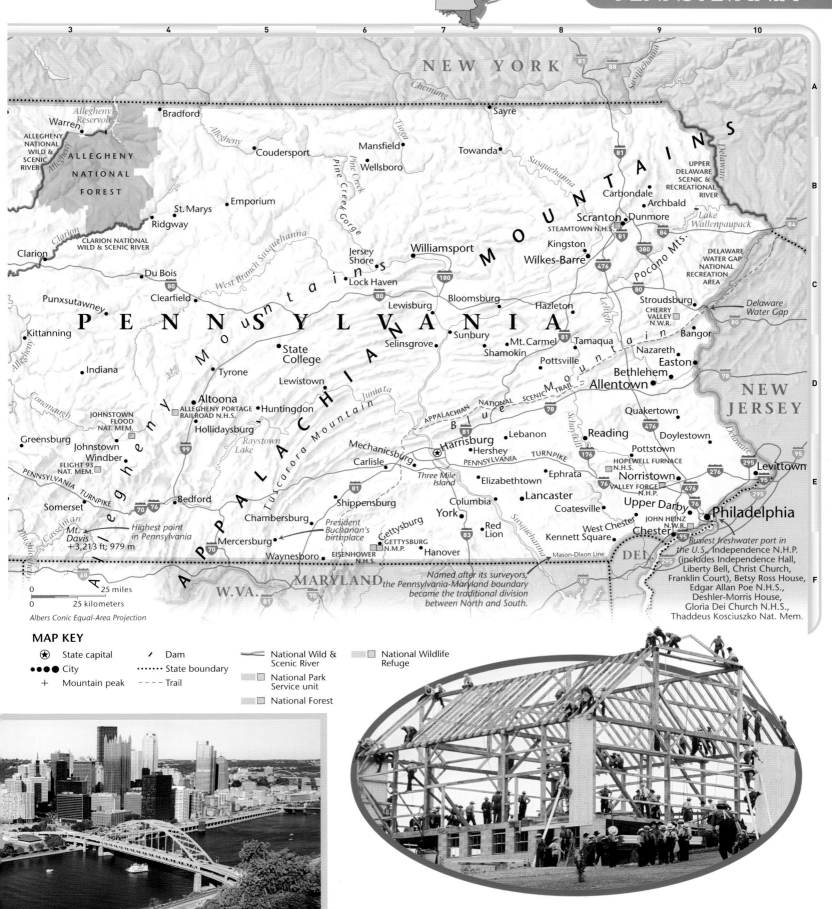

NEW YORK

Warren
Allegheny Reservoir
Bradford
ALLEGHENY NATIONAL WILD & SCENIC RIVER
ALLEGHENY NATIONAL FOREST
Coudersport
Mansfield
Wellsboro
Chemung
Sayre
Towanda
Susquehanna
St. Marys
Emporium
Ridgway
Carbondale
Archbald
Scranton
Dunmore
STEAMTOWN N.H.S.
UPPER DELAWARE SCENIC & RECREATIONAL RIVER
Clarion
CLARION NATIONAL WILD & SCENIC RIVER
Du Bois
Jersey Shore
Williamsport
Lock Haven
Kingston
Wilkes-Barre
Lake Wallenpaupack
Pocono Mts.
DELAWARE WATER GAP NATIONAL RECREATION AREA
Clarion
West Branch Susquehanna
Clearfield
Lewisburg
Bloomsburg
Hazleton
Stroudsburg
CHERRY VALLEY N.W.R.
Delaware Water Gap
Punxsutawney
PENNSYLVANIA
Kittanning
Selinsgrove
Sunbury
Mt. Carmel
Tamaqua
Bangor
Indiana
State College
Shamokin
Pottsville
Nazareth
Easton
Allegheny
Tyrone
Lewistown
Bethlehem
Allentown
APPALACHIAN NATIONAL SCENIC
Blue
Conemaugh
Altoona
ALLEGHENY PORTAGE RAILROAD N.H.S.
Huntingdon
Juniata
Quakertown
Greensburg
Hollidaysburg
JOHNSTOWN FLOOD NAT. MEM.
Johnstown
Windber
FLIGHT 93 NAT. MEM.
Raystown Lake
Mechanicsburg
Harrisburg
Hershey
Lebanon
PENNSYLVANIA
TURNPIKE
Reading
Pottstown
HOPEWELL FURNACE N.H.S.
Doylestown
Three Mile Island
Norristown
VALLEY FORGE N.H.P.
Levittown
PENNSYLVANIA TURNPIKE
Somerset
Bedford
Carlisle
Shippensburg
Elizabethtown
Ephrata
Upper Darby
Casselman
Mt. Davis +3,213 ft; 979 m
Highest point in Pennsylvania
Chambersburg
President Buchanan's birthplace
Gettysburg
GETTYSBURG N.M.P.
Columbia
York
Red Lion
Lancaster
Coatesville
West Chester
Kennett Square
JOHN HEINZ N.W.R.
Chester
Philadelphia
Mercersburg
Waynesboro
EISENHOWER N.H.S.
Hanover
Mason-Dixon Line
DEL.
Busiest freshwater port in the U.S. Independence N.H.P. (includes Independence Hall, Liberty Bell, Christ Church, Franklin Court), Betsy Ross House, Edgar Allan Poe N.H.S., Deshler-Morris House, Gloria Dei Church N.H.S., Thaddeus Kosciuszko Nat. Mem.
Named after its surveyors, the Pennsylvania-Maryland boundary became the traditional division between North and South.
W.VA.
MARYLAND
NEW JERSEY

0 — 25 miles
0 — 25 kilometers
Albers Conic Equal-Area Projection

MAP KEY
⊛ State capital
●●●● City
+ Mountain peak
／ Dam
⋯⋯ State boundary
--- Trail
National Wild & Scenic River
National Park Service unit
National Forest
National Wildlife Refuge

⬙ **TEAMWORK.** Amish people in Lancaster County work together to erect a barn. The Amish, who came to Pennsylvania in the early 1700s from Switzerland and Germany, live in traditional farming communities and shun modern technology.

THE OCEAN STATE:
RHODE ISLAND

Rhode Island

In 1524 Italian navigator Giovanni da Verrazzano was the first European explorer to visit Rhode Island, but place-names such as Quonochontaug and Narragansett tell of an earlier Native American population. In 1636 Roger Williams, seeking greater religious freedom, left Massachusetts and established the first European settlement in what was to become the colony of Rhode Island. In the years following the Revolutionary War, Rhode Island pressed for fairness in trade, taxes, and representation in Congress as well as greater freedom of worship before becoming the 13th state. By the 19th century Rhode Island had become an important center of trade and textile factories, attracting many immigrants from Europe. In addition to its commercial activities, Rhode Island's coastline became a popular vacation retreat for the wealthy. Today, Rhode Island, like many other states, has seen its economy shift toward high-tech jobs and service industries. It is also promoting its scenic coastline and bays as well as its rich history to attract tourists.

⬟ **CLUES TO THE PAST.**
Fossils embedded in rocks left behind 10,000 years ago by retreating glaciers tell of Block Island's past.

THE BASICS

Statehood
May 29, 1790; 13th state

**Total area
(land and water)**
1,545 sq mi
(4,001 sq km)

Land area
1,034 sq mi
(2,678 sq km)

Population
1,057,315

Capital
Providence
Population 179,335

Largest city
Providence
Population 179,335

Racial/ethnic groups
84.1% white; 8.2% African American; 3.7% Asian; 1.0% Native American; 15.5% Hispanic origin (any race)

Foreign born
13.7%

Urban population
90.7%

Population density
1,022.5 per sq mi
(394.8 per sq km)

GEO WHIZ

Providence is home to the world's largest artificial bug—a 58-foot (17.6-m)-long termite, weighing almost two tons (1.8 t), that is the mascot of a local pest control company.

Wild coyotes are living and thriving on islands in Narragansett Bay. Researchers have outfitted some of the animals with GPS tracking collars so that their numbers and whereabouts can be studied online—even by schoolkids.

VIOLET

RHODE ISLAND RED

◗ **SETTING SAIL.** Newport Harbor invites sailors of all ages. From 1930 to 1983 the prestigious America's Cup yacht race took place in the waters off Newport. Today, the town provides moorings for boats of all types.

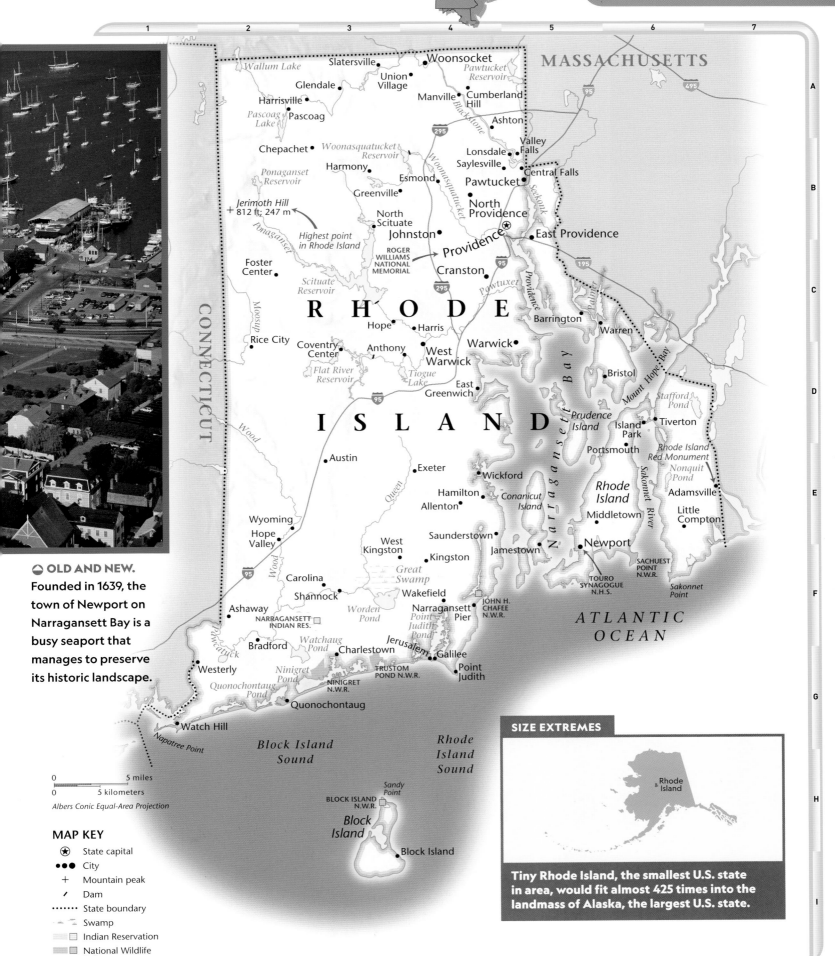

MASSACHUSETTS

CONNECTICUT

RHODE ISLAND

Wallum Lake · Slatersville · Woonsocket · Pawtucket Reservoir
Glendale · Union Village · Manville · Cumberland Hill
Harrisville · Pascoag Lake · Pascoag · Ashton
Chepachet · Woonasquatucket Reservoir · Valley Falls · Lonsdale · Saylesville · Central Falls
Ponaganset Reservoir · Harmony · Esmond · Pawtucket
Jerimoth Hill +812 ft; 247 m · Greenville · North Scituate · North Providence
Highest point in Rhode Island · Johnston · Providence · East Providence
ROGER WILLIAMS NATIONAL MEMORIAL
Foster Center · Cranston
Scituate Reservoir
Hope · Harris · Barrington · Warren
Rice City · Coventry Center · Anthony · West Warwick · Warwick · Bristol
Flat River Reservoir · Tiogue Lake · East Greenwich · Prudence Island · Island Park · Tiverton
Stafford Pond
Portsmouth · Rhode Island Red Monument · Nonquit Pond
Austin · Exeter · Wickford · Conanicut Island · Rhode Island · Adamsville
Hamilton · Allenton · Middletown · Little Compton
Wyoming · Saunderstown
Hope Valley · West Kingston · Kingston · Jamestown · Newport
Carolina · Great Swamp · SACHUEST POINT N.W.R.
Shannock · Wakefield · TOURO SYNAGOGUE N.H.S. · Sakonnet Point
Ashaway · NARRAGANSETT INDIAN RES. · Worden Pond · Narragansett Pier · JOHN H. CHAFEE N.W.R.
Bradford · Watchaug Pond · Charlestown · Jerusalem · Galilee · Point Judith Pond
Westerly · Ninigret Pond · TRUSTOM POND N.W.R. · Point Judith
Quonochontaug Pond · NINIGRET N.W.R.
Watch Hill · Quonochontaug
Napatree Point

Blackstone · *Woonasquatucket* · *Seekonk* · *Pawtuxet* · *Providence* · *Moshassuck* · *Narragansett Bay* · *Mount Hope Bay* · *Sakonnet River* · *Moosup* · *Pawcatuck* · *Wood* · *Queen* · *Pawcatuck*

ATLANTIC OCEAN

Block Island Sound · Rhode Island Sound

OLD AND NEW.
Founded in 1639, the town of Newport on Narragansett Bay is a busy seaport that manages to preserve its historic landscape.

0   5 miles
0   5 kilometers
Albers Conic Equal-Area Projection

Sandy Point
BLOCK ISLAND N.W.R.
Block Island
Block Island

SIZE EXTREMES

Rhode Island

Tiny Rhode Island, the smallest U.S. state in area, would fit almost 425 times into the landmass of Alaska, the largest U.S. state.

MAP KEY
- ★ State capital
- ●●● City
- + Mountain peak
- ⟋ Dam
- ⋯⋯ State boundary
- Swamp
- ☐ Indian Reservation
- National Wildlife Refuge

Vermont

When French explorer Jacques Cartier arrived in Vermont in 1535, Native Americans living in woodland villages had been there for hundreds of years. Settled first by the French in 1666 and then by the English in 1724, the territory of Vermont became an area of tensions between these colonial powers. The French finally withdrew, but conflict continued between New York and New Hampshire, both of which wanted to take over Vermont. The people of Vermont declared their independence in 1777, and Vermont became the 14th U.S. state in 1791. Vermont's name, which means "green mountain," comes from the extensive forests that cover much of the state and provide the basis for furniture and pulp industries. Vermont also boasts the largest deep-hole granite quarry in the world and the largest underground marble quarry. Both produce valuable building materials. Tourism and recreation are also important.

Lakes, rivers, and mountain trails are popular summer attractions, and snow-covered mountains lure skiers throughout the winter.

THE BASICS

Statehood
March 4, 1791; 14th state

Total area (land and water)
9,616 sq mi (24,906 sq km)

Land area
9,217 sq mi (23,871 sq km)

Population
626,299

Capital
Montpelier
Population 7,436

Largest city
Burlington
Population 42,417

Racial/ethnic groups
94.5% white; 1.4% African American; 1.8% Asian; 0.4% Native American; 1.9% Hispanic origin (any race)

Foreign born
4.5%

Urban population
38.9%

Population density
68.0 per sq mi
(26.2 per sq km)

GEO WHIZ

Burlington is the home of Ben & Jerry's ice cream. The company gives its leftovers to local farmers, who feed it to their hogs.

From 1777 until it became a state in 1791, Vermont was an independent country.

Vermont is the only state in New England that does not border the Atlantic Ocean.

⬤ **LIQUID GOLD.** In spring, sap from maple trees is collected in buckets by drilling a hole in the tree trunk—called "tapping." The sap is boiled to remove water, then filtered, and finally bottled.

RED CLOVER
HERMIT THRUSH

⬤ **WINTER FUN.** One of the snowiest places in the Northeast, Jay Peak averages 355 inches (900 cm) of snow each year. With 76 trails, the mountain, near Vermont's border with Canada, attracts beginner and expert skiers from near and far.

SWEET DELIGHT

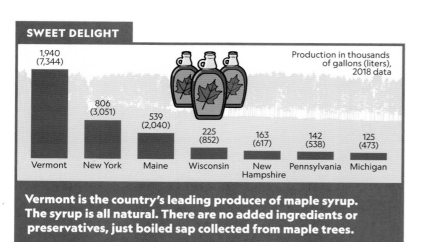

Production in thousands of gallons (liters), 2018 data

State	Production
Vermont	1,940 (7,344)
New York	806 (3,051)
Maine	539 (2,040)
Wisconsin	225 (852)
New Hampshire	163 (617)
Pennsylvania	142 (538)
Michigan	125 (473)

Vermont is the country's leading producer of maple syrup. The syrup is all natural. There are no added ingredients or preservatives, just boiled sap collected from maple trees.

QUEBEC
CANADA
U.S.

Alburg
MISSISQUOI N.W.R.
Swanton
Richford
North Troy
Lake Memphremagog
Derby Line
Derby Center
Canaan

North Hero Island
Saint Albans
Missisquoi
Enosburg Falls
Jay Peak
3,862 ft
1,177 m
Newport
Seymour Lake
SILVIO O. CONTE N.W.R.

North Hero
President Arthur's birthplace
Fairfield
Orleans
Island Pond

Grand Isle
South Hero Island
Lamoille
Johnson
Barton
Lake Willoughby
East Mountain
3,420 ft
1,042 m

Lake Champlain
Milton
Morrisville
Lyndonville

Mt. Mansfield
4,393 ft
1,339 m
Highest point in Vermont
Hardwick

Winooski
Essex Junction
Jericho
Stowe
St. Johnsbury
Moore Reservoir

Burlington
South Burlington
Richmond
Waterbury
Plainfield

Shelburne
Winooski
Camels Hump
4,083 ft
1,244 m
★ Montpelier
Barre

Vergennes
Bristol
Northfield
Graniteville
Wells River
Newbury

MAP KEY

⊛ State capital
•• City
▪ Point of interest
+ Mountain peak
⟋ Dam
⋯⋯ State or national boundary
--- Trail
▨ National Park Service unit
▨ National Forest
▨ National Wildlife Refuge

0 ————— 20 miles
0 ————— 20 kilometers
Albers Conic Equal-Area Projection

VERMONT

MORGAN HORSE FARM
Middlebury
GREEN MOUNTAIN NATIONAL FOREST

Randolph Center
Bradford

Lake Dunmore
Randolph

NEW HAMPSHIRE

Brandon
White

Chittenden Reservoir

NEW YORK

Pittsford
Proctor
Castleton
Lake Bomoseen
NATIONAL SCENIC
MARSH-BILLINGS-ROCKEFELLER N.H.P.
Norwich
Wilder
White River Junction

Fair Haven
Rutland
Woodstock
Otter Creek

W. Rutland
Killington Peak
4,235 ft; 1,291 m
Hartland

Poultney
Poultney
Plymouth
Windsor

APPALACHIAN
President Coolidge's birthplace

Lake St. Catherine
Wallingford
WHITE ROCKS NATIONAL RECREATION AREA
Ludlow
Black
North Springfield

Taconic Range
Green Mountains
Metawee
Springfield
Chester

LONG TRAIL

Manchester Center
Bromley Mt.
3,260 ft
994 m

Mt. Equinox
3,816 ft
1,163 m
Batten Kill

Stratton Mt.
3,936 ft
1,200 m
Bellows Falls

Arlington
GREEN MOUNTAIN
Somerset Reservoir
West

NATIONAL
Mt. Snow
3,556 ft
1,084 m
Putney

N. Bennington
FOREST
Hoosic

Bennington
Harriman Reservoir
Brattleboro

Pownal Center
Deerfield

Connecticut

MASSACHUSETTS

🌉 BRIDGE TO THE PAST.

More than 100 covered bridges mark the state's rural landscape. In the 1800s, bridges were covered to protect them from foul weather. Typical toll charges were one cent for a person on foot and four cents for a person on horseback.

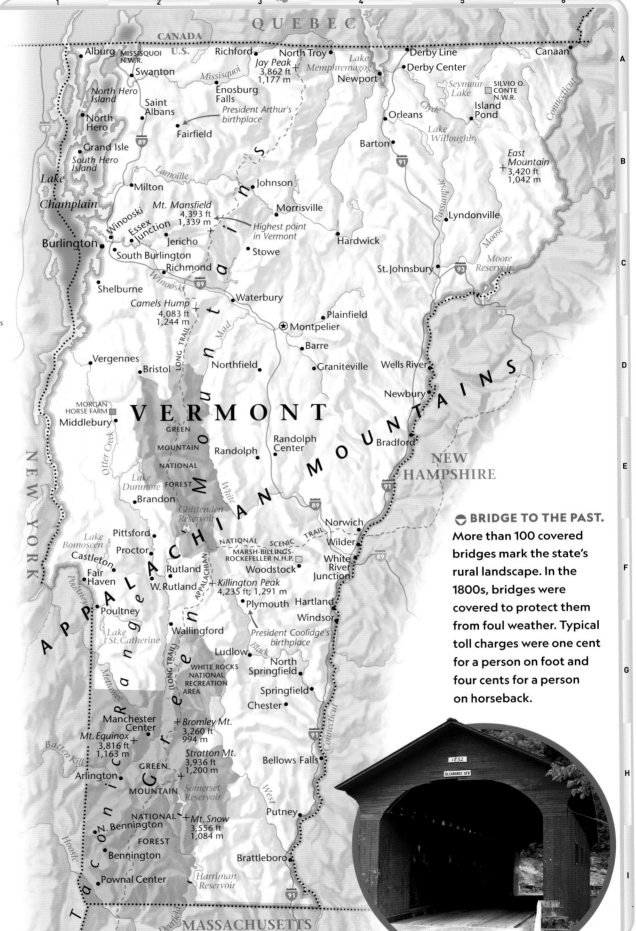

THE REGION

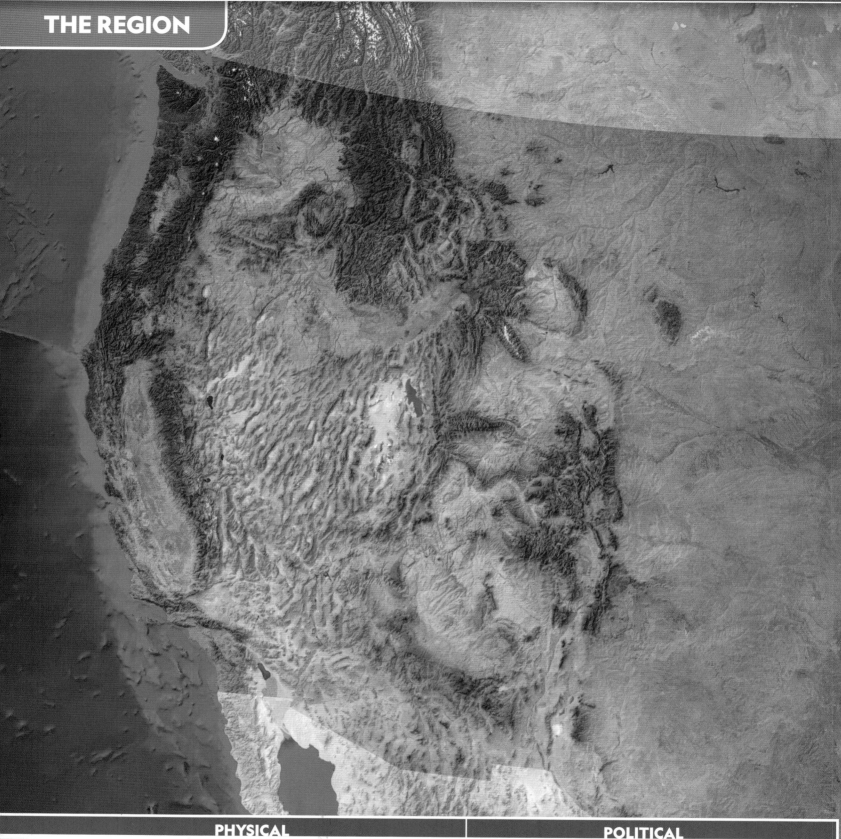

PHYSICAL

Land area
566,988 sq mi
(1,468,492 sq km)

Highest point
Mount Mitchell, NC
6,684 ft (2,037 m)

Lowest point
New Orleans, LA
8 ft (2.4 m) below sea level

Longest rivers
Mississippi, Arkansas, Red, Ohio

Largest lakes
Okeechobee, Pontchartrain,
Kentucky (reservoir)

Vegetation
Needleleaf, broadleaf, and
mixed forest

Climate
Continental to mild, ranging from cool summers
in the north to humid,
subtropical conditions in
the south

POLITICAL

Total population
84,396,680

States (12):
Alabama, Arkansas, Florida, Georgia,
Kentucky, Louisiana, Mississippi, North
Carolina, South Carolina, Tennessee,
Virginia, West Virginia

Largest state
Florida: 65,758 sq mi (170,312 sq km)

Smallest state
West Virginia: 24,230 sq mi
(62,756 sq km)

Most populous state
Florida: 21,299,325

Least populous state
West Virginia: 1,805,832

Largest city proper
Jacksonville, FL: 903,889

THE SOUTHEAST

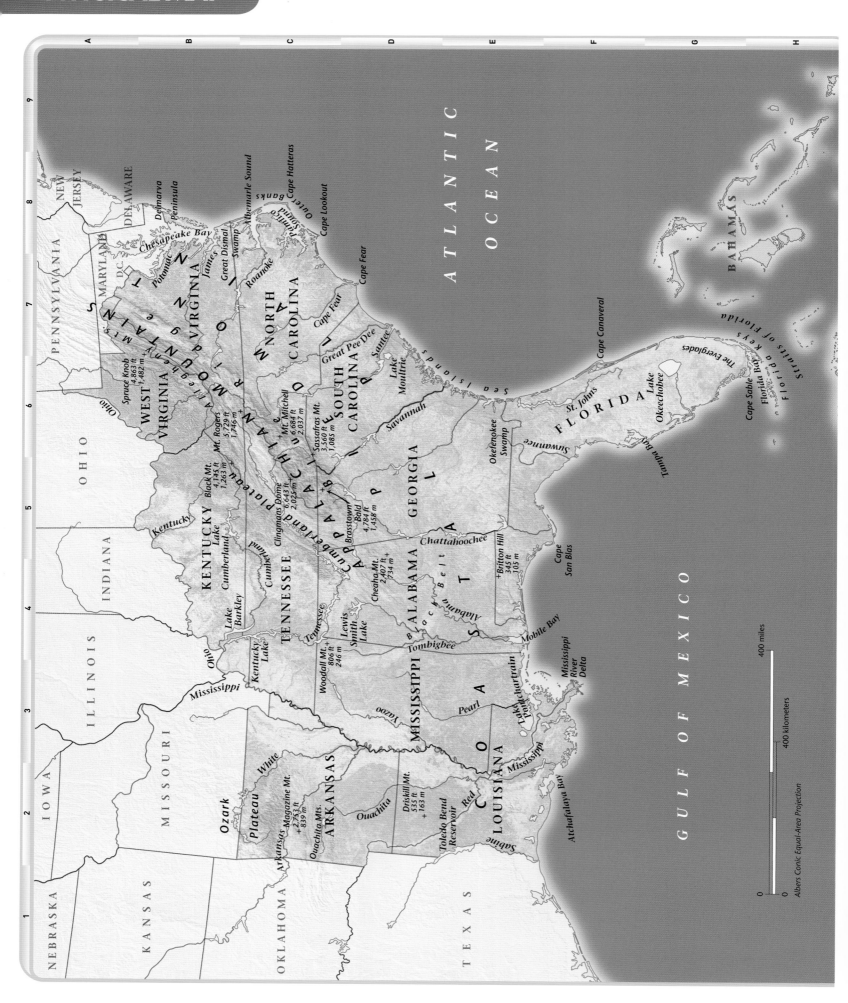

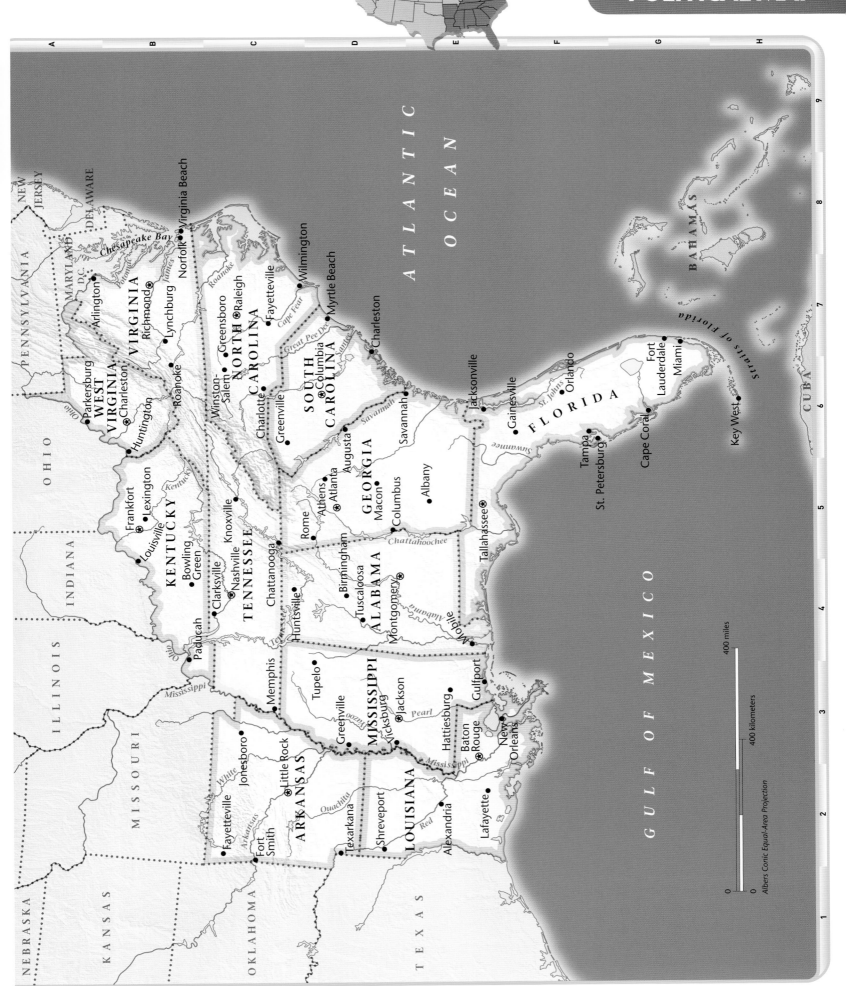

A   B   C   D   E   F   G   H

NEW JERSEY
DELAWARE
PENNSYLVANIA
MARYLAND
D.C.
Arlington

Chesapeake Bay
Potomac
VIRGINIA
⊛Richmond
James
Norfolk
Virginia Beach

Roanoke
Parkersburg
WEST VIRGINIA
⊛Charleston
Huntington
Lynchburg
Roanoke

Winston-Salem
Greensboro
⊛Raleigh
NORTH CAROLINA
Fayetteville
Cape Fear

Wilmington
Myrtle Beach

Great Pee Dee
Charlotte
Greenville
SOUTH CAROLINA
⊛Columbia
Santee
Charleston

OHIO
Ohio

Frankfort
Lexington
KENTUCKY
Kentucky
Louisville
Bowling Green

ILLINOIS
INDIANA

Knoxville
Clarksville
⊛Nashville
TENNESSEE
Chattanooga

Rome
Athens
Atlanta⊛
GEORGIA
Augusta
Macon
Columbus
Savannah
Savannah
Albany

ATLANTIC

OCEAN

BAHAMAS

Jacksonville
Gainesville
St. Johns
Orlando
FLORIDA
Suwannee
Tampa
St. Petersburg
Cape Coral
Fort Lauderdale
Miami

Straits of Florida
Key West
CUBA

Paducah
Ohio
Memphis
Mississippi

Birmingham
Huntsville
Tuscaloosa
ALABAMA
Montgomery⊛
Chattahoochee
Alabama
Mobile
Tallahassee⊛

Tupelo
Greenville
MISSISSIPPI
Vicksburg
Jackson
Yazoo
Pearl
Hattiesburg
Gulfport

Baton Rouge
New Orleans

GULF OF MEXICO

Fayetteville
Jonesboro
White
⊛Little Rock
ARKANSAS
Fort Smith
Arkansas
Ouachita
Texarkana
Shreveport
LOUISIANA
Red
Alexandria
Lafayette
Mississippi

MISSOURI
NEBRASKA
KANSAS
OKLAHOMA
TEXAS

400 miles
400 kilometers
0
0

Albers Conic Equal-Area Projection

ABOUT THE
SOUTHEAST

The Southeast
TRADITION MEETS TECHNOLOGY

◐ **OPEN WIDE.** An American alligator in Florida's Big Cypress Swamp shows off its sharp teeth.

From deeply weathered mountains in West Virginia to warm, humid wetlands in south Florida and the Mississippi River's sprawling delta in southern Louisiana, the Southeast is marked by great physical diversity. The region's historical roots are in agriculture—especially cotton and tobacco. The Civil War brought economic and political upheaval in the mid-19th century, but today the Southeast, which is part of the Sunbelt, has three of the country's top 20 metropolitan areas. High-tech industries are redefining the way people in the Southeast earn a living as well as the way the region is connected to the global economy.

◑ **ENCHANTED KINGDOM.** Fireworks light up the night sky above Cinderella Castle at Walt Disney World near Orlando, Florida. The park attracts millions of tourists from around the world each year.

◯ **SOCIAL CONSCIENCE.** Members of the Big Nine Social Aid and Pleasure Club of New Orleans's Lower Ninth Ward march in a parade through a neighborhood devastated by Hurricane Katrina. Such clubs date to the late 19th century and bring support to needy communities.

WHERE THE PICTURES ARE

Banjo playing p. 67
Horse race p. 66
Black bear family p. 76
Watts Bar Dam p. 77
Cherokee woman p. 73
Grand Ole Opry p. 77
Rocket display p. 58-59
Race car p. 57
Rock climber p. 60
Bird-watchers p. 60
Diamond hunter p. 61
Paddleboat p. 70
Blues museum p. 70
Catfish p. 71
New Orleans musicians p. 68
Katrina parade p. 56
Shrimp fisherman p. 68

River rafting p. 81
Atlanta p. 64
Oil rig p. 58
Peanuts p. 64
Manatee p. 62
Cinderella's Castle p. 56, Girl in parade p. 62

Coal miner p. 80
Cyclists on outcrop pp. 56-57
Harpers Ferry p. 80
Pentagon p. 79
Luray Caverns p. 78-79
Dice p. 78
Wright Brothers Memorial p. 72
Blackbeard's cannon p. 57
Boys playing basketball p. 72
Beach scene p. 74
Wild turkey p. 75
Historic Charleston pp. 74-75
Aerial of Sea Islands p. 64
Rocket launch p. 63
Alligator p. 56

VIEW FROM ABOVE. Cyclists look out from a rocky ledge across West Virginia's Germany Valley. The area took its name from German immigrants who moved there in the mid-1700s from North Carolina and Pennsylvania and established farming villages.

CAR STARS. For more than 50 years, auto racing has been a leading sport in the U.S., especially in the Southeast. The International Motorsports Hall of Fame, located adjacent to the Talladega Superspeedway in Alabama, features racing cars, motorcycles, and vintage cars.

PIRATE'S DEFENSE. This cannon was salvaged from the 1718 wreck of the *Queen Anne's Revenge* off North Carolina's coast. The ship probably belonged to the pirate Blackbeard.

THE BASICS

Statehood
December 14, 1819; 22nd state

Total area (land and water)
52,420 sq mi (135,767 sq km)

Land area
50,645 sq mi (131,171 sq km)

Population
4,887,871

Capital
Montgomery
Population 198,218

Largest city
Birmingham
Population 209,880

Racial/ethnic groups
69.2% white; 26.8% African American; 1.5% Asian; 0.7% Native American; 4.3% Hispanic (any race)

Foreign born
3.5%

Urban population
59.0%

Population density
96.5 per sq mi (37.3 per sq km)

GEO WHIZ

Russell Cave, near Bridgeport, was home to prehistoric peoples for more than 10,000 years. Today, visitors can tour the cave and see tools and weapons that were used by these early inhabitants.

In 2004 Hurricane Ivan, one of the worst storms to batter Alabama's Gulf Coast since 1900, struck Orange Beach.

Alabama

In 1702 the French established the first permanent European settlement at Mobile Bay in what is now Alabama, but different groups—British, Native Americans, and U.S. settlers—struggled over control of the land for more than 100 years. In 1819 Alabama became the 22nd state, but in 1861 it joined the Confederacy. During the Civil War, Montgomery was the capital of the secessionist South for a time. After the war Alabama struggled to rebuild its agriculture-based economy. By 1900 the state was producing more than one million bales of cotton annually. In the mid-20th century Alabama was at the center of the civil rights movement, which pressed for equal rights for all people regardless of race or social status. Martin Luther King, Jr., and Rosa Parks were among the key players. Modern industries, including the NASA space program and assembly plants built by automakers from Asia, have given the state's economy a big boost.

○ **UNDERWATER RESOURCE.** A massive drill descends from an offshore oil rig to tap petroleum deposits beneath the water of the Gulf of Mexico off Alabama's shore.

NORTHERN FLICKER

CAMELLIA

○ **ROCKET POWER.** A giant Saturn V moon rocket dominates a display of rockets in front of the U.S. Space and Rocket Center at NASA's Marshall Space Flight Center in Huntsville. Since it opened in 1970, almost 16 million people have visited the center.

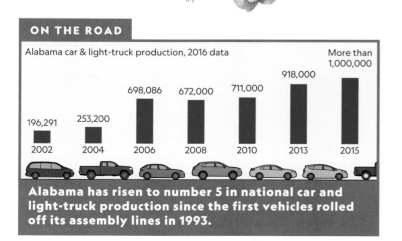

ON THE ROAD

Alabama car & light-truck production, 2016 data

Year	Production
2002	196,291
2004	253,200
2006	698,086
2008	672,000
2010	711,000
2013	918,000
2015	More than 1,000,000

Alabama has risen to number 5 in national car and light-truck production since the first vehicles rolled off its assembly lines in 1993.

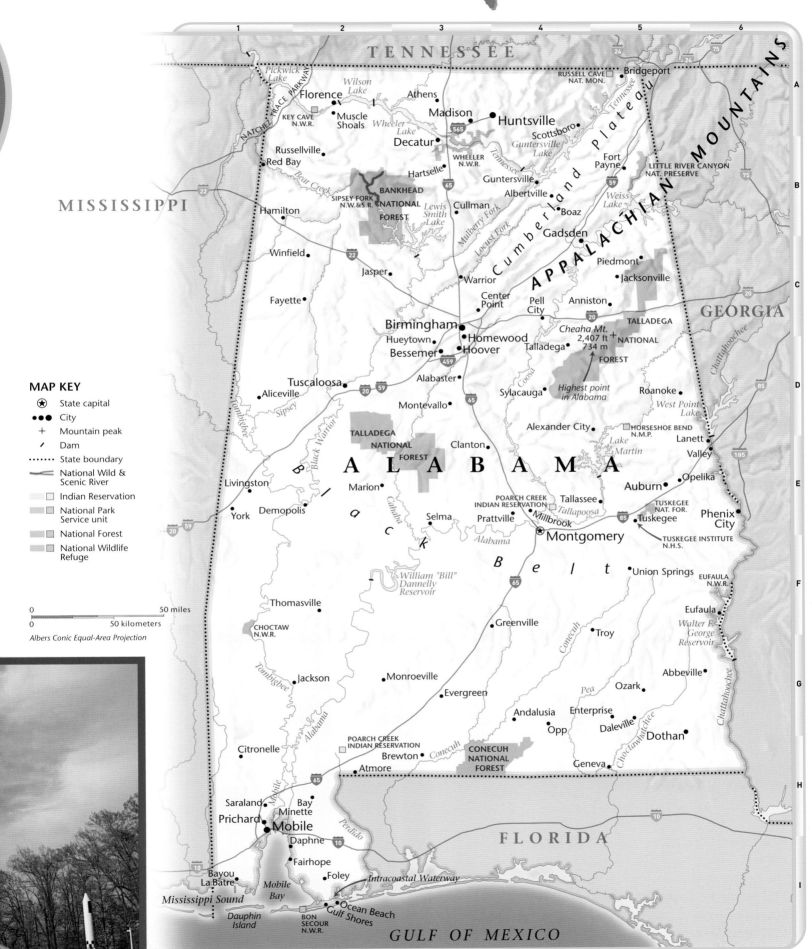

TENNESSEE

MISSISSIPPI

GEORGIA

FLORIDA

GULF OF MEXICO

MAP KEY

⊛ State capital
●●● City
+ Mountain peak
╱ Dam
········ State boundary
〰 National Wild & Scenic River
▢ Indian Reservation
▢ National Park Service unit
▢ National Forest
▢ National Wildlife Refuge

0 ———— 50 miles
0 ———— 50 kilometers
Albers Conic Equal-Area Projection

Pickwick Lake
Wilson Lake
Wheeler Lake
RUSSELL CAVE NAT. MON.
Bridgeport
Florence
Athens
Madison
Huntsville
KEY CAVE N.W.R.
Muscle Shoals
Scottsboro
Decatur
Guntersville Lake
Russellville
Red Bay
WHEELER N.W.R.
Fort Payne
LITTLE RIVER CANYON NAT. PRESERVE
Hartselle
Guntersville
Hamilton
BANKHEAD NATIONAL FOREST
Albertville
Weiss Lake
SIPSEY FORK N.W.&S.R.
Lewis Smith Lake
Cullman
Boaz
Winfield
Gadsden
Jasper
Warrior
Piedmont
Fayette
Center Point
Jacksonville
Pell City
Anniston
Birmingham
Cheaha Mt. 2,407 ft 734 m
TALLADEGA
Hueytown
Homewood
Hoover
Talladega
NATIONAL
Bessemer
Highest point in Alabama
FOREST
Tuscaloosa
Aliceville
Alabaster
Roanoke
Montevallo
Sylacauga
West Point Lake
Lanett
TALLADEGA NATIONAL FOREST
Alexander City
HORSESHOE BEND N.M.P.
Lake Martin
Valley
Clanton
ALABAMA
Auburn
Opelika
Livingston
Marion
Tallassee
York
Demopolis
POARCH CREEK INDIAN RESERVATION
Tallapoosa
Tallassee
TUSKEGEE NAT. FOR.
Phenix City
Selma
Prattville
Millbrook
Tuskegee
William "Bill" Dannelly Reservoir
Union Springs
EUFAULA N.W.R.
Thomasville
Montgomery
TUSKEGEE INSTITUTE N.H.S.
CHOCTAW N.W.R.
Greenville
Troy
Eufaula
Jackson
Monroeville
Walter F. George Reservoir
Evergreen
Ozark
Abbeville
Andalusia
Enterprise
Daleville
Citronelle
Opp
Dothan
POARCH CREEK INDIAN RESERVATION
Brewton
CONECUH NATIONAL FOREST
Geneva
Saraland
Atmore
Bay Minette
Prichard
Mobile
Daphne
Fairhope
Bayou La Batre
Foley
Intracoastal Waterway
Mobile Bay
Ocean Beach
Gulf Shores
Mississippi Sound
Dauphin Island
BON SECOUR N.W.R.

THE BASICS

Statehood
June 15, 1836; 25th state

Total area (land and water)
53,179 sq mi (137,732 sq km)

Land area
52,035 sq mi (134,771 sq km)

Population
3,013,825

Capital
Little Rock
Population 197,881

Largest city
Little Rock
Population 197,881

Racial/ethnic groups
79.3% white; 15.7% African American; 1.6% Asian; 1.0% Native American; 7.6% Hispanic (any race)

Foreign born
4.7%

Urban population
56.2%

Population density
57.9 per sq mi (22.4 per sq km)

GEO WHIZ

In 1924 Arkansas's Crater of Diamonds State Park yielded the largest natural diamond ever found in the United States—a 40.23-carat whopper named "Uncle Sam."

Stuttgart has been the site of the annual World's Championship Duck Calling Contest since 1936, when the winner received a hunting coat valued at $6.60. Today, the prize package is worth more than $15,000.

Texarkana is divided by the Arkansas-Texas border. It has two governments, one for each state.

Arkansas

The land that is Arkansas was explored by the Spanish in 1541 and later by the French, but it came under U.S. control with the Louisiana Purchase in 1803. Native Americans were pushed out as settlers arrived, and cotton fields spread across the fertile valleys of the Arkansas and Mississippi Rivers. Arkansas became the 25th state in 1836, but joined the Confederacy in 1861. Following the war Arkansas faced hard times, and many people moved away in search of jobs. Today, agriculture is still an important part of the economy. Rice has replaced cotton as the state's main crop, and poultry and grain production are also important. Natural gas, in the northwestern part of the state, and petroleum, along the southern border with Louisiana, are key mining products in Arkansas. The state is headquarters for Walmart, the world's largest retail chain, and tourism is growing as visitors are attracted to the natural beauty of the Ozark and Ouachita Mountains.

⊖ **HOLD ON!** A climber scales the face of Mount Magazine, the highest point in Arkansas, where the Ozark and Ouachita Mountains make up the country's Interior Highlands. Ouachita means "good hunting land" in the language of the Caddo people.

APPLE BLOSSOM
MOCKINGBIRD

◗ **BIRD-WATCHERS.** Biologists and volunteers scan the treetops for a rare ivory-billed woodpecker in the White River National Wildlife Refuge. Established in 1935 along the White River near where it joins the Mississippi, the refuge provides a protected habitat for migratory birds.

THE NATURAL STATE:
ARKANSAS

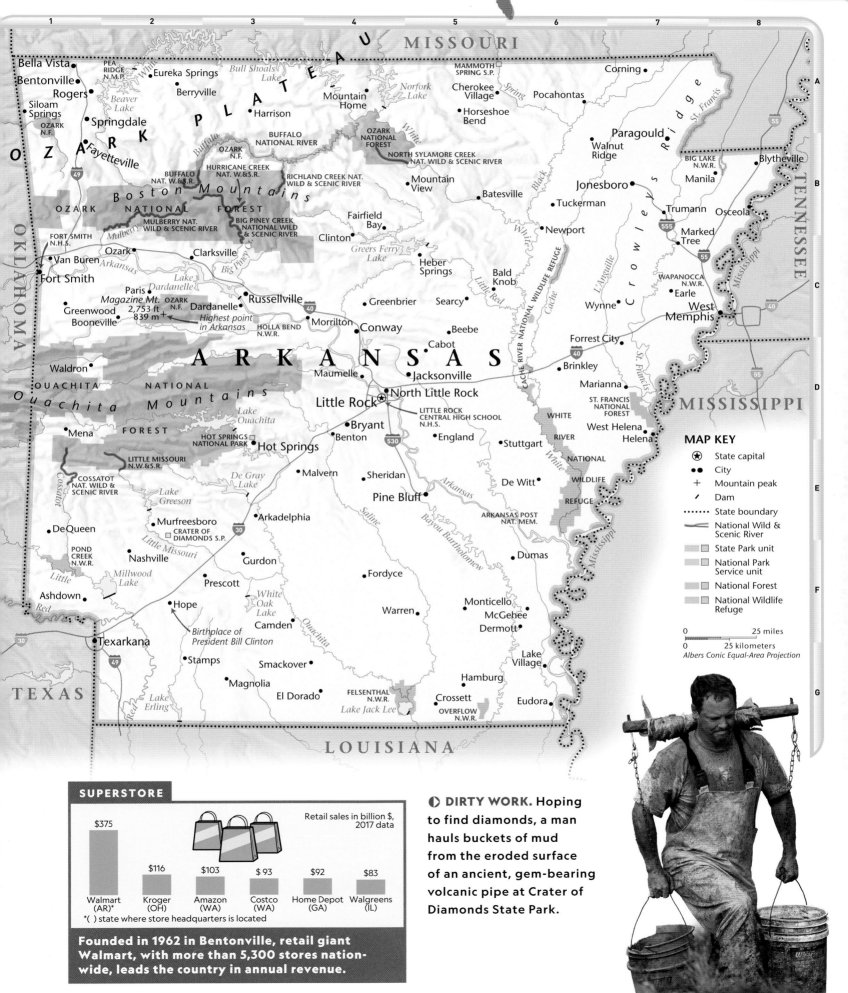

MISSOURI

Bella Vista
Bentonville
Rogers
Siloam Springs
Springdale
OZARK N.F.
Fayetteville

PEA RIDGE N.M.P.
Eureka Springs
Berryville
Harrison
Beaver Lake
Bull Shoals Lake
White

OZARK PLATEAU

Norfork Lake
Mountain Home
White

MAMMOTH SPRING S.P.
Cherokee Village
Horseshoe Bend
Spring
Pocahontas

Corning

St. Francis Ridge

Paragould
Walnut Ridge

BIG LAKE N.W.R.
Manila
Blytheville

BUFFALO NATIONAL RIVER
Buffalo
OZARK N.F.
HURRICANE CREEK NAT. W.&S.R.
RICHLAND CREEK NAT. WILD & SCENIC RIVER

OZARK NATIONAL FOREST
NORTH SYLAMORE CREEK NAT. WILD & SCENIC RIVER

Mountain View
Batesville

Jonesboro
Tuckerman

Osceola
Trumann
Marked Tree

Boston Mountains

OZARK NATIONAL FOREST
MULBERRY NAT. WILD & SCENIC RIVER
BIG PINEY CREEK NATIONAL WILD & SCENIC RIVER

Fairfield Bay
Clinton

Greers Ferry Lake

Heber Springs

Newport

Bald Knob

L'Anguille

Crowleys Ridge

WAPANOCCA N.W.R.

Earle

West Memphis

FORT SMITH N.H.S.
Van Buren
Fort Smith

Mulberry
Ozark
Clarksville
Arkansas
Lake Dardanelle
Big Piney

White

Cache River

Cache

Wynne

40

55

Greenwood
Booneville
Paris
Magazine Mt. 2,753 ft 839 m
Highest point in Arkansas
OZARK N.F.
Dardanelle
Russellville
Morrilton
HOLLA BEND N.W.R.

Conway
Greenbrier
Searcy

Beebe
Cabot

Forrest City

Brinkley
Marianna

ST. FRANCIS NATIONAL FOREST

West Helena
Helena

St. Francis

MISSISSIPPI

Waldron

A R K A N S A S

Maumelle
Jacksonville

OUACHITA NATIONAL Mountains

Mena

FOREST

Lake Ouachita

Little Rock
North Little Rock
LITTLE ROCK CENTRAL HIGH SCHOOL N.H.S.

Bryant
Benton
England

WHITE

RIVER

Stuttgart

NATIONAL

LITTLE MISSOURI N.W.&S.R.

COSSATOT NAT. WILD & SCENIC RIVER
Cossatot

HOT SPRINGS NATIONAL PARK
Hot Springs

De Gray Lake

Malvern

Sheridan

De Witt

WILDLIFE

REFUGE

Lake Greeson

Arkadelphia

Arkansas

DeQueen

POND CREEK N.W.R.

Murfreesboro
CRATER OF DIAMONDS S.P.
Little Missouri

Nashville
Gurdon

Fordyce

Pine Bluff

Saline

Bayou Bartholomew

ARKANSAS POST NAT. MEM.

Dumas

Ashdown

Millwood Lake

Prescott

White Oak Lake

Warren

Monticello
McGehee
Dermott

Little

Hope
Birthplace of President Bill Clinton

Camden

Ouachita

Red

Texarkana

Stamps

Smackover

Magnolia
El Dorado

FELSENTHAL N.W.R.
Lake Jack Lee

Hamburg

Crossett
OVERFLOW N.W.R.

Lake Village

Eudora

Lake Erling

TEXAS

LOUISIANA

MAP KEY

- ⊛ State capital
- •• City
- + Mountain peak
- ⌐ Dam
- ⋯ State boundary
- National Wild & Scenic River
- State Park unit
- National Park Service unit
- National Forest
- National Wildlife Refuge

0 ——— 25 miles
0 ——— 25 kilometers
Albers Conic Equal-Area Projection

SUPERSTORE

Retail sales in billion $, 2017 data

$375	Walmart (AR)*
$116	Kroger (OH)
$103	Amazon (WA)
$93	Costco (WA)
$92	Home Depot (GA)
$83	Walgreens (IL)

*( ) state where store headquarters is located

Founded in 1962 in Bentonville, retail giant Walmart, with more than 5,300 stores nationwide, leads the country in annual revenue.

◖ **DIRTY WORK.** Hoping to find diamonds, a man hauls buckets of mud from the eroded surface of an ancient, gem-bearing volcanic pipe at Crater of Diamonds State Park.

BASICS

Statehood
March 3, 1845;
27th state

**Total area
(land and water)**
65,758 sq mi
(170,312 sq km)

Land area
53,625 sq mi
(138,887 sq km)

Population
21,299,325

Capital
Tallahassee
Population 193,551

Largest city
Jacksonville
Population 903,889

Racial/ethnic groups
77.4% white; 16.9% African
American; 2.9% Asian; 0.5%
Native American; 25.6%
Hispanic (any race)

Foreign born
20.2%

Urban population
91.2%

Population density
397.2 per sq mi
(153.4 per sq km)

GEO WHIZ

In 1937 Amelia Earhart and
her navigator took off from
Miami with the goal of making
an around-the-world flight,
but they disappeared over the
Pacific Ocean and were never
seen again.

Everglades National Park,
the largest subtropical
wilderness in the United
States, is home to rare and
endangered species such as the
Florida panther and the West
Indian manatee.

Lightning strikes occur more
often in Florida than in any
other U.S. state.

ORANGE BLOSSOM

MOCKINGBIRD

Florida

Florida is home to St. Augustine, the country's oldest permanent European settlement, established by the Spanish in 1565. But various Native American tribes had called Florida home long before then. Florida became a U.S. territory in 1821 and a state in 1845. The state's turbulent early history included the Civil War and three wars with native tribes over control of the land. Railroads opened Florida to migration from northern states as early as the 1890s. Its mild climate and sandy beaches continue to attract people seeking to escape cold winters. Today, the state draws both tourists and retirees. South Florida has a large Hispanic population that has migrated from all over Latin America—especially from nearby Cuba. Florida is working to solve many challenges: competition between city dwellers and farmers for limited water resources; the risk of annual tropical storms; and the need to preserve its natural environment, including the vast Everglades wetland.

CULTURAL PRIDE. A young girl marches in Orlando's Puerto Rican Parade, a celebration of the music, dance, and culture of this U.S. island territory.

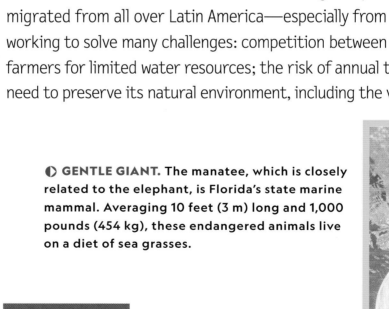

GENTLE GIANT. The manatee, which is closely related to the elephant, is Florida's state marine mammal. Averaging 10 feet (3 m) long and 1,000 pounds (454 kg), these endangered animals live on a diet of sea grasses.

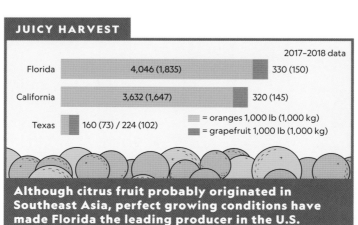

JUICY HARVEST

		2017–2018 data
Florida	4,046 (1,835)	330 (150)
California	3,632 (1,647)	320 (145)
Texas	160 (73) / 224 (102)	= oranges 1,000 lb (1,000 kg) = grapefruit 1,000 lb (1,000 kg)

Although citrus fruit probably originated in Southeast Asia, perfect growing conditions have made Florida the leading producer in the U.S.

GEORGIA

ATLANTIC OCEAN

Marianna
Lake Seminole
Tallahassee ★
Panama City

OKEFENOKEE NATIONAL WILDLIFE REFUGE

Fernandina Beach

TIMUCUAN ECOLOGICAL AND HISTORIC PRESERVE
FORT CAROLINE NAT. MEM.

APALACHICOLA NATIONAL FOREST
ST. MARKS N.W.R.
Perry
Live Oak
Lake City
OSCEOLA NAT. FOREST
Jacksonville
Jacksonville Beach

ST. VINCENT N.W.R.

CASTILLO DE SAN MARCOS NAT. MON.
St. Augustine

FLORIDA

Gainesville
Palatka
FORT MATANZAS NAT. MON.
Palm Coast

Oldest permanent European settlement in the U.S., established 1565

LOWER SUWANNEE NATIONAL WILDLIFE REFUGE
Ocala
Lake George
OCALA NATIONAL FOREST
LAKE WOODRUFF N.W.R.
De Land
Deltona
Ormond Beach
Daytona Beach
New Smyrna Beach

CEDAR KEYS N.W.R.
CRYSTAL RIVER N.W.R.
The Villages
Leesburg
Sanford
CANAVERAL NATIONAL SEASHORE
Titusville
MERRITT ISLAND N.W.R.

Homosassa Springs
CHASSAHOWITZKA N.W.R.
Apopka
Winter Garden
Orlando
JOHN F. KENNEDY SPACE CENTER

Spring Hill
WALT DISNEY WORLD
Kissimmee
Poinciana
Cape Canaveral
Merritt Island
Melbourne
Palm Bay

Bayonet Point
Tarpon Springs
Lakeland
Haines City
FLORIDA'S TURNPIKE
PELICAN ISLAND N.W.R.

TAMPA I.R.
Winter Haven
Vero Beach

Clearwater
Tampa
St. Petersburg
Tampa Bay
PINELLAS N.W.R.
EGMONT KEY N.W.R.
DE SOTO NAT. MEM.
Bradenton

Sebring
Kissimmee
Fort Pierce
FORT PIERCE I.R.
Port St. Lucie

Sarasota
Venice
Arcadia
Peace
BRIGHTON SEMINOLE I.R.
Lake Okeechobee
St. Lucie
St. Lucie Canal
HOBE SOUND N.W.R.
LOXAHATCHEE NAT. WILD & SCENIC RIVER

Port Charlotte
Punta Gorda
Caloosahatchee
Jupiter

ISLAND BAY N.W.R.
Belle Glade
West Palm Beach

Charlotte Harbor
Cape Coral
Fort Myers
Lehigh Acres
Miami Canal
ARTHUR R. MARSHALL LOXAHATCHEE N.W.R.
Delray Beach
Boca Raton

J. N. "DING" DARLING N.W.R.
Immokalee
IMMOKALEE I.R.
COCONUT CREEK I.R.
Coral Springs

Sanibel Island
Bonita Springs
BIG CYPRESS SEMINOLE I.R.
MICCOSUKEE INDIAN RES.
Fort Lauderdale
SEMINOLE I.R.

Golden Gate
Big Cypress
BIG CYPRESS
HOLLYWOOD I.R.
Hollywood

Naples
Swamp
NATIONAL PRESERVE
Hialeah
Miami

GULF OF MEXICO
Ten Thousand Islands
Kendall
Miami Beach

EVERGLADES
Biscaynе Bay
BISCAYNE N.P.

Largest subtropical wilderness in the United States
NATIONAL
Homestead

PARK
Cape Sable
Florida Bay
Key Largo

MAP KEY

- ★ State capital
- ●●● City
- ▪ Point of interest
- + Mountain peak
- ⟋ Dam
- ⋯⋯ State boundary
- Swamp
- National Wild & Scenic River
- ▢ Indian Reservation
- ▢ National Park Service unit
- ▢ National Forest
- ▢ National Wildlife Refuge
- ▢ National Marine Sanctuary

0 ——— 50 miles
0 ——— 50 kilometers
Albers Conic Equal-Area Projection

FLORIDA KEYS NATIONAL MARINE SANCTUARY
DRY TORTUGAS NATIONAL PARK
GREAT WHITE HERON N.W.R.
KEY WEST N.W.R.
NAT. KEY DEER REFUGE
Marathon
FLORIDA KEYS
STRAITS OF FLORIDA

Key West
Southernmost incorporated place in the continental United States

🚀 **LIFTOFF!** A NASA rocket rises amid clouds of steam from John F. Kennedy Space Center on Florida's Atlantic coast. The center has been the launch site for many U.S. space exploration projects.

THE EMPIRE STATE OF THE SOUTH:
GEORGIA

Georgia

When Spanish explorers arrived in the mid-1500s in what would become Georgia, they found the land already occupied by Cherokee, Creek, and other native people. Georgia was the frontier separating Spanish Florida and English South Carolina, but in 1733 James Oglethorpe founded a new colony on the site of present-day Savannah. Georgia became the fourth state in 1788 and built an economy based on agriculture and slave labor. During the Civil War Georgia was part of the Confederacy. The state experienced a long period of poverty following the war. But modern-day Georgia is part of the fast-changing Sunbelt region. Agriculture—especially poultry, cotton, peanuts, and forest products—remains important. Atlanta has emerged as a regional center of banking, telecommunications, and transportation, and Savannah is a major container port near the Atlantic coast, linking the state to the global economy. Historic sites, sports, and beaches draw thousands of tourists to the state every year.

◔ **LIGHT SHOW.** Busy interstate traffic appears as ribbons of light below Atlanta's nighttime skyline. Atlanta is a center of economic growth, with 18 Fortune 500 companies headquartered within its metropolitan area.

◔ **CASH CROP.** Peanuts are a big money-maker in Georgia, where almost half the U.S. crop is grown—about half of which is used to make peanut butter.

BASICS

Statehood
January 2, 1788;
4th state

Total area
(land and water)
59,425 sq mi
(153,910 sq km)

Land area
57,513 sq mi
(148,959 sq km)

Population
10,519,475

Capital
Atlanta
Population 498,044

Largest city
Atlanta
Population 498,044

Racial/ethnic groups
60.8% white; 32.2% African American; 4.2% Asian; 0.5% Native American; 9.6% Hispanic (any race)

Foreign born
10.0%

Urban population
75.1%

Population density
182.9 per sq mi
(70.6 per sq km)

GEO WHIZ

The Okefenokee Swamp, the largest swamp in North America, has meat-eating plants that capture insects and spiders for food.

Founded in 1836 in Macon as the Georgia Female College, Wesleyan College was the first college in the world established to grant degrees to women.

CHEROKEE ROSE
BROWN THRASHER

◔ **PAST MEETS PRESENT.** Georgia's 100-mile (160-km) coastline is laced with barrier islands, wetlands, and winding streams. In the 19th century, plantations grew Sea Island cotton here. Today, tourists are attracted to the area's natural beauty and beaches.

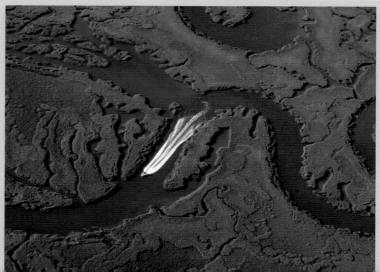

FLYING HIGH

Total passengers in millions, 2017 data

City	Passengers
Atlanta	103.9
Los Angeles	84.6
Chicago O'Hare	79.8
Dallas–Ft. Worth	67.1
Denver	61.4

Moving more than 103 million passengers in 2017, Atlanta's Hartsfield-Jackson International Airport is the busiest in the world.

MAP KEY

⊛ State capital
●●● City
■ Point of interest
+ Mountain peak
⟋ Dam
••••• State boundary
— — Trail
⌁⌁ Swamp
≋ National Wild &
   Scenic River
□ State Park unit
□ National Park
   Service unit
□ National Forest
□ National Wildlife
   Refuge
▭▮ National Marine
   Sanctuary

0 _____ 25 miles
0 _____ 25 kilometers

Albers Conic Equal-
Area Projection

TENNESSEE

NORTH CAROLINA

SOUTH CAROLINA

ALABAMA

GEORGIA

FLORIDA

ATLANTIC OCEAN

SEA ISLANDS

CHICKAMAUGA AND
CHATTANOOGA N.M.P.
LaFayette
Dalton
CHATTAHOOCHEE
NATIONAL
FOREST
Rome
Calhoun
NEW ECHOTA
S.H.S.
Dahlonega
Springer Mt.
3,782 ft
1,153 m
Brasstown
Bald
4,784 ft; 1,458 m
Highest point
in Georgia
Rabun
Gap
CHATTOOGA
NATIONAL
WILD &
SCENIC
RIVER
CHATTAHOOCHEE NATIONAL FOREST
APPALACHIAN MOUNTAINS
Blue Ridge
Toccoa
Hartwell L.
Hartwell
Elberton
Richard B.
Russell Lake
Broad
Lake
Sidney
Lanier
Gainesville
Allatoona
Lake
Etowah
Coosa
Oostanaula
Coosawattee
Roswell
KENNESAW
MOUNTAIN N.B.P.
CHATTAHOOCHEE RIVER N.R.A.
Marietta
Smyrna
MARTIN LUTHER KING, JR.
N.H.S.
Sandy Springs
Atlanta
STONE MOUNTAIN
Athens
Monroe
Washington
J. Strom Thurmond
Reservoir
Martinez
SOUTH
CAROLINA
Carrollton
East Point
Stockbridge
Peachtree
City
Newnan
Covington
OCONEE
Lake
Oconee
Thomson
Evans
Augusta
Griffin
NATIONAL
Eatonton
Lake
Sinclair
Waynesboro
La Grange
West Point
Lake
FOREST
PIEDMONT
N.W.R.
Milledgeville
Sandersville
Thomaston
Macon
OCMULGEE NATIONAL
MONUMENT
Savannah
Millen
GEORGIA
Warner
Robins
Perry
Dublin
Swainsboro
Statesboro
SAVANNAH
N.W.R.
Columbus
Lake Harding
Lake Oliver
Flint
Chattahoochee
ANDERSONVILLE
N.H.S.
JIMMY CARTER
N.H.S.
EUFAULA
N.W.R.
Plains
President Carter's
birthplace
Americus
Cordele
Eastman
Vidalia
Hinesville
FORT PULASKI NAT. MONUMENT
Tybee Island
WASSAW N.W.R.
Ossabaw Sound
Ossabaw Island
St. Catherines Sound
St. Catherines Island
Sapelo Sound
BLACKBEARD ISLAND
N.W.R.
Sapelo Island
GRAY'S REEF
N.M.S.
HARRIS NECK
N.W.R.
Walter F. George
Reservoir
Dawson
Fitzgerald
Hazlehurst
Jesup
Albany
Douglas
WOLF ISLAND
N.W.R.
FORT FREDERICA
NAT. MONUMENT
Blakely
Tifton
Satilla
Camilla
Moultrie
Adel
Waycross
Brunswick
St. Simons Island
Jekyll Island
St. Andrew Sound
BANKS LAKE
N.W.R.
Cumberland Island
Bainbridge
Cairo
Thomasville
Quitman
Valdosta
Ochlockonee
Withlacoochee
Alapaha
OKEFENOKEE
NATIONAL
WILDLIFE
REFUGE
Okefenokee
Swamp
Kingsland
St. Marys
CUMBERLAND ISLAND
NATIONAL SEASHORE
Lake Seminole
Suwannee
Flint
Oconee
Ocmulgee
Ohoopee
Altamaha
Canoochee
Ogeechee
Savannah
Tugaloo

BASICS

Statehood
June 1, 1792; 15th state

Total area (land and water)
40,408 sq mi (104,656 sq km)

Land area
39,486 sq mi (102,269 sq km)

Population
4,468,402

Capital
Frankfort
Population 27,679

Largest city
Louisville/Jefferson County
Population 620,118

Racial/ethnic groups
87.8% white; 8.4% African
American; 1.6% Asian; 0.3%
Native American; 3.7% Hispanic
(any race)

Foreign born
3.6%

Urban population
58.4%

Population density
113.2 per sq mi (43.7 per sq km)

GEO WHIZ

A favorite Kentucky dessert
is Derby Pie, a rich chocolate-
and-walnut pastry that was
first created by George Kern,
manager of the Melrose Inn,
in Prospect, in the 1950s. It
became so popular that the
name was registered with
the U.S. Patent Office and the
Commonwealth of Kentucky.

Pleasant Hill, near Lexington,
was the site of a Shaker
religious community. It is now
a National Historic Site with a
living history museum.

"Happy Birthday to You," one
of the most popular songs in
the English language, was the
creation of two Louisville
sisters in 1893.

GOLDENROD

CARDINAL

Kentucky

The original inhabitants of the area known today as Kentucky were Native Americans, but a treaty with the Cherokee, signed in 1775, opened the territory to settlers—including the legendary Daniel Boone—from the soon-to-be-independent eastern colonies. In 1776 Kentucky became a western county of the state of Virginia. In 1792 it became the 15th state. Eastern Kentucky is a part of Appalachia, a region rich in bituminous (soft) coal but burdened with the environmental problems that often accompany the mining industry. The region is known for crafts and music that can be traced back to Scotch-Irish immigrants who settled there. In central Kentucky, the Bluegrass region produces some of the finest thoroughbred horses in the world, and the Kentucky Derby, held in Louisville, is a part of racing's coveted Triple Crown. In western Kentucky, coal found near the surface is strip-mined, leaving scars on the landscape. Federal laws now require that the land be restored after mining.

THEY'RE OFF! Riders and horses press for the finish line at Churchill Downs, in Louisville. Kentucky is a major breeder of Thoroughbred race horses, and horses are the leading source of farm income in the state.

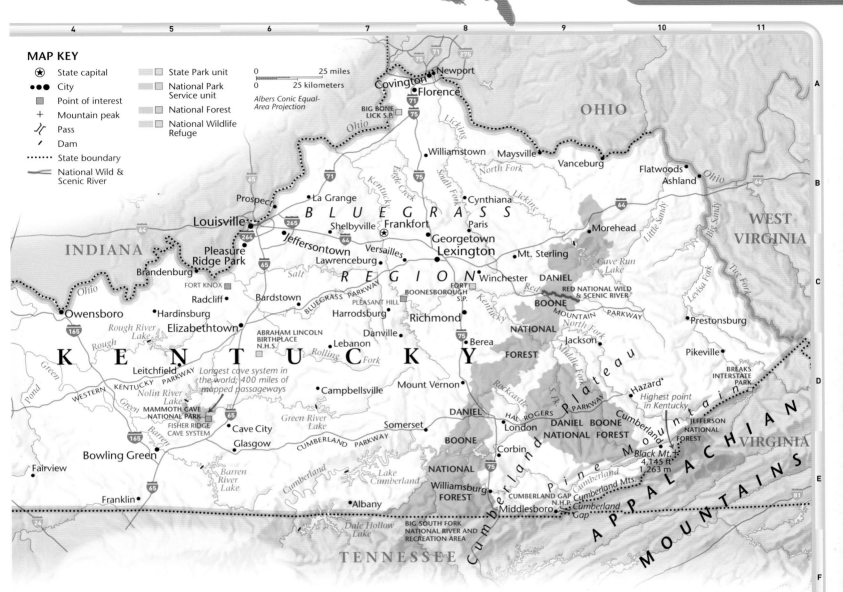

MAP KEY

- ★ State capital
- ●●● City
- ■ Point of interest
- + Mountain peak
-)(Pass
- / Dam
- ···· State boundary
- National Wild & Scenic River

- State Park unit
- National Park Service unit
- National Forest
- National Wildlife Refuge

0 — 25 miles
0 — 25 kilometers
Albers Conic Equal-Area Projection

STRUMMING A TUNE. Music is an important part of Kentucky's cultural heritage, especially in remote mountain areas, where a banjo can become the focus of a family gathering.

BENEATH THE SURFACE

Cave	Length
Mammoth Cave System, KY	367 miles (591 km)
Jewel Cave, SD	140 miles (225 km)
Wind Cave, SD	125 miles (201 km)
Lechuguilla Cave, NM	121 miles (195 km)
Fisher Ridge Cave System, KY	110 miles (177 km)

Caves, natural openings in Earth's surface extending beyond the reach of sunlight, are often created by water dissolving limestone.

THE PELICAN STATE:
LOUISIANA

Louisiana

BASICS

Statehood
April 30, 1812;
18th state

**Total area
(land and water)**
52,378 sq mi
(135,659 sq km)

Land area
43,204 sq mi
(111,898 sq km)

Population
4,659,978

Capital
Baton Rouge
Population 221,599

Largest city
New Orleans
Population 391,006

Racial/ethnic groups
63.0% white; 32.6% African
American; 1.9% Asian; 0.8%
Native American; 5.2% Hispanic
(any race)

Foreign born
4.2%

Urban population
73.2%

Population density
107.9 per sq mi (41.6 per sq km)

GEO WHIZ

The magnolia, Louisiana's
state flower, is the oldest
flowering plant in the world.
Some species are believed to
be 100 million years old.

Cajuns are people whose
French-speaking ancestors
were exiled by the British from
Acadia, in what is now Canada.
They live primarily in the
bayou region of Louisiana.

△ **TASTY HARVEST.**
The Gulf region,
led by Louisiana,
produces more than
200 million pounds
(90 million t) of
shrimp—more than
three-quarters of the
country's annual catch.

Louisiana's Native American heritage is evident in place-names such as Natchitoches and Opelousas. Spanish sailors explored the area in 1528, but the French, traveling down the Mississippi River, established permanent settlements in the mid-17th century and named the region for King Louis XIV. The United States gained possession of the territory as part of the Louisiana Purchase in 1803, and Louisiana became the 18th state in 1812. The Port of South Louisiana, located near the delta of the Mississippi River, and New Orleans are Louisiana's main ports. Trade from the interior of the United States moves through these ports and out to world markets. Oil and gas are drilled in the Mississippi Delta area and Gulf of Mexico. The explosion of an offshore oil rig in 2010 brought serious environmental damage to coastal areas still recovering from Hurricane Katrina. This massive storm roared in off the Gulf in 2005, flooding towns, breaking through levees, and changing the lives of everyone in southern Louisiana.

**MAGNOLIA
BROWN PELICAN**

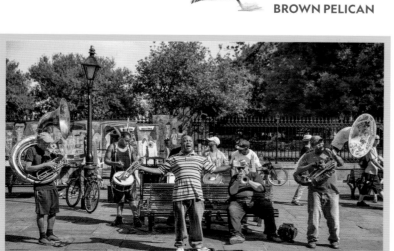

◑ **MUSIC IN THE AIR.** Street musicians, called buskers, are a common sight in New Orleans, where they play blues, jazz, folk, or country music for tips from passersby.

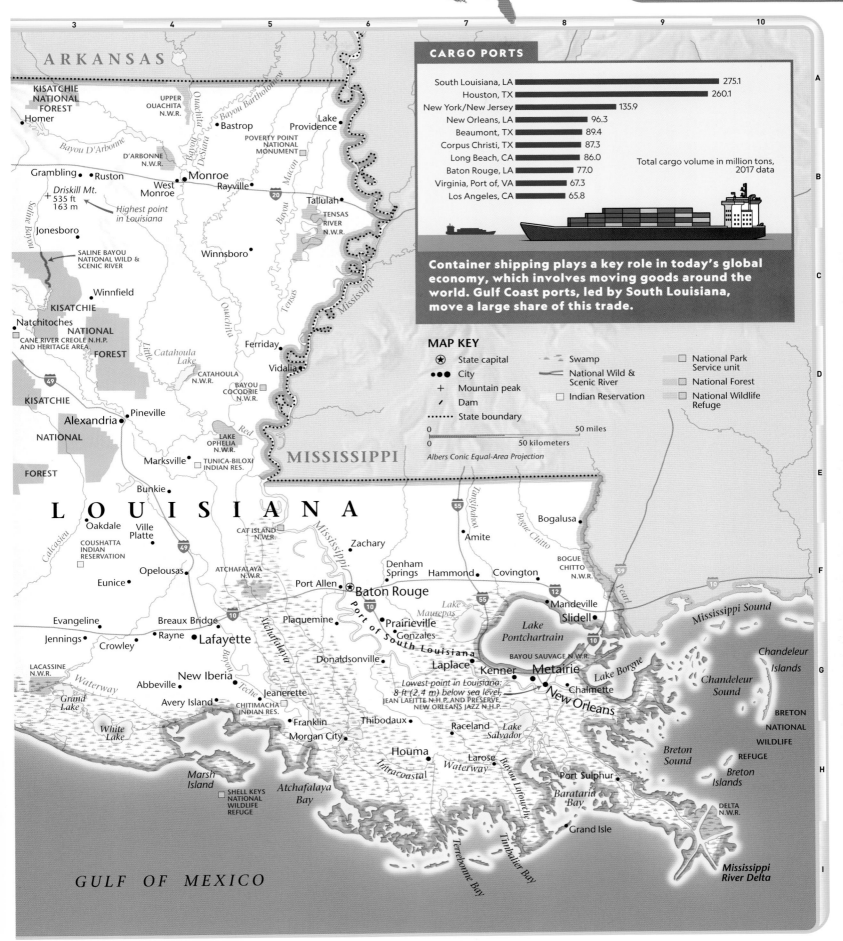

CARGO PORTS

Port	Total cargo volume (million tons)
South Louisiana, LA	275.1
Houston, TX	260.1
New York/New Jersey	135.9
New Orleans, LA	96.3
Beaumont, TX	89.4
Corpus Christi, TX	87.3
Long Beach, CA	86.0
Baton Rouge, LA	77.0
Virginia, Port of, VA	67.3
Los Angeles, CA	65.8

Total cargo volume in million tons, 2017 data

Container shipping plays a key role in today's global economy, which involves moving goods around the world. Gulf Coast ports, led by South Louisiana, move a large share of this trade.

MAP KEY

- ★ State capital
- ••• City
- + Mountain peak
- ⌿ Dam
- •••• State boundary
- ~~ Swamp
- ～ National Wild & Scenic River
- ☐ Indian Reservation
- ☐ National Park Service unit
- ▨ National Forest
- ▨ National Wildlife Refuge

0 — 50 miles
0 — 50 kilometers
Albers Conic Equal-Area Projection

ARKANSAS

KISATCHIE NATIONAL FOREST
Homer
Grambling • Ruston
Bastrop
Lake Providence
UPPER OUACHITA N.W.R.
POVERTY POINT NATIONAL MONUMENT
D'ARBONNE N.W.R.
Bayou D'Arbonne
West Monroe • Monroe
Rayville
Driskill Mt. + 535 ft 163 m
Highest point in Louisiana
Tallulah
TENSAS RIVER N.W.R.
Jonesboro
Winnsboro
Saline Bayou
SALINE BAYOU NATIONAL WILD & SCENIC RIVER
Winnfield
KISATCHIE
Natchitoches
NATIONAL
CANE RIVER CREOLE N.H.P. AND HERITAGE AREA
FOREST
Ferriday
Vidalia
Catahoula Lake
CATAHOULA N.W.R.
BAYOU COCODRIE N.W.R.
KISATCHIE
Alexandria • Pineville
NATIONAL
LAKE OPHELIA N.W.R.
Marksville
TUNICA-BILOXI INDIAN RES.
FOREST
MISSISSIPPI

LOUISIANA
Bunkie
Oakdale
Ville Platte
COUSHATTA INDIAN RESERVATION
CAT ISLAND N.W.R.
Zachary
Amite
Bogalusa
BOGUE CHITTO N.W.R.
Eunice
Opelousas
ATCHAFALAYA N.W.R.
Denham Springs
Hammond
Covington
Mandeville
Slidell
Evangeline
Breaux Bridge
Port Allen
Baton Rouge
Plaquemine
Prairieville
Gonzales
Lake Maurepas
Lake Pontchartrain
Jennings
Rayne
Lafayette
Port of South Louisiana
Donaldsonville
Laplace
Kenner • Metairie
Crowley
BAYOU SAUVAGE N.W.R.
Lake Borgne
LACASSINE N.W.R.
Abbeville
New Iberia
Jeanerette
Lowest point in Louisiana: 8 ft (2.4 m) below sea level, JEAN LAFITTE N.H.P. AND PRESERVE, NEW ORLEANS JAZZ N.H.P.
Chalmette
New Orleans
Grand Lake
White Lake
Franklin
Morgan City
Thibodaux
Raceland
Lake Salvador
Houma
Larose
Breton Sound
Port Sulphur
Marsh Island
SHELL KEYS NATIONAL WILDLIFE REFUGE
Atchafalaya Bay
Intracoastal Waterway
Barataria Bay
Grand Isle
DELTA N.W.R.
CHITIMACHA INDIAN RES.
Avery Island
Terrebonne Bay
Timbalier Bay
Bayou Lafourche
Mississippi Sound
Chandeleur Islands
Chandeleur Sound
BRETON NATIONAL WILDLIFE REFUGE
Breton Islands
Mississippi River Delta

GULF OF MEXICO

THE MAGNOLIA STATE:
MISSISSIPPI

BASICS

Statehood
December 10, 1817; 20th state

Total area (land and water)
48,432 sq mi (125,438 sq km)

Land area
46,923 sq mi (121,531 sq km)

Population
2,986,530

Capital
Jackson
Population 164,422

Largest city
Jackson
Population 164,422

Racial/ethnic groups
59.2% white; 37.8% African American; 1.1% Asian; 0.6% Native American; 3.2% Hispanic (any race)

Foreign born
2.3%

Urban population
49.4%

Population density
63.6 per sq mi (24.6 per sq km)

GEO WHIZ

The Marine Life Oceanarium in Gulfport was almost completely destroyed by Hurricane Katrina in 2005. Eight of its 14 bottlenose dolphins were swept into the Gulf of Mexico by a 40-foot (12-m) wave. These animals and two sea lions named Splash and Elliot were eventually rescued. Others were not so lucky.

Greenville is the birthplace of Jim Henson, creator of Kermit the Frog, Miss Piggy, Big Bird, and other famous *Sesame Street* Muppets.

Mississippi

Mississippi is named for the river that forms its western boundary. The name comes from the Chippewa words *mici zibi*, meaning "great river." Indeed it is a great river, draining much of the interior United States and providing a trade artery to the world. Explored by the Spanish in 1540 and claimed by the French in 1699, the territory of Mississippi passed to the United States in 1783 and became the 20th state in 1817. For more than a hundred years following statehood, Mississippi was the center of U.S. cotton production and trade. The fertile soils and mild climate of the delta region in northwestern Mississippi provided a perfect environment for cotton, a crop that depended on slave labor. When the Civil War broke out, Mississippi joined the Confederacy. The war took a heavy toll on the state's economy. Today, poverty, especially in rural areas, is a major challenge for the state, where agriculture, including poultry, cotton, soybeans, and rice, is still the base of the economy.

SINGING THE BLUES. The Gateway to the Blues Museum in Tunica traces the blues, a uniquely American music form, to Mississippi's cotton fields where West Africans, brought on slave ships, toiled in the 1800s.

MOCKINGBIRD
MAGNOLIA

BIG WHEEL TURNING. Now popular with tourists, paddleboats made the Mississippi River a major artery for trade and travel in the 19th century.

GONE FISHIN'

Total sales, 2017 data

Mississippi	$196,745,000
Alabama	$114,029,000
Arkansas	$18,144,000
Texas	$15,540,000

The Southeast, especially Mississippi, is the leading producer of pond-raised catfish. Mississippi also tops all other states in revenue from catfish sales.

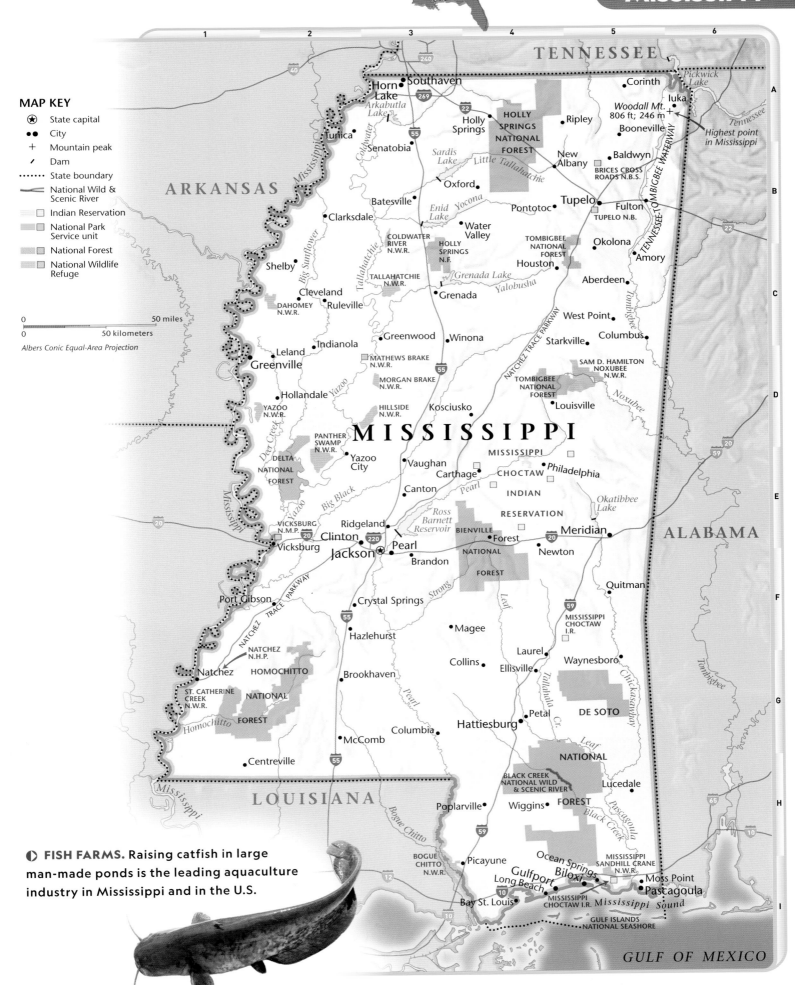

MAP KEY

★ State capital
•• City
+ Mountain peak
⟋ Dam
•••• State boundary
〰 National Wild & Scenic River
▨ Indian Reservation
▨ National Park Service unit
▨ National Forest
▨ National Wildlife Refuge

0   50 miles
0   50 kilometers

Albers Conic Equal-Area Projection

TENNESSEE

ARKANSAS

ALABAMA

LOUISIANA

MISSISSIPPI

GULF OF MEXICO

Southaven
Horn Lake
Arkabutla Lake
Tunica
Senatobia
Holly Springs
Holly Springs National Forest
Ripley
Corinth
Pickwick Lake
Iuka
Woodall Mt. 806 ft; 246 m
Highest point in Mississippi
Booneville
Sardis Lake
Oxford
Little Tallahatchie
New Albany
Baldwyn
BRICES CROSS ROADS N.B.S.
Tupelo
Fulton
TUPELO N.B.
Batesville
Enid Lake
Yocona
Pontotoc
Clarksdale
Water Valley
COLDWATER RIVER N.W.R.
HOLLY SPRINGS N.F.
TOMBIGBEE NATIONAL FOREST
Okolona
Amory
Houston
Shelby
Cleveland
Ruleville
DAHOMEY N.W.R.
Tallahatchie
TALLAHATCHIE N.W.R.
Grenada Lake
Yalobusha
Grenada
Aberdeen
West Point
Columbus
Greenwood
Winona
Starkville
Big Sunflower
Indianola
MATHEWS BRAKE N.W.R.
SAM D. HAMILTON NOXUBEE N.W.R.
Leland
Greenville
MORGAN BRAKE N.W.R.
TOMBIGBEE NATIONAL FOREST
Noxubee
Hollandale
Yazoo
HILLSIDE N.W.R.
Kosciusko
Louisville
YAZOO N.W.R.
Deer Creek
PANTHER SWAMP N.W.R.
DELTA NATIONAL FOREST
Yazoo City
Vaughan
MISSISSIPPI
Philadelphia
Okatibbee Lake
Carthage
CHOCTAW
INDIAN
Canton
Pearl
RESERVATION
VICKSBURG N.M.P.
Ridgeland
Ross Barnett Reservoir
BIENVILLE
Forest
Meridian
Vicksburg
Clinton
Jackson
Pearl
NATIONAL
Newton
Brandon
FOREST
Quitman
Port Gibson
Crystal Springs
Strong
Leaf
NATCHEZ TRACE PARKWAY
Hazlehurst
MISSISSIPPI CHOCTAW I.R.
Natchez
NATCHEZ N.H.P.
Magee
Laurel
Waynesboro
Collins
Ellisville
HOMOCHITTO
Brookhaven
DE SOTO
ST. CATHERINE CREEK N.W.R.
NATIONAL
Petal
Chickasawhay
Columbia
Hattiesburg
FOREST
Homochitto
McComb
Leaf
NATIONAL
Centreville
Lucedale
BLACK CREEK NATIONAL WILD & SCENIC RIVER
Mississippi
Poplarville
Wiggins
FOREST
Black Creek
BOGUE CHITTO N.W.R.
Bogue Chitto
Picayune
Ocean Springs
MISSISSIPPI SANDHILL CRANE N.W.R.
Moss Point
Gulfport
Biloxi
Pastagoula
Long Beach
Bay St. Louis
MISSISSIPPI CHOCTAW I.R.
Mississippi Sound
GULF ISLANDS NATIONAL SEASHORE
Pascagoula
Tombigbee
Coldwater
Mississippi
Bienville
TENNESSEE-TOMBIGBEE WATERWAY

◗ **FISH FARMS.** Raising catfish in large man-made ponds is the leading aquaculture industry in Mississippi and in the U.S.

North Carolina

Early attempts by English colonists to settle the area that would become North Carolina met with strong resistance from Native American groups already living there. Despite ongoing tensions, in 1663 King Charles II approved establishment of the Carolina colony, which included present-day North Carolina, South Carolina, and part of Georgia. In 1789 North Carolina became the 12th state, but in 1861 it joined the Confederacy and supplied more men and equipment to the Civil War than any other southern state. In 1903 the Wright brothers piloted the first success-ful airplane near Kitty Hawk, foreshadowing the change and growth coming to the Tar Heel State. Traditional industries included agriculture, textiles, and furniture making. Today, these, plus high-tech industries and education in the Raleigh-Durham Research Triangle area, as well as banking and finance in Charlotte, are important to the economy.

BASICS

Statehood
November 21, 1789; 12th state

Total area (land and water)
53,819 sq mi (139,391 sq km)

Land area
48,618 sq mi (125,920 sq km)

Population
10,383,620

Capital
Raleigh
Population 469,298

Largest city
Charlotte
Population 872,498

Racial/ethnic groups
70.8% white; 22.2% African American; 3.1% Asian; 1.6% Native American; 9.5% Hispanic (any race)

Foreign born
7.8%

Urban population
66.1%

Population density
213.6 per sq mi
(82.5 per sq km)

GEO WHIZ

The University of North Carolina at Chapel Hill, dating to 1795, is the oldest public university in the U.S.

At 208 feet (63 m) high, Cape Hatteras Lighthouse is the tallest lighthouse in the U.S.

CARDINAL

FLOWERING
DOGWOOD

FAVORITE PASTIME. With four of the state's schools represented in the powerful Atlantic Coast Conference, basketball is a popular sport whether on the court or in the driveway.

TAKING FLIGHT. The Wright Brothers Memorial on Kill Devil Hill, near Kitty Hawk on the Outer Banks, marks the site of the first successful airplane flight in 1903.

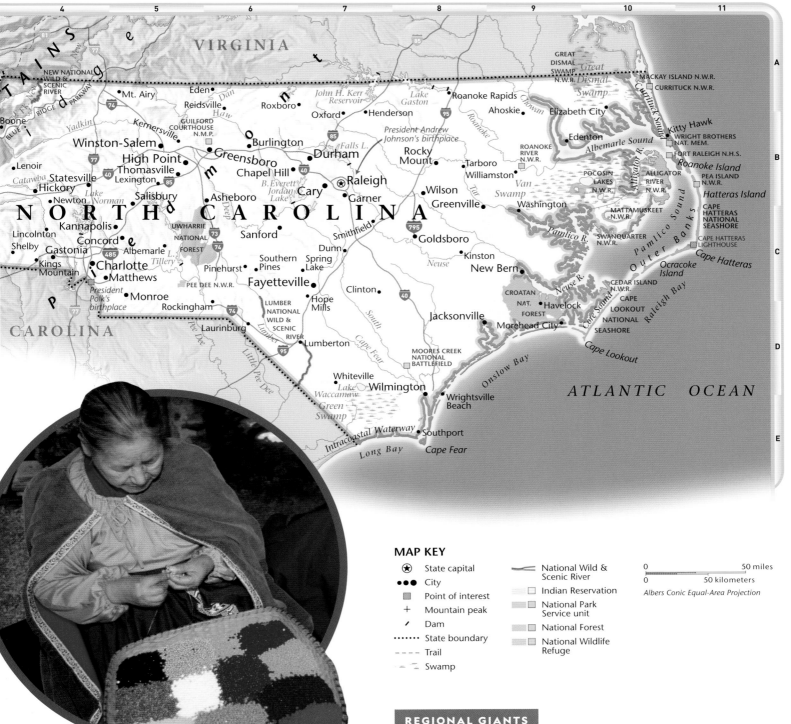

VIRGINIA

NORTH CAROLINA

CAROLINA

ATLANTIC OCEAN

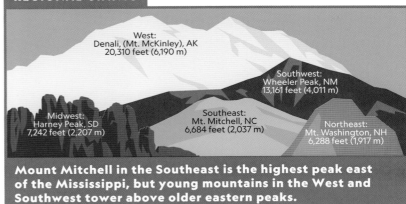

⬤ **SKILLED ARTISAN.** A Cherokee woman sews a beaded belt in Oconaluftee Indian Village in western North Carolina. Cherokee in this region are descendants of tribal members who hid in the mountains to avoid the forced removal known as the Trail of Tears. This living history site preserves traditional 18th-century crafts and customs.

MAP KEY

⭐ State capital

●●● City

◼ Point of interest

✛ Mountain peak

╱ Dam

········· State boundary

- - - - Trail

〜 Swamp

〜 National Wild & Scenic River

▢ Indian Reservation

▢ National Park Service unit

▢ National Forest

▢ National Wildlife Refuge

```
0                    50 miles
0                    50 kilometers
```
Albers Conic Equal-Area Projection

REGIONAL GIANTS

West:
Denali, (Mt. McKinley), AK
20,310 feet (6,190 m)

Southwest:
Wheeler Peak, NM
13,161 feet (4,011 m)

Midwest:
Harney Peak, SD
7,242 feet (2,207 m)

Southeast:
Mt. Mitchell, NC
6,684 feet (2,037 m)

Northeast:
Mt. Washington, NH
6,288 feet (1,917 m)

Mount Mitchell in the Southeast is the highest peak east of the Mississippi, but young mountains in the West and Southwest tower above older eastern peaks.

South Carolina

Attempts in the 16th century by the Spanish and the French to colonize the area that would become South Carolina met fierce resistance from local Native American tribes. But in 1670 the English became the first to establish a permanent European settlement at present-day Charleston. The colony prospered by relying on slave labor to produce first cotton, then rice and indigo. South Carolina became the eighth state in 1788 and the first to leave the Union just months before the first shots of the Civil War were fired on Fort Sumter in 1861. After the war South Carolina struggled to rebuild its economy. Early in the 20th century, textile mills introduced new jobs. Today, agriculture remains important, manufacturing and high-tech industries are expanding along interstate highway corridors, and tourists and retirees are drawn to the state's Atlantic coastline. But these coastal areas are not without risk. In 1989 Hurricane Hugo's 135-mile-an-hour (217-km/h) winds left a trail of destruction.

BASICS

Statehood
May 23, 1788; 8th state

**Total area
(land and water)**
32,020 sq mi
(82,933 sq km)

Land area
30,061 sq mi
(77,857 sq km)

Population
5,084,127

Capital
Columbia
Population 133,451

Largest city
Charleston
Population 136,208

Racial/ethnic groups
68.5% white; 27.3% African American; 1.7% Asian; 0.5% Native American; 5.7% Hispanic (any race)

Foreign born
4.9%

Urban population
66.3%

Population density
158.8 per sq mi
(61.3 per sq km)

GEO WHIZ

The loggerhead sea turtle, which is the state reptile of South Carolina, is threatened throughout its range.

Sweetgrass basketmaking, a traditional African art form, has been a part of the Mount Pleasant community for more than 300 years.

◔ **GLOW OF DAWN.**
The rising sun reflects off the water along the Atlantic coast. Beaches attract visitors year-round, contributing to tourism, the state's largest industry.

**YELLOW JESSAMINE
CAROLINA WREN**

Map labels
Highest point in South Carolina
Sassafras Mt. 3,560 ft 1,085 m
CHATTOOGA NATIONAL WILD & SCENIC RIVER
SUMTER NATIONAL FOREST
Blue Ridge
Lake Keowee
Tugaloo
Greenville
Easley • Gantt
Seneca •
• Clemson
85
Belton
Anderson
Hartwell Lake
Savannah
Richard B. Russell Lake
Abbeville
P

TRADE PARTNERS

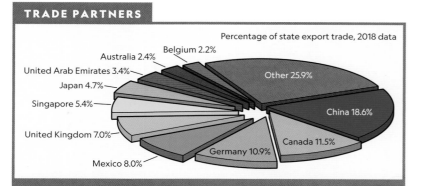

Percentage of state export trade, 2018 data

- Australia 2.4%
- Belgium 2.2%
- United Arab Emirates 3.4%
- Japan 4.7%
- Singapore 5.4%
- United Kingdom 7.0%
- Mexico 8.0%
- Germany 10.9%
- Canada 11.5%
- China 18.6%
- Other 25.9%

With more than $34.6 billion in export goods in 2018, export industries are an important source of employment in South Carolina. Transportation equipment is the leading manufactured export.

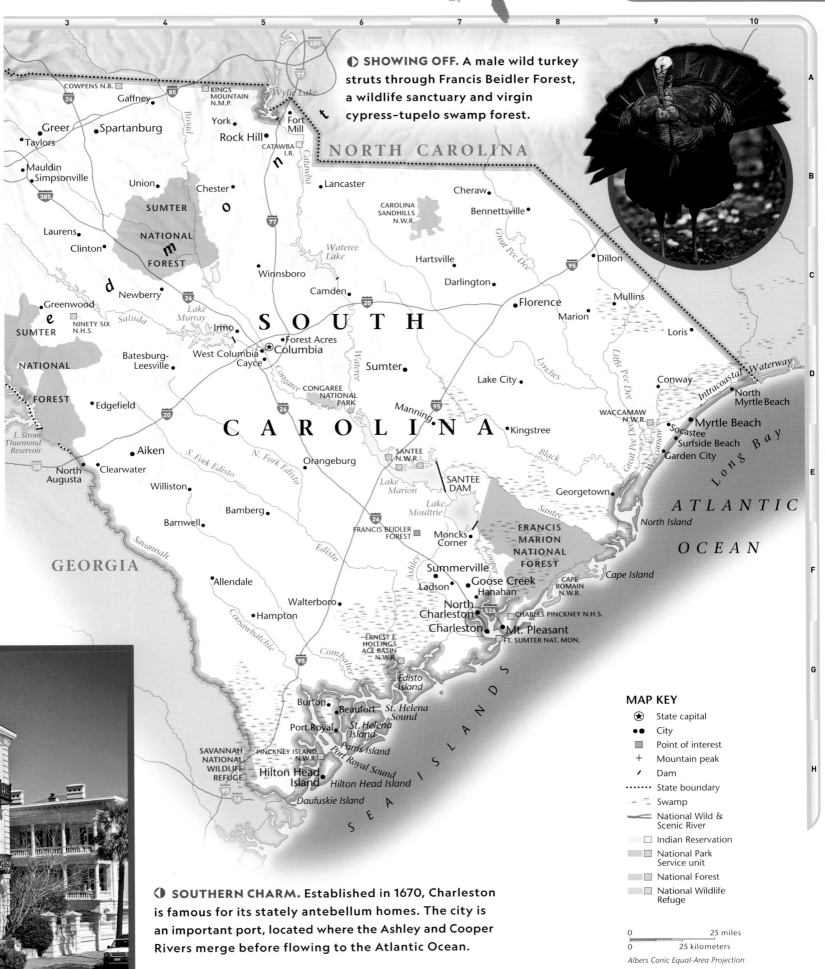

3 4 5 6 7 8 9 10

A

◗ **SHOWING OFF.** A male wild turkey struts through Francis Beidler Forest, a wildlife sanctuary and virgin cypress-tupelo swamp forest.

COWPENS N.B.
Gaffney
KINGS MOUNTAIN N.M.P.
Wylie Lake
Greer
Spartanburg
York
Rock Hill
CATAWBA I.R.
Fort Mill
NORTH CAROLINA

B

Taylors
Mauldin
Simpsonville
Union
Chester
Lancaster
Cheraw
Bennettsville
CAROLINA SANDHILLS N.W.R.

Laurens
SUMTER NATIONAL FOREST
Wateree Lake
Hartsville
Darlington
Dillon
Great Pee Dee

C

Clinton
Newberry
Winnsboro
Camden
Florence
Marion
Mullins
Greenwood
Saluda
Lake Murray
Irmo
S O U T H
Loris
SUMTER
NINETY SIX N.H.S.
West Columbia
Forest Acres
Columbia
Cayce
Batesburg-Leesville
Sumter
Lake City
Conway
Waccamaw
Intracoastal Waterway

D

NATIONAL
Edgefield
CONGAREE NATIONAL PARK
Manning
Kingstree
WACCAMAW N.W.R.
North Myrtle Beach
C A R O L I N A
FOREST
J. Strom Thurmond Reservoir
Aiken
S. Fork Edisto
N. Fork Edisto
Orangeburg
SANTEE N.W.R.
Black
Myrtle Beach
Socastee
Surfside Beach
Garden City
Long Bay

E

North Augusta
Clearwater
Williston
Bamberg
Lake Marion
SANTEE DAM
Lake Moultrie
Georgetown
North Island
ATLANTIC
Barnwell
FRANCIS MARION NATIONAL FOREST
Santee
OCEAN

F

GEORGIA
Savannah
Allendale
FRANCIS BEIDLER FOREST
Edisto
Moncks Corner
Cooper
Summerville
Ladson
Goose Creek
Hanahan
CAPE ROMAIN N.W.R.
Cape Island
Walterboro
Hampton
Coosawhatchie
North Charleston
Charleston
CHARLES PINCKNEY N.H.S.
Mt. Pleasant
FT. SUMTER NAT. MON.
Ashley

G

Combahee
Edisto Island
ERNEST F. HOLLINGS ACE BASIN N.W.R.
Burton
Beaufort
St. Helena Sound
St. Helena Island
S E A   I S L A N D S
Port Royal
SAVANNAH NATIONAL WILDLIFE REFUGE
PINCKNEY ISLAND N.W.R.
Parris Island
Port Royal Sound
Hilton Head Island
Hilton Head Island
Daufuskie Island

H

MAP KEY
⍟ State capital
●● City
▢ Point of interest
+ Mountain peak
⟋ Dam
······· State boundary
⬝⬝ Swamp
── National Wild & Scenic River
▢ Indian Reservation
▢ National Park Service unit
▢ National Forest
▢ National Wildlife Refuge

◑ **SOUTHERN CHARM.** Established in 1670, Charleston is famous for its stately antebellum homes. The city is an important port, located where the Ashley and Cooper Rivers merge before flowing to the Atlantic Ocean.

0   25 miles
0   25 kilometers
Albers Conic Equal-Area Projection

BASICS

Statehood
June 1, 1796; 16th state

Total area (land and water)
42,144 sq mi (109,153 sq km)

Land area
41,235 sq mi (106,798 sq km)

Population
6,770,010

Capital
Nashville/Davidson County
Population 669,053

Largest city
Nashville/Davidson County
Population 669,053

Racial/ethnic groups
78.6% white; 17.1% African
American; 1.9% Asian; 0.5%
Native American; 5.5% Hispanic
(any race)

Foreign born
5.0%

Urban population
66.4%

Population density
160.6 per sq mi
(62.0 per sq km)

GEO WHIZ

**Great Smoky Mountains
National Park** has earned the
title Salamander Capital of
the World in recognition
of the 30 species of sala-
manders that live there,
including the five-foot
(1.5-m)-long hellbender.

**The New Madrid
Earthquakes** of 1811–1812,
some of the largest
earthquakes in U.S.
history, created Reelfoot
Lake in northwestern
Tennessee. It is the
state's only large, natural
lake; others were created
by damming waterways.

**The Tennessee-Tombigbee
Waterway** is a 234-mile
(376-km) artificial waterway
that connects the Tennessee
and Tombigbee Rivers. This
water transportation route
provides inland ports with an
outlet to the Gulf of Mexico.

Tennessee

Following the last ice age, ancestors of today's Native Americans moved onto the fertile lands of Tennessee. The earliest Europeans in Tennessee were Spanish explorers who passed through in 1541. In 1673 both the English and French made claims on the land, hoping to develop trade with the powerful Cherokee, whose town, called Tanasi, gave the state its name. Originally part of North Carolina, Tennessee was ceded to the federal government and became the 16th state in 1796. Tennessee was the last state to join the Confederacy and endured years of hardship after the war. Beginning in the 1930s, the federally funded Tennessee Valley Authority (TVA) set a high standard in water management in the state, and the hydro-power that it generated supported major industrial development. Tennessee played a key role in the civil rights movement of the 1960s. Today, visitors to Tennessee are drawn to national parks, Nashville's country music, and the mournful sound of the blues in Memphis.

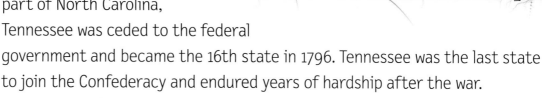

MOCKINGBIRD

IRIS

◗ **OUT FOR A STROLL.**
Black bear cubs are usually
born in January and
remain with their mother
for about 18 months.
Great Smoky Mountains
National Park is one of the
few remaining natural
habitats for black bears in
the eastern United States.

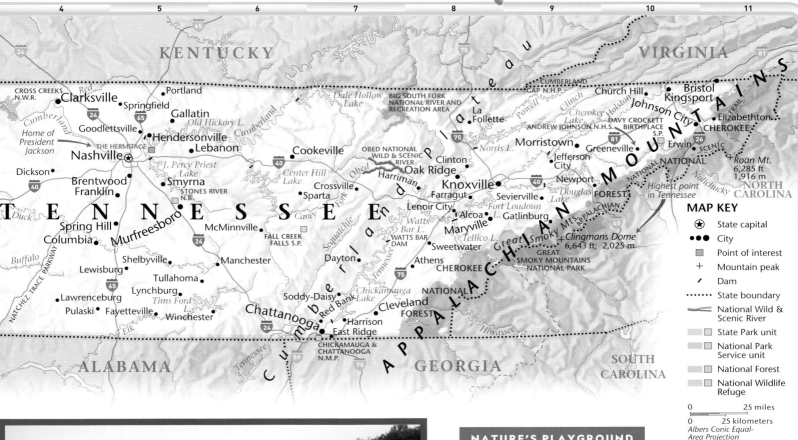

KENTUCKY

VIRGINIA

CROSS CREEKS N.W.R.
Clarksville
Portland
Springfield
Gallatin
Goodlettsville
Home of President Jackson
Old Hickory L.
THE HERMITAGE
Hendersonville
Lebanon
Nashville ★
Dickson
J. Percy Priest Lake
Brentwood
Smyrna
Franklin
STONES RIVER N.B.
Spring Hill
Columbia
Murfreesboro
Shelbyville
Lewisburg
Tullahoma
Lawrenceburg
Lynchburg
Pulaski
Fayetteville
Winchester

Dale Hollow Lake
BIG SOUTH FORK NATIONAL RIVER AND RECREATION AREA
Cookeville
Center Hill Lake
Crossville
Sparta
McMinnville
FALL CREEK FALLS S.P.
Manchester
Dayton
Soddy-Daisy
Red Bank
Chattanooga
Harrison
East Ridge
CHICKAMAUGA & CHATTANOOGA N.M.P.

CUMBERLAND GAP N.H.P.
La Follette
OBED NATIONAL WILD & SCENIC RIVER
Obed
Clinton
Oak Ridge
Harriman
Knoxville
Farragut
Lenoir City
Sweetwater
WATTS BAR DAM
Athens
CHEROKEE
NATIONAL
FOREST
Chickamauga Lake
Cleveland

Norris L.
ANDREW JOHNSON N.H.S.
Morristown
Jefferson City
Newport
Sevierville
Alcoa
Maryville
Gatlinburg
Tellico L.
Great Smoky Mts.
Clingmans Dome 6,643 ft; 2,025 m
GREAT SMOKY MOUNTAINS NATIONAL PARK

Church Hill
Johnson City
Bristol
Kingsport
DAVY CROCKETT BIRTHPLACE S.P.
Greeneville
Erwin
Elizabethton
CHEROKEE
NATIONAL FOREST
Highest point in Tennessee
Roan Mt. 6,285 ft 1,916 m

NORTH CAROLINA

TENNESSEE
Cumberland Plateau
APPALACHIAN MOUNTAINS

ALABAMA
GEORGIA
SOUTH CAROLINA

MAP KEY
★ State capital
●●● City
■ Point of interest
+ Mountain peak
∕ Dam
⋯⋯ State boundary
National Wild & Scenic River
State Park unit
National Park Service unit
National Forest
National Wildlife Refuge

0 — 25 miles
0 — 25 kilometers
Albers Conic Equal-Area Projection

NATURE'S PLAYGROUND

🚶 One million national park visitors, 2017 data

Great Smoky Mountains N.P. 🚶🚶🚶🚶🚶🚶🚶🚶🚶🚶🚶 11.39
Grand Canyon N.P. 🚶🚶🚶🚶🚶🚶 6.25
Zion N.P. 🚶🚶🚶🚶 4.50
Rocky Mountain N.P. 🚶🚶🚶🚶 4.44
Yosemite N.P. 🚶🚶🚶🚶 4.37

Great Smoky Mountains National Park, on the Tennessee-North Carolina border, attracts more visitors than any other U.S. national park.

WATER POWER. Watts Bar Dam is one of nine TVA dams built on the Tennessee River to aid navigation and flood control and to supply power. The large reservoir behind the dam provides a recreation area that attracts millions of vacationers each year. Without the dam, cities such as Chattanooga would face devastating floods.

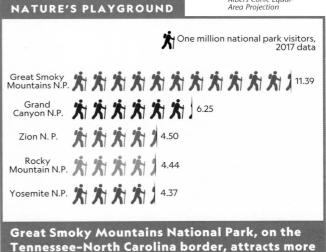

SOUTHERN TRADITION. Nashville's Grand Ole Opry is the home of country music. Originally a 1925 radio show called WSM Barn Dance, the Opry now occupies a theater that seats 4,400. The Opry is the longest running radio show in the U.S. Country music, using mainly stringed instruments, evolved from traditional folk tunes of the Appalachians.

BASICS

Statehood
June 25, 1788; 10th state

Total area (land and water)
42,775 sq mi (110,787 sq km)

Land area
39,490 sq mi (102,279 sq km)

Population
8,517,685

Capital
Richmond
Population 228,783

Largest city
Virginia Beach
Population 450,189

Racial/ethnic groups
69.7% white; 19.8% African American; 6.8% Asian; 0.5% Native American; 9.4% Hispanic (any race)

Foreign born
12.1%

Urban population
75.5%

Population density
215.7 per sq mi (83.3 per sq km)

GEO WHIZ

In the early 1700s, the bustling port of Hampton was a major target for pirates, including the notorious Blackbeard. Today, the city hosts the Blackbeard Festival each spring, complete with pirate reenactors, live music, games, and fireworks.

During the Battle of Hampton Roads in 1862, the ships U.S.S. *Monitor* and the C.S.S. *Virginia* (a rebuilt version of the U.S.S. *Merrimack*) met in one of the most famous naval engagements in U.S. history. The battle marked the dawn of a new era of naval warfare.

Virginia

Long before Europeans arrived in present-day Virginia, Native Americans populated the area. Early Spanish attempts to establish a colony failed, but in 1607 merchants established the first permanent English settlement in North America at Jamestown. Virginia became a prosperous colony, growing tobacco using slave labor. Virginia played a key role in the drive for independence, and the final battle of the Revolutionary War was at Yorktown, near Jamestown.

In 1861 Virginia joined the Confederacy and became a major battleground of the Civil War, which left the state in financial ruin. Today, Virginia has a diversified economy. Farmers still grow tobacco, along with other crops. The Hampton Roads area, near the mouth of Chesapeake Bay, is a center for shipbuilding and home to major U.S. naval bases. Northern Virginia, across the Potomac River from Washington, D.C., boasts federal government offices and high-tech businesses. The state's natural beauty and many historic sites attract tourists from around the world.

⊜ **EARLY ENTERTAINMENT. Dice made of bone, ivory, and lead, dating to 1607, were excavated at Jamestown.**

FLOWERING DOGWOOD

CARDINAL

◗ **NATURAL WONDER. Winding under the Appalachian Mountains, Luray Caverns were formed as water dissolved limestone rocks and deposited minerals to form dramatic stalactites and stalagmites.**

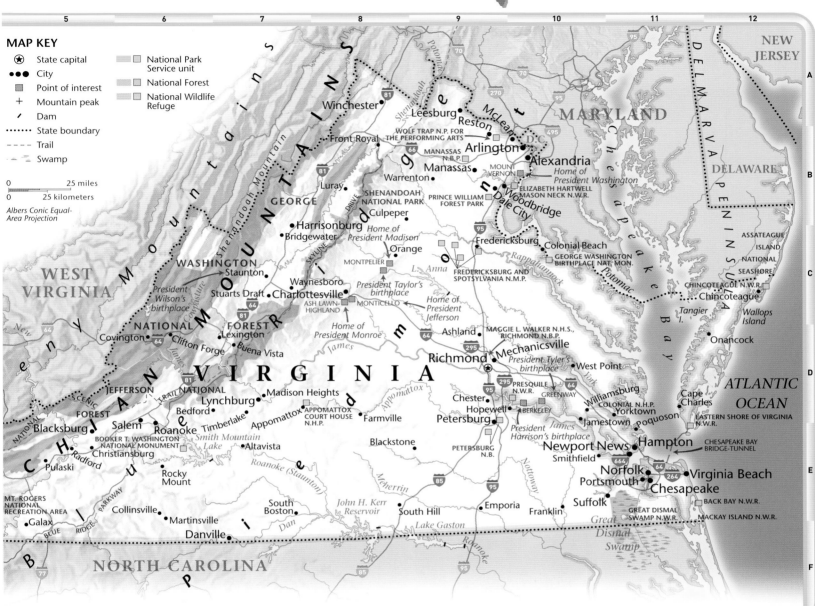

MAP KEY

- ★ State capital
- ●●● City
- ■ Point of interest
- + Mountain peak
- ⟋ Dam
- ····· State boundary
- ----- Trail
- Swamp
- ▢ National Park Service unit
- ▢ National Forest
- ▢ National Wildlife Refuge

0 ——— 25 miles
0 ——— 25 kilometers

Albers Conic Equal-Area Projection

NEW JERSEY

MARYLAND

DELAWARE

DELMARVA PENINSULA

WEST VIRGINIA

Winchester
Leesburg
McLean
Reston
Front Royal
WOLF TRAP N.P. FOR THE PERFORMING ARTS
Arlington
D.C.
Alexandria
MANASSAS N.B.P.
Manassas
Warrenton
MOUNT VERNON
Home of President Washington
ELIZABETH HARTWELL MASON NECK N.W.R.
Luray
GEORGE
SHENANDOAH NATIONAL PARK
PRINCE WILLIAM FOREST PARK
Woodbridge
Dale City
Harrisonburg
Bridgewater
Home of President Madison
Orange
Colonial Beach
GEORGE WASHINGTON BIRTHPLACE NAT. MON.
ASSATEAGUE ISLAND NATIONAL SEASHORE
WASHINGTON
MONTPELIER
L. Anna
FREDERICKSBURG AND SPOTSYLVANIA N.M.P.
Rappahannock
Fredericksburg
CHINCOTEAGUE N.W.R.
Chincoteague
Staunton
President Wilson's birthplace
Waynesboro
President Taylor's birthplace
Tangier I.
Wallops Island
Stuarts Draft
Charlottesville
ASH LAWN-HIGHLAND
MONTICELLO
Home of President Jefferson
MAGGIE L. WALKER N.H.S., RICHMOND N.B.P.
Ashland
Onancock
NATIONAL
Lexington
Home of President Monroe
Mechanicsville
President Tyler's birthplace
West Point
Covington
Clifton Forge
FOREST
Richmond
Williamsburg
Cape Charles
ATLANTIC OCEAN
Buena Vista
James
PRESQUILE N.W.R.
GREENWAY
COLONIAL N.H.P.
Yorktown
EASTERN SHORE OF VIRGINIA N.W.R.
JEFFERSON
VIRGINIA
Chester
Hopewell
BERKELEY
Jamestown
Poquoson
Lynchburg
Madison Heights
Appomattox
Petersburg
President Harrison's birthplace
James
Newport News
Hampton
CHESAPEAKE BAY BRIDGE-TUNNEL
Bedford
APPOMATTOX COURT HOUSE N.H.P.
Farmville
Smithfield
Blacksburg
Salem
Roanoke
Timberlake
PETERSBURG N.B.
Norfolk
Virginia Beach
BOOKER T. WASHINGTON NATIONAL MONUMENT
Smith Mountain Lake
Blackstone
Portsmouth
Chesapeake
Pulaski
Christiansburg
Altavista
Back BAY N.W.R.
Radford
Rocky Mount
Suffolk
GREAT DISMAL SWAMP N.W.R.
MACKAY ISLAND N.W.R.
MT. ROGERS NATIONAL RECREATION AREA
Collinsville
South Boston
South Hill
Emporia
Franklin
Great Dismal Swamp
Galax
Martinsville
John H. Kerr Reservoir
Lake Gaston
BLUE RIDGE PARKWAY
Danville
Dan
Meherrin
Nottoway
Roanoke

NORTH CAROLINA

Shenandoah
Potomac
Allegheny Mountains
Shenandoah Mountains
Piedmont
Chesapeake Bay
Appomattox
Roanoke (Staunton)
New
James

🔵 **DEFENSE CENTRAL.** The Pentagon, located just outside of Washington, D.C., in Arlington, Virginia, is the world's largest office building, with 17.5 miles (28.2 km) of corridors. It is the headquarters of the U.S. Department of Defense.

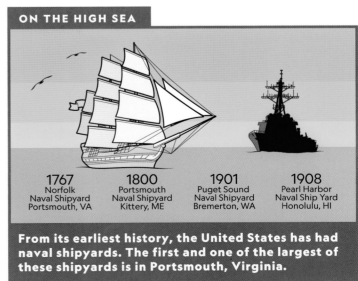

ON THE HIGH SEA

1767	1800	1901	1908
Norfolk Naval Shipyard Portsmouth, VA	Portsmouth Naval Shipyard Kittery, ME	Puget Sound Naval Shipyard Bremerton, WA	Pearl Harbor Naval Ship Yard Honolulu, HI

From its earliest history, the United States has had naval shipyards. The first and one of the largest of these shipyards is in Portsmouth, Virginia.

West Virginia

West Virginia was first settled by Native Americans who favored the wooded region for hunting. The first Europeans to settle in what originally was an extension of Virginia were Germans and Scotch-Irish, who came through mountain valleys in Pennsylvania in the early 1700s. Because farms in West Virginia were not dependent on slave labor, residents opposed secession during the Civil War and broke away from Virginia, becoming the 35th state in 1863. In the early 1800s, West Virginia harvested forest products and mined salt, but it was the discovery of vast coal deposits that brought industrialization to the state. Coal fueled steel mills, steamboats, and trains, and jobs in the mines attracted immigrants from far and near to the state. However, poor work conditions resulted in a legacy of poverty, illness, and environmental degradation— problems the state continues to face. Today, the state is working to build a tourist industry based on its natural beauty as well as its mountain crafts and culture.

BASICS

Statehood
June 20, 1863; 35th state

Total area (land and water)
24,230 sq mi (62,756 sq km)

Land area
24,038 sq mi (62,259 sq km)

Population
1,805,832

Capital
Charleston
Population 47,215

Largest city
Charleston
Population 47,215

Racial/ethnic groups
93.6% white; 3.6% African American; 0.8% Asian; 0.2% Native American; 1.6% Hispanic (any race)

Foreign born
1.6%

Urban population
48.7%

Population density
75.1 per sq mi (29.0 per sq km)

GEO WHIZ

Weirton, the only U.S. city that sits in one state and borders two others, is nestled in West Virginia's panhandle between Ohio and Pennsylvania.

The first rural free mail delivery in the U.S. started in Charles Town on October 1, 1896.

⊖ HARD LABOR. Coal miners work under difficult conditions—some in underground mines; others in surface mines.

CARDINAL

RHODODENDRON

O H I O

Point Pleasant

Hurricane

Huntington
Kenova

Kanawha

Big Sandy

Guyandotte

Tug Fork

Logan

Williamson

KENTUCKY

◑ STRATEGIC LOCATION. Harpers Ferry, established at the site of a ferry crossing over the Shenandoah River, was the target of John Brown's historic 1859 raid on the town's U.S. military arsenal. This anti-slavery movement was a precursor to the Civil War.

A

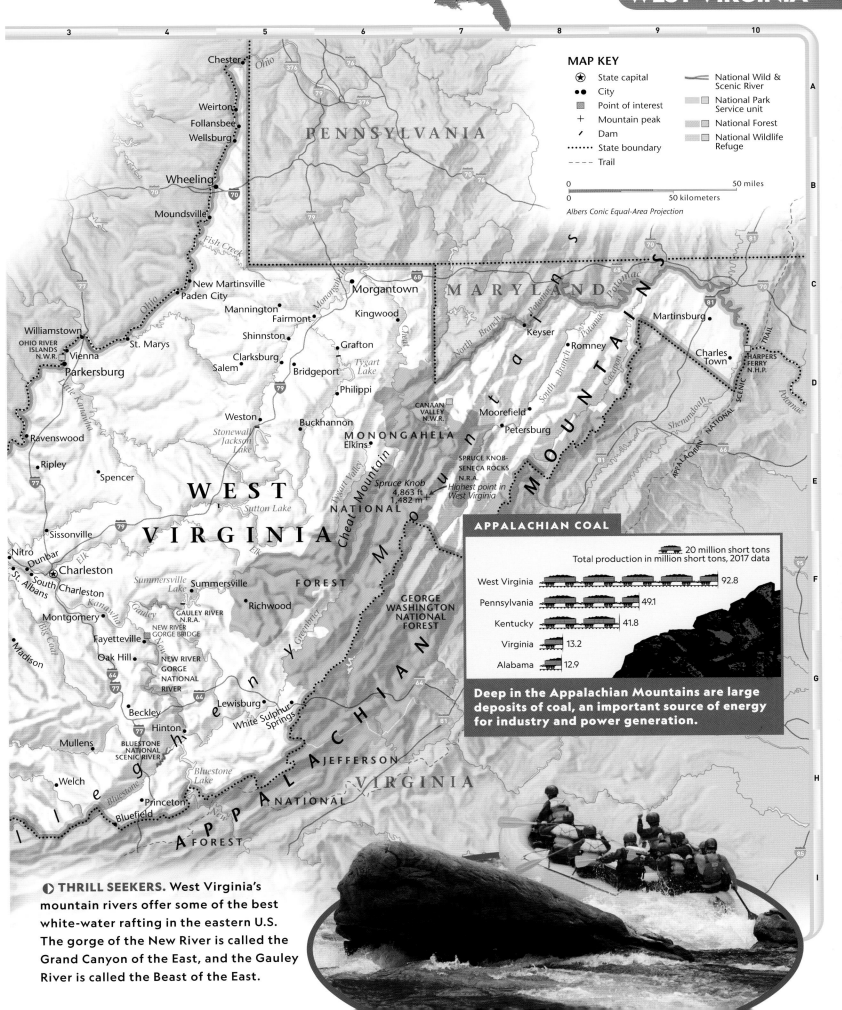

MAP KEY

⊛ State capital
●● City
▪ Point of interest
+ Mountain peak
╱ Dam
· · · State boundary
- - - Trail

〰 National Wild & Scenic River
▨ National Park Service unit
▨ National Forest
▨ National Wildlife Refuge

0 — 50 miles
0 — 50 kilometers

Albers Conic Equal-Area Projection

PENNSYLVANIA

MARYLAND

VIRGINIA

WEST VIRGINIA

Chester
Ohio
Weirton
Follansbee
Wellsburg
Wheeling
Moundsville
New Martinsville
Paden City
Williamstown
OHIO RIVER ISLANDS N.W.R.
Vienna
Parkersburg
St. Marys
Mannington
Fairmont
Shinnston
Clarksburg
Salem
Morgantown
Kingwood
Grafton
Bridgeport
Philippi
Tygart Lake
Martinsburg
Keyser
Romney
Charles Town
HARPERS FERRY N.H.P.
Ravenswood
Ripley
Spencer
Weston
Stonewall Jackson Lake
Buckhannon
CANAAN VALLEY N.W.R.
Moorefield
Petersburg
MONONGAHELA
Elkins
Fish Creek
Monongahela
Cheat
Potomac
North Branch
South Branch
Potomac
Shenandoah
Potomac
APPALACHIAN NATIONAL SCENIC TRAIL
Sissonville
Nitro
Dunbar
Charleston
St. Albans
South Charleston
Montgomery
Summersville Lake
Summersville
Richwood
Fayetteville
GAULEY RIVER N.R.A.
NEW RIVER GORGE BRIDGE
Oak Hill
NEW RIVER GORGE NATIONAL RIVER
Beckley
Hinton
Mullens
BLUESTONE NATIONAL SCENIC RIVER
Welch
Princeton
Bluefield
Bluestone Lake
Lewisburg
White Sulphur Springs
GEORGE WASHINGTON NATIONAL FOREST
JEFFERSON NATIONAL FOREST
Madison
Cheat Mountain
Spruce Knob 4,863 ft 1,482 m
SPRUCE KNOB-SENECA ROCKS N.R.A.
Highest point in West Virginia
NATIONAL
FOREST
Sutton Lake
Elk
Kanawha
Gauley
Greenbrier
New
Bluestone
Big Coal
Little Kanawha
Tygart Valley
Cheat
Allegheny Mountains
Appalachian

APPALACHIAN COAL

🚃 20 million short tons
Total production in million short tons, 2017 data

West Virginia	92.8
Pennsylvania	49.1
Kentucky	41.8
Virginia	13.2
Alabama	12.9

Deep in the Appalachian Mountains are large deposits of coal, an important source of energy for industry and power generation.

◗ **THRILL SEEKERS.** West Virginia's mountain rivers offer some of the best white-water rafting in the eastern U.S. The gorge of the New River is called the Grand Canyon of the East, and the Gauley River is called the Beast of the East.

THE REGION

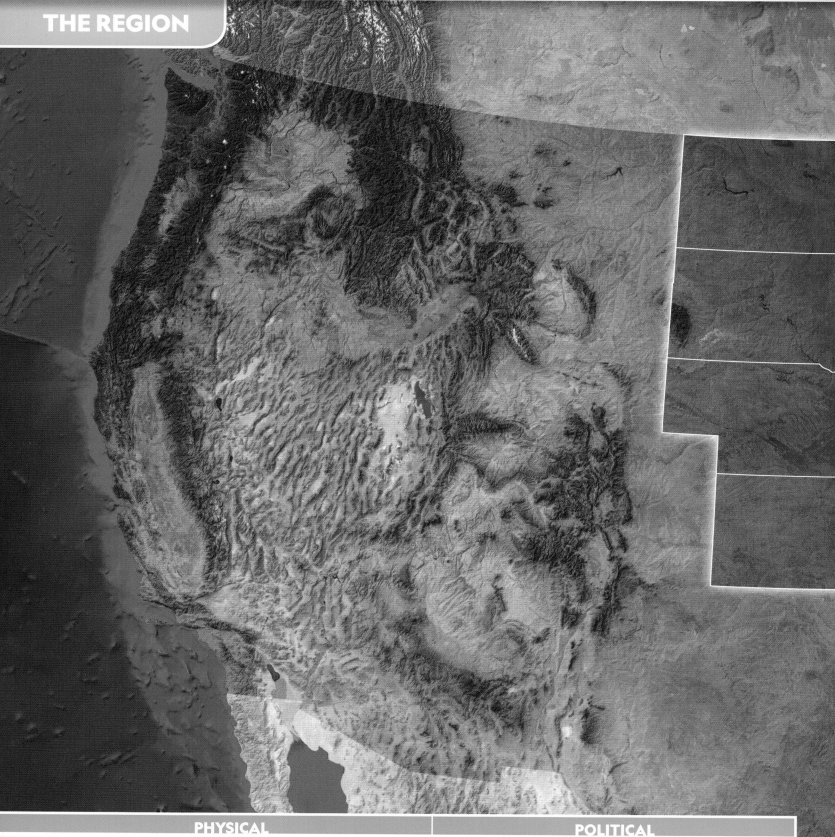

PHYSICAL

Total area (land and water)
821,726 sq mi (2,128,257 sq km)

Highest point
Harney Peak, SD 7,242 ft (2,207 m)

Lowest point
St. Francis River, MO 230 ft (70 m)

Longest rivers
Mississippi, Missouri, Arkansas, Ohio

Largest lakes
Superior, Michigan, Huron, Erie

Vegetation
Grassland; broadleaf, needleleaf, and mixed forest

Climate
Continental to mild, ranging from cold winters and cool summers in the north to mild winters and humid summers in the south

POLITICAL

Total population
68,308,744

States (12):
Illinois, Indiana, Iowa, Kansas, Michigan, Minnesota, Missouri, Nebraska, North Dakota, Ohio, South Dakota, Wisconsin

Largest state
Michigan: 96,714 sq mi (250,487 sq km)

Smallest state
Indiana: 36,420 sq mi (94,326 sq km)

Most populous state
Illinois: 12,741,080

Least populous state
North Dakota: 760,077

Largest city proper
Chicago, IL: 2,705,994

THE MIDWEST

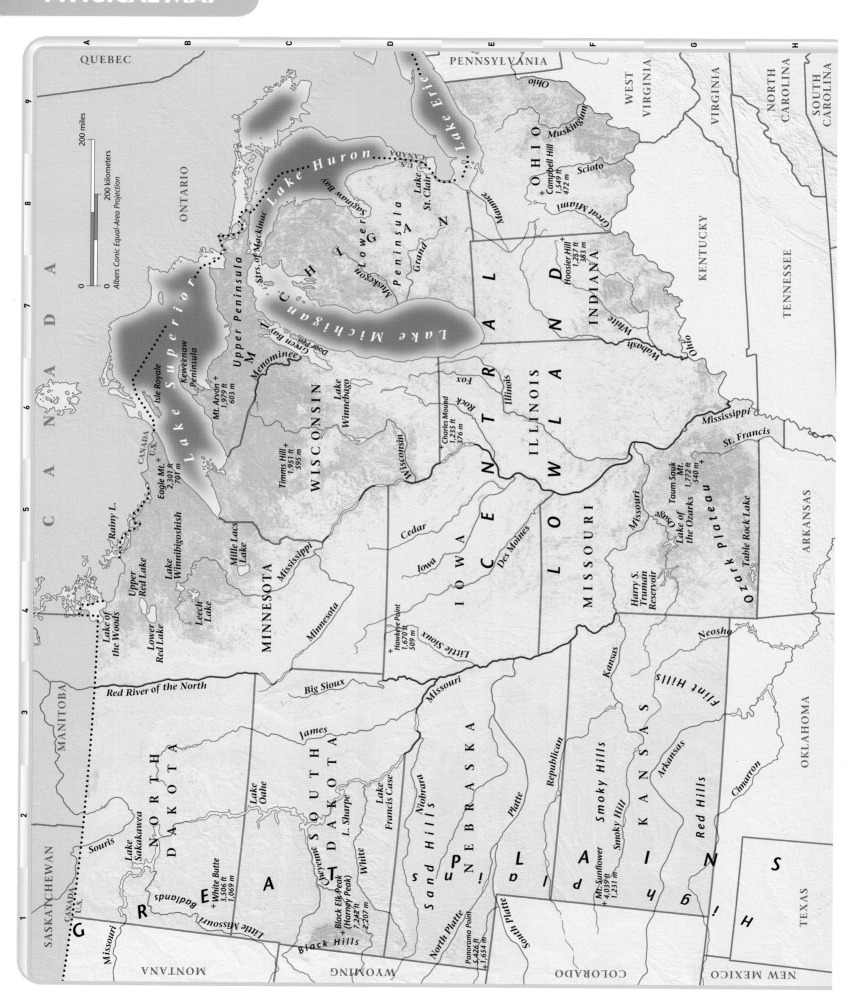

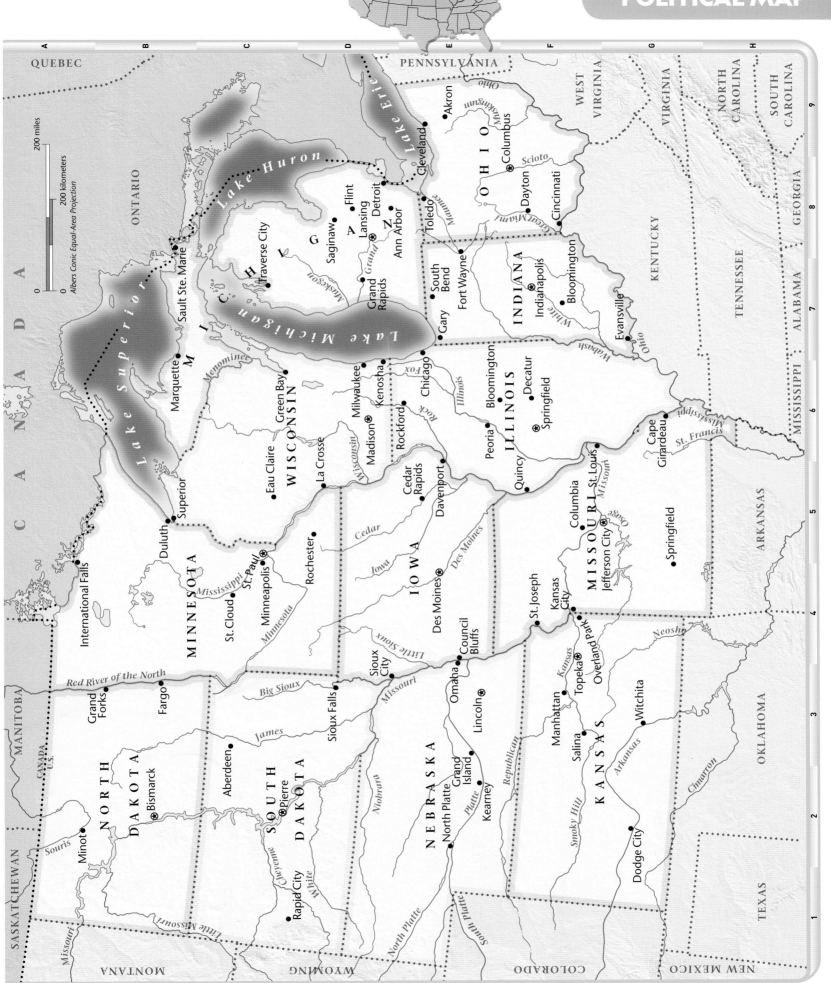

A   B   C   D   E   F   G   H

QUEBEC

PENNSYLVANIA

ONTARIO

Lake Erie

Lake Huron

Lake Superior

Lake Michigan

CANADA

200 miles
200 kilometers
Albers Conic Equal-Area Projection

• Akron

OHIO

Ohio

Muskingum

• Columbus ⊛

Scioto

• Dayton

Cincinnati •

WEST VIRGINIA

VIRGINIA

NORTH CAROLINA

SOUTH CAROLINA

9

Cleveland •

Great Miami

KENTUCKY

TENNESSEE

GEORGIA

ALABAMA

8

• Flint

Saginaw •

Lansing ⊛

Detroit •

M I C H I G A N

Ann Arbor •

Toledo •

Maumee

• Fort Wayne

• South Bend

INDIANA

• Bloomington

Indianapolis ⊛

White

MISSISSIPPI

7

Traverse City •

Grand

Muskegon

Grand Rapids •

Gary •

Wabash

Ohio

Evansville •

Marquette •

Sault Ste. Marie •

M

Menominee

Green Bay •

WISCONSIN

Milwaukee •

Kenosha •

Chicago •

Fox

Rock

Bloomington •

ILLINOIS

Decatur •

Springfield ⊛

Illinois

Cape Girardeau •

Mississippi

St. Francis

6

Superior •

Duluth •

Eau Claire •

La Crosse •

Madison ⊛

Rockford •

Wisconsin

Cedar Rapids •

Davenport •

Peoria •

Quincy •

St. Louis •

Missouri

Columbia •

Springfield •

ARKANSAS

5

International Falls •

MINNESOTA

St. Paul ⊛

Rochester •

Minneapolis •

St. Cloud •

Mississippi

Cedar

Iowa

I O W A

Des Moines ⊛

Des Moines

MISSOURI

Jefferson City ⊛

Osage

4

Red River of the North

Grand Forks •

Fargo •

Minnesota

Sioux City •

Council Bluffs •

Omaha •

St. Joseph •

Kansas City •

Overland Park •

Topeka ⊛

Osage

Neosho

Little Sioux

Big Sioux

Missouri

Sioux Falls •

Manhattan •

Salina •

Kansas

Witchita •

3

James

Aberdeen •

Lincoln ⊛

NEBRASKA

Grand Island •

North Platte •

Kearney •

Platte

Republican

KANSAS

Arkansas

Smoky Hill

Neosho

Niobrara

CANADA
U.S.

Souris

Minot •

NORTH DAKOTA

Bismarck ⊛

SOUTH DAKOTA

Pierre ⊛

Rapid City •

White

Cheyenne

Missouri

Little Missouri

Dodge City •

Cimarron

2

MANITOBA

SASKATCHEWAN

MONTANA

WYOMING

COLORADO

NEW MEXICO

TEXAS

OKLAHOMA

North Platte

South Platte

1

The Midwest

GREAT LAKES, GREAT RIVERS

◑ FIERCE GIANT. This *Tyrannosaurus rex* at Chicago's Field Museum roamed North America 65 million years ago.

The Midwest's early white settlers arrived from eastern U.S. states or Europe, but recent immigrants come from all parts of the world. Hispanics, for example, are settling in communities large and small throughout the region, and many Arabs reside in Detroit and Dearborn, Michigan. Drained by three mighty rivers—the Mississippi, Missouri, and Ohio—the Midwest's lowlands and plains are one of the world's most bountiful farmlands. Though the number of farmers has declined, new technologies and equipment have made farms larger and more productive. Meanwhile, industrial cities of the Rust Belt are adjusting to an economy focused more on information and services than on manufacturing.

◑ CROP CIRCLES. Much of the western part of the region receives less than 20 inches (50 cm) of rain yearly—not enough to support agriculture. Large, circular, center-pivot irrigation systems draw water from underground reserves called aquifers to provide life-giving water to crops.

◑ DAIRY HEARTLAND. Dairy cows, such as these in Wisconsin, are sometimes treated with growth hormones to increase milk production. These animals play an important role in the economy of the Midwest, which supplies much of the country's milk, butter, and cheese.

◐ **MIDWEST URBAN HUB.** Chicago, the third largest metropolitan area in the U.S., is the economic and cultural core of the Midwest.

◑ **PROUD LEADER.**
A statue of Menominee Chief Oshkosh stands near Lake Winnebago in Oshkosh, Wisconsin, which was named for him.

◒ **NATURE'S MOST VIOLENT STORMS.**
Parts of the midwestern U.S. have earned the nickname Tornado Alley because these destructive, swirling storms, which develop in association with thunderstorms along eastward-moving cold fronts, occur here more than any other place on Earth.

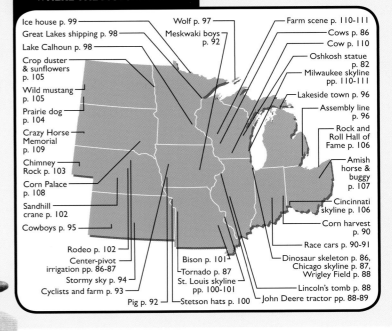

WHERE THE PICTURES ARE

Ice house p. 99
Great Lakes shipping p. 98
Lake Calhoun p. 98
Crop duster & sunflowers p. 105
Wild mustang p. 105
Prairie dog p. 104
Crazy Horse Memorial p. 109
Chimney Rock p. 103
Corn Palace p. 108
Sandhill crane p. 102
Cowboys p. 95
Rodeo p. 102
Center-pivot irrigation pp. 86-87
Stormy sky p. 94
Cyclists and farm p. 93

Wolf p. 97
Meskwaki boys p. 92
Bison p. 101
Tornado p. 87
St. Louis skyline pp. 100-101
Pig p. 92
Stetson hats p. 100

Farm scene p. 110-111
Cows p. 86
Cow p. 110
Oshkosh statue p. 82
Milwaukee skyline pp. 110-111
Lakeside town p. 96
Assembly line p. 96
Rock and Roll Hall of Fame p. 106
Amish horse & buggy p. 107
Cincinnati skyline p. 106
Corn harvest p. 90
Race cars p. 90-91
Dinosaur skeleton p. 86, Chicago skyline p. 87, Wrigley Field p. 88
Lincoln's tomb p. 88
John Deere tractor pp. 88-89

ILLINOIS

THE BASICS

Statehood
December 3, 1818; 21st state

Total area (land and water)
57,914 sq mi (149,995 sq km)

Land area
55,519 sq mi (143,793 sq km)

Population
12,741,080

Capital
Springfield
Population 114,694

Largest city
Chicago
Population 2,705,994

Racial/ethnic groups
77.1% white; 14.6% African American; 5.7% Asian; 0.6% Native American; 17.3% Hispanic (any race)

Foreign born
14.0%

Urban population
88.5%

Population density
229.5 per sq mi (88.6 per sq km)

GEO WHIZ

A giant, fossilized rainforest has been unearthed in an eastern Illinois coal mine near Danville. Scientists believe it was buried by an earthquake 300 million years ago.

The Great Chicago Fire of 1871 destroyed the city's waterworks, so firemen had to drag water in buckets from Lake Michigan and the Chicago River.

Illinois

Two rivers that now form the borders of Illinois were key to the state's early white settlement. French explorers traveled down the Mississippi in 1673, and many 19th-century settlers followed the Ohio to southern Illinois. By the 1830s many Native Americans had been forced out of Illinois. Chicago, the most populous city in the Midwest, is an economic giant and one of the country's busiest transportation hubs. Barges from Chicago's port on Lake Michigan reach the Gulf of Mexico via rivers and canals; ships reach the Atlantic Ocean via the Great Lakes and St. Lawrence Seaway. Flat terrain and fertile soils in the northern and central regions of the state help make Illinois a top producer of corn and soybeans. The more rugged, forested south has deposits of coal. Springfield, capital of the Land of Lincoln, welcomes tourists visiting the home and tomb of the country's 16th president.

◖ **REMEMBERING A PRESIDENT. Dedicated in 1874, the National Lincoln Monument in Springfield honors Abraham Lincoln, who was assassinated in 1865. A special vault holds the remains of the slain president, who led the country during the Civil War.**

VIOLET

CARDINAL

◖ **PLAY BALL! Wrigley Field, home to the Chicago Cubs baseball team, is affected by wind conditions more than any other major league park due to its location near Lake Michigan.**

ALTERNATIVE ENERGY

Production in million megawatt hours*, 2017 data

97,191,142	83,199,832	54,344,554	42,651,973	42,374,264
Illinois	Pennsylvania	South Carolina	Alabama	North Carolina

*1 Megawatt hour (Mwh) = 1000 Kilowatt hours (Kwh)

Illinois ranks first among the 30 states that produce nuclear power. The state has six nuclear power plants with 11 reactors.

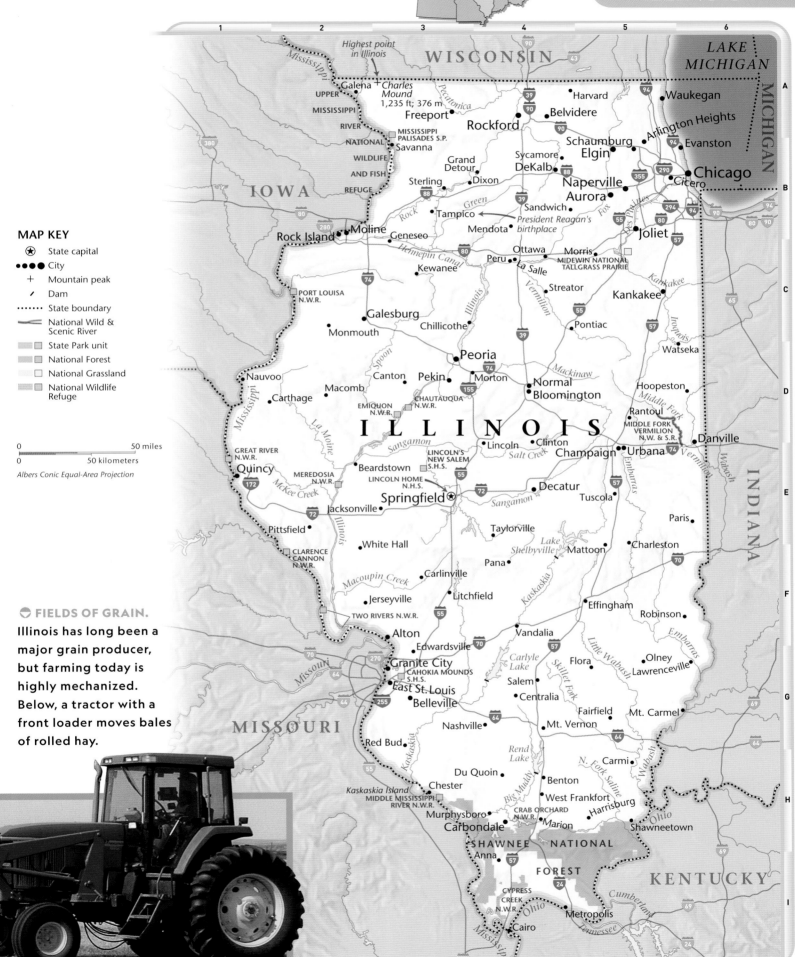

1 2 3 4 5 6

WISCONSIN

LAKE MICHIGAN

MICHIGAN

Mississippi R.

Highest point in Illinois

Galena · *Charles Mound* 1,235 ft; 376 m
UPPER
MISSISSIPPI
RIVER
NATIONAL
WILDLIFE
AND FISH
REFUGE

Pecatonica

90
43

Harvard
Waukegan

Freeport
Belvidere
39
90

Rockford
90

Arlington Heights
94

MISSISSIPPI PALISADES S.P.
Savanna

Grand Detour
Sycamore
DeKalb

Schaumburg
Elgin

Evanston

IOWA

Sterling
88
Dixon

Naperville
Aurora
355
290

Chicago
Cicero

MAP KEY

Rock R.
Green R.

Sandwich

55
80
94

90

94

⊛ State capital
•••● City
+ Mountain peak
⟋ Dam
········ State boundary
～～ National Wild & Scenic River
▨ State Park unit
▨ National Forest
☐ National Grassland
▨ National Wildlife Refuge

80
Rock Island
Moline
Geneseo

Tampico ←
President Reagan's birthplace

Joliet
57

Hennepin Canal
80

Ottawa
Peru
La Salle
Morris
294
MIDEWIN NATIONAL TALLGRASS PRAIRIE

Mendota

Kewanee

Streator

Illinois R.
Vermilion R.

Kankakee

Kankakee R.

65

PORT LOUISA
N.W.R.

Galesburg

Chillicothe

55

Pontiac

Iroquois R.

57

Monmouth

39

Watseka

0 ——— 50 miles
0 ——— 50 kilometers
Albers Conic Equal-Area Projection

Spoon R.

Peoria

Canton
Pekin
Morton
74
155

Normal
Bloomington

Mackinaw R.

Hoopeston

Middle Fork

Nauvoo

Macomb

EMIQUON
N.W.R.

CHAUTAUQUA
N.W.R.

Rantoul

MIDDLE FORK VERMILION N.W. & S.R.

Carthage

La Moine R.

Sangamon R.

Lincoln
Clinton

Danville

I L L I N O I S

Salt Creek

Champaign
Urbana
74

Vermilion R.

INDIANA

Wabash R.

GREAT RIVER
N.W.R.

Quincy
172

MEREDOSIA
N.W.R.

Beardstown

LINCOLN'S NEW SALEM S.H.S.
55

Embarras R.

LINCOLN HOME N.H.S.

72

McKee Creek

Mississippi R.

Jacksonville
72

Springfield ⊛

Decatur
57

Sangamon R.

Tuscola

Paris

Pittsfield

White Hall

Taylorville

Lake Shelbyville

Charleston

70

CLARENCE CANNON
N.W.R.

Pana

Mattoon

Macoupin Creek

Carlinville

Jerseyville
Litchfield

Kaskaskia R.

Effingham

Robinson

Embarras R.

TWO RIVERS N.W.R.
55

FIELDS OF GRAIN.
Illinois has long been a major grain producer, but farming today is highly mechanized. Below, a tractor with a front loader moves bales of rolled hay.

Alton
Edwardsville
70
Vandalia
157

Carlyle Lake

Flora

Olney
Lawrenceville

Little Wabash R.

70

Missouri R.

270
Granite City
CAHOKIA MOUNDS S.H.S.
East St. Louis
255
Belleville

64

64

Salem

Centralia

Fairfield

Mt. Carmel

69

MISSOURI

Nashville

64

Mt. Vernon

Skillet Fork

64

Red Bud

Kaskaskia R.

Rend Lake

Carmi

Wabash R.

Du Quoin

Benton

N. Fork Saline R.

55

Chester

Kaskaskia Island
MIDDLE MISSISSIPPI RIVER N.W.R.

Big Muddy R.

West Frankfort

Harrisburg

Ohio R.

Shawneetown

69

Murphysboro
Carbondale

CRAB ORCHARD N.W.R.

Marion

SHAWNEE NATIONAL

Anna
57

FOREST

KENTUCKY

CYPRESS CREEK
N.W.R.

24

Ohio R.
Cumberland R.

Metropolis

69

Tennessee R.

Cairo
55
Mississippi R.

380
280

THE BASICS

Statehood
December 11, 1816; 19th state

Total area (land and water)
36,420 sq mi (94,326 sq km)

Land area
35,826 sq mi (92,789 sq km)

Population
6,691,878

Capital
Indianapolis
Population 867,125

Largest city
Indianapolis
Population 867,125

Racial/ethnic groups
85.4% white; 9.7% African American; 2.4% Asian; 0.4% Native American; 7.0% Hispanic (any race)

Foreign born
5.0%

Urban population
72.4%

Population density
186.8 per sq mi
(72.1 per sq km)

GEO WHIZ

Every year Fort Wayne hosts the Johnny Appleseed Festival to honor John Chapman, who planted apple orchards from Pennsylvania to Illinois.

The Children's Museum of Indianapolis, the world's largest children's museum, features life-size dinosaur replicas, hands-on science labs, and much more.

Indiana

Indiana's name, meaning "Land of the Indians," honors the tribes who lived in the region before the arrival of Europeans. The first permanent white settlement was Vincennes, established by the French in the early 1700s. Following statehood in 1816, most Native Americans were forced out to make way for white settlement. Lake Michigan, in the state's northwest corner, brings economic and recreational opportunities. The lakefront city of Gary anchors a major industrial region. Nearby, the natural beauty and shifting sands of the Indiana Dunes National Lakeshore attract many visitors. Corn, soybeans, and hogs are the most important products from Indiana's many farms. True to the state motto, "The Crossroads of America," highways from all directions converge at Indianapolis. Traveling at a much higher speed are cars on that city's famed Motor Speedway, home to the Indy 500 auto race since 1911. Cheering for a favorite high school or college team is a popular pastime for many Hoosiers who catch basketball fever.

START YOUR ENGINES. The Indianapolis Motor Speedway seats up to 250,000 sports fans. Nicknamed the Brickyard, its track was once paved with 3.2 million bricks.

CARDINAL

PEONY

FARM TO TABLE

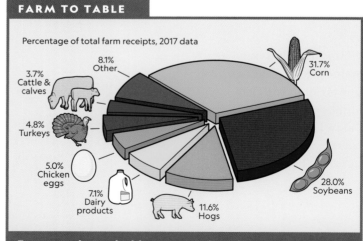

Percentage of total farm receipts, 2017 data

- 8.1% Other
- 3.7% Cattle & calves
- 4.8% Turkeys
- 5.0% Chicken eggs
- 7.1% Dairy products
- 11.6% Hogs
- 31.7% Corn
- 28.0% Soybeans

Farm products, led by corn and soybeans, account for more than $10 billion of Indiana's cash receipts. The state produces 15 percent of the total U.S. output in these two crops.

FUEL FARMING. Indiana farmers grow corn for many uses—livestock feed, additives used in human food products, and production of ethanol, a non-fossil fuel energy source.

LAKE MICHIGAN

MICHIGAN

MAP KEY

⊛ State capital

•●● City

◼ Point of interest

+ Mountain peak

╱ Dam

⋯⋯ State boundary

State Park unit

National Park Service unit

National Forest

National Wildlife Refuge

0   50 miles

0   50 kilometers

Albers Conic Equal-Area Projection

INDIANA

ILLINOIS

OHIO

KENTUCKY

East Chicago

Michigan City

INDIANA DUNES NATIONAL PARK

South Bend

Elkhart

Mishawaka

Goshen

Angola

Hammond

Gary

Portage

LaPorte

Merrillville

Nappanee

Kendallville

Auburn

Valparaiso

Crown Point

Plymouth

Lake Wawasee

Columbia City

Lowell

Warsaw

Rochester

Fort Wayne

North Manchester

Huntington

Decatur

Rensselaer

Lake Shafer

Monticello

Logansport

Peru

Wabash

Salamonie Lake

Lake Freeman

Mississinewa Lake

Marion

Gas City

Portland

Kokomo

Hartford City

Lafayette

Wildcat Creek

Frankfort

Elwood

Alexandria

Muncie

Winchester

Crawfordsville

Lebanon

Noblesville

Anderson

Highest point in Indiana

Hoosier Hill 1,257 ft 383 m +

Carmel

New Castle

Cecil M. Harden Lake

Indianapolis ⊛

Lawrence

Greenfield

Richmond

Clinton

Plainfield

Beech Grove

Connersville

Greencastle

Greenwood

Rushville

Brookville Lake

Terre Haute

Brazil

Franklin

Shelbyville

Martinsville

Greensburg

Cagles Mill Lake

Lake Lemon

Columbus

U.S. center of population in 1900

Lawrenceburg

Bloomington

BROWN COUNTY STATE PARK

Linton

Monroe Lake

North Vernon

Seymour

BIG OAKS N.W.R.

HOOSIER

MUSCATATUCK N.W.R.

Bedford

Madison

GEORGE ROGERS CLARK N.H.P.

Vincennes

Washington

Scottsburg

NATIONAL

Salem

Charlestown

Princeton

Jasper

Patoka Lake

Jeffersonville

New Albany

PATOKA RIVER N.W.R.

Huntingburg

FOREST

WYANDOTTE CAVE

Corydon

NEW HARMONY S.H.S.

LINCOLN BOYHOOD NATIONAL MEMORIAL

Santa Claus

Mount Vernon

Boonville

Tell City

Evansville

IOWA

THE BASICS

Statehood
December 28, 1846; 29th state

Total area (land and water)
56,273 sq mi (145,746 sq km)

Land area
55,857 sq mi (144,669 sq km)

Population
3,156,145

Capital
Des Moines
Population 216,853

Largest city
Des Moines
Population 216,853

Racial/ethnic groups
91.1% white; 3.8% African
American; 2.6% Asian; 0.5%
Native American; 6.0%
Hispanic (any race)

Foreign born
5.0%

Urban population
64.0%

Population density
56.5 per sq mi (21.8 per sq km)

GEO WHIZ

One of America's most famous houses is in Eldon. It was immortalized in Grant Wood's famous painting "American Gothic." The pitchfork-holding man and his wife shown in the art were not farmers at all. Wood's dentist and his sister posed for the painting.

Effigy Mounds National Monument, in northeast Iowa, is the only place in the country with such a large collection of mounds in the shapes of birds, mammals, and reptiles. Eastern Woodland Indians built these mounds from about 500 B.C. to A.D. 1300.

Iowa ranks second, after Texas, among U.S. wind energy producers.

WILD ROSE

AMERICAN
GOLDFINCH

Iowa

Iowa's earliest inhabitants built earthen mounds—some shaped like birds and bears—that are visible in the state's northeast. Nineteenth-century white settlers found rolling prairies covered by a sea of tall grasses that soon yielded to the plow. A decade after statehood in 1846, a group of religious German immigrants established the Amana Colonies, a communal society that still draws visitors. Blessed with ample precipitation and rich soils, Iowa is the heart of one of the world's most productive farming regions. The state is a major producer of corn, soybeans, hogs, and eggs. Much of the grain crop feeds livestock destined to reach dinner plates throughout the United States and around the world. An increasing amount of corn is used to make ethanol, which is mixed with gasoline to fuel cars and trucks. Two of the state's biggest industries are food processing and the manufacture of machinery. Des Moines, the capital and largest city, is a center of insurance and publishing.

◯ **PIG BUSINESS.**
Hogs outnumber people more than seven to one in Iowa. The state is the leading hog producer in the U.S.

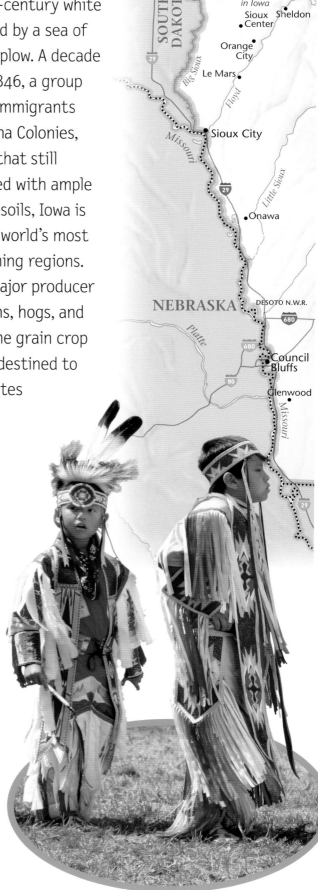

◗ **CELEBRATING CULTURE.**
Young Meskwaki boys dance at a powwow near Tama. Such gatherings allow Native Americans to preserve their traditions.

MINNESOTA

Spirit Lake
West Okoboji L.
East Okoboji Lake
Estherville
Spencer
Cherokee
Storm Lake
Des Moines
Union Slough N.W.R.
Forest City
Emmetsburg
Algona
Clear Lake
Mason City
Winnebago
Humboldt
Fort Dodge
Webster City
Iowa
Boone
Story City
I O W A
Ames
Nevada
Perry
Ankeny
Urbandale
Windsor Heights
Des Moines
West Des Moines
Neal Smith N.W.R.
Atlantic
Winterset
Indianola
Lake Red Rock
Pella
Knoxville
Harlan
Carroll
Denison
Jefferson
Red Oak
Creston
Osceola
Chariton
Centerville
Shenandoah
Clarinda
Blanchard
Bedford

Osage
Cresco
Decorah
Waukon
Charles City
New Hampton
Waverly
Oelwein
Cedar Falls
Independence
Manchester
Dyersville
Waterloo
Eldora
Vinton
Central City
Anamosa
Marion
Cedar Rapids
De Witt
Maquoketa
Clinton
Tama
Marshalltown
Amana Colonies
Newton
Grinnell
Coralville
Iowa City
Bettendorf
Davenport
Muscatine
Washington
Oskaloosa
Ottumwa
Fairfield
Mount Pleasant
Eldon
Burlington
Bloomfield
Fort Madison
Keokuk

Sac and Fox/Meskwaki Indian Reservation
Herbert Hoover N.H.S.
Port Louisa N.W.R.

MISSOURI
WISCONSIN
ILLINOIS

Upper Iowa
Wapsipinicon
Cedar
Shell Rock
Boone
Iowa
Turkey
Maquoketa
Cedar
Des Moines
Thompson
E. Nodaway
Chariton
Rathbun Lake
Des Moines
Mississippi
North Raccoon
Boyer

Effigy Mounds N.M.
Dubuque
UPPER MISSISSIPPI RIVER NATIONAL WILDLIFE AND FISH REFUGE

MAP KEY
★ State capital
●●● City
▪ Point of interest
+ Mountain peak
⌐ Dam
···· State boundary
☐ Indian Reservation
☐ National Park Service unit
☐ National Wildlife Refuge

0 — 25 miles
0 — 25 kilometers
Albers Conic Equal-Area Projection

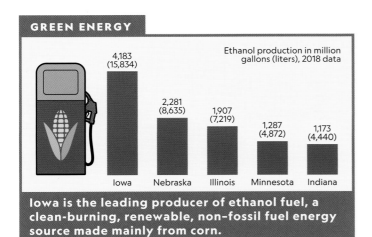

GREEN ENERGY

Ethanol production in million gallons (liters), 2018 data

Iowa	4,183 (15,834)
Nebraska	2,281 (8,635)
Illinois	1,907 (7,219)
Minnesota	1,287 (4,872)
Indiana	1,173 (4,440)

Iowa is the leading producer of ethanol fuel, a clean-burning, renewable, non-fossil fuel energy source made mainly from corn.

⬭ FITNESS RALLY. Cyclists pass a farm community during the Annual Great Bicycle Ride Across Iowa. Begun in 1973, it is the oldest and longest recreational bicycle event in the world.

KANSAS

KANSAS

THE BASICS

Statehood
January 29, 1861; 34th state

Total area (land and water)
82,278 sq mi (213,100 sq km)

Land area
81,759 sq mi (211,754 sq km)

Population
2,911,505

Capital
Topeka
Population 125,904

Largest city
Wichita
Population 389,255

Racial/ethnic groups
86.5% white; 6.2% African American; 3.1% Asian; 1.2% Native American; 11.9% Hispanic (any race)

Foreign born
7.0%

Urban population
74.2%

Population density
35.6 per sq mi (13.7 per sq km)

GEO WHIZ

Plesiosaur skeletons and many other marine reptile fossils have been unearthed in Kansas.

The Tallgrass Prairie National Preserve, one of the last great expanses of tallgrass prairie, is in the Flint Hills.

Lindsborg is proud of its Swedish heritage and the fact that it is home to the Anatoly Karpov International School of Chess, named for the Russian who succeeded American Bobby Fischer as world champion in 1975.

SUNFLOWER

WESTERN MEADOWLARK

Kansas

Considered by the government to be unsuitable for settlement, Kansas was made part of Indian Territory—a vast tract of land between Missouri and the Rockies—in the 1830s. By the 1850s white settlers were fighting Native Americans for more land and among themselves over the issue of slavery. In 1861 Kansas entered the Union as a free state. After the Civil War, cowboys drove Texas cattle to the Wild West railroad towns of Abilene and Dodge City, where waiting trains hauled cattle to slaughterhouses in the East. Today, the state remains a major producer of beef, oil and natural gas wells dot the landscape, and factories in Wichita make aircraft equipment. Heading west toward the High Plains and the Rockies in neighboring Colorado, the elevation gradually increases, and the climate becomes drier. Threats of fierce thunderstorms accompanied by tornadoes have many Kansans keeping an eye on the sky.

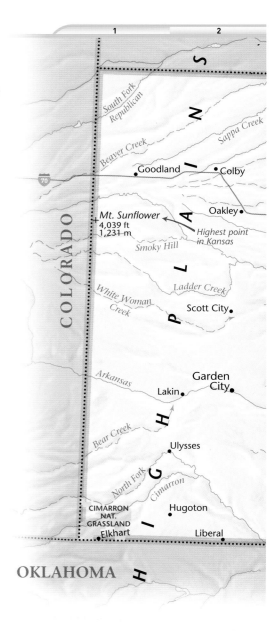

◗ OMINOUS SKY. Lightning splits the sky as black clouds of a thunderstorm roll across a field of wheat. Such storms bring heavy rain and often spawn dangerous tornadoes.

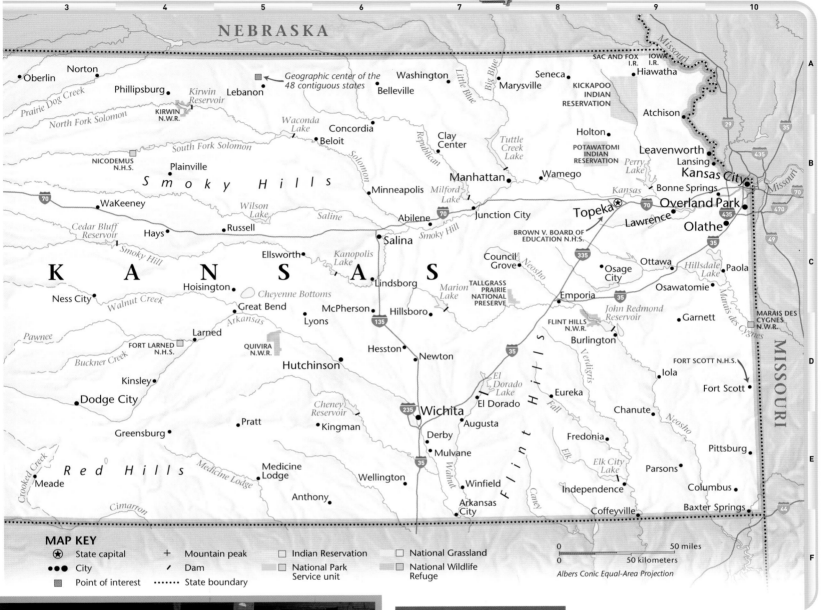

NEBRASKA

Oberlin • Norton • Phillipsburg • *Kirwin Reservoir* Lebanon • ← Geographic center of the 48 contiguous states

Washington • Belleville • Marysville • Seneca • SAC AND FOX I.R. IOWA I.R. • Hiawatha

Prairie Dog Creek *North Fork Solomon* KIRWIN N.W.R.

KICKAPOO INDIAN RESERVATION

Atchison

NICODEMUS N.H.S. Plainville • Concordia • Beloit • *Waconda Lake* Clay Center • *Tuttle Creek Lake*

Holton

POTAWATOMI INDIAN RESERVATION *Perry Lake* Leavenworth • Lansing

South Fork Solomon

S m o k y   H i l l s

WaKeeney • *Wilson Lake* Minneapolis • *Milford Lake* Manhattan • Wamego • *Kansas* Bonne Springs • Kansas City

Abilene • Junction City • Topeka ★ Overland Park

Hays • Russell • *Saline* *Smoky Hill* BROWN V. BOARD OF EDUCATION N.H.S. Lawrence • Olathe

K   A   N   S   A   S

Ellsworth • *Kanopolis Lake* Salina • Council Grove • *Neosho* Ottawa • *Hillsdale Lake* Paola

Ness City • *Walnut Creek* Hoisington • *Cheyenne Bottoms* Lindsborg • *Marion Lake* TALLGRASS PRAIRIE NATIONAL PRESERVE Osage City • Osawatomie

Great Bend • McPherson • Hillsboro • Emporia

Arkansas Lyons • FLINT HILLS N.W.R. *John Redmond Reservoir* Garnett

Larned • FORT LARNED N.H.S. QUIVIRA N.W.R. Hesston • Newton • F l i n t   H i l l s Burlington • FORT SCOTT N.H.S. Iola • Fort Scott

Buckner Creek Kinsley • Hutchinson • *El Dorado Lake* MARAIS DES CYGNES N.W.R.

Pawnee Dodge City • *Cheney Reservoir* Wichita • El Dorado • Eureka • Chanute • *Neosho*

Pratt • Kingman • Augusta • Fredonia • Pittsburg

Greensburg • Derby • Mulvane • Winfield • Independence • *Elk City Lake* Parsons • Columbus

R e d   H i l l s *Medicine Lodge* Medicine Lodge • Wellington • *Elk* Coffeyville • Baxter Springs

Meade • *Crooked Creek* Anthony • Arkansas City

Cimarron

MISSOURI

MAP KEY

★ State capital
●●● City
■ Point of interest
✛ Mountain peak
✓ Dam
□ Indian Reservation
□ National Park Service unit
□ National Grassland
□ National Wildlife Refuge

0   50 miles
0   50 kilometers

Albers Conic Equal-Area Projection

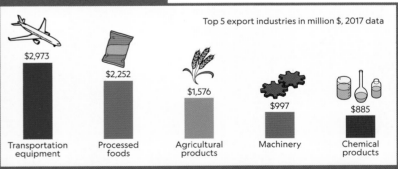

SELLING TO THE WORLD

Top 5 export industries in million $, 2017 data

$2,973	$2,252	$1,576	$997	$885
Transportation equipment	Processed foods	Agricultural products	Machinery	Chemical products

Participation in the global economy earns Kansas more than $11 billion each year. Top markets are Canada and Mexico. Aircraft and processed meat products make up much of its export sales.

◑ **MODERN-DAY COWBOYS.** Dodge City traces its history to Fort Dodge, built on the Santa Fe Trail in 1865 to protect pioneer wagon trains and the mail service from attacks by outlaws or bands of Native Americans. The town, frequented by cattle herders and bison hunters, was known for its lawlessness.

THE BASICS

Statehood
January 26, 1837; 26th state

Total area (land and water)
96,714 sq mi (250,487 sq km)

Land area
56,539 sq mi (146,435 sq km)

Population
9,995,915

Capital
Lansing
Population 118,427

Largest city
Detroit
Population 672,662

Racial/ethnic groups
79.4% white; 14.1% African American; 3.2% Asian; 0.7% Native American; 5.1% Hispanic (any race)

Foreign born
6.6%

Urban population
74.6%

Population density
176.8 per sq mi
(68.3 per sq km)

GEO WHIZ

Researchers at the Seney National Wildlife Refuge on the Upper Peninsula have discovered that loons change their call as they move to different territories.

The Great Lakes, which contain 20 percent of Earth's freshwater, are at risk due to industrial and municipal dumping and agricultural runoff.

APPLE BLOSSOM

ROBIN

Michigan

Native Americans had friendly relations with early French fur traders who came to what is now Michigan, but they waged battles with the British who later assumed control. Completion of New York's Erie Canal in 1825 made it easier for settlers to reach the area, and statehood came in 1837. Michigan consists of two large peninsulas that border four of the five Great Lakes—Erie, Huron, Michigan, and Superior. Most of the population is on the state's Lower Peninsula, while the Upper Peninsula, once a productive mining area, now is popular among vacationing nature lovers. The five-mile (8-km)-long Mackinac Bridge has linked the peninsulas since 1957. In the 20th century Michigan became the center of the American auto industry, and the state's fortunes have risen and fallen with those of major car companies. Though it remains a big producer of cars and trucks, the state is working to diversify its economy. Michigan's farms grow crops ranging from grains to fruits and vegetables.

ASSEMBLY LINE. **For more than 100 years the Ford Motor Company's Rouge Complex in Dearborn has been a leader in motor vehicle production, which is a major part of the state economy. Today, the plant turns out a truck every 53 seconds.**

DRIVING FORCE

$39,283

Top 5 manufacturing sectors in million $, 2016 data

$7,823

$7,789

$7,524

$6,156

Motor vehicles & parts | Machinery | Fabricated metal products | Chemical products | Food, beverage, & tobacco products

Once the main hub of automotive production in the U.S., Michigan is still among the top auto manufacturing states.

REFLECTION OF THE PAST. **Victorian-style summer homes, built on Mackinac Island in the late 19th century by wealthy railroad families, now welcome vacationers to the island. To protect the environment, cars are not allowed.**

1 2 3 4 5 6 7 8

ONTARIO

MINNESOTA

CANADA
U.S.

ISLE ROYALE NATIONAL PARK

Isle Royale

LAKE SUPERIOR

CANADA
U.S.

◗ **TOP PREDATOR.**

Wolves on Isle Royale, in upper Lake Superior, live in packs that hunt moose in this isolated national park.

KEWEENAW N.H.P.

Laurium

Keweenaw Peninsula

ONTONAGON INDIAN RESERVATION

Houghton

HURON N.W.R.

PORCUPINE MTS. S.P.

BLACK N.W.&S.R.

PRESQUE ISLE N.W.&S.R.

Ironwood

OTTAWA

NAT.

FOREST

ONTONAGON N.W.&S.R.

STURGEON N.W.&S.R.

PAINT N.W.&S.R.

LAC VIEUX DESERT I.R.

L'Anse

L'ANSE I.R.

Mt. Arvon
1,979 ft
+603 m

Highest point in Michigan

OTTAWA N.F.

YELLOW DOG N.W.&S.R.

Marquette

GRAND ISLAND N.R.A.

Munising

PICTURED ROCKS NATIONAL LAKESHORE

TAHQUAMENON FALLS S.P.

TAHQUAMENON (EAST BRANCH) N.W.&S.R.

Whitefish Bay

Soo Canals: among the busiest ship canals in the Western Hemisphere

Sault Sainte Marie

SAULT SAINTE MARIE I.R.

ONTARIO

Ishpeming

SENEY N.W.R.

BAY MILLS I.R.

BAY MILLS I.R.

St. Marys

HARBOR ISLAND N.W.R.

U P P E R   P E N I N S U L A

INDIAN N.W.&S.R.

HIAWATHA NATIONAL FOREST

CARP N.W.&S.R.

Brule

Ford

WHITEFISH N.W.&S.R.

Manistique

FATHER MARQUETTE NATIONAL MEMORIAL

St. Ignace

Mackinac I.

Drummond Island

HANNAHVILLE I.R.

Gladstone

STURGEON N.W.&S.R.

Straits of Mackinac

Bois Blanc I.

Iron Mountain

Escanaba

Garden Peninsula

Beaver I.

Cheboygan

Burt Lake

Mullett L.

Rogers City

Cedar

Menominee

Site of at least 50 shipwrecks

LITTLE TRAVERSE BAY I.R.

Petoskey

Pigeon

LAKE HURON

Menominee

Green Bay

Manitou Islands

Grand Traverse Bay

GRAND TRAVERSE I.R.

Boyne City

Gaylord

Thunder Bay

Alpena

Thunder Bay

WISCONSIN

Manitou Passage

SLEEPING BEAR DUNES NAT. LAKESHORE

Kalkaska

Au Sable

Mio

Hubbard L.

AU SABLE N.W.&S.R.

Traverse City

Houghton Lake

HURON

NAT.

MAP KEY

★ State capital

••• City

+ Mountain peak

····· State or national boundary

∿ National Wild & Scenic River

☐ Indian Reservation

☐ State Park unit

☐ National Park Service unit

☐ National Forest

☐ National Wildlife Refuge

BEAR CREEK N.W.&S.R.

LITTLE RIVER I.R.

PINE N.W.&S.R.

Cadillac

Houghton Lake

Rifle

Tawas City

Manistee

MANISTEE N.W.&S.R.

MANISTEE

Manistee

L O W E R

ISABELLA I.R.

Saginaw Bay

Bad Axe

Harbor Beach

FOREST

Ludington

PERE MARQUETTE N.W.&S.R.

NATIONAL

Big Rapids

Muskegon

ISABELLA I.R.

Midland

Bay City

Caro

Cass

Sandusky

Black

FOREST

Fremont

Mt. Pleasant

Alma

SHIAWASSEE N.W.R.

Saginaw

0   50 miles

0   50 kilometers

Albers Conic Equal-Area Projection

White

P E N I N S U L A

Greenville

Flint

Port Huron

Muskegon

Grand Haven

Belding

Ionia

St. Johns

Owosso

Burton

St. Clair

LAKE MICHIGAN

Grand Rapids

Kentwood

Grand

Looking Glass

East Lansing

Pontiac

Troy

Warren

St. Clair Shores

Lake St. Clair

Holland

Zeeland

MATCH-E-BE-NASH-SHE-WISH BAND OF POTTAWATOMI I.R.

Hastings

Lansing

Mason

Livonia

ONTARIO

Charlotte

Kalamazoo

South Haven

Battle Creek

Jackson

Ann Arbor

Detroit

Kalamazoo

Portage

Marshall

Albion

Ypsilanti

Dearborn

Benton Harbor

HURON POTAWATOMI I.R.

St. Joseph

Tecumseh

Monroe

DETROIT RIVER INTERNATIONAL WILDLIFE REFUGE

Dowagiac

Three Rivers

Coldwater

Hillsdale

Adrian

Temperance

Lambertville

CANADA
U.S.

Niles

Sturgis

LAKE ERIE

ILLINOIS

INDIANA

OHIO

Mississippi

THE BASICS

Statehood
May 11, 1858; 32nd state

Total area (land and water)
86,936 sq mi (225,163 sq km)

Land area
79,627 sq mi (206,232 sq km)

Population
5,611,179

Capital
St. Paul
Population 307,695

Largest city
Minneapolis
Population 425,403

Racial/ethnic groups
84.4% white; 6.5% African American; 5.1% Asian; 1.4% Native American; 5.4% Hispanic (any race)

Foreign born
8.2%

Urban population
73.3%

Population density
70.5 per sq mi
(27.2 per sq km)

GEO WHIZ

The Mayo Clinic, a world-famous medical research center, is in Rochester.

The Boundary Waters Canoe Area Wilderness was the first U.S. wilderness area set aside for canoeing.

COMMON LOON

SHOWY LADY'S SLIPPER

Minnesota

French fur traders began arriving in present-day Minnesota in the mid-17th century. Statehood was established in 1858, and most remaining Native Americans were forced from the state after a decisive battle in 1862. During the late 1800s, large numbers of Scandinavians, Germans, and other immigrants settled a land rich in wildlife, timber, minerals, and fertile soils. Today, farming is concentrated in the south and west. In the northeast, the Mesabi Range's open-pit mines make the state the country's leading source of iron ore. Most of the ore is shipped from Duluth. Both Duluth and nearby Superior in Wisconsin (see page 111) are leading Great Lakes ports. From these ports, ships can reach the Atlantic Ocean via the St. Lawrence Seaway. Scattered across the state's landscape are thousands of lakes—ancient footprints of retreating glaciers—that draw anglers and canoeists. One of those lakes, Lake Itasca, is the source of the mighty Mississippi River, which flows through the Twin Cities of Minneapolis and St. Paul.

⊖ **SUMMER FUN.** Lake Calhoun, also known by its Dakota name Bde Maka Ska, which means "White Earth Lake," is surrounded by a Minneapolis city park that is popular with bikers and pedestrians.

SHOPPER'S PARADISE

Retail space in square feet (square meters), 2017 data

Mall	Retail space
Mall of America (MN)	4,870,000 (452,438)
King of Prussia Mall (PA)	2,900,000 (269,419)
South Coast Plaza (CA)	2,700,000 (250,838)
Aventura Mall (FL)	2,700,000 (250,838)
Del Amo Fashion Center (CA)	2,600,000 (241,548)

Americans love to shop, and Bloomington's Mall of America includes more retail space than any other mall in the country.

◐ **INLAND PORT.** Duluth, on the northern shore of Lake Superior, is the westernmost deep-water port on the St. Lawrence Seaway. Barges and container ships move products such as iron ore and grain along the Great Lakes to the Atlantic Ocean and to markets around the world.

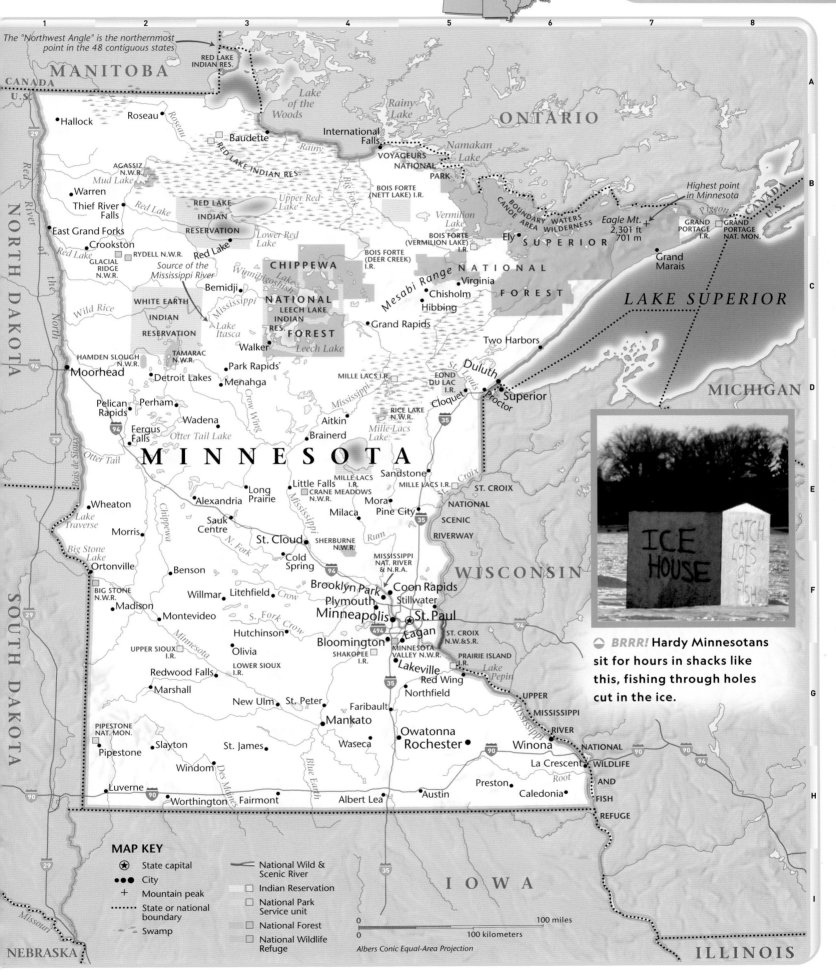

The "Northwest Angle" is the northernmost point in the 48 contiguous states

MANITOBA

CANADA
U.S.

1 2 3 4 5 6 7 8

A

B

C

D

E

F

G

H

I

NORTH DAKOTA

Hallock
Roseau
Roseau
RED LAKE INDIAN RES.
Baudette
Lake of the Woods
Rainy
International Falls
ONTARIO
Rainy Lake
Namakan Lake
VOYAGEURS NATIONAL PARK
BOIS FORTE (NETT LAKE) I.R.
Vermilion Lake
BOUNDARY WATERS CANOE AREA WILDERNESS
Eagle Mt. 2,301 ft 701 m
Highest point in Minnesota
CANADA U.S.
GRAND PORTAGE
GRAND PORTAGE I.R.
GRAND PORTAGE NAT. MON.
Pigeon

AGASSIZ N.W.R.
Mud Lake
Warren
Thief River Falls
East Grand Forks
Crookston
RYDELL N.W.R.
GLACIAL RIDGE N.W.R.
Red Lake
RED LAKE INDIAN RESERVATION
Upper Red Lake
RED LAKE INDIAN RES.
Red Lake
Lower Red Lake
Source of the Mississippi River
BOIS FORTE (VERMILION LAKE) I.R.
BOIS FORTE (DEER CREEK) I.R.
Ely
SUPERIOR
Mesabi Range
Virginia
Chisholm
Hibbing
NATIONAL FOREST
Grand Marais

Red Lake
Wild Rice
WHITE EARTH INDIAN RESERVATION
Bemidji
Lake Winnibigoshish
CHIPPEWA NATIONAL FOREST
LEECH LAKE INDIAN RES.
Lake Itasca
Walker
Leech Lake
Grand Rapids
St. Louis
Two Harbors

LAKE SUPERIOR

MICHIGAN

HAMDEN SLOUGH N.W.R.
Moorhead
Detroit Lakes
Menahga
TAMARAC N.W.R.
Park Rapids
Crow Wing
Mississippi
MILLE LACS I.R.
FOND DU LAC I.R.
Duluth
Cloquet
Proctor
Superior

Red River of the North
29
94
Pelican Rapids
Perham
Wadena
Fergus Falls
Otter Tail Lake
RICE LAKE N.W.R.
Mille Lacs Lake
Aitkin
Brainerd
St. Croix

MINNESOTA

Otter Tail
Bois de Sioux
94
Wheaton
Lake Traverse
Morris
Big Stone Lake
Ortonville
BIG STONE N.W.R.
Benson
Chippewa
Alexandria
Long Prairie
Sauk Centre
St. Cloud
Mississippi
Little Falls
MILLE LACS I.R.
CRANE MEADOWS N.W.R.
Mora
Milaca
Pine City
Rum
MILLE LACS I.R.
Sandstone
ST. CROIX NATIONAL SCENIC RIVERWAY

ICE HOUSE
CATCH LOTS OF FISH

🖱 *BRRR!* Hardy Minnesotans sit for hours in shacks like this, fishing through holes cut in the ice.

SOUTH DAKOTA

29
Madison
Montevideo
N. Fork
Cold Spring
SHERBURNE N.W.R.
94
MISSISSIPPI NAT. RIVER & N.R.A.
WISCONSIN
Willmar
Litchfield
Crow
Brooklyn Park
Plymouth
Coon Rapids
Stillwater
UPPER SIOUX I.R.
Minnesota
S. Fork Crow
Hutchinson
Minneapolis
494
St. Paul
Eagan
ST. CROIX N.W.&S.R.
Olivia
LOWER SIOUX I.R.
Bloomington
SHAKOPEE I.R.
MINNESOTA VALLEY N.W.R.
PRAIRIE ISLAND I.R.
Lake Pepin
Redwood Falls
35
Lakeville
Red Wing
Marshall
New Ulm
St. Peter
Faribault
Northfield
UPPER MISSISSIPPI RIVER

PIPESTONE NAT. MON.
Mankato
Waseca
Owatonna
Rochester
Winona
NATIONAL WILDLIFE AND FISH REFUGE
Pipestone
Slayton
St. James
Des Moines
Windom
Blue Earth
Luverne
90
Worthington
Fairmont
Albert Lea
Austin
Preston
Caledonia
La Crescent
Root
90
90
94

NEBRASKA

IOWA

ILLINOIS

35

MAP KEY

⭐ State capital
●●● City
+ Mountain peak
⋯⋯ State or national boundary
〜 Swamp

━ National Wild & Scenic River
☐ Indian Reservation
☐ National Park Service unit
☐ National Forest
☐ National Wildlife Refuge

0   100 miles
0   100 kilometers
Albers Conic Equal-Area Projection

THE BASICS

Statehood
August 10, 1821; 24th state

Total area (land and water)
69,707 sq mi (180,540 sq km)

Land area
68,742 sq mi (178,040 sq km)

Population
6,126,452

Capital
Jefferson City
Population 42,838

Largest city
Kansas City
Population 491,918

Racial/ethnic groups
83.1% white; 11.8% African American; 2.1% Asian; 0.6% Native American; 4.2% Hispanic (any race)

Foreign born
4.0%

Urban population
70.4%

Population density
89.1 per sq mi (34.4 per sq km)

GEO WHIZ

Camp Wood, near St. Louis, was the starting point for Lewis and Clark's Corps of Discovery, commissioned by President Thomas Jefferson to seek a water route to the Pacific. Along the way they encountered hundreds of new plants and animal species, nearly 50 native tribes, and the Rocky Mountains.

In Ash Grove, near Springfield, Father Moses Berry has turned his family history into a museum for slavery education. The museum is the only one of its kind in the Ozark region.

EASTERN
BLUEBIRD

HAWTHORN

Missouri

The Osage people were among the largest Native American tribes in present-day Missouri when the French began establishing permanent settlements in the 1700s. The United States obtained the territory as part of the 1803 Louisiana Purchase, and Lewis and Clark began exploring the vast wilderness by paddling up the Missouri River from the St. Louis area. Missouri entered the Union as a slave state in 1821. Though it remained in the Union during the Civil War, sympathies were split between the North and South. For much of the 1800s the state was the staging ground for pioneers traveling to western frontiers on the Santa Fe and Oregon Trails. Today, Missouri leads the country in lead mining. Farmers raise cattle, hogs, poultry, corn, and soybeans. Cotton and rice are grown in the southeastern Bootheel region. Cross-state riverport rivals St. Louis and Kansas City are centers of transportation, manufacturing, and finance. Scenic views, lakes, caves, and Branson's country music shows bring many tourists to the Ozarks.

TALL HATS. Since its founding in 1865 in St. Joseph, the Stetson Company has been associated with Western hats worn by men and women around the world.

NATIONAL LANDMARK. Named a national historic landmark in 1987, the steel and concrete Gateway Arch is the tallest arch in the world. Here it frames St. Louis and the Mississippi River.

THE SHOW-ME STATE:
MISSOURI

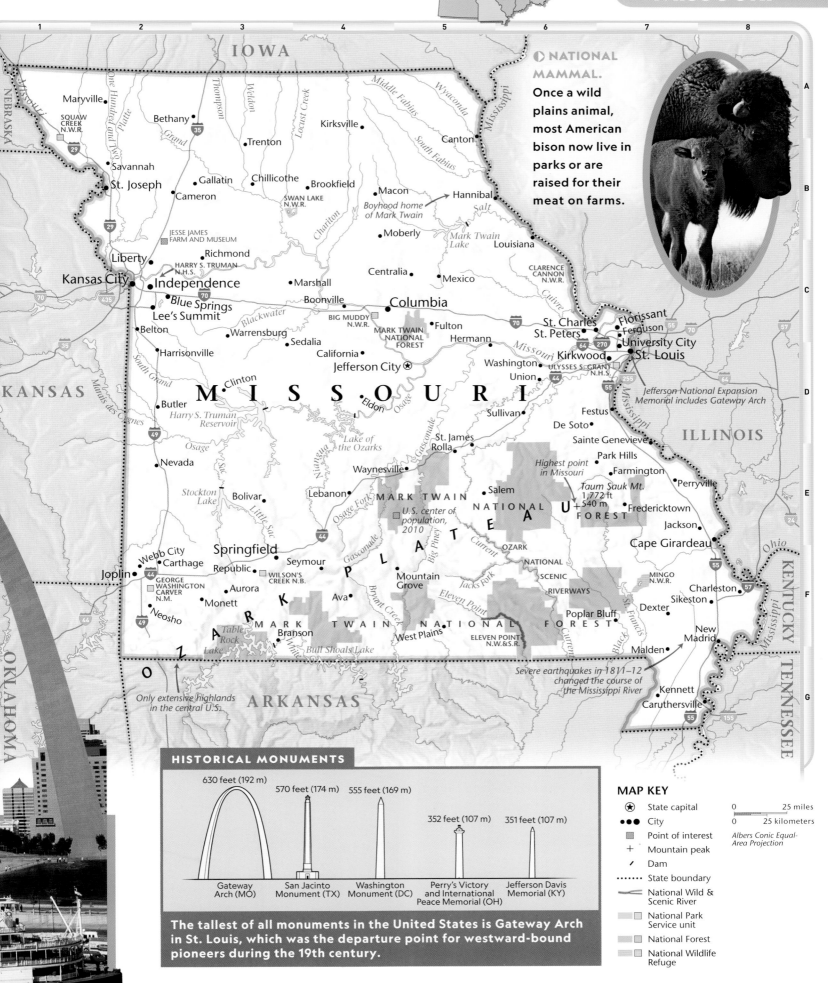

IOWA

NEBRASKA

KANSAS

OKLAHOMA

ARKANSAS

ILLINOIS

KENTUCKY

TENNESSEE

M I S S O U R I

Maryville
SQUAW CREEK N.W.R.
Bethany
Kirksville
Canton
Savannah
Trenton
St. Joseph
Gallatin
Chillicothe
Brookfield
Macon
Hannibal
Cameron
SWAN LAKE N.W.R.
Moberly
Louisiana
Richmond
JESSE JAMES FARM AND MUSEUM
Liberty
Kansas City
HARRY S. TRUMAN N.H.S.
Independence
Marshall
Boonville
Columbia
Centralia
Mexico
CLARENCE CANNON N.W.R.
Blue Springs
Lee's Summit
Belton
Warrensburg
BIG MUDDY N.W.R.
St. Charles
St. Peters
Florissant
Ferguson
Harrisonville
Sedalia
MARK TWAIN NATIONAL FOREST
Fulton
Hermann
University City
Kirkwood
St. Louis
Clinton
California
Jefferson City
Washington
Union
ULYSSES S. GRANT N.H.S.
Butler
Eldon
Harry S. Truman Reservoir
Sullivan
Festus
De Soto
Sainte Genevieve
Nevada
Lake of the Ozarks
St. James
Rolla
Park Hills
Farmington
Waynesville
Salem
Taum Sauk Mt. 1,772 ft +540 m
Fredericktown
Perryville
Stockton Lake
Bolivar
Lebanon
MARK TWAIN
NATIONAL FOREST
U.S. center of population, 2010
Jackson
Cape Girardeau
Webb City
Carthage
Springfield
Seymour
OZARK
NATIONAL
SCENIC
RIVERWAYS
MINGO N.W.R.
Charleston
Joplin
Republic
WILSON'S CREEK N.B.
Mountain Grove
GEORGE WASHINGTON CARVER N.M.
Aurora
Ava
Sikeston
Dexter
Monett
Neosho
MARK TWAIN NATIONAL FOREST
Branson
West Plains
ELEVEN POINT N.W.&S.R.
Poplar Bluff
New Madrid
Table Rock Lake
Bull Shoals Lake
Malden
Kennett
Caruthersville

O Z A R K P L A T E A U

NATIONAL MAMMAL. Once a wild plains animal, most American bison now live in parks or are raised for their meat on farms.

Boyhood home of Mark Twain

Jefferson National Expansion Memorial includes Gateway Arch

Highest point in Missouri

Severe earthquakes in 1811–12 changed the course of the Mississippi River

Only extensive highlands in the central U.S.

HISTORICAL MONUMENTS

630 feet (192 m) — Gateway Arch (MO)
570 feet (174 m) — San Jacinto Monument (TX)
555 feet (169 m) — Washington Monument (DC)
352 feet (107 m) — Perry's Victory and International Peace Memorial (OH)
351 feet (107 m) — Jefferson Davis Memorial (KY)

The tallest of all monuments in the United States is Gateway Arch in St. Louis, which was the departure point for westward-bound pioneers during the 19th century.

MAP KEY

⊛ State capital
●●● City
▪ Point of interest
+ Mountain peak
⟋ Dam
······ State boundary
National Wild & Scenic River
National Park Service unit
National Forest
National Wildlife Refuge

0 — 25 miles
0 — 25 kilometers

Albers Conic Equal-Area Projection

THE BASICS

Statehood
March 1, 1867; 37th state

Total area (land and water)
77,348 sq mi (200,330 sq km)

Land area
**76,824 sq mi
(198,974 sq km)**

Population
1,929,268

Capital
**Lincoln
Population 287,401**

Largest city
**Omaha
Population 468,262**

Racial/ethnic groups
**88.6% white; 5.1% African
American; 2.6% Asian; 1.5%
Native American; 11.0%
Hispanic (any race)**

Foreign born
6.9%

Urban population
73.1%

Population density
25.1 per sq mi (9.7 per sq km)

GEO WHIZ

**Many of Nebraska's early
white settlers were called
sodbusters because they cut
chunks of the grassy prairie
(sod) to build their houses.
These building blocks became
known as "Nebraska marble."**

**Nebraska's state fossil is the
mammoth. The state estimates
that as many as 10 of these
prehistoric elephants are
buried beneath an average
square mile of territory.**

**Boys Town, a village-style
community founded near
Omaha in 1917 as a home
for troubled boys, has
provided a haven for girls,
too, since 1979.**

GOLDENROD

WESTERN
MEADOWLARK

Nebraska

For thousands of westbound pioneers on the Oregon and California Trails, Scotts Bluff and Chimney Rock were unforgettable landmarks, towering above the North Platte River. Much of the Nebraska Territory was reserved by the U.S. government for Native Americans, who hunted bison and farmed there, but in 1854 Nebraska was opened to settlers from the East. Following statehood in 1867, ranchers clashed with farmers in an unsuccessful bid to preserve open rangelands. Today, farms and ranches cover nearly all of the state. Ranchers graze beef cattle on the grass-covered Sand Hills, and farmers grow corn, soybeans, and wheat elsewhere. The vast underground Ogallala Aquifer feeds center-pivot irrigation systems needed to water crops in areas that do not receive enough rain. Processing the state's farm products, especially meatpacking, is a big part of the economy. Omaha, which sits along the Missouri River, is a center of finance, insurance, and agribusiness. Lincoln, the state capital, has the only unicameral, or one-house, legislature in the country.

⬤ **TAKING FLIGHT.**
**Migratory sandhill
cranes pass through
in late winter, stop-
ping in the Platte
River Valley to feed
and rest.**

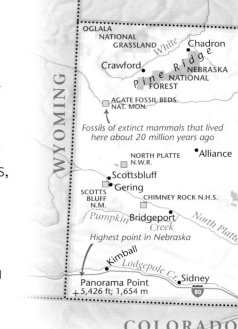

Fossils of extinct mammals that lived here about 20 million years ago

Highest point in Nebraska

Panorama Point
+5,426 ft; 1,654 m

◗ **RIDER DOWN.** The
Big Rodeo is an annual
event in tiny Burwell
(population 1,191) in
Nebraska's Sand Hills.
The town, sometimes
called "the place where
the Wild West meets
the 21st century," has
hosted the rodeo for
more than 80 years.

MAP KEY
- ★ State capital
- ••• City
- ▪ Point of interest
- + Mountain peak
- ⌐ Dam
- ···· State boundary
- ~ National Wild & Scenic River
- ☐ Indian Reservation
- ☐ State Park unit
- ☐ National Park Service unit
- National Forest
- National Grassland
- National Wildlife Refuge

SOUTH DAKOTA

Gordon · Rushville · Valentine · FORT NIOBRARA N.W.R. · NIOBRARA NATIONAL SCENIC RIVER · SANTEE INDIAN RES. · Hartington · South Sioux City

SAMUEL R. McKELVIE NATIONAL FOREST · Gordon Cr. · Ainsworth · Atkinson · O'Neill · Wayne · WINNEBAGO I.R.

Sand Hills · 20,000 square miles of grass-covered dunes, the largest such area in North America · VALENTINE N.W.R. · JOHN W. AND LOUISE SEIER N.W.R. · Holt Creek · Neligh · Norfolk · Pender · OMAHA I.R.

PLAINS · Mullen · CRESCENT LAKE N.W.R. · Dismal · North Loup · Calamus · Calamus Reservoir · Cedar · Madison · West Point · Tekamah

NEBRASKA · NEBRASKA NAT. FOREST · Middle Loup · Burwell · Ord · Albion · Shell Cr. · Columbus · Schuyler · Blair · DE SOTO N.W.R. · BOYER CHUTE N.W.R. · Fremont

Lake C.W. McConaughy · Wild West Show began in 1883 · Broken Bow · South Loup · St. Paul · Fullerton · Loup · David City · Wahoo · Omaha · President Ford's birthplace

Ogallala · North Platte · BUFFALO BILL S.H.P. · South Platte · Platte · Ravenna · Central City · Big Blue · Seward · Ashland · Waverly · Papillion · Bellevue · Plattsmouth

Grant · Gothenburg · Cozad · Lexington · Gibbon · Grand Island · Aurora · York · NINE-MILE PRAIRIE · Lincoln · Milford · Nebraska City · IOWA

Imperial · Largest mammoth fossil ever found, 1922 · Kearney · Hastings · Crete · Wilber · Auburn

Frenchman Cr. · Hugh Butler Lake · Minden · Holdrege · Geneva · HOMESTEAD NAT. MON. OF AMERICA · Beatrice · Big Nemaha

Cambridge · Swanson Res. · McCook · Republican · Little Blue · Hebron · Fairbury · Falls City

HIGH · Alma · Harlan County Lake · Red Cloud · Superior · SAC AND FOX I.R. · IOWA I.R.

KANSAS

Lewis and Clark Lake · MISSOURI NATIONAL RECREATIONAL RIVER · Missouri · Keya Paha · Niobrara · Verdigre Cr. · Logan Creek · Elkhorn · Big Blue · Platte · MISSOURI

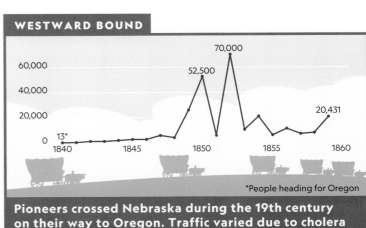

WESTWARD BOUND

70,000
60,000
52,500
40,000
20,000 — 20,431
13*
0
1840 · 1845 · 1850 · 1855 · 1860

*People heading for Oregon

Pioneers crossed Nebraska during the 19th century on their way to Oregon. Traffic varied due to cholera epidemics and conflicts with Native Americans.

◖ **THE WAY WEST.** Longhorn cattle and a bison stand knee-deep in grass below Chimney Rock, which rises more than 300 feet (91 m) above western Nebraska's rolling landscape. An important landmark on the Oregon Trail for 19th-century westbound pioneers and now a national historic site, the formation is being worn away by forces of erosion.

North Dakota

THE BASICS

Statehood
November 2, 1889; 39th state

Total area (land and water)
70,698 sq mi
(183,108 sq km)

Land area
69,001 sq mi
(178,711 sq km)

Population
760,077

Capital
Bismarck
Population 73,112

Largest city
Fargo
Population 124,844

Racial/ethnic groups
87.5% white; 3.1% African
American; 1.6% Asian; 5.5%
Native American; 3.7%
Hispanic (any race)

Foreign born
3.6%

Urban population
59.9%

Population density
11.0 per sq mi (4.3 per sq km)

GEO WHIZ

The state's largest reservoir is
named in honor of Sacagawea
(also known as Sakakawea),
the young Shoshone guide
who joined the Lewis and
Clark expedition in the
spring of 1805.

Devils Lake has earned the title
Perch Capital of the World for
the large number of walleye—
a kind of perch—caught there.

North Dakota's landscape
boasts some of the world's
largest outdoor animal sculp-
tures, including Salem Sue, the
world's largest Holstein cow;
a giant grasshopper; and a
snowmobiling turtle.

WILD PRAIRIE ROSE

WESTERN
MEADOWLARK

During the winter of 1804–05 Lewis and Clark camped at a Mandan village where they met Sacagawea, the young Shoshone woman who helped guide them through the Rockies and on to the Pacific Ocean. White settlement of the vast grassy plains coin-cided with the growth of railroads, and statehood was gained in 1889. The geo-graphic center of North America is southwest of Rugby. The state's interior location helps give it a huge annual temperature range: A record low temperature of -60°F (-51°C) and record high of 121°F (49°C) were recorded in 1936. Fargo, located on the northward flowing Red River of the North, is the state's largest city. Garrison Dam, on the Missouri River, generates electricity and provides water for irrigation. The state is a major producer of flaxseed, canola, sunflowers, and barley, but it is wheat, cattle, and soybeans that provide the greatest income. Oil and lignite coal are important in the western part of the state.

⊖ **ALERT LOOKOUT.**
A black-tailed prairie dog watches for signs of danger. This member of the squirrel family lives in burrows in the Great Plains.

BREADBASKET

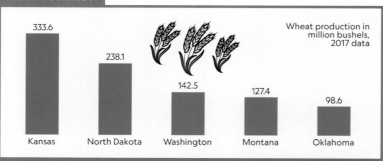

Wheat production in
million bushels,
2017 data

Kansas	North Dakota	Washington	Montana	Oklahoma
333.6	238.1	142.5	127.4	98.6

Favorable climate and soil along with technology advances have made North Dakota one of the leading producers of wheat in the United States.

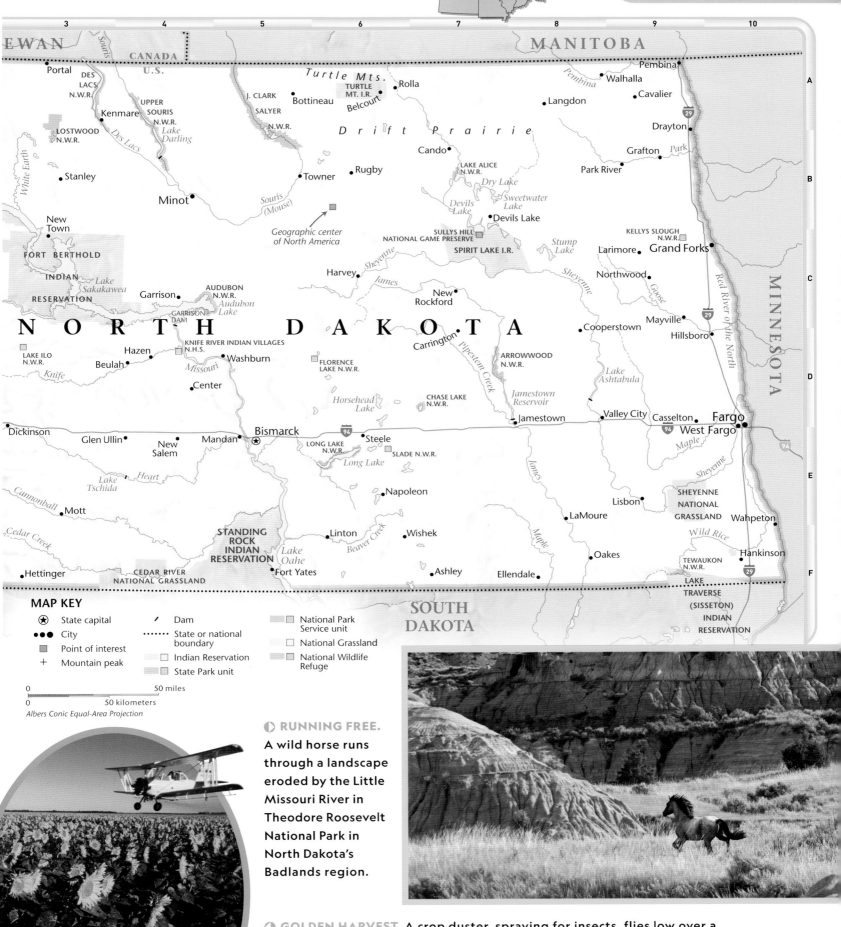

EWAN

Portal

DES LACS N.W.R.

U.S.

CANADA

Souris

Turtle Mts.

TURTLE MT. I.R.

Rolla

MANITOBA

Pembina

Walhalla

Cavalier

Langdon

UPPER SOURIS N.W.R.

Kenmare

J. CLARK

SALYER N.W.R.

Bottineau

Belcourt

Drift Prairie

Cando

Drayton

Grafton

Park

LOSTWOOD N.W.R.

Des Lacs

Lake Darling

Stanley

White Earth

Minot

Towner

Rugby

Souris (Mouse)

Park River

LAKE ALICE N.W.R.

Dry Lake

Devils Lake

Sweetwater Lake

Devils Lake

Stump Lake

KELLYS SLOUGH N.W.R.

Larimore

Grand Forks

New Town

Geographic center of North America

SULLYS HILL NATIONAL GAME PRESERVE

SPIRIT LAKE I.R.

FORT BERTHOLD INDIAN RESERVATION

Lake Sakakawea

Garrison

AUDUBON N.W.R.

Audubon Lake

GARRISON DAM

Harvey

Sheyenne

James

New Rockford

Northwood

Sheyenne

Goose

Cooperstown

Mayville

Hillsboro

N O R T H   D A K O T A

MINNESOTA

Red River of the North

LAKE ILO N.W.R.

Hazen

Beulah

KNIFE RIVER INDIAN VILLAGES N.H.S.

Washburn

FLORENCE LAKE N.W.R.

Carrington

Pipestem Creek

ARROWWOOD N.W.R.

Lake Ashtabula

Knife

Center

Missouri

Horsehead Lake

CHASE LAKE N.W.R.

Jamestown Reservoir

Valley City

Casselton

Fargo

Dickinson

Glen Ullin

New Salem

Mandan

Bismarck

LONG LAKE N.W.R.

Steele

SLADE N.W.R.

Jamestown

West Fargo

Maple

Lake Tschida

Heart

Long Lake

Napoleon

James

Lisbon

SHEYENNE NATIONAL GRASSLAND

Sheyenne

Wahpeton

Cannonball

Mott

LaMoure

Wild Rice

Hankinson

Cedar Creek

Linton

Beaver Creek

Wishek

Maple

Oakes

TEWAUKON N.W.R.

Hettinger

STANDING ROCK INDIAN RESERVATION

CEDAR RIVER NATIONAL GRASSLAND

Lake Oahe

Fort Yates

Ashley

Ellendale

LAKE TRAVERSE (SISSETON) INDIAN RESERVATION

SOUTH DAKOTA

MAP KEY

⊛ State capital

●●● City

▪ Point of interest

+ Mountain peak

⟋ Dam

⋯ State or national boundary

▫ Indian Reservation

▪ State Park unit

▫ National Park Service unit

▫ National Grassland

▪ National Wildlife Refuge

0 — 50 miles
0 — 50 kilometers

Albers Conic Equal-Area Projection

◗ **RUNNING FREE.**
A wild horse runs through a landscape eroded by the Little Missouri River in Theodore Roosevelt National Park in North Dakota's Badlands region.

◖ **GOLDEN HARVEST.** A crop duster, spraying for insects, flies low over a field of sunflowers in the Red River Valley in eastern North Dakota. In the valley's fertile soil, farmers grow sunflowers mainly for the oil in their seeds.

THE BASICS

Statehood
March 1, 1803; 17th state

Total area (land and water)
44,826 sq mi (116,098 sq km)

Land area
40,861 sq mi (105,829 sq km)

Population
11,689,442

Capital
Columbus
Population 892,533

Largest city
Columbus
Population 892,533

Racial/ethnic groups
82.2% white; 12.9% African American; 2.3% Asian; 0.3% Native American; 3.8% Hispanic (any race)

Foreign born
4.3%

Urban population
77.9%

Population density
286.1 per sq mi
(110.5 per sq km)

GEO WHIZ

Cedar Point Amusement Park, in Sandusky, is known as the Roller Coaster Capital of the World. Top Thrill Dragster has a maximum speed of 120 miles an hour (193 km/h).

Ohio's state tree is the buckeye, so called because the nut it produces resembles the eye of a male deer, or buck.

Ohio

Ohio and the rest of the land north and west of the Ohio River became part of the United States after the Revolutionary War. The movement of white settlers into the region led to conflicts with Native Americans until 1794, when the native people were defeated at Fallen Timbers. Ohio entered the Union nine years later. Lake Erie in the north and the Ohio River in the south, along with canals and railroads, provided transportation links that spurred early immigration and commerce. The state became an industrial giant, producing steel, machinery, rubber, and glass. From 1869 to 1923, seven of twelve U.S. presidents were Ohioans. With 18 electoral votes, the seventh highest number in the country, Ohio is still a big player in presidential elections. Education, government, and finance employ many people in Columbus, the capital and largest city. Manufacturing in Cleveland, Toledo, Cincinnati, and other cities remains a vital segment of the state's economy. Farmers on Ohio's western plains, which were created by glaciers, grow soybeans and corn, the two largest cash crops.

◯ **INLAND URBAN CENTER.** Cincinnati's skyline sparkles in the red glow of twilight. Founded in 1788, the modern city boasts education and medical centers as well as headquarters for companies such as Procter & Gamble.

SCARLET CARNATION
CARDINAL

TRADITIONAL CULTURE

Amish population, 2017 data

Pennsylvania	Ohio	Indiana	Wisconsin	New York
74,250	73,780	53,075	20,095	18,575

The Amish, who migrated to the United States from Europe beginning in the mid-1700s, observe simple lifestyles and hold conservative values.

ROCK AND ROLL HALL OF

◯ **SOUND OF MUSIC.** Colorful guitars mark the entrance to the Rock and Roll Hall of Fame in downtown Cleveland. The museum, through its Rockin' the Schools program, attracts thousands of students annually to experience the sounds of rock and roll music and learn about its history.

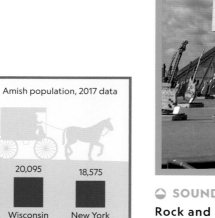

ONTARIO

CANADA
U.S.

L A K E   E R I E

MICHIGAN

Sylvania
Toledo
Maumee
Perrysburg
Oregon
Maumee Bay
Port Clinton
S. Bass I.
PERRY'S VICTORY AND INT'L. PEACE MEMORIAL
OTTAWA N.W.R.
Kelleys I.
Sandusky Bay
Painesville
Mentor
Euclid
Conneaut
Ashtabula
Geneva
Grand
Pymatuning Reservoir

Wauseon
Bryan
Napoleon
Defiance
Bowling Green
Fremont
Sandusky
Bellevue
Norwalk
Lorain
North Olmsted
Cleveland
Elyria
Parma
Strongsville
Brunswick
Shaker Heights
CUYAHOGA VALLEY N.P.
Cuyahoga Falls
Kent
Austintown
Warren
Niles
President McKinley's birthplace
DAVID BERGER NAT. MEM.
JAMES A. GARFIELD N.H.S.
Mosquito Creek Lake

St. Joseph
Findlay
Fostoria
Tiffin
Willard
Medina
Akron
Barberton
Alliance
Youngstown
Lake Milton
Berlin Lake
Mahoning

Blanchard

Van Wert
Delphos
Lima
Upper Sandusky
Bucyrus
Shelby
Ashland
Wooster
Orrville
Massillon
North Canton
Canton
Salem
East Liverpool
LITTLE BEAVER CREEK SCENIC RIVER
FIRST LADIES N.H.S.
Atwood Lake

Auglaize
St. Marys
Celina
Wapakoneta
St. Marys
Kenton
Marion
Blooming Grove
Galion
Mansfield
Loudonville
President Harding's birthplace
Dover
New Philadelphia
Uhrichsville
Leesville Lake
Toronto
Steubenville

PENNSYLVANIA

Grand Lake (St. Marys)
Indian Lake
Campbell Hill + 1,549 ft 472 m
Highest point in Ohio
Bellefontaine
Sidney
Piqua
Greenville
Troy
Urbana
Marysville
Delaware
Mt. Vernon
President Hayes' birthplace
Coshocton
Tuscarawas
Ohio

O H I O

Stillwater
Great Miami
Darby C.
Dublin
Westerville
Upper Arlington
Gahanna
Reynoldsburg
Newark
Cambridge
Salt Fork Lake
Piedmont L.
Martins Ferry
Bellaire

INDIANA

Englewood
Huber Heights
Springfield
Columbus
Big and Little Darby Creeks National Scenic River
Zanesville
Buckeye Lake
Senecaville Lake

Trotwood
Fairborn
Dayton
Kettering
Xenia
Centerville
CHARLES YOUNG BUFFALO SOLDIERS NAT. MON.
Lancaster
New Lexington
DAYTON AVIATION HERITAGE N.H.P.

Middletown
Hamilton
Oxford
Lebanon
Mason
Fairfield
President Benjamin Harrison's birthplace
Caesar Creek Lake
Washington Court House
Wilmington
Deer Creek Lake
Circleville
Logan
Nelsonville
Marietta
WAYNE NATIONAL FOREST
Belpre
Athens
Hocking

North Bend
Cincinnati
Norwood
WILLIAM HOWARD TAFT N.H.S.
Greenfield
Hillsboro
HOPEWELL CULTURE N.H.P.
Chillicothe
Waverly
Wellston
Jackson

WEST VIRGINIA

SERPENT MOUND STATE MEMORIAL
William H. Harsha Lake
President Grant's birthplace
Point Pleasant
Georgetown
Manchester
Portsmouth
Wheelersburg
WAYNE NATIONAL FOREST
Gallipolis
Raccoon Cr.
Ohio

KENTUCKY

Ironton
South Point

TRADITIONAL TRAVEL. A horse and buggy is a familiar sight in central Ohio, location of a large Amish population.

MAP KEY

★ State capital
••• City
+ Mountain peak
⌐ Dam
•••• State or national boundary
~ National Wild & Scenic River

☐ State Park unit
☐ National Park Service unit
☐ National Forest
☐ National Wildlife Refuge

0   50 miles
0   50 kilometers

Albers Conic Equal-Area Projection

THE BASICS

Statehood
November 2, 1889; 40th state

Total area (land and water)
77,116 sq mi (199,729 sq km)

Land area
75,811 sq mi (196,350 sq km)

Population
882,235

Capital
Pierre
Population 13,980

Largest city
Sioux Falls
Population 181,883

Racial/ethnic groups
84.9% white; 2.1% African American; 1.5% Asian; 9.0% Native American; 3.8% Hispanic origin (any race)

Foreign born
3.3%

Urban population
56.7%

Population density
11.6 per sq mi (4.5 per sq km)

GEO WHIZ

Thanks to captive breeding programs, the world's largest population of wild black-footed ferrets is thriving in a blacktailed prairie dog colony in south-central South Dakota.

Sometimes known as the Shrine of Democracy, Mount Rushmore National Monument features the faces of four presidents: Washington, Jefferson, Lincoln, and Theodore Roosevelt.

South Dakota

After the discovery of Black Hills gold in 1874, prospectors poured in and established lawless mining towns such as Deadwood. Native Americans fought this invasion but were defeated, and statehood came in 1889. Today, South Dakota has several reservations, and 9 percent of the state's people are Native Americans. The Missouri River flows through the center of the state, creating two distinct regions: To the east, farmers grow corn and soybeans on the fertile, rolling prairie; to the west, where it is too dry for most crops, farmers grow wheat and graze cattle and sheep on the vast plains. In the southwest the Black Hills, named for the dark coniferous trees blanketing their slopes, are still a rich source of gold. Millions of tourists visit the area to see Mount Rushmore and a giant sculpture of Lakota leader Crazy Horse, which has been in the works since 1948. Nearby, the fossil-rich Badlands, a region of eroded buttes and pinnacles, dominates the landscape.

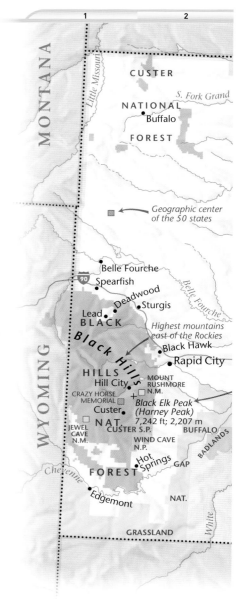

PASQUEFLOWER

RING-NECKED PHEASANT

◗ **HONORING AGRICULTURE.**
The face of the Corn Palace in Mitchell is renewed each year using thousands of bushels of grain to create pictures depicting the role of agriculture in the state's history.

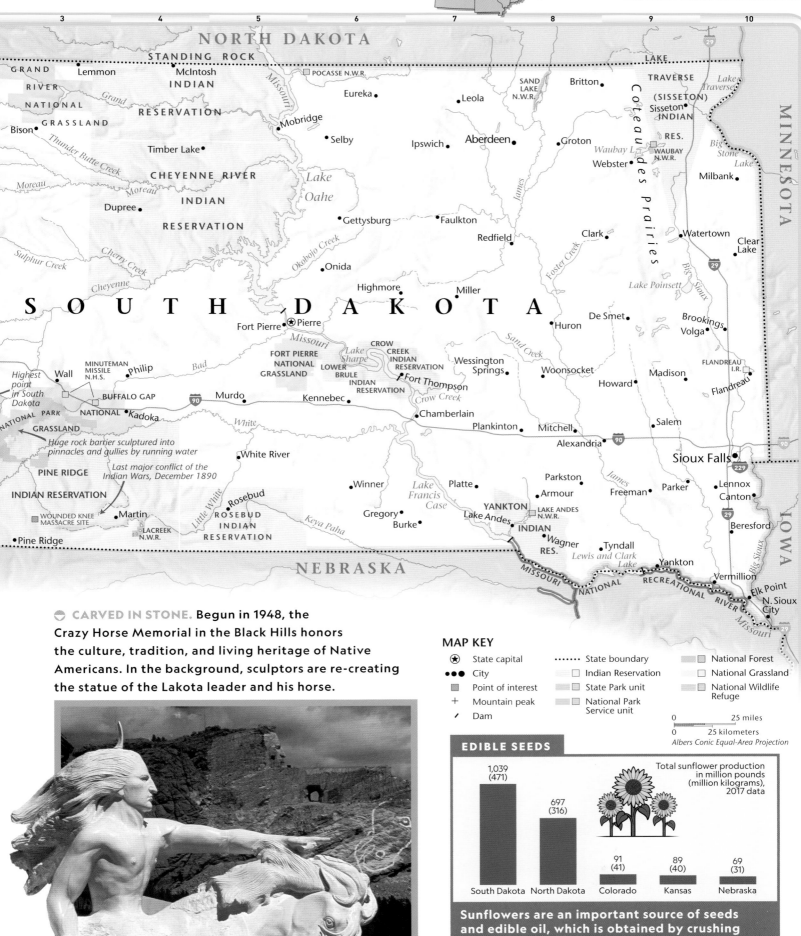

NORTH DAKOTA

STANDING ROCK

GRAND RIVER NATIONAL GRASSLAND

Lemmon

McIntosh

INDIAN

RESERVATION

POCASSE N.W.R.

SAND LAKE N.W.R.

Eureka

Leola

Britton

Coteau des prairies

LAKE TRAVERSE (SISSETON)

Lake Traverse

Sisseton

SISSETON INDIAN RES.

MINNESOTA

Bison

Grand

Moreau

Timber Lake

Mobridge

Selby

Ipswich

Aberdeen

Groton

Waubay L.

WAUBAY N.W.R.

Webster

Milbank

Big Stone Lake

Thunder Butte Creek

CHEYENNE RIVER

Lake Oahe

INDIAN

RESERVATION

Dupree

Moreau

Gettysburg

Faulkton

Redfield

Clark

Watertown

Clear Lake

Sulphur Creek

Cherry Creek

Okobojo Creek

Onida

Highmore

Miller

Lake Poinsett

Big Sioux

Foster Creek

Cheyenne

S O U T H   D A K O T A

Fort Pierre

Pierre

Huron

De Smet

Brookings

Volga

Missouri

CROW CREEK INDIAN RESERVATION

Sand Creek

Highest point in South Dakota

Wall

MINUTEMAN MISSILE N.H.S.

Philip

Bad

FORT PIERRE NATIONAL GRASSLAND

Lake Sharpe

LOWER BRULE INDIAN RESERVATION

Fort Thompson

Wessington Springs

Woonsocket

Madison

FLANDREAU I.R.

Flandreau

NATIONAL PARK

BUFFALO GAP

Murdo

Kennebec

Crow Creek

Chamberlain

Howard

Salem

GRASSLAND

Kadoka

White

Plankinton

Mitchell

Alexandria

Sioux Falls

Huge rock barrier sculptured into pinnacles and gullies by running water

White River

James

PINE RIDGE

Last major conflict of the Indian Wars, December 1890

INDIAN RESERVATION

Winner

Lake Francis Case

Platte

Parkston

Armour

Freeman

Parker

Lennox

Canton

WOUNDED KNEE MASSACRE SITE

Martin

Rosebud

ROSEBUD INDIAN RESERVATION

Gregory

Burke

YANKTON

LAKE ANDES N.W.R.

Lake Andes

INDIAN RES.

Beresford

LACREEK N.W.R.

Little White

Keya Paha

Wagner

Tyndall

Big Sioux

IOWA

Pine Ridge

Lewis and Clark Lake

Yankton

Vermillion

Elk Point

NEBRASKA

MISSOURI NATIONAL RECREATIONAL RIVER

Missouri

N. Sioux City

⬢ **CARVED IN STONE.** Begun in 1948, the Crazy Horse Memorial in the Black Hills honors the culture, tradition, and living heritage of Native Americans. In the background, sculptors are re-creating the statue of the Lakota leader and his horse.

MAP KEY

- ⊛ State capital
- ●●● City
- ▣ Point of interest
- + Mountain peak
- ⟋ Dam
- ⋯⋯ State boundary
- ▢ Indian Reservation
- ▢ State Park unit
- ▢ National Park Service unit
- ▨ National Forest
- ▢ National Grassland
- ▨ National Wildlife Refuge

0 — 25 miles
0 — 25 kilometers
Albers Conic Equal-Area Projection

EDIBLE SEEDS

1,039 (471) — South Dakota
697 (316) — North Dakota
91 (41) — Colorado
89 (40) — Kansas
69 (31) — Nebraska

Total sunflower production in million pounds (million kilograms), 2017 data

Sunflowers are an important source of seeds and edible oil, which is obtained by crushing the seeds of the flower.

WISCONSIN

1848

THE BASICS

Statehood
May 29, 1848; 30th state

Total area (land and water)
65,496 sq mi (169,635 sq km)

Land area
54,158 sq mi (140,268 sq km)

Population
5,813,568

Capital
Madison
Population 258,054

Largest city
Milwaukee
Population 592,025

Racial/ethnic groups
87.3% white; 6.7% African American; 2.9% Asian; 1.2% Native American; 6.9% Hispanic (any race)

Foreign born
4.9%

Urban population
70.2%

Population density
107.3 per sq mi (41.4 per sq km)

GEO WHIZ

The Indian Community School in Milwaukee has courses in numerous native languages, history, and rituals, all stressing seven core values: bravery, love, truth, wisdom, humility, loyalty, and respect.

Bogs left by retreating ice-age glaciers provide excellent conditions for raising cranberries. Wisconsin leads the country in harvesting this fruit.

Wisconsin's nickname— Badger State—comes not from the animal but from miners who dug living spaces by burrowing like badgers into the hillsides during the 1820s.

Wisconsin

Frenchman Jean Nicolet was the first European to reach present-day Wisconsin when he landed on the shore of Green Bay in 1634. As more settlers arrived, tensions with the region's Native Americans increased, but the Black Hawk War in 1832 brought an end to most conflicts. Wisconsin became a state in 1848. Although health care and other services have increased in importance, food processing and the manufacture of machinery and metal products remain significant for the state economy. More than one million dairy cows graze in America's Dairyland, as the state is often called, and Wisconsin leads the country in cheese production. It is second only to California in the production of milk and butter. Farmers also grow crops ranging from corn and soybeans to potatoes and cranberries. Northern Wisconsin is sparsely populated but heavily forested and is an important source of paper and paper products.

CITY BY THE LAKE. Milwaukee derives its name from the Algonquian word for "beautiful land." Known for brewing and manufacturing, the city also has a growing service sector.

TASTY GRAZING. The largest concentration of Brown Swiss cows in the United States is in Wisconsin. The milk of this breed is prized by cheese manufacturers.

RURAL ECONOMY. The dairy industry is an important part of Wisconsin's rural economy, and dairy farmers control most of the state's farmland.

WOOD VIOLET

ROBIN

DAIRY HEARTLAND

Cheese production in million lb (million kg), 2017 data

3400 (1500)	2500 (1100)	959 (435)	861 (391)	766 (347)
Wisconsin	California	Idaho	New York	New Mexico

Wisconsin, with more than 1.27 million dairy cows, is known for dairy products and leads the country in cheese production.

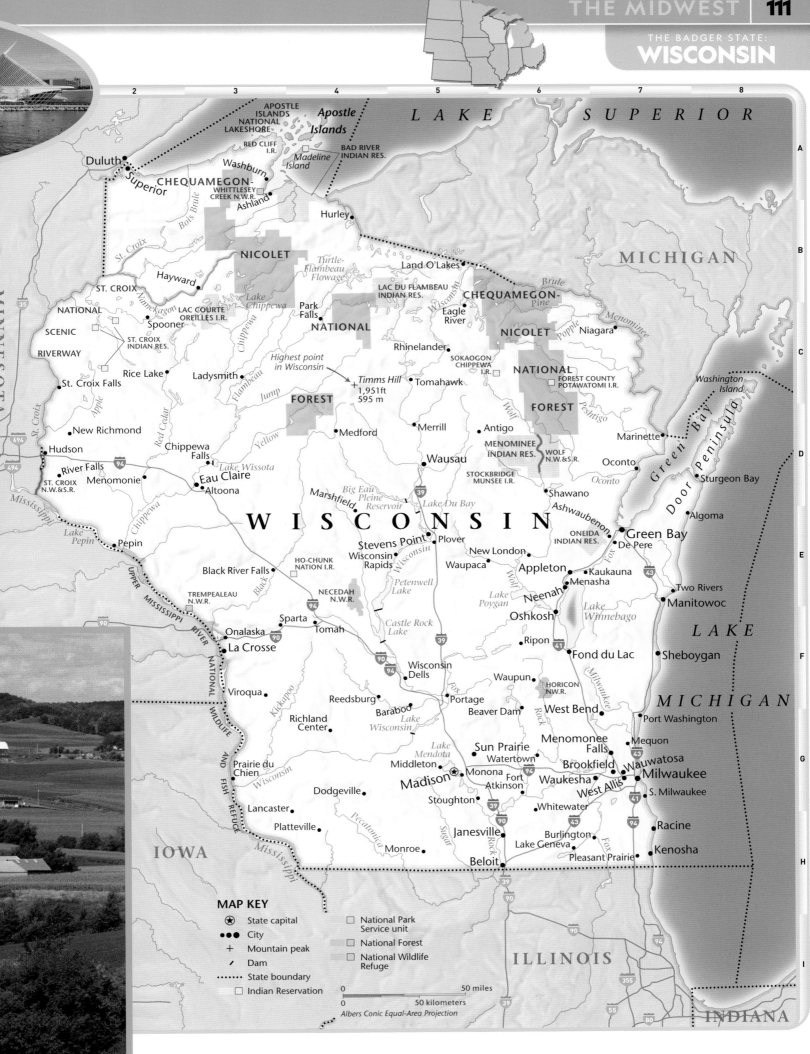

LAKE SUPERIOR

Apostle Islands

MINNESOTA

MICHIGAN

Duluth
Superior
Washburn
APOSTLE ISLANDS NATIONAL LAKESHORE
RED CLIFF I.R.
Madeline Island
BAD RIVER INDIAN RES.
WHITTLESEY CREEK N.W.R.
Ashland
CHEQUAMEGON-
Hurley
NICOLET
Land O'Lakes
Turtle-Flambeau Flowage
Hayward
Lake Chippewa
LAC DU FLAMBEAU INDIAN RES.
CHEQUAMEGON-
Pine
ST. CROIX
Park Falls
Eagle River
NICOLET
Menominee
Niagara
NATIONAL
LAC COURTE OREILLES I.R.
Spooner
Rhinelander
SCENIC
ST. CROIX INDIAN RES.
NATIONAL
SOKAOGON CHIPPEWA I.R.
RIVERWAY
Rice Lake
Ladysmith
Highest point in Wisconsin
Timms Hill 1,951ft 595 m
Tomahawk
FOREST COUNTY POTAWATOMI I.R.
Washington Island
St. Croix Falls
FOREST
NATIONAL
New Richmond
Medford
Merrill
Antigo
FOREST
Marinette
Hudson
Chippewa Falls
Wausau
MENOMINEE INDIAN RES.
WOLF N.W.&S.R.
Oconto
Sturgeon Bay
River Falls
Eau Claire
Oconto
Menomonie
Altoona
Marshfield
Big Eau Pleine Reservoir
Lake Du Bay
Shawano
STOCKBRIDGE MUNSEE I.R.
Ashwaubenon
Algoma
Green Bay
WISCONSIN
Stevens Point
Plover
New London
ONEIDA INDIAN RES.
Green Bay
De Pere
Lake Pepin
Pepin
HO-CHUNK NATION I.R.
Wisconsin Rapids
Waupaca
Appleton
Kaukauna
Menasha
Two Rivers
Black River Falls
Petenwell Lake
Lake Poygan
Neenah
Manitowoc
TREMPEALEAU N.W.R.
NECEDAH N.W.R.
Castle Rock Lake
Lake Winnebago
Oshkosh
LAKE
Sparta
Onalaska
Tomah
Ripon
Fond du Lac
Sheboygan
La Crosse
Wisconsin Dells
Waupun
HORICON N.W.R.
MICHIGAN
Viroqua
Reedsburg
Portage
Beaver Dam
West Bend
Port Washington
Baraboo
Lake Wisconsin
Richland Center
Menomonee Falls
Mequon
Sun Prairie
Watertown
Wauwatosa
Lake Mendota
Middleton
Prairie du Chien
Monona
Brookfield
Milwaukee
Madison
Fort Atkinson
Waukesha
West Allis
S. Milwaukee
Dodgeville
Stoughton
Whitewater
Lancaster
Janesville
Burlington
Racine
Platteville
Monroe
Lake Geneva
Pleasant Prairie
Kenosha
Beloit

IOWA

ILLINOIS

INDIANA

MAP KEY
★ State capital
●●● City
+ Mountain peak
⌐ Dam
···· State boundary
□ Indian Reservation
□ National Park Service unit
National Forest
National Wildlife Refuge

0   50 miles
0   50 kilometers
Albers Conic Equal-Area Projection

THE SOUTHWEST

PHYSICAL

Total area (land and water) 574,075 sq mi (1,486,850 sq km)	**Lowest point** Sea level, shores of the Gulf of Mexico	**Vegetation** Mixed, broadleaf, and needle-leaf forest; grassland; desert
Highest point Wheeler Peak, NM 13,161 ft (4,011 m)	**Longest rivers** Rio Grande, Arkansas, Colorado	**Climate** Humid subtropical, semiarid and arid, with warm to hot summers and cool winters
	Largest lakes Toledo Bend, Sam Rayburn, Eufaula (all reservoirs)	

POLITICAL

Total population 41,911,998	**Smallest state** Oklahoma: 69,899 sq mi (181,037 sq km)
States (4): Arizona, New Mexico, Oklahoma, Texas	**Most populous state** Texas: 28,701,845
Largest state Texas: 268,596 sq mi (695,662 sq km)	**Least populous state** New Mexico: 2,095,428
	Largest city proper Houston, TX: 2,325,502

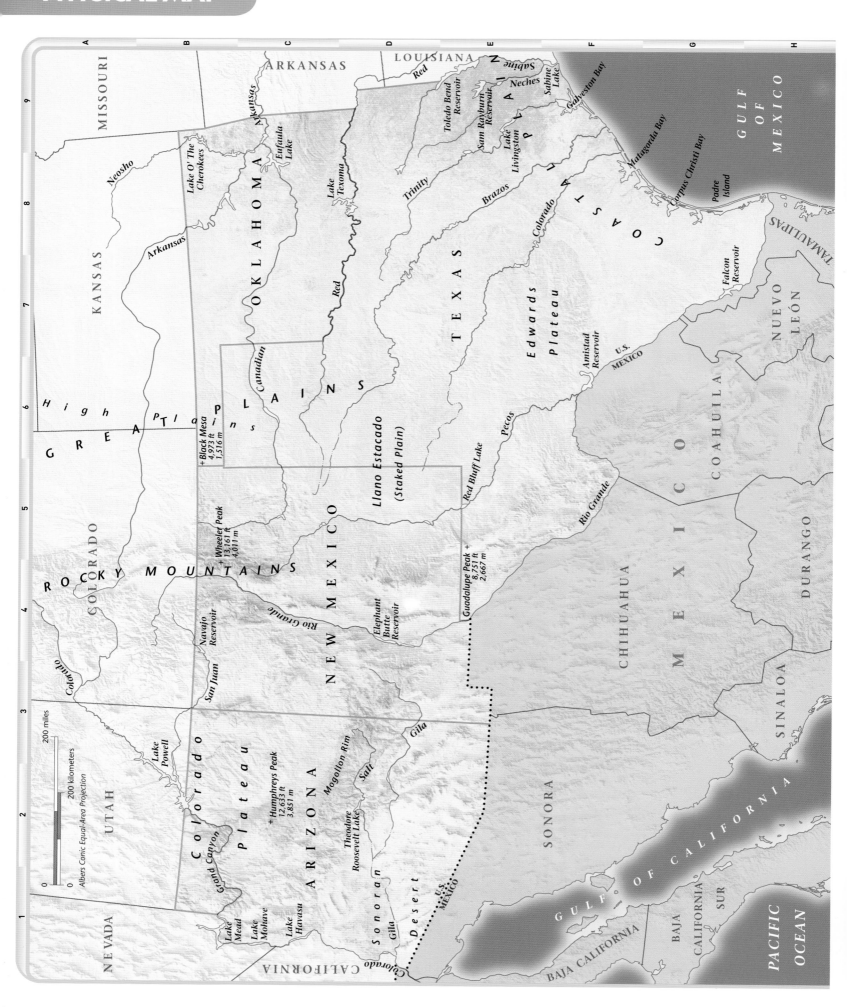

MISSOURI

ARKANSAS

LOUISIANA

Red

Neches

Sabine

Toledo Bend Reservoir

Sam Rayburn Reservoir

Lake Livingston

Galveston Bay

Matagorda Bay

GULF OF MEXICO

Corpus Christi Bay

Padre Island

TAMAULIPAS

KANSAS

Neosho

Lake O' The Cherokees

OKLAHOMA

Arkansas

Eufaula Lake

Arkansas

Lake Texoma

Red

Trinity

Brazos

Colorado

TEXAS

COASTAL PLAIN

Edwards Plateau

Falcon Reservoir

NUEVO LEÓN

High

GREAT PLAINS

Black Mesa
4,973 ft
1,516 m

Canadian

Pecos

Red Bluff Lake

Amistad Reservoir

U.S.
MEXICO

COAHUILA

M E X I C O

COLORADO

ROCKY MOUNTAINS

Wheeler Peak
13,161 ft
4,011 m

NEW MEXICO

Llano Estacado
(Staked Plain)

Rio Grande

Guadalupe Peak
8,751 ft
2,667 m

Rio Grande

CHIHUAHUA

DURANGO

Colorado

San Juan

Navajo Reservoir

Rio Grande

Elephant Butte Reservoir

UTAH

Lake Powell

Colorado Plateau

Humphreys Peak
12,633 ft
3,851 m

Mogollon Rim

Salt

Gila

SONORA

SINALOA

Grand Canyon

ARIZONA

Theodore Roosevelt Lake

Sonoran Desert

Gila

U.S.
MEXICO

GULF OF CALIFORNIA

NEVADA

Lake Mead

Lake Mohave

Lake Havasu

Colorado

CALIFORNIA

BAJA CALIFORNIA

BAJA CALIFORNIA SUR

PACIFIC OCEAN

200 miles

200 kilometers

Albers Conic Equal-Area Projection

MISSOURI

ARKANSAS

LOUISIANA

Red

Sabine

MEXICO

GULF
OF
MEXICO

Galveston Bay

Beaumont

Houston

Matagorda Bay

Corpus Christi Bay

KANSAS

Neosho

Arkansas

Trinity

Brazos

Colorado

Austin

San Antonio

Corpus
Christi

Brownsville

McAllen

TAMAULIPAS

Tulsa

O K L A H O M A

Oklahoma City ✪

Norman

Lawton

Red

Fort Worth

Dallas

T E X A S

Waco

Laredo

NUEVO
LEÓN

Wichita Falls

Canadian

Abilene

San Angelo

U.S.
MEXICO

Amarillo

Midland

Pecos

Lubbock

Odessa

Rio Grande

C O A H U I L A

M E X I C O

COLORADO

KANSAS

Santa Fe ✪

Albuquerque

N E W   M E X I C O

Roswell

Las Cruces

El Paso

CHIHUAHUA

DURANGO

Farmington

Colorado

San Juan

Gila

Rio Grande

SONORA

SINALOA

200 miles

200 kilometers

Albers Conic Equal-Area Projection

UTAH

NEVADA

Flagstaff

A R I Z O N A

Prescott

Mesa

Phoenix ✪

Salt

Tucson

U.S.
MEXICO

G U L F   O F   C A L I F O R N I A

BAJA
CALIF.
SUR

PACIFIC
OCEAN

Gila

Yuma

Colorado

CALIFORNIA

BAJA CALIFORNIA

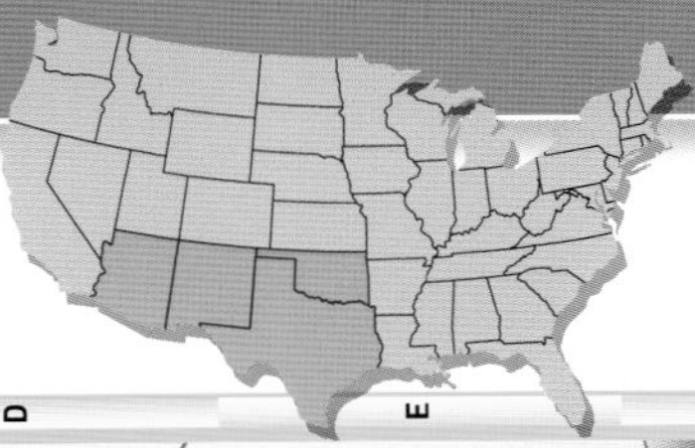

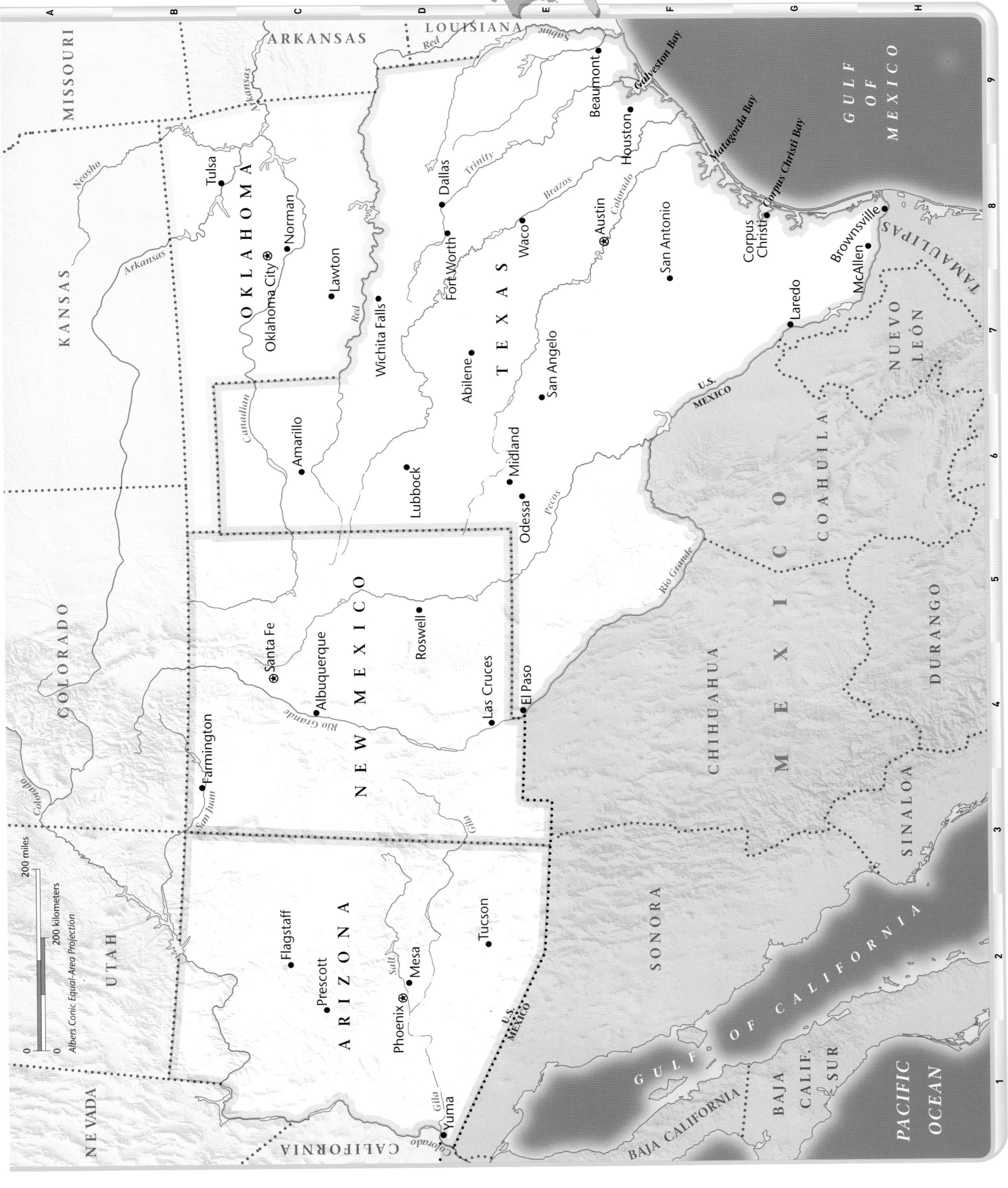

ABOUT THE
SOUTHWEST

The Southwest

SKY STONE. According to Pueblo legend, turquoise stole its color from the sky. This Zuni woman is wearing turquoise rings and bracelets for a festival in Phoenix.

FROM CANYONS TO GRASSLANDS

In the 1500s, legendary cities of gold lured Spanish conquistadors to the Southwest—land inhabited by ancestors of present-day Native Americans. Today, the promise of economic opportunities brings people from other states as well as immigrants from countries south of the border. This part of the Sunbelt region boasts future-oriented cities while preserving Wild West tales and Native American traditions. Its climate ranges from humid subtropical along the Gulf Coast to arid in Arizona's deserts, and the landscape ranges from sprawling plains in the east to plateaus cut by dramatic canyons in the west. Water is a major concern in the Southwest, one of the country's fastest-growing regions.

HIGH SOCIETY. A young woman participates in the Society of Martha Washington pageant in Laredo, Texas. This event presents daughters of wealthy and long-established Hispanic families to the local community.

◖ MODERN METROPOLIS. Towering skyscrapers tell a story of success and wealth. Although incorporated as a town in 1856, it was not until 1930 that Dallas, Texas, experienced explosive growth and prosperity due to the discovery of oil. Today, the city is a center of the U.S. oil industry and a leader in technology-based industries.

◖ DEADLY VIPER. Shaking the rattles on the tip of its tail, this diamondback rattlesnake—coiled for attack—warns intruders to stay away. Common throughout the arid Southwest, the snake eats mainly small rodents.

◖ STANDING TALL.
The saguaro cactus, which often rises more than 30 feet (9 m) above the shrubs of the Sonoran Desert, frequently has several branches and produces creamy-white flowers that bloom at night. The Sonoran, the hottest desert in North America, is located in the borderlands of southern Arizona and California and extends into northern Mexico.

WHERE THE PICTURES ARE

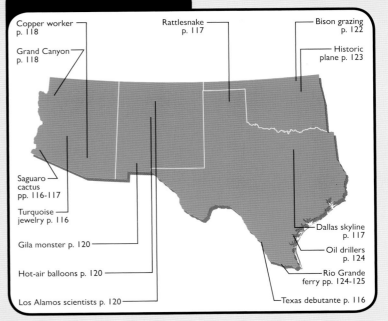

Copper worker p. 118
Grand Canyon p. 118
Rattlesnake p. 117
Bison grazing p. 122
Historic plane p. 123
Saguaro cactus pp. 116-117
Turquoise jewelry p. 116
Gila monster p. 120
Hot-air balloons p. 120
Los Alamos scientists p. 120
Dallas skyline p. 117
Oil drillers p. 124
Rio Grande ferry pp. 124-125
Texas debutante p. 116

THE GRAND CANYON STATE:
ARIZONA

THE BASICS

Statehood
February 14, 1912; 48th state

Total area (land and water)
113,990 sq mi (295,234 sq km)

Land area
113,594 sq mi (294,207 sq km)

Population
7,171,646

Capital
Phoenix
Population 1,660,272

Largest city
Phoenix
Population 1,660,272

Racial/ethnic groups
83.1% white; 5.0% African American; 3.5% Asian; 5.3% Native American; 31.4% Hispanic (any race)

Foreign born
13.4%

Urban population
89.8%

Population density
63.1 per sq mi (24.4 per sq km)

GEO WHIZ

California condors, once common in the Southwest, nearly became extinct in 1987, but conservation measures have led to their reintroduction into the wild.

People have carved pictures called petroglyphs into rock cliffs near Flagstaff for thousands of years, but the meanings of most petroglyphs remain a mystery.

Arizona

The first Europeans to visit what is now Arizona were the Spanish in the 1500s. The territory passed from Spain to Mexico and then to the United States over the next three centuries. In the 1800s settlers clashed with the Apache people led by Cochise and Geronimo—and with one another in lawless towns like Tombstone. Youngest of the 48 contiguous states, Arizona achieved statehood in 1912. Arizona's economy was long based on the Five C's: copper, cattle, cotton, citrus, and climate—but manufacturing and service industries have gained prominence. A fast-growing population, sprawling cities, and agricultural irrigation strain limited water supplies in this dry state, which depends on water from the Colorado River and underground aquifers. Tourists flock to the Colorado Plateau in the north to see stunning vistas of the Grand Canyon, Painted Desert, and Monument Valley. To the south, the Sonoran Desert's unique ecosystem includes the giant saguaro cactus. Reservations scattered around the state offer visitors the chance to learn about Native American history and culture.

⬡ **HOT WORK. A man in protective clothing works near a furnace that melts and refines copper ore at Magma Copper Company near Tucson. Arizona is one of the largest copper-producing regions in the world.**

CACTUS WREN
SAGUARO

⬡ **NATURAL WONDER. Carved by the rushing waters of the Colorado River, the Grand Canyon's geologic features and fossil record reveal almost two billion years of Earth's history. Archaeological evidence indicates human habitation dating back 12,000 years.**

INDIAN RESERVATIONS

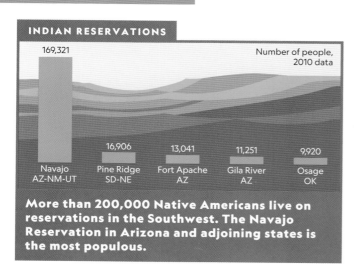

Number of people, 2010 data

169,321	16,906	13,041	11,251	9,920
Navajo AZ-NM-UT	Pine Ridge SD-NE	Fort Apache AZ	Gila River AZ	Osage OK

More than 200,000 Native Americans live on reservations in the Southwest. The Navajo Reservation in Arizona and adjoining states is the most populous.

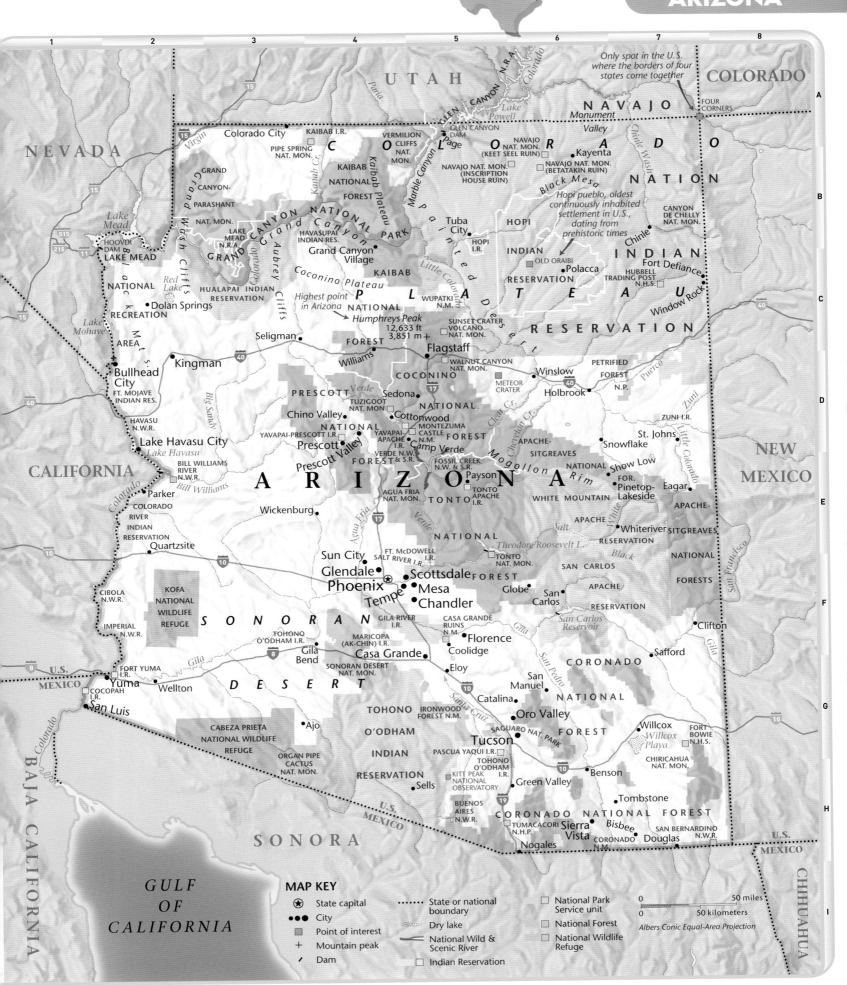

Only spot in the U.S. where the borders of four states come together

UTAH

NEVADA

COLORADO

CALIFORNIA

NEW MEXICO

Highest point in Arizona → Humphreys Peak 12,633 ft 3,851 m +

Hopi pueblo, oldest continuously inhabited settlement in U.S., dating from prehistoric times

FOUR CORNERS

NAVAJO **NATION** **INDIAN** **RESERVATION**

COLORADO PLATEAU

Colorado City
KAIBAB I.R.
VERMILION CLIFFS NAT. MON.
PIPE SPRING NAT. MON.
Page
GLEN CANYON DAM
Lake Powell
Monument Valley
Kayenta
NAVAJO NAT. MON. (KEET SEEL RUIN)
NAVAJO NAT. MON. (BETATAKIN RUIN)
NAVAJO NAT. MON. (INSCRIPTION HOUSE RUIN)
Black Mesa
CANYON DE CHELLY NAT. MON.
Chinle
Tuba City
HOPI I.R.
HOPI INDIAN RESERVATION
OLD ORAIBI
Polacca
Fort Defiance
HUBBELL TRADING POST N.H.S.
Window Rock

GRAND CANYON-PARASHANT NAT. MON.
KAIBAB NATIONAL FOREST
Kaibab Plateau
GRAND CANYON NATIONAL PARK
Grand Canyon Village
KAIBAB
Coconino Plateau

Lake Mead
HOOVER DAM
LAKE MEAD
LAKE MEAD N.R.A.
Red Lake
HUALAPAI INDIAN RESERVATION
NATIONAL RECREATION AREA
Dolan Springs
Lake Mohave

SUNSET CRATER VOLCANO NAT. MON.
NATIONAL FOREST
Seligman
Flagstaff
WALNUT CANYON NAT. MON.
COCONINO
Winslow
PETRIFIED FOREST N.P.
Williams
Kingman
Bullhead City
FT. MOJAVE INDIAN RES.
Holbrook
METEOR CRATER
ZUNI I.R.
ZUNI
St. Johns
Snowflake
NATIONAL
Show Low
APACHE-SITGREAVES
Pinetop-Lakeside
Eagar

PRESCOTT
Verde
Sedona
Chino Valley
TUZIGOOT NAT. MON.
Cottonwood
MONTEZUMA CASTLE N.M.
YAVAPAI-PRESCOTT I.R.
NATIONAL
YAVAPAI-APACHE I.R.
Camp Verde
FOREST
Lake Havasu City
Lake Havasu
Prescott
Prescott Valley
VERDE N.W. & S.R.
FOSSIL CREEK N.W. & S.R.
FOR.
BILL WILLIAMS RIVER N.W.R.
Bill Williams
A R I Z O N A
Payson
TONTO APACHE I.R.
Mogollon Rim
WHITE MOUNTAIN
Whiteriver
APACHE-SITGREAVES
NATIONAL FORESTS

Parker
COLORADO RIVER INDIAN RESERVATION
Wickenburg
AGUA FRIA NAT. MON.
TONTO
NATIONAL
Theodore Roosevelt L.
TONTO NAT. MON.
APACHE
SAN CARLOS
Black
San Francisco

Quartzsite
Sun City
FT. McDOWELL SALT RIVER I.R.
Glendale
Scottsdale
Phoenix
Mesa
Tempe
Chandler
Globe
San Carlos
APACHE RESERVATION
Clifton

KOFA NATIONAL WILDLIFE REFUGE
CIBOLA N.W.R.
IMPERIAL N.W.R.
S O N O R A N
GILA RIVER I.R.
CASA GRANDE RUINS N.M.
Florence
Gila
San Carlos Reservoir
CORONADO
Safford
Gila

FORT YUMA I.R.
TOHONO O'ODHAM I.R.
MARICOPA (AK-CHIN) I.R.
Coolidge
Casa Grande
Gila Bend
SONORAN DESERT NAT. MON.
Eloy
San Manuel
NATIONAL
Yuma
COCOPAH I.R.
Wellton
D E S E R T
Catalina
FOREST

San Luis
Ajo
CABEZA PRIETA NATIONAL WILDLIFE REFUGE
TOHONO O'ODHAM INDIAN RESERVATION
IRONWOOD FOREST N.M.
Oro Valley
SAGUARO NAT. PARK
Willcox
Willcox Playa
FORT BOWIE N.H.S.
ORGAN PIPE CACTUS NAT. MON.
Tucson
PASCUA YAQUI I.R.
CHIRICAHUA NAT. MON.
Benson

Sells
KITT PEAK NATIONAL OBSERVATORY
Green Valley
Tombstone
BUENOS AIRES N.W.R.
TUMACACORI N.H.P.
Sierra Vista
Bisbee
SAN BERNARDINO N.W.R.
CORONADO NATIONAL FOREST
CORONADO N.M.
Nogales
Douglas

U.S. MEXICO

BAJA CALIFORNIA

GULF OF CALIFORNIA

SONORA

CHIHUAHUA

MAP KEY

⊛ State capital
●●● City
▪ Point of interest
+ Mountain peak
⌐ Dam

···· State or national boundary
Dry lake
National Wild & Scenic River

☐ National Park Service unit
☐ National Forest
☐ National Wildlife Refuge
☐ Indian Reservation

0   50 miles
0   50 kilometers
Albers Conic Equal-Area Projection

THE BASICS

Statehood
January 6, 1912; 47th state

Total area (land and water)
121,590 sq mi (314,917 sq km)

Land area
121,298 sq mi (314,161 sq km)

Population
2,095,428

Capital
Santa Fe
Population 84,612

Largest city
Albuquerque
Population 560,218

Racial/ethnic groups
82.2% white; 2.5% African American; 1.7% Asian; 10.9% Native American; 48.8% Hispanic (any race)

Foreign born
9.7%

Urban population
77.4%

Population density
17.3 per sq mi (6.7 per sq km)

GEO WHIZ

Carlsbad Caverns National Park has more than a hundred caves, including the deepest limestone cavern in the U.S. From May through October thousands of Mexican free-tailed bats emerge from the caverns on their nightly search for food.

Taos Pueblo, near Taos in north-central New Mexico, has been continuously inhabited by Pueblo people for more than 1,000 years.

New Mexico

New Mexico is among the youngest states—statehood was established in 1912—but its capital city is the country's oldest. The Spanish founded Santa Fe in 1610, a decade before the *Mayflower* reached America. Beginning in the 1820s, the Santa Fe Trail brought trade and settlers, and the United States acquired the territory from Mexico by 1853. Most large cities are in the center of the state, along the Rio Grande. The Rocky Mountains divide the plains in the east from eroded mesas and canyons in the west. Cattle and sheep ranching on the plains is the chief agricultural activity, but hay, onions, and chili peppers are also important. Copper, potash, and natural gas are sources of mineral wealth. Cultural richness created by the historic interaction of Native American, Hispanic, and Anglo peoples abounds. Visitors experience this unique culture in the state's spicy cuisine, the famous art galleries of Taos, and Native American crafts.

◯ **FLYING HIGH.** Brightly colored balloons rise into a brilliant blue October sky during Albuquerque's annual International Balloon Fiesta, the largest such event in the world. During the nine-day festival more than 500 hot-air balloons drift on variable air currents created by surrounding mountains.

◯ **PAINFUL BITE.**
The most venomous lizard native to the United States is the strikingly patterned Gila monster, which lives in desert areas of the Southwest.

ROADRUNNER
YUCCA

SPICY HOT!

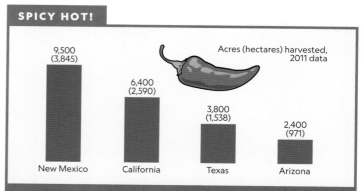

Acres (hectares) harvested, 2011 data

New Mexico	California	Texas	Arizona
9,500 (3,845)	6,400 (2,590)	3,800 (1,538)	2,400 (971)

Chili peppers help give southwestern food its distinctive taste. New Mexico leads the country in acres planted with this fiery flavor enhancer.

◑ **NUCLEAR MYSTERIES.** Scientists at Los Alamos National Laboratory, a leading scientific and engineering research institution, use 3D simulations to study nuclear explosions.

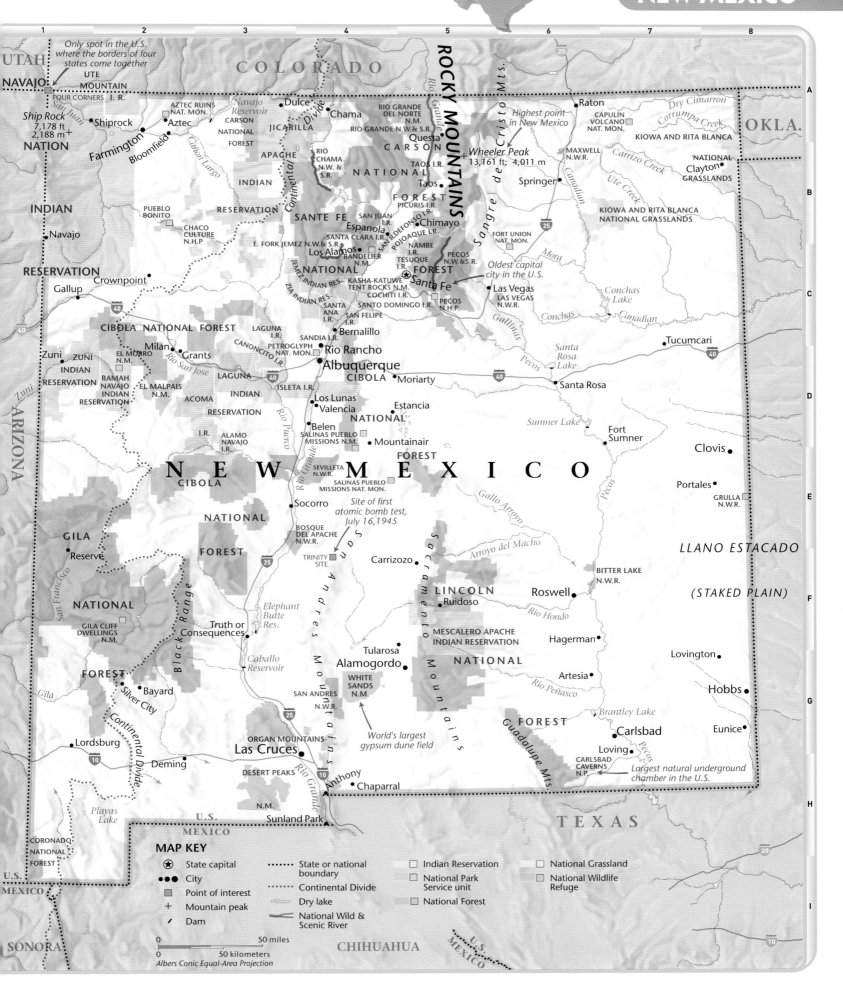

UTAH

NAVAJO

Only spot in the U.S. where the borders of four states come together

NATION

INDIAN

RESERVATION

FOUR CORNERS I. R.

UTE MOUNTAIN

Ship Rock 7,178 ft 2,188 m

Shiprock

Farmington

Bloomfield

Navajo

Crownpoint

Gallup

AZTEC RUINS NAT. MON.

Aztec

CARSON NATIONAL FOREST

APACHE

INDIAN

RESERVATION

PUEBLO BONITO

CHACO CULTURE N.H.P.

COLORADO

Navajo Reservoir

Dulce

Chama

JICARILLA

RIO CHAMA N.W. & S.R.

Continental Divide

RIO GRANDE DEL NORTE N.M.

RIO GRANDE N.W.& S.R.

Questa

CARSON

NATIONAL

FOREST

ROCKY MOUNTAINS

Sangre de Cristo Mts.

Wheeler Peak 13,161 ft; 4,011 m

Highest point in New Mexico

Raton

CAPULIN VOLCANO NAT. MON.

MAXWELL N.W.R.

Springer

Dry Cimarron

Corrumpa Creek

KIOWA AND RITA BLANCA

Carrizo Creek

Ute Creek

NATIONAL

Clayton

GRASSLANDS

OKLA.

ARIZONA

Zuni

ZUNI INDIAN RESERVATION

RAMAH NAVAJO INDIAN RESERVATION

Milan

EL MORRO N.M.

Grants

EL MALPAIS N.M.

ACOMA

INDIAN

RESERVATION

CIBOLA NATIONAL FOREST

Rio San Jose

LAGUNA

I.R.

ALAMO NAVAJO I.R.

CANONCITO I.R.

PETROGLYPH NAT. MON.

ISLETA I.R.

SANDIA I.R.

Bernalillo

Rio Rancho

Albuquerque

CIBOLA

Los Lunas

Valencia

Belen

SALINAS PUEBLO MISSIONS N.M.

Rio Puerco

SEVILLETA N.W.R.

Moriarty

Estancia

NATIONAL

Mountainair

SALINAS PUEBLO MISSIONS NAT. MON.

NEW

CIBOLA

GILA

Reserve

NATIONAL

FOREST

San Francisco

GILA CLIFF DWELLINGS N.M.

FOREST

Gila

Silver City

Bayard

Lordsburg

Continental Divide

Deming

Playas Lake

CORONADO NATIONAL FOREST

U.S. MEXICO

SONORA

ESPANOLA

SANTE FE

SAN JUAN I.R.

SANTA CLARA I.R.

Los Alamos

BANDELIER N.M.

NATIONAL

JEMEZ INDIAN RES.

KASHA-KATUWE TENT ROCKS N.M.

ZIA INDIAN RES.

SANTA ANA I.R.

SAN FELIPE I.R.

LAGUNA

E. FORK JEMEZ N.W.& S.R.

PICURIS I.R.

San Juan I.R.

SAN ILDEFONSO I.R.

POJOAQUE I.R.

NAMBE I.R.

TESUQUE I.R.

COCHITI I.R.

SANTO DOMINGO I.R.

TAOS I.R.

Taos

Chimayo

FOREST

PECOS N.W.&S.R.

Santa Fe

Oldest capital city in the U.S.

Las Vegas

LAS VEGAS N.W.R.

PECOS N.H.P.

FORT UNION NAT. MON.

Mora

Gallinas

Conchas

KIOWA AND RITA BLANCA NATIONAL GRASSLANDS

Conchas Lake

Canadian

Tucumcari

Santa Rosa Lake

Santa Rosa

MEXICO

Socorro

BOSQUE DEL APACHE N.W.R.

TRINITY SITE

Site of first atomic bomb test, July 16, 1945

Elephant Butte Res.

Truth or Consequences

Caballo Reservoir

Black Range

FOREST

Rio Grande

Tularosa

Alamogordo

WHITE SANDS N.M.

SAN ANDRES N.W.R.

San Andres Mountains

Organ Mountains

Las Cruces

DESERT PEAKS N.M.

Rio Grande

Sunland Park

Anthony

Chaparral

U.S. MEXICO

CHIHUAHUA

MEXICO

Pecos

Gallo Arroyo

Arroyo del Macho

Carrizozo

Sacramento Mountains

LINCOLN

Ruidoso

MESCALERO APACHE INDIAN RESERVATION

NATIONAL

World's largest gypsum dune field

Sacramento Mountains

FOREST

Rio Hondo

Roswell

Hagerman

Rio Peñasco

Artesia

Guadalupe Mts.

CARLSBAD CAVERNS N.P.

Largest natural underground chamber in the U.S.

Carlsbad

Loving

Pecos

BITTER LAKE N.W.R.

Sumner Lake

Fort Sumner

Clovis

Portales

GRULLA N.W.R.

LLANO ESTACADO

(STAKED PLAIN)

Lovington

Hobbs

Eunice

Brantley Lake

TEXAS

OKLAHOMA

THE BASICS

Statehood
November 16, 1907; 46th state

Total area (land and water)
69,899 sq mi (181,037 sq km)

Land area
68,595 sq mi (177,660 sq km)

Population
3,943,079

Capital
Oklahoma City
Population 649,021

Largest city
Oklahoma City
Population 649,021

Racial/ethnic groups
74.3% white; 7.8% African American; 2.3% Asian; 9.2% Native American; 10.6% Hispanic (any race)

Foreign born
5.9%

Urban population
66.2%

Population density
57.5 per sq mi (22.2 per sq km)

GEO WHIZ

An area of Oklahoma City has earned the nickname Little Saigon. In the 1960s the city opened its doors to tens of thousands of refugees from Vietnam. Today, the area is a thriving business district that includes people of many Asian nationalities.

"Pocket dinosaur" is one of several nicknames for the armadillo. Native to South America, large populations of this armor-plated mammal are found throughout Oklahoma and in much of the southern United States.

Before it became a state in 1907, Oklahoma was known as Indian Territory. Today, 39 tribes have their headquarters in the state.

ROSE

SCISSOR-TAILED
FLYCATCHER

Oklahoma

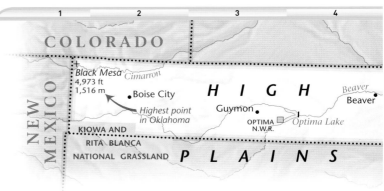

The U.S. government declared most of present-day Oklahoma as Indian Territory in 1834. To reach this new homeland, the Cherokee and other south-eastern tribes were forced to travel the Trail of Tears, named for its brutal conditions. By 1889 areas were opened for white homesteaders, who staked claims in frenzied land runs. White and Native American lands were combined to form the state of Oklahoma in 1907. During the 1930s many Oklahomans fled drought and dust storms that smothered everything in sight. Some traveled as far as California in search of work. Better farming methods and the return of rain helped agriculture recover, and today cattle and wheat are among the chief products. Oil and natural gas wells are found throughout the state. The Red River, colored by the region's iron-rich soils, marks the state's southern boundary. Along the eastern border, the Ozark Plateau and Ouachita Mountains form rugged bluffs and valleys. To the west, rolling plains rise toward the High Plains in the state's panhandle.

⊘ **NATURAL LANDSCAPE. Bison graze in the Joseph H. Williams Tallgrass Prairie Preserve, near Pawhuska. Tallgrass prairie once covered 140 million acres (57 million ha), extending from Minnesota to Texas, but today less than 4 percent remains because of urban sprawl and cropland expansion. The preserve is the largest protected tallgrass prairie remaining on Earth.**

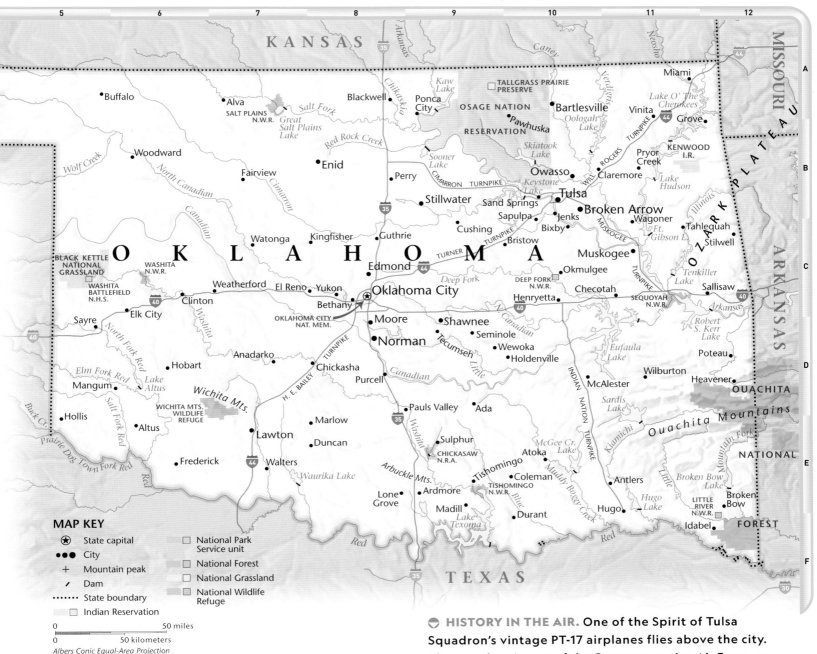

MAP KEY

- ⊛ State capital
- ••• City
- + Mountain peak
- ⌐ Dam
- ······ State boundary
- ☐ Indian Reservation
- ☐ National Park Service unit
- ☐ National Forest
- ☐ National Grassland
- ☐ National Wildlife Refuge

0 —— 50 miles
0 —— 50 kilometers
Albers Conic Equal-Area Projection

FOOD SUPPLIER

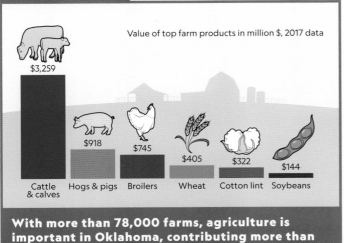

Value of top farm products in million $, 2017 data

Product	Value
Cattle & calves	$3,259
Hogs & pigs	$918
Broilers	$745
Wheat	$405
Cotton lint	$322
Soybeans	$144

With more than 78,000 farms, agriculture is important in Oklahoma, contributing more than $8 billion each year to the state's economy.

⬤ **HISTORY IN THE AIR.** One of the Spirit of Tulsa Squadron's vintage PT-17 airplanes flies above the city. The squadron is part of the Commemorative Air Force, an organization committed to preserving aviation history.

Texas

Various groups of Plains Native Americans were the early inhabitants of what would become Texas. In fact, the name Texas is derived from the word *Taysha*, which means "friend" in the Caddo language. Texas was an independent republic from 1836 until it became a state in 1845. Today, it is the second largest state in population (after California) and area (after Alaska), and a top producer of many agricultural products, including cattle, sheep, cotton, citrus fruits, vegetables, rice, and pecans. It also has huge oil and natural gas fields and is a manufacturing powerhouse. Pine forests cover East Texas while barrier islands protect the Gulf Coast, and grassy plains cover the northern panhandle. Wildflowers flourish in the Hill Country, and mountains and sandy plains sprawl across dry West Texas. The Rio Grande, sometimes barely a trickle, separates Texas and Mexico.

THE BASICS

Statehood
December 29, 1845; 28th state

Total area (land and water)
268,596 sq mi (695,662 sq km)

Land area
261,232 sq mi (676,587 sq km)

Population
28,701,845

Capital
Austin
Population 964,254

Largest city
Houston
Population 2,325,502

Racial/ethnic groups
79.2% white; 12.7% African American; 5.0% Asian; 1.0% Native American; 39.4% Hispanic (any race)

Foreign born
16.9%

Urban population
84.7%

Population density
109.9 per sq mi (42.4 per sq km)

GEO WHIZ

The Fossil Rim Wildlife Center in the Hill Country breeds endangered African animals. Offspring will be returned to the wild in Africa whenever possible.

Defeat at the 1836 Battle of the Alamo gave rise to the battle cry "Remember the Alamo" and inspired General Sam Houston's forces to win Texas independence from Mexico.

MOCKINGBIRD
BLUEBONNET

⬥ **BLACK GOLD. Workers plug an oil well. Discovery of oil early in the 20th century transformed life in Texas. Today, the state leads the U.S. in oil and natural gas production.**

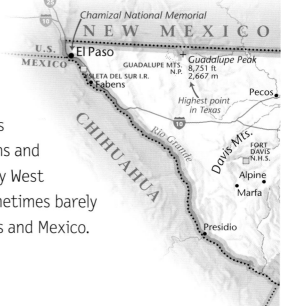

Chamizal National Memorial
NEW MEXICO
U.S.
MEXICO
El Paso
GUADALUPE MTS. N.P.
Guadalupe Peak
8,751 ft
2,667 m
YSLETA DEL SUR I.R.
Fabens
Highest point in Texas
Pecos
CHIHUAHUA
Rio Grande
Davis Mts.
FORT DAVIS N.H.S.
Alpine
Marfa
Presidio

WHIRLING DANGER

147 — Texas
92 — Kansas
65 — Florida
55 — Oklahoma
55 — Nebraska

Average annual number of tornadoes, 1991–2015

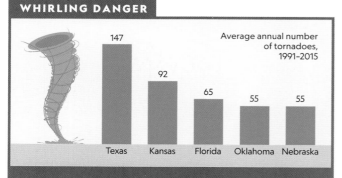

Every state in the U.S. has experienced a tornado, but Texas has more than any other. These violent storms occur when cold air collides with warm, moist air.

◗ **BORDER RELIC.**
Los Ebanos Ferry, near Mission, Texas, takes its name from a nearby grove of ebony trees. It is the last remaining government-licensed, hand-pulled ferry on any U.S. border. It can carry three cars as it crosses the Rio Grande.

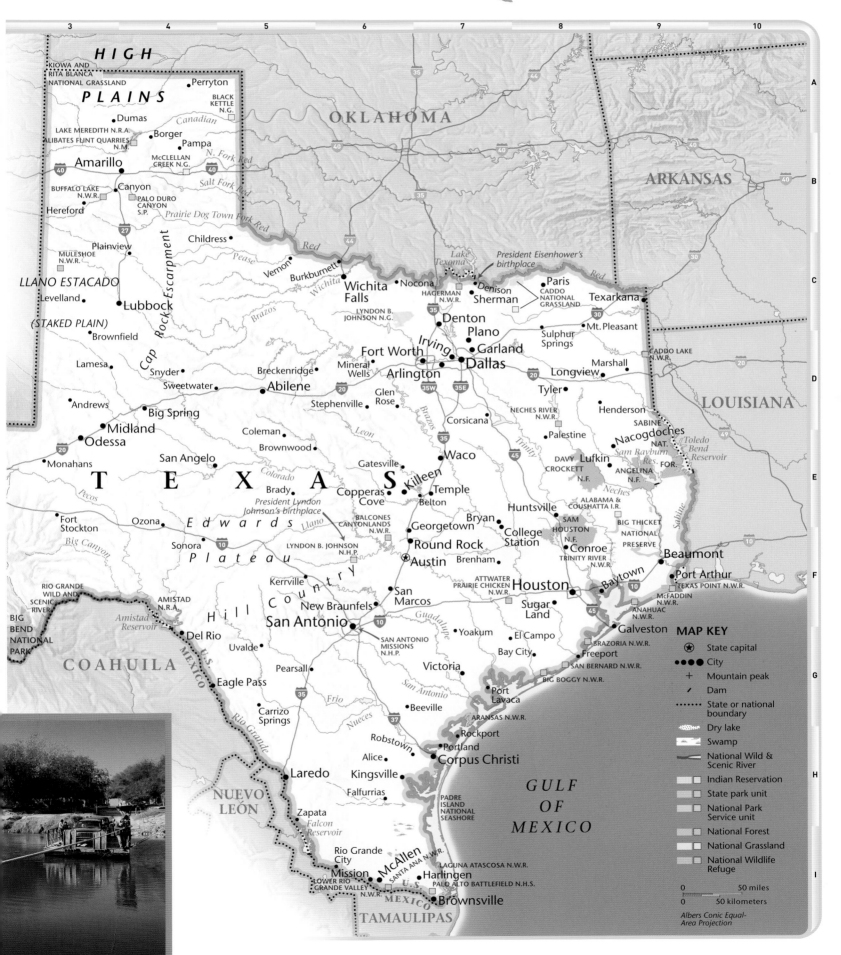

OKLAHOMA

ARKANSAS

LOUISIANA

HIGH
P L A I N S

KIOWA AND
RITA BLANCA
NATIONAL GRASSLAND

Perryton

BLACK
KETTLE
N.G.

Dumas

LAKE MEREDITH N.R.A.
ALIBATES FLINT QUARRIES
N.M.

Borger

Pampa

McCLELLAN
CREEK N.G.

N. Fork Red

Amarillo

Canyon

BUFFALO LAKE
N.W.R.

PALO DURO
CANYON
S.P.

Hereford

Salt Fork Red

Prairie Dog Town Fork Red

MULESHOE
N.W.R.

Plainview

Childress

Red

Pease

Vernon

LLANO ESTACADO

Wichita

Burkburnett

Levelland

Lubbock

Brazos

Wichita
Falls

Nocona

HAGERMAN
N.W.R.

Denison

Sherman

President Eisenhower's
birthplace

Paris

CADDO
NATIONAL
GRASSLAND

Texarkana

Mt. Pleasant

CADDO LAKE
N.W.R.

(STAKED PLAIN)

Cap Rock Escarpment

Brownfield

LYNDON B.
JOHNSON N.G.

Denton

Plano

Sulphur
Springs

Lamesa

Snyder

Breckenridge

Fort Worth

Irving

Garland

Dallas

Marshall

Longview

Sweetwater

Mineral
Wells

Arlington

Henderson

SABINE

Andrews

Abilene

Glen
Rose

Tyler

NECHES RIVER
N.W.R.

Nacogdoches

NAT.

Toledo
Bend
Reservoir

Big Spring

Stephenville

Corsicana

Palestine

FOR.

Midland

Coleman

Brownwood

Leon

Brazos

Waco

DAVY
CROCKETT
N.F.

Lufkin

Sam Rayburn
Res.

ANGELINA
N.F.

Odessa

Monahans

San Angelo

Colorado

Gatesville

Killeen

Temple

Neches

Pecos

Brady

Copperas
Cove

Belton

Bryan

Huntsville

ALABAMA &
COUSHATTA I.R.

BIG THICKET
NATIONAL
PRESERVE

Fort
Stockton

Ozona

President Lyndon
Johnson's birthplace

Edwards

Llano

BALCONES
CANYONLANDS
N.W.R.

Georgetown

College
Station

SAM
HOUSTON
N.F.

Beaumont

Big Canyon

Sonora

Plateau

LYNDON B. JOHNSON
N.H.P.

Round Rock

Brenham

Conroe

TRINITY RIVER
N.W.R.

Port Arthur

Austin

ATTWATER
PRAIRIE CHICKEN
N.W.R.

Houston

Baytown

TEXAS POINT N.W.R.

RIO GRANDE
WILD AND
SCENIC
RIVER

Kerrville

Hill

Country

San
Marcos

Sugar
Land

McFADDIN
N.W.R.

ANAHUAC
N.W.R.

AMISTAD
N.R.A.

Amistad
Reservoir

New Braunfels

Guadalupe

Yoakum

El Campo

Galveston

BIG
BEND
NATIONAL
PARK

COAHUILA

Del Rio

San Antonio

SAN ANTONIO
MISSIONS
N.H.P.

Bay City

MAP KEY

BRAZORIA N.W.R.

Uvalde

Freeport

SAN BERNARD N.W.R.

★ State capital

•••• City

Pearsall

Victoria

BIG BOGGY N.W.R.

+ Mountain peak

MEXICO

U.S.

Eagle Pass

Frio

San Antonio

Port
Lavaca

ARANSAS N.W.R.

∕ Dam

Carrizo
Springs

Beeville

Rockport

State or national
boundary

Nueces

Robstown

Portland

Dry lake

NUEVO
LEÓN

Rio Grande

Alice

Corpus Christi

Swamp

Laredo

Kingsville

National Wild &
Scenic River

Falfurrias

Indian Reservation

Zapata

Falcon
Reservoir

PADRE
ISLAND
NATIONAL
SEASHORE

GULF
OF
MEXICO

State park unit

National Park
Service unit

Rio Grande
City

McAllen

SANTA ANA N.W.R.

LAGUNA ATASCOSA N.W.R.

National Forest

National Grassland

Mission

Harlingen

PALO ALTO BATTLEFIELD N.H.S.

National Wildlife
Refuge

LOWER RIO
GRANDE VALLEY
N.W.R.

U.S.

MEXICO

Brownsville

TAMAULIPAS

0   50 miles
0   50 kilometers

Albers Conic Equal-
Area Projection

T E X A S

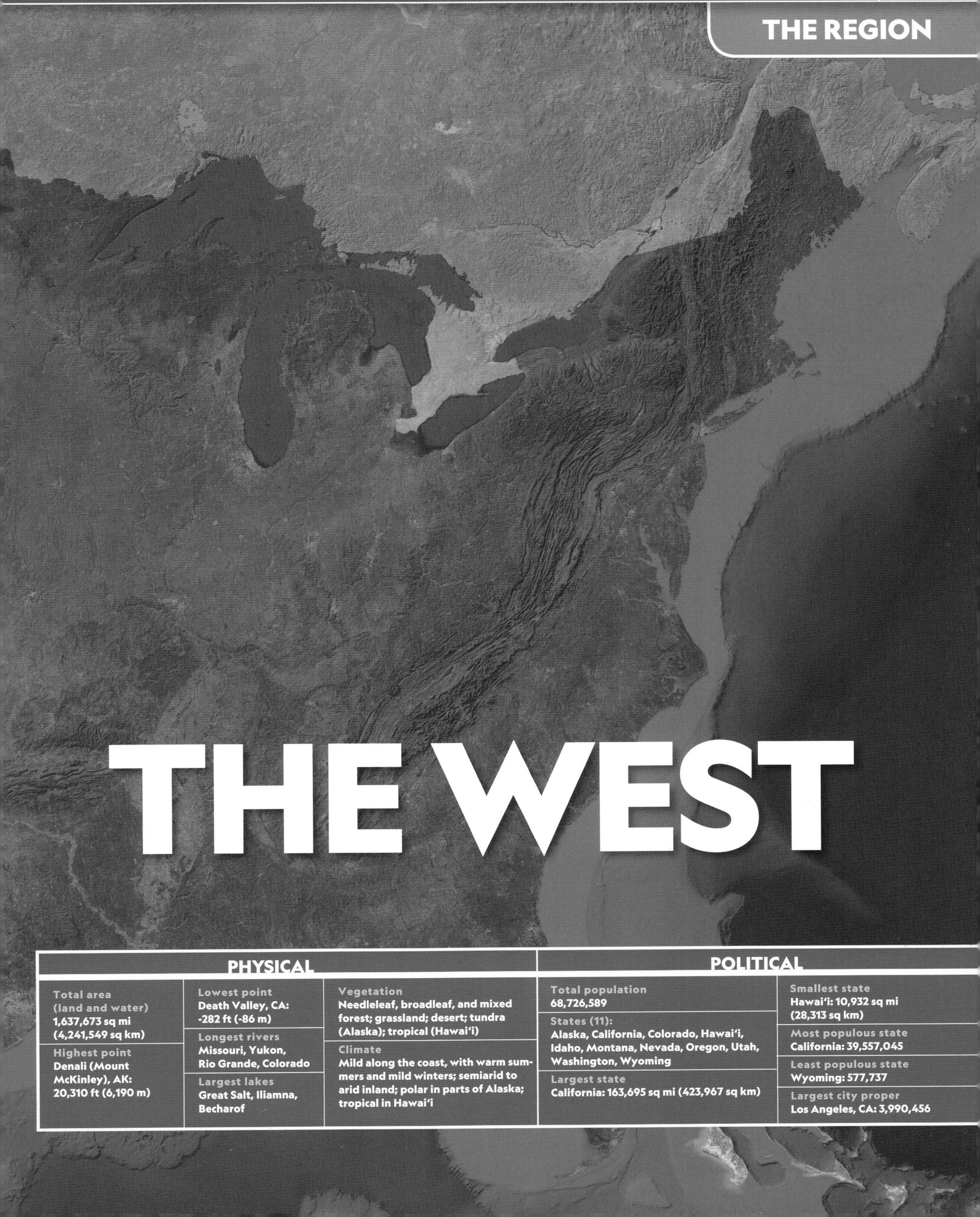

THE WEST

PHYSICAL

Total area (land and water)
1,637,673 sq mi (4,241,549 sq km)

Highest point
Denali (Mount McKinley), AK:
20,310 ft (6,190 m)

Lowest point
Death Valley, CA:
-282 ft (-86 m)

Longest rivers
Missouri, Yukon, Rio Grande, Colorado

Largest lakes
Great Salt, Iliamna, Becharof

Vegetation
Needleleaf, broadleaf, and mixed forest; grassland; desert; tundra (Alaska); tropical (Hawai'i)

Climate
Mild along the coast, with warm summers and mild winters; semiarid to arid inland; polar in parts of Alaska; tropical in Hawai'i

POLITICAL

Total population
68,726,589

States (11):
Alaska, California, Colorado, Hawai'i, Idaho, Montana, Nevada, Oregon, Utah, Washington, Wyoming

Largest state
California: 163,695 sq mi (423,967 sq km)

Smallest state
Hawai'i: 10,932 sq mi (28,313 sq km)

Most populous state
California: 39,557,045

Least populous state
Wyoming: 577,737

Largest city proper
Los Angeles, CA: 3,990,456

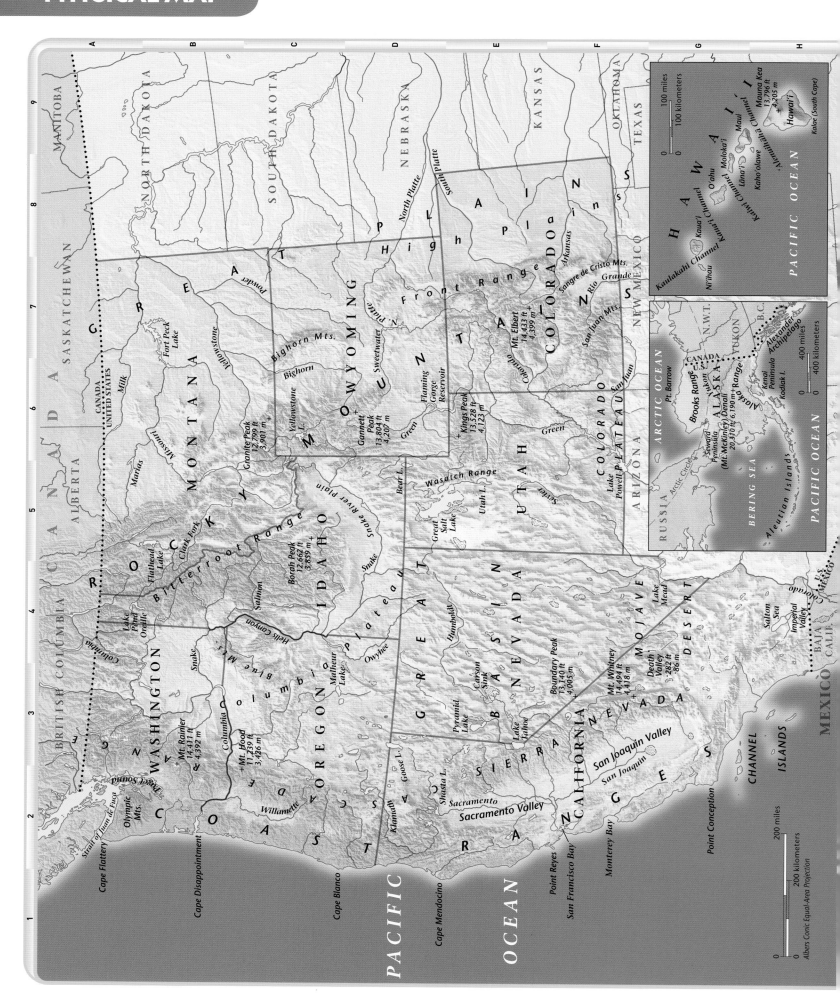

A B C D E F G H

9 8 7 6 5 4 3 2 1

MANITOBA

NORTH DAKOTA

SOUTH DAKOTA

NEBRASKA

KANSAS

OKLAHOMA

TEXAS

SASKATCHEWAN

CANADA
UNITED STATES

ALBERTA

C A N A D A

BRITISH COLUMBIA

MONTANA
• Great Falls
• Billings
• Bozeman
• Butte
Helena ⊛
• Missoula
Milk
Marias
Missouri
Yellowstone
Powder
Bighorn

WYOMING
• Gillette
• Casper
• Cody
Rock Springs •
Sweetwater
Green

COLORADO
Fort Collins •
Boulder • • Denver
Cheyenne ⊛
Laramie •
• Colorado Springs
• Pueblo
• Grand Junction
North Platte
South Platte
Arkansas
Colorado
Rio Grande

NEW MEXICO

IDAHO
Idaho Falls •
Pocatello •
• Boise ⊛
Twin Falls •
Snake
Salmon
Owyhee

UTAH
Logan •
Ogden •
⊛ Salt Lake City
Provo •
St. George •
Great Salt Lake
Sevier
Green

ARIZONA

NEVADA
• Elko
• Reno
Carson City ⊛
Las Vegas •
• Henderson
Humboldt

WASHINGTON
• Bellingham
• Seattle
• Tacoma
Olympia ⊛
• Spokane
• Yakima
• Vancouver
Walla Walla •
• Coeur d'Alene
• Lewiston
Columbia
Snake

OREGON
• Pendleton
• Portland
• Salem ⊛
• Eugene
• Bend
• Medford
• Klamath Falls
Columbia
Klamath

CALIFORNIA
• Redding
• Eureka
• Santa Rosa
• San Francisco
• Oakland
• San Jose
• Sacramento ⊛
• Stockton
• Salinas
• Fresno
• Bakersfield
• San Bernardino
• Riverside
• Los Angeles
• Long Beach
• Oceanside
• San Diego
Sacramento
San Joaquin
U.S.
MEXICO

BAJA CALIF.
MEXICO
SONORA
Colorado

PACIFIC OCEAN

Albers Conic Equal-Area Projection

200 miles
200 kilometers

HAWAI'I
Ni'ihau
Kaua'i
O'ahu
Honolulu
Moloka'i
Lāna'i
Maui
Kaho'olawe
Hawai'i
Hilo
PACIFIC OCEAN
100 miles
100 kilometers

ALASKA
Barrow
Prudhoe Bay
Nome
Fairbanks
Anchorage
Juneau
Kodiak I.
Aleutian Islands
ARCTIC OCEAN
Arctic Circle
BERING SEA
PACIFIC OCEAN
RUSSIA
CANADA U.S.
N.W.T.
YUKON
B.C.
Yukon
San Juan
400 miles
400 kilometers

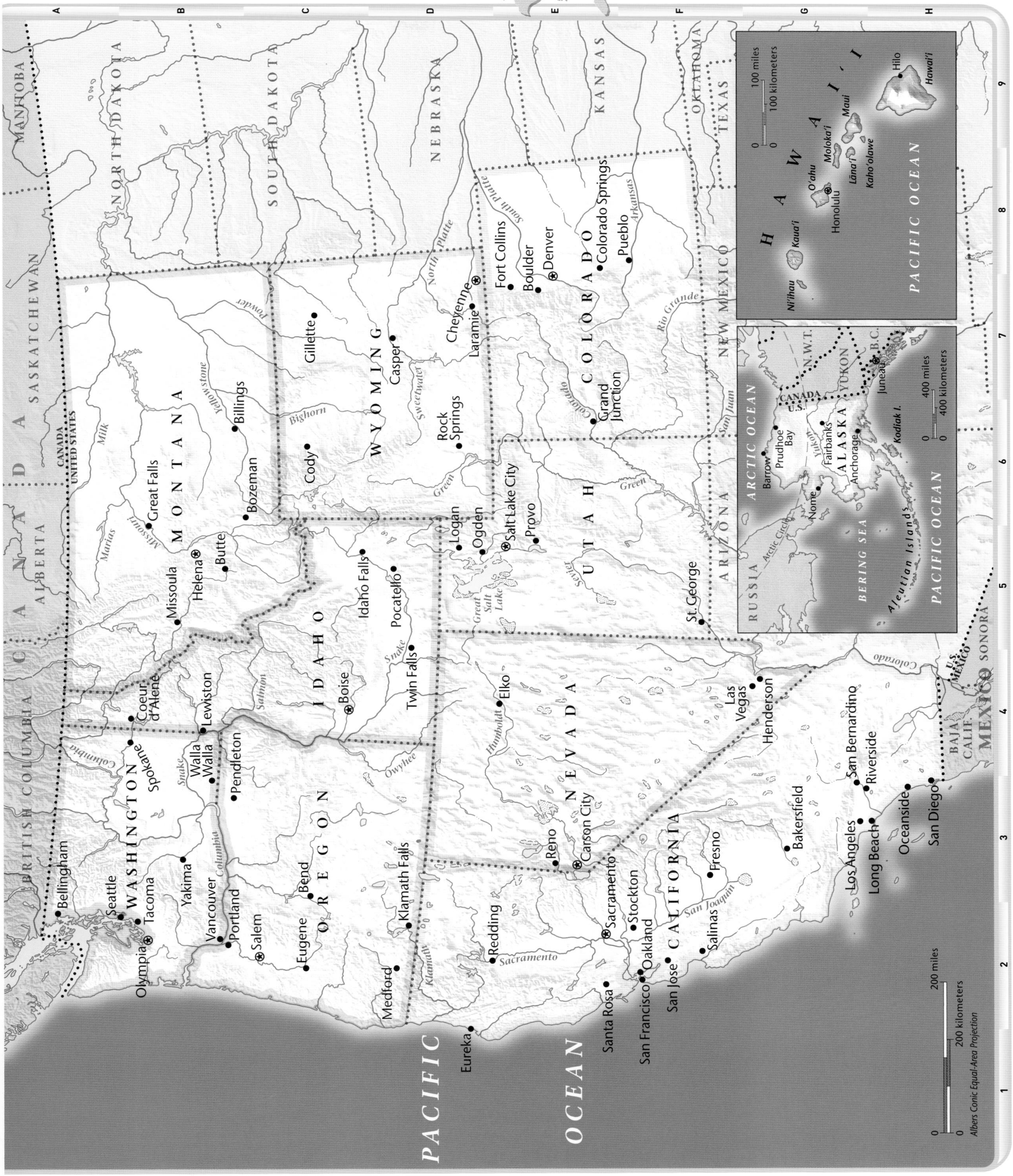

The West

THE HIGH FRONTIER

OLD AND NEW.
A cable car carries passengers in San Francisco. In the background, modern buildings rise above older neighborhoods in this earthquake-prone city.

T he western states, which make up almost half of the country's land area, have diverse landscapes and climates, ranging from the frozen heights of Denali, in Alaska, to the desolation of Death Valley, in California, and the lush, tropical islands of Hawai'i. More than half the region's population lives in California, and the Los Angeles metropolitan area is second in population only to that of New York City. Yet many parts of the region are sparsely populated, and much of the land is set aside as parkland and military bases. The region also faces many natural hazards—earthquakes, landslides, wildfires, and even volcanic eruptions.

NORTHERN GIANT.
Denali, a name meaning "High One" in the Athabascan language, rises more than 20,000 feet (6,100 m) in the Alaska Range. Also known as Mount McKinley, it is North America's highest peak. The same tectonic forces that trigger earthquakes in Alaska are slowly pushing this huge block of granite ever higher.

WHERE THE PICTURES ARE

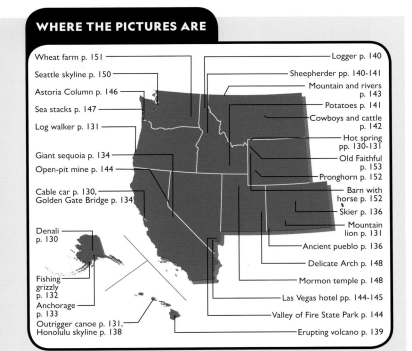

Wheat farm p. 151
Seattle skyline p. 150
Astoria Column p. 146
Sea stacks p. 147
Log walker p. 131
Giant sequoia p. 134
Open-pit mine p. 144
Cable car p. 130,
Golden Gate Bridge p. 134
Denali p. 130
Fishing grizzly p. 132
Anchorage p. 133
Outrigger canoe p. 131,
Honolulu skyline p. 138

Logger p. 140
Sheepherder pp. 140-141
Mountain and rivers p. 143
Potatoes p. 141
Cowboys and cattle p. 142
Hot spring pp. 130-131
Old Faithful p. 153
Pronghorn p. 152
Barn with horse p. 152
Skier p. 136
Mountain lion p. 131
Ancient pueblo p. 136
Delicate Arch p. 148
Mormon temple p. 148
Las Vegas hotel pp. 144-145
Valley of Fire State Park p. 144
Erupting volcano p. 139

ELUSIVE PREDATOR. Known by many names, including cougar and mountain lion, these big cats are found mainly in remote mountainous areas of the West, where they hunt deer and smaller animals.

STEAMY BATH. Mineral-rich hot springs are a colorful feature of Yellowstone National Park. Runoff from rain and snowmelt seeps into cracks in the ground, sinking to a depth of 10,000 feet (3,050 m), where it is heated by molten rock before rising back to the surface.

BALANCING ACT. For many years rivers have been used to move logs from forest to market, taking advantage of the buoyancy of logs and the power of moving water. A logger stands on a floating log raft in Coos Bay, Oregon.

TRADITIONAL SAILING CRAFT. A Hawaiian outrigger canoe on Waikiki Beach promises fun in the surf for visitors to the 50th state. An important part of Polynesian culture, the canoes were once used to travel from island to island.

Alaska

Alaska—from *Alyeska*, an Aleut word meaning "great land"—was purchased by the U.S. from Russia in 1867 for just two cents an acre. Many people thought it was a bad investment, but it soon paid off when gold was discovered, and again when major petroleum deposits were discovered in 1968. Today, an 800-mile (1,287-km)-long pipeline links North Slope oil fields to the ice-free port at Valdez, but critics worry about the long-term environmental impact. Everything is big in Alaska. It is the largest state, with one-sixth of the country's land area; it has the highest peak in the United States as well as in North America, Denali (Mount McKinley); and the largest earthquake ever recorded in the United States—a 9.2 magnitude—occurred there in 1964. It is first in forestland, a leading source of seafood, and a major oil producer. Alaska's population has a higher percentage of native people than that of any other state.

THE BASICS

Statehood
January 3, 1959; 49th state

Total area
(land and water)
665,384 sq mi
(1,723,337 sq km)

Land area
570,641 sq mi
(1,477,953 sq km)

Population
737,438

Capital
Juneau
Population 32,113

Largest city
Anchorage
Population 291,538

Racial/ethnic groups
65.8% white; 3.7% African American; 6.5% Asian; 15.3% Native American; 7.1% Hispanic (any race)

Foreign born
7.6%

Urban population
66.0%

Population density
1.3 per sq mi (0.5 per sq km)

GEO WHIZ

During summer, migrating humpback whales work together in Alaskan waters to catch fish. While swimming in circles, the whales blow bubbles that form a net around schools of herring. Each whale can eat hundreds of fish in one gulp.

Climate change and population growth are changing the route of the famous Iditarod sled-dog race. Since 2002, lack of snow in Wasilla has forced the starting point for the competition first to Willow and then as far north as Fairbanks.

The Tongass National Forest in southeastern Alaska is the largest U.S. national forest.

◯ TIME FOR LUNCH.
A grizzly bear fishes for salmon at Brooks Falls in Katmai National Park and Preserve.

FORGET-ME-NOT
WILLOW PTARMIGAN

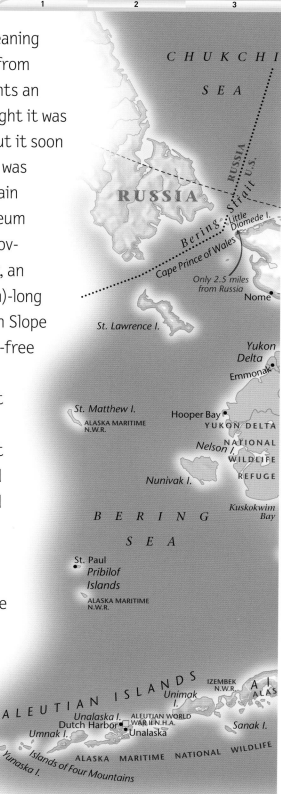

◑ NORTHERN METROPOLIS. Anchorage, established in 1915 as a construction port for the Alaska Railroad, sits in the shadow of the snow-covered Chugach Mountains.

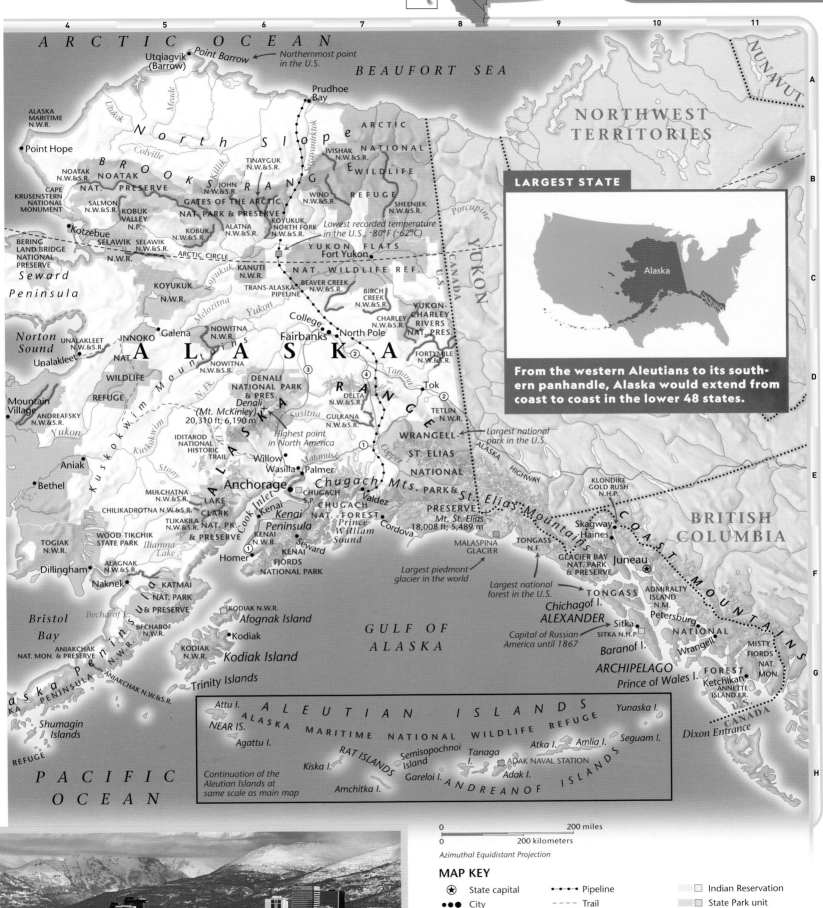

ARCTIC OCEAN

Utqiagvik (Barrow)
Point Barrow ← Northernmost point in the U.S.
BEAUFORT SEA

Point Hope

ALASKA MARITIME N.W.R.

Utukok
Meade
North Slope
Colville
Prudhoe Bay

ARCTIC NATIONAL WILDLIFE REFUGE

NUNAVUT

NORTHWEST TERRITORIES

BROOKS RANGE
NOATAK N.W.&S.R.
NOATAK NAT. PRESERVE
Killik
TINAYGUK N.W.&S.R.
JOHN N.W.&S.R.
GATES OF THE ARCTIC NAT. PARK & PRESERVE
IVISHAK N.W.&S.R.
Sagavanirktok
WIND N.W.&S.R.

CAPE KRUSENSTERN NATIONAL MONUMENT
SALMON N.W.&S.R.
KOBUK VALLEY N.P.
ALATNA N.W.&S.R.
KOYUKUK, NORTH FORK N.W.&S.R.
SHEENJEK N.W.&S.R.
Porcupine

Kotzebue
SELAWIK N.W.R.
SELAWIK N.W.&S.R.
KOBUK N.W.&S.R.
Koyukuk
Lowest recorded temperature in the U.S., -80°F (-62°C)
ARCTIC CIRCLE
YUKON FLATS
Fort Yukon
U.S. CANADA
YUKON

BERING LAND BRIDGE NATIONAL PRESERVE
Seward Peninsula
KANUTI N.W.R.
TRANS-ALASKA PIPELINE
NAT. WILDLIFE REF.
BEAVER CREEK N.W.&S.R.
BIRCH CREEK N.W.&S.R.
CHARLEY N.W.&S.R.
YUKON-CHARLEY RIVERS NAT. PRES.

LARGEST STATE

Alaska

From the western Aleutians to its southern panhandle, Alaska would extend from coast to coast in the lower 48 states.

Norton Sound
UNALAKLEET N.W.&S.R.
INNOKO NAT.
Galena
KOYUKUK N.W.R.
NOWITNA N.W.R.
Melozitna
Yukon
College
Fairbanks
North Pole
FORTYMILE N.W.&S.R.
Tanana

Unalakleet
WILDLIFE REFUGE
NOWITNA N.W.&S.R.
N. Fk.
②
③
④
DELTA N.W.&S.R.
Tok
②
TETLIN N.W.R.
Largest national park in the U.S.

Mountain Village
ANDREAFSKY N.W.&S.R.
Yukon
DENALI NATIONAL PARK & PRES.
Denali (Mt. McKinley) 20,310 ft; 6,190 m
Highest point in North America
Susitna
GULKANA N.W.&S.R.
①
WRANGELL-ST. ELIAS NATIONAL PARK & PRESERVE
ALASKA HIGHWAY

Aniak
Kuskokwim Mountains
IDITAROD NATIONAL HISTORIC TRAIL
Willow
Wasilla Palmer
Matanuska
Copper
Mt. St. Elias 18,008 ft; 5,489 m
①
KLONDIKE GOLD RUSH N.H.P.

Bethel
Kuskokwim
Stony
MULCHATNA N.W.&S.R.
Anchorage
CHUGACH S.P.
Valdez
St. Elias Mountains
BRITISH COLUMBIA

LAKE CLARK
CHILIKADROTNA N.W.&S.R.
TLIKAKILA N.W.&S.R.
LAKE CLARK NAT. PK. & PRESERVE
Cook Inlet
Kenai
Kenai Peninsula
CHUGACH Mts.
CHUGACH NAT. FOREST
Prince William Sound
Cordova
PRESERVE
MALASPINA GLACIER
TONGASS N.F.
Skagway
Haines
COAST MOUNTAINS

TOGIAK N.W.R.
WOOD-TIKCHIK STATE PARK
Iliamna Lake
KENAI N.W.R.
Seward
KENAI FJORDS NATIONAL PARK
①
Largest piedmont glacier in the world
Largest national forest in the U.S.
GLACIER BAY NAT. PARK & PRESERVE
Juneau ✪
ADMIRALTY ISLAND N.M.

Dillingham
ALAGNAK N.W.&S.R.
Homer
①
Largest national forest in the U.S.
Chichagof I.
ALEXANDER
TONGASS
Sitka
Petersburg
NATIONAL

Naknek
KATMAI NAT. PARK & PRESERVE
Bechorof L.
KODIAK N.W.R.
Afognak Island
GULF OF ALASKA
Capital of Russian America until 1867
SITKA N.H.P.
Baranof I.
Wrangell
MISTY FIORDS NAT. MON.

Bristol Bay
BECHAROF N.W.R.
BECHAROF N.W.R.
Kodiak
KODIAK N.W.R.
Kodiak Island
ARCHIPELAGO
Prince of Wales I.
FOREST
Ketchikan
ANNETTE ISLAND I.R.

ANIAKCHAK NAT. MON. & PRESERVE
Alaska Peninsula
ANIAKCHAK N.W.&S.R.
Trinity Islands
Dixon Entrance
U.S. CANADA

Shumagin Islands
Attu I.
NEAR IS.
ALASKA MARITIME NATIONAL WILDLIFE REFUGE
Yunaska I.

REFUGE
Agattu I.
RAT ISLANDS
Semisopochnoi Island
Tanaga I.
Atka I.
Amlia I.
Seguam I.

PACIFIC OCEAN
ALEUTIAN ISLANDS
Kiska I.
Garioi I.
ADAK NAVAL STATION
Adak I.
ANDREANOF ISLANDS
Continuation of the Aleutian Islands at same scale as main map
Amchitka I.

0   200 miles
0   200 kilometers
Azimuthal Equidistant Projection

MAP KEY

✪ State capital	•••• Pipeline	Indian Reservation
••• City	- - - Trail	State Park unit
▪ Point of interest	••••• State or national boundary	National Park Service unit
+ Mountain peak	Glacier	National Forest
③ State highway shield	National Wild & Scenic River	National Wildlife Refuge
- - - Arctic Circle		

CALIFORNIA REPUBLIC

THE BASICS

Statehood
September 9, 1850; 31st state

Total area (land and water)
163,695 sq mi (423,967 sq km)

Land area
155,779 sq mi (403,466 sq km)

Population
39,557,045

Capital
Sacramento
Population 508,529

Largest city
Los Angeles
Population 3,990,456

Racial/ethnic groups
72.4% white; 6.5% African American; 15.2% Asian; 1.6% Native American; 39.1% Hispanic (any race)

Foreign born
27.0%

Urban population
95.0%

Population density
253.9 per sq mi (98.0 per sq km)

GEO WHIZ

The Monterey Bay Aquarium has worked to save endangered sea otters for more than 20 years.

Castroville, south of San Jose, is known as the Artichoke Capital of the World.

California

The coast of what is now California was visited by Spanish and English explorers in the mid-1500s, but colonization did not begin until 1769 when the first of 21 Spanish missions was established in San Diego. The missions, built mainly to convert (often forcibly) Native Americans to Christianity, eventually extended up the coast as far as Sonoma along a road known as El Camino Real. The United States gained control of California in 1847, following a war with Mexico. The next year gold was discovered near Sutter's Mill, triggering a gold rush and migration from the eastern United States and around the world. Today, California is the most populous state, and its economy ranks above that of most of the world's countries. It is a major source of fruits, nuts, and vegetables and a leader in the entertainment industry and in the production of high-tech equipment.

⊖ **ENGINEERING WONDER.** Stretching more than a mile (1.6 km) across the entrance to San Francisco Bay, the Golden Gate Bridge opened to traffic in 1937. The bridge is painted vermilion orange, a color chosen in part because it is visible in fog.

CALIFORNIA QUAIL
GOLDEN POPPY

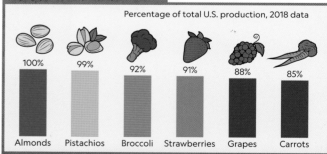

BOUNTIFUL HARVEST

Percentage of total U.S. production, 2018 data

Almonds	Pistachios	Broccoli	Strawberries	Grapes	Carrots
100%	99%	92%	91%	88%	85%

Fresh fruits and vegetables are part of a healthy diet. California leads the country in the overall production of these beneficial crops.

◑ **FOREST GIANT.** Sequoias in Yosemite National Park's Mariposa Grove exceed 200 feet (61 m), making them the world's tallest trees. The trees, some of which are 3,000 years old, grow in isolated groves on the western slopes of the Sierra Nevada.

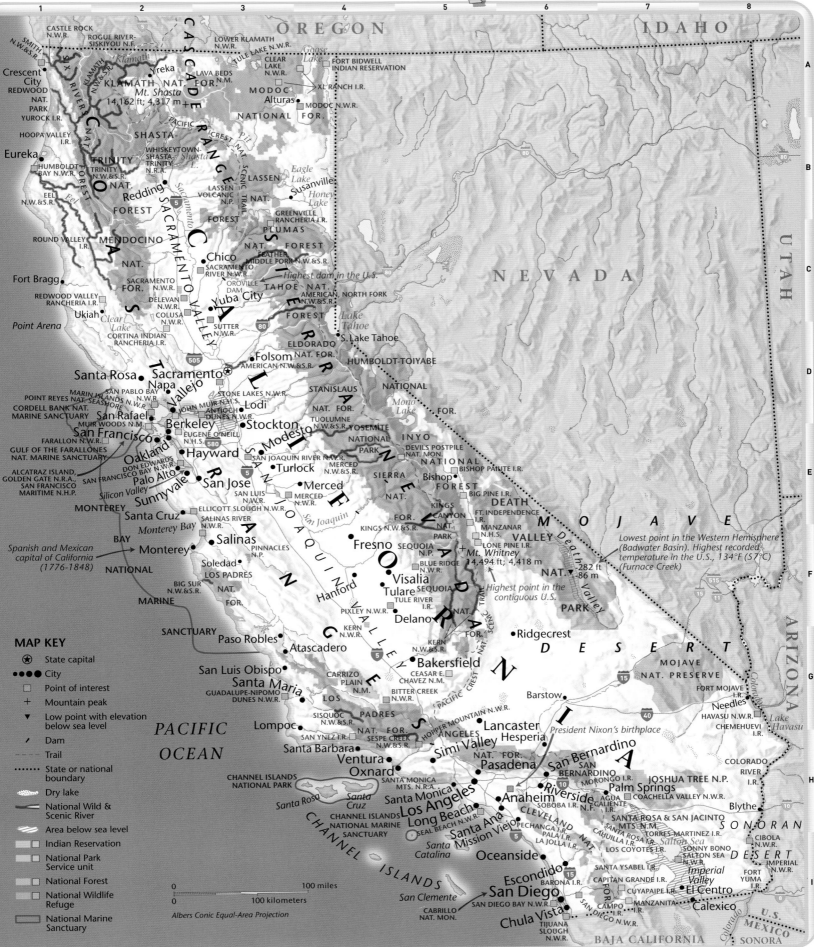

OREGON | IDAHO

CASTLE ROCK
N.W.R.&S.R.
ROGUE RIVER-
SISKIYOU N.F.
LOWER KLAMATH
N.W.R.
TULE LAKE N.W.R.
CLEAR
LAKE
N.W.R.
FORT BIDWELL
INDIAN RESERVATION

Crescent
City
REDWOOD
NAT.
PARK
YUROK I.R.

Yreka
KLAMATH NAT. FOR.
Mt. Shasta
14,162 ft; 4,317 m +
SHASTA-
LAVA BEDS
N.M.
MODOC
XL RANCH I.R.
Alturas
MODOC N.W.R.

Eureka

WHISKEYTOWN-
SHASTA-
TRINITY
N.R.A.
Shasta L.
Redding
NATIONAL FOR.

HUMBOLDT
BAY N.W.R.
TRINITY
NAT.
FOREST
Eagle
Lake
LASSEN
VOLCANIC
N.P.
LASSEN
NAT.
FOR.
Susanville
Honey
Lake

EEL
N.W.&S.R.
Eel
ROUND VALLEY
I.R.
MENDOCINO
NAT.
FOR.
Chico
GREENVILLE
RANCHERIA I.R.
PLUMAS
NAT.
FOR.
FEATHER
MIDDLE FORK N.W.&S.R.

NEVADA

Fort Bragg
REDWOOD VALLEY
RANCHERIA I.R.
SACRAMENTO
FOR.
DELEVAN
N.W.R.
COLUSA
N.W.R.
Yuba City
OROVILLE
DAM
Highest dam in the U.S.
TAHOE NAT.
AMERICAN, NORTH FORK
N.W.&S.R.

Ukiah
Clear
Lake
CORTINA INDIAN
RANCHERIA I.R.
SUTTER
N.W.R.
Folsom
ELDORADO
NAT. FOR.
FOREST
Lake
Tahoe
S. Lake Tahoe
HUMBOLDT-TOIYABE

Point Arena

Santa Rosa
Napa
Vallejo
Sacramento
AMERICAN N.W.&S.R.
STONE LAKES N.W.R.
Lodi
STANISLAUS
NAT. FOR.
NATIONAL
Mono
Lake
FOR.

Point Reyes
MARIN ISLANDS
SAN PABLO BAY
N.W.R.
JOHN MUIR N.H.S.
ANTIOCH
DUNES N.W.R.
Stockton
TUOLUMNE
N.W.&S.R.
YOSEMITE
NATIONAL

POINT REYES NAT. SEASHORE
CORDELL BANK NAT.
MARINE SANCTUARY
San Rafael
Berkeley
EUGENE O'NEILL
N.H.S.
Modesto
PARK
DEVILS
POSTPILE
NAT. MON.

MUIR WOODS N.M.
San Francisco
FARALLON N.W.R.
GULF OF THE FARALLONES
NAT. MARINE SANCTUARY
Oakland
Hayward
SAN JOAQUIN RIVER N.W.R.
Turlock
MERCED
N.W.R.
INYO
NATIONAL
BISHOP PAIUTE I.R.
Bishop
FOREST

ALCATRAZ ISLAND,
GOLDEN GATE N.R.A.,
SAN FRANCISCO
MARITIME N.H.P.
DON EDWARDS
SAN FRANCISCO BAY N.W.R.
Palo Alto
San Jose
SAN LUIS
N.W.R.
Merced
SIERRA
NAT.
BIG PINE I.R.
DEATH

MONTEREY
Sunnyvale
Silicon Valley
ELLIOTT SLOUGH N.W.R.
San Joaquin
KINGS
CANYON
NAT.
FT. INDEPENDENCE
I.R.
MANZANAR
N.H.S.

Santa Cruz
SALINAS RIVER
N.W.R.
Salinas
FOR.
PARK
VALLEY

Monterey Bay
BAY
Monterey
PINNACLES
N.P.
KINGS N.W.&S.R.
MOJAVE
Lowest point in the Western Hemisphere
(Badwater Basin). Highest recorded
temperature in the U.S., 134°F (57°C)
(Furnace Creek)

Spanish and Mexican
capital of California
(1776-1848)
Soledad
LOS PADRES
Fresno
SEQUOIA
N.P.
BLUE RIDGE
N.W.R.
+ Mt. Whitney
14,494 ft; 4,418 m
Highest point in the
contiguous U.S.
Death Valley
NAT.
-282 ft
-86 m
PARK

BIG SUR
N.W.&S.R.
NAT.
FOR.
Visalia
Hanford
Tulare
SEQUOIA
NAT.
TULE RIVER
I.R.
MARINE
SANCTUARY
Paso Robles
PIXLEY N.W.R.
Delano
KERN
N.W.&S.R.
Ridgecrest

MAP KEY
Atascadero
CARRIZO
PLAIN
N.M.
KERN
N.W.&S.R.
Bakersfield
DESERT
MOJAVE
NAT. PRESERVE

⭐ State capital
●●●● City
□ Point of interest
+ Mountain peak
▼ Low point with elevation
below sea level
San Luis Obispo
Santa Maria
GUADALUPE-NIPOMO
DUNES N.W.R.
LOS
CEASAR E.
CHAVEZ N.M.
BITTER CREEK
N.W.R.
Barstow
FORT MOJAVE
I.R.
Needles
HAVASU N.W.R.

PACIFIC
OCEAN
Lompoc
SISQUOC
N.W.&S.R.
PADRES
NAT. FOR.
SAN YNEZ I.R.
SESPE CREEK
N.W.&S.R.
HOPPER MOUNTAIN N.W.R.
ANGELES
Lancaster
Hesperia
President Nixon's birthplace
CHEMEHUEVI
I.R.
Lake
Havasu

/ Dam
--- Trail
...... State or national
boundary
Dry lake
National Wild &
Scenic River
Area below sea level
CHANNEL ISLANDS
NATIONAL PARK
Santa Rosa
Santa Barbara
Ventura
Oxnard
SANTA MONICA
MTS. N.R.A.
NAT.
FOR.
Simi Valley
Pasadena
San Bernardino
SAN
BERNARDINO
JOSHUA TREE N.P.
COLORADO
RIVER
I.R.
Blythe

Indian Reservation
National Park
Service unit
National Forest
National Wildlife
Refuge
National Marine
Sanctuary
Santa
Cruz
CHANNEL ISLANDS
NATIONAL MARINE
SANCTUARY
Santa
Catalina
SEAL BEACH N.W.R.
Santa Monica
Los Angeles
Long Beach
Santa Ana
Mission Viejo
Oceanside
MORONGO I.R.
Riverside
Anaheim
AGUA
CALIENTE
SOBOBA I.R.
Palm Springs
COACHELLA VALLEY N.W.R.
SANTA ROSA & SAN JACINTO
MTS. N.M.
TORRES-MARTINEZ I.R.
CLEVELAND NAT.
PECHANGA I.R.
PALA I.R.
LA JOLLA I.R.
LOS COYOTES I.R.
SANTA ROSA
CAHUILLA I.R.
Salton Sea
SONNY BONO
SALTON SEA N.W.R.
CIBOLA N.W.R.
SONORAN

0   100 miles
0   100 kilometers
Albers Conic Equal-Area Projection
CHANNEL ISLANDS
San Clemente
Escondido
San Diego
SANTA YSABEL I.R.
BARONA I.R.
SAN DIEGO BAY N.W.R.
CABRILLO NAT. MON.
Chula Vista
TIJUANA
SLOUGH
N.W.R.
CUYAPAIPE I.R.
CAMPO I.R.
SAN
DIEGO
CAPITAN GRANDE I.R.
MANZANITA I.R.
El Centro
Calexico
Imperial
Valley
FORT
YUMA
I.R.
IMPERIAL
N.W.R.
DESERT
Colorado

BAJA CALIFORNIA | SONORA
U.S.
MEXICO

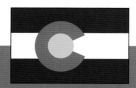

THE BASICS

Statehood
August 1, 1876; 38th state

Total area (land and water)
104,094 sq mi (269,601 sq km)

Land area
103,642 sq mi (268,431 sq km)

Population
5,695,564

Capital
Denver
Population 716,492

Largest city
Denver
Population 716,492

Racial/ethnic groups
87.3% white; 4.5% African
American; 3.4% Asian; 1.6%
Native American; 21.5%
Hispanic (any race)

Foreign born
9.8%

Urban population
86.2%

Population density
55.0 per sq mi (21.2 per sq km)

GEO WHIZ

The Black Canyon of the Gunnison is one of the newest national parks in the Rockies. As it flows through the canyon, the Gunnison River drops an average of 95 feet (29 m) per mile—one of the steepest descents in North America. The craggy rock walls are a mecca for rock climbers.

Colorado's lynx population is making a comeback, thanks to a program that, between 1999 and 2006, released 214 wild cats captured in Canada and Alaska into Colorado's southern Rockies. Based on data from tracking and camera traps, the program has been declared a success.

Colorado

Ancestors of today's Native Americans were the earliest inhabitants of present-day Colorado. Some were cliff dwellers; others were plains dwellers. Spanish explorers arrived in Colorado in 1541. In 1803 eastern Colorado became a U.S. territory as part of the Louisiana Purchase. Gold was discovered in 1858, and thousands were attracted by the prospect of quick wealth. The sudden jump in population led to conflict with the Cheyenne and Arapaho tribes over control of the land, but the settlers prevailed. Completion of the transcontinental railroad in 1869 helped link Colorado to the eastern states and opened its doors for growth. Cattle ranching and farming developed on the High Plains of eastern Colorado, while mining was the focus in the mountainous western part of the state. Mining is still important in Colorado, but the focus has shifted to energy resources—oil, natural gas, coal, and wind. Agriculture is also a major source of income, with cattle accounting for half of farm income. And Colorado's majestic mountains attract thousands of tourists each year.

◯ **THRILLING SPORT.** Colorado's snow-covered mountains attract winter sports enthusiasts from near and far. In the past, skis were used by gold prospectors. Today, skiing and snowboarding are big moneymakers in the state's recreation and tourism industry.

COLUMBINE

LARK BUNTING

◗ **ANCIENT CULTURE.** Ancestors of today's pueblo-dwelling people lived from about A.D. 600 to 1300 in the canyons that today are part of Mesa Verde National Park. More than 600 stone structures were built on protected cliffs of the canyon walls; others were located on mesas. These dwellings hold many clues to a past way of life.

WYOMING

NEBRASKA

KANSAS

OKLAHOMA

NEW MEXICO

COLORADO

GREAT PLAINS

ROCKY MOUNTAINS

- Powder Wash
- Elkhead Mts.
- Craig
- Steamboat Springs
- Danforth Hills
- Meeker
- WHITE RIVER PLATEAU
- WHITE RIVER NATIONAL FOREST
- Rifle
- Glenwood Springs
- Carbondale
- GRAND MESA NAT. FOR.
- Grand Mesa
- Aspen
- Orchard City
- Gunnison City
- Delta
- BLACK CANYON OF THE GUNNISON N.P.
- GUNNISON NATIONAL FOREST
- Gunnison
- Montrose
- UNCOMPAHGRE PLATEAU
- Blue Mesa Reservoir
- CURECANTI N.R.A.
- Telluride
- SAN JUAN NATIONAL FOREST
- Durango
- CHIMNEY ROCK N.M.
- Pagosa Springs
- SOUTHERN UTE INDIAN RES.

- ROUTT NATIONAL FOREST
- ARAPAHO N.W.R.
- Park Range
- Medicine Bow Mts.
- Laramie Mts.
- ROOSEVELT NATIONAL FOREST
- CACHE LA POUDRE N.W. & S.R.
- Continental Divide
- ROCKY MOUNTAIN NAT. PARK
- Estes Park
- L. Granby
- ARAPAHO N.R.A.
- ARAPAHO NATIONAL FOREST
- Vail
- Gore Range
- Blue R.
- ROCKY FLATS N.W.R.
- TWO PONDS N.W.R.
- Leadville
- Highest city in the U.S. PIKE
- Sawatch Range
- Mt. Elbert 14,433 ft 4,399 m — Highest point in Colorado
- BROWNS CANYON N.M.
- Salida
- FLORISSANT FOSSIL BEDS N.M.
- SAN ISABEL NATIONAL FOREST
- Woodland Park
- Pikes Peak 14,110 ft 4,301 m
- Cañon City
- Florence
- BACA N.W.R.
- GREAT SAND DUNES N.P. AND PRESERVE
- Wet Mountains
- Cochetopa Hills
- RIO GRANDE NATIONAL FOREST
- Monte Vista
- MONTE VISTA N.W.R.
- Alamosa
- ALAMOSA N.W.R.
- San Luis Lake
- San Luis Valley
- Sangre de Cristo Mountains
- Culebra Range
- Walsenburg
- Trinidad

- Fort Collins
- Greeley
- Loveland
- Longmont
- Boulder
- Louisville
- Lafayette
- Brighton
- Thornton
- Westminster
- Arvada
- ROCKY MOUNTAIN ARSENAL N.W.R.
- Denver ✪
- Aurora
- Littleton
- Castle Rock
- Kiowa
- Colorado Springs
- Fountain
- Pueblo
- St. Charles
- Huerfano

- Hereford
- Sterling
- Sterling Reservoir
- Frenchman Creek
- Holyoke
- Fort Morgan
- Brush
- Akron
- Yuma
- Last Chance
- South Platte
- Cheyenne Wells
- Burlington
- Limon
- Big Sandy Creek
- Arikaree R.
- South Fork Republican
- Punkin Center
- Rush Creek
- Ordway
- Lake Meredith
- Great Plains Reservoirs
- BENT'S OLD FORT N.H.S.
- John Martin Res.
- Rocky Ford
- La Junta
- Las Animas
- Lamar
- Arkansas
- SAND CREEK MASSACRE N.H.S.
- COMANCHE NATIONAL GRASSLAND
- Apishapa R.
- Purgatoire R.
- Chacuaco Canyon
- Smith Canyon
- Mesa de Maya
- Bear Cr.
- Springfield
- Sand Arroyo
- North Fork
- Two Butte Creek
- Cimarron R.

Rivers and features: Little Snake, Yampa, Colorado R., N. Platte R., Laramie R., Continental Divide, Crow Cr., South Platte, Arkansas R., San Luis Creek, Saguache Creek, Rio Grande, Conejos R., Alamosa R., Piedra R., Animas R., Los Pinos R., San Juan R., Uncompahgre R.

PAWNEE NATIONAL GRASSLAND

RISING HIGH

Average state elevation

Colorado	Wyoming	Utah	New Mexico	Nevada
6,800 feet (2,073 m)	6,700 feet (2,042 m)	6,100 feet (1,859 m)	5,700 feet (1,737 m)	5,500 feet (1,676 m)

Because of their mountain cores, states in the western region, led by Colorado, have the country's highest average elevations.

MAP KEY

- ✪ State capital
- ●●● City
- ▢ Point of interest
- + Mountain peak
- ⟋ Dam
- ▭ Indian Reservation
- ······· State boundary
- ········· Continental Divide
- ═══ National Wild & Scenic River
- ▨ National Park Service unit
- ▨ National Forest
- ▢ National Grassland
- ▨ National Wildlife Refuge

0 — 50 miles
0 — 50 kilometers

Albers Conic Equal-Area Projection

THE BASICS

Statehood
August 21, 1959; 50th state

Total area (land and water)
10,932 sq mi (28,313 sq km)

Land area
6,423 sq mi (16,635 sq km)

Population
1,420,491

Capital
Honolulu/Honolulu County
Population 980,080

Largest city
Honolulu/Honolulu County
Population 980,080

Racial/ethnic groups
25.7% white; 2.2% African American; 37.8% Asian; 10.2% Pacific Islander; 10.5% Hispanic (any race)

Foreign born
18.1%

Urban population
91.9%

Population density
129.9 per sq mi (50.2 per sq km)

GEO WHIZ

Hawai'i is the world's most isolated population center — 2,300 miles (3,700 km) from California; and 3,850 miles (6,196 km) from Japan.

You can ski two ways in Hawai'i: on the water at the beach and on snow at Mauna Kea on the Big Island.

HIBISCUS

HAWAIIAN GOOSE
(NENE)

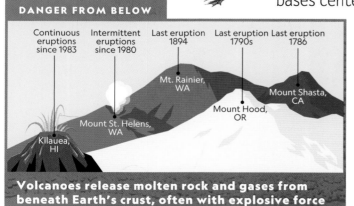

Continuous eruptions since 1983 — Kīlauea, HI

Intermittent eruptions since 1980 — Mount St. Helens, WA

Last eruption 1894 — Mt. Rainier, WA

Last eruption 1790s — Mount Hood, OR

Last eruption 1786 — Mount Shasta, CA

Volcanoes release molten rock and gases from beneath Earth's crust, often with explosive force that can put people and property at great risk.

Hawai'i

Some 1,500 years ago Polynesians traveling in large canoes arrived from the south to settle the volcanic islands that make up Hawai'i. In 1778 Captain James Cook claimed the islands for Britain, and soon Hawai'i became a center of the whaling industry and a major producer of sugarcane. The spread of sugarcane plantations led to the importation of workers from Asia. Hawai'i became a U.S. territory in 1900. Naval installations, established as fueling depots and to protect U.S. interests in the Pacific, were attacked by the Japanese in 1941, an act that officially brought the United States into World War II. In 1959 Hawai'i became the 50th state. Tourism, agriculture, and the military, with bases centered on O'ahu's Pearl Harbor, are the cornerstone of Hawai'i's economy today. Jet airline service makes the state accessible to tourists from both the mainland United States and Asia as well as from Australia and New Zealand. Hawai'i is still a major producer of sugarcane and other plant products.

⛱ **ISLAND PARADISE.**
Waikiki, where sandy beaches attract thousands of visitors, is the center of Honolulu's tourist industry.

KAUA'I

One of the world's rainiest spots

Princeville
KILAUEA POINT N.W.R.
HANALEI N.W.R.
Wai'ale'ale 5,148 ft 1,569 m
Kapa'a
Hanamā'ulu
Līhu'e
Lehua I.
HULEIA N.W.R.
Kekaha
Kalāheo
Pu'uwai
NI'IHAU
Kaulakahi Channel

Kure Atoll
Midway Islands
MIDWAY ATOLL N.W.R.
Pearl and Hermes Atoll
Lisianski I.
Laysan I.
Maro Reef
NORTHWESTERN HAW

0   400 miles
0   400 kilometers
Oblique Mercator Projection

3 4 5 6 7 8 9 10

MAP KEY

⊛ State capital
•• City
☐ Point of interest
+ Mountain peak
▭ National Park Service unit
▭ National Wildlife Refuge
▭ National Marine Sanctuary

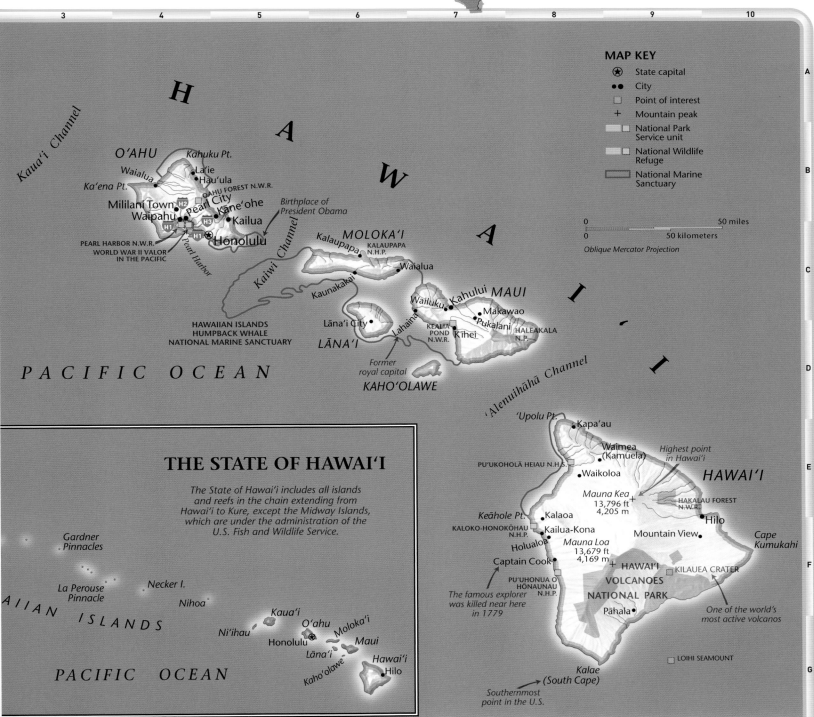

H A W A I I

Kaua'i Channel

O'AHU
Kahuku Pt.
Waialua
La'ie
Hau'ula
Ka'ena Pt.
OAHU FOREST N.W.R.
Mililani Town
Pearl City
Kāne'ohe
Waipahu
Kailua
PEARL HARBOR N.W.R.
WORLD WAR II VALOR IN THE PACIFIC
Pearl Harbor
Honolulu
Birthplace of President Obama

Kaiwi Channel

MOLOKA'I
Kalaupapa
KALAUPAPA N.H.P.
Waialua
Kaunakakai

HAWAIIAN ISLANDS HUMPBACK WHALE NATIONAL MARINE SANCTUARY

Lāna'i City
LĀNA'I
Lahaina
Former royal capital

Wailuku
Kahului MAUI
Makawao
Pukalani
KEALIA POND N.W.R.
Kīhei
HALEAKALA N.P.

PACIFIC OCEAN

KAHO'OLAWE

0 _____ 50 miles
0 _____ 50 kilometers
Oblique Mercator Projection

'Alenuihāhā Channel

'Upolu Pt.
Kapa'au
Waimea (Kamuela)
Highest point in Hawai'i
PU'UKOHOLĀ HEIAU N.H.S.
Waikoloa
HAWAI'I
HAKALAU FOREST N.W.R.
Mauna Kea 13,796 ft 4,205 m
Keāhole Pt.
Kalaoa
KALOKO-HONOKŌHAU N.H.P.
Kailua-Kona
Mountain View
Hilo
Holualoa
Mauna Loa 13,679 ft 4,169 m
Cape Kumukahi
Captain Cook
PU'UHONUA O HŌNAUNAU N.H.P.
The famous explorer was killed near here in 1779
HAWAI'I
VOLCANOES
NATIONAL PARK
KILAUEA CRATER
One of the world's most active volcanos
Pāhala
☐ LOIHI SEAMOUNT
Kalae (South Cape)
Southernmost point in the U.S.

A
B
C
D
E
F
G

THE STATE OF HAWAI'I

The State of Hawai'i includes all islands and reefs in the chain extending from Hawai'i to Kure, except the Midway Islands, which are under the administration of the U.S. Fish and Wildlife Service.

Gardner Pinnacles
La Perouse Pinnacle
Necker I.
Nihoa
HAWAIIAN ISLANDS
Kaua'i
Ni'ihau
O'ahu
Moloka'i
Honolulu
Lāna'i
Maui
Kaho'olawe
Hawai'i
Hilo

PACIFIC OCEAN

⟩ **FIERY CREATION.** Hawai'i is the fastest-growing U.S. state—not in people, but in land. Active volcanoes are constantly creating new land as lava continues to flow. Recent eruptions on Kilauea, Hawai'i's most active volcano, have added more than 700 acres (283 ha) of new land to the state.

THE BASICS

Statehood
July 3, 1890; 43rd state

Total area (land and water)
83,569 sq mi (216,443 sq km)

Land area
82,643 sq mi (214,045 sq km)

Population
1,754,208

Capital
Boise
Population 228,790

Largest city
Boise
Population 228,790

Racial/ethnic groups
93.2% white; 0.9% African American; 1.5% Asian; 1.7% Native American; 12.5% Hispanic (any race)

Foreign born
5.9%

Urban population
70.6%

Population density
21.2 per sq mi (8.2 per sq km)

GEO WHIZ

Before the last ice age, huge mammals roamed what is now Idaho. Fossils of these creatures are displayed at the Museum of Idaho, in Idaho Falls.

Apollo astronauts trained for their moon mission in the harsh environment of Craters of the Moon National Monument and Preserve.

SYRINGA
(MOCK ORANGE)

MOUNTAIN BLUEBIRD

Idaho

Some of the earliest Native American sites in what is now Idaho date back more than 10,000 years. In the 18th century, contact between native people and Europeans not only brought trade and cultural change, but also diseases that wiped out many native groups. Present-day Idaho was part of the 1803 Louisiana Purchase and was explored during the Lewis and Clark expedition. In 1843 wagons crossed into Idaho on the Oregon Trail. The arrival of white settlers caused conflict with Native Americans, which continued until 1890 when Idaho became a state. Today, almost half the land is planted with crops, especially wheat, sugar beets, barley, and potatoes. The state encourages the use of alternative energy, such as wind, geothermal, and biomass, including ethanol. Manufacturing and high-tech industries have diversified the economy, and the state's natural beauty attracts tourists.

◐ **WOOLLY RUSH HOUR.** Sheep fill a roadway in Idaho's Salmon River Valley. The herds move twice a year. In the spring they migrate north to mountain pastures. In the fall they return to the Snake River Plain in the south.

ANCIENT STAPLE FOOD

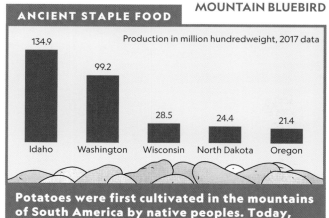

Production in million hundredweight, 2017 data

Idaho	134.9
Washington	99.2
Wisconsin	28.5
North Dakota	24.4
Oregon	21.4

Potatoes were first cultivated in the mountains of South America by native peoples. Today, Idaho leads in U.S. potato production.

◐ **TIMBER!** More than 60 percent of Idaho's land area is tree-covered, much of it in national forests. Lumber and paper products, most of which are sold to other states, are important to the state economy.

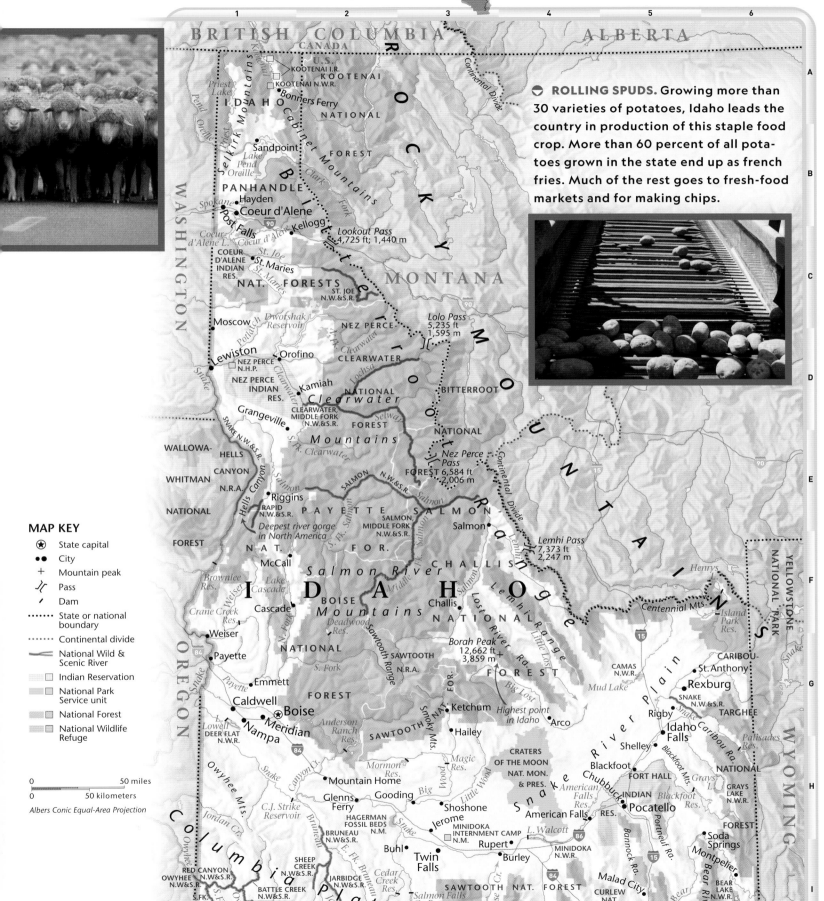

ROLLING SPUDS. Growing more than 30 varieties of potatoes, Idaho leads the country in production of this staple food crop. More than 60 percent of all potatoes grown in the state end up as french fries. Much of the rest goes to fresh-food markets and for making chips.

BRITISH COLUMBIA | ALBERTA

CANADA

ROCKY

WASHINGTON

MONTANA

MAP KEY

⊛ State capital
•• City
+ Mountain peak
)(Pass
⌐ Dam
······· State or national boundary
······· Continental divide
⤚ National Wild & Scenic River
☐ Indian Reservation
☐ National Park Service unit
☐ National Forest
☐ National Wildlife Refuge

0 ——— 50 miles
0 ——— 50 kilometers
Albers Conic Equal-Area Projection

OREGON

IDAHO

WYOMING

YELLOWSTONE NATIONAL PARK

Borah Peak 12,662 ft 3,859 m
Highest point in Idaho

Lemhi Pass 7,373 ft 2,247 m

Nez Perce Pass 6,584 ft 2,006 m

Lolo Pass 5,235 ft 1,595 m

Lookout Pass 4,725 ft; 1,440 m

Deepest river gorge in North America

NEVADA | UTAH

MONTANA

THE BASICS

Statehood
November 8, 1889; 41st state

Total area (land and water)
147,040 sq mi (380,831 sq km)

Land area
145,546 sq mi (376,962 sq km)

Population
1,062,305

Capital
Helena
Population 32,315

Largest city
Billings
Population 109,550

Racial/ethnic groups
89.1% white; 0.6% African American; 0.8% Asian; 6.7% Native American; 3.8% Hispanic (any race)

Foreign born
2.1%

Urban population
55.9%

Population density
7.3 per sq mi (2.8 per sq km)

GEO WHIZ

The fossil of a turkey-size dinosaur is being called the missing link between Asian and North American horned dinosaurs. Paleontologist Paul Horner discovered the fossil while sitting on it during a lunch break at a dig near Choteau.

Montana is the only state with river systems that empty southeast into the Gulf of Mexico, north into Canada's Hudson Bay, and west into the Pacific Ocean.

WESTERN
MEADOWLARK

BITTERROOT

Montana

Long before the arrival of Europeans, numerous native groups lived and hunted in the plains and mountains of present-day Montana. Although contact between European explorers and these Native Americans was often peaceful, Montana was the site of the historic 1876 Battle of the Little Bighorn, in which Lakota (Sioux) and Cheyenne warriors defeated George Armstrong Custer's troops. In the mid-19th century, the discovery of gold and silver attracted many prospectors, and later cattle ranching became big business, adding to tensions with the native people. Montana became the 41st state in 1889. Today, Native Americans make up almost 7 percent of the state's population—only four other states have a larger percentage. Agriculture is important to the economy, producing wheat, hay, and barley as well as beef cattle. Mining and timber industries have seen a decline, but service industries and tourism are growing. Montana's natural environment, including Glacier and Yellowstone National Parks, remains one of its greatest resources.

◗ **STEP BACK IN TIME.** Just like in the past, Montana ranchers move their cattle herds from low winter pastures to higher elevations for summer grazing. Some ranches allow adventurous tourists to participate in the drives.

ALBERTA

SASKATCHEWAN

CANADA

U.S.

BLACKFEET INDIAN RES.

Browning

Cut Bank

Shelby

Conrad

Choteau

Lake Elwell

Marias

Teton

CREEDMAN COULEE N.W.R.

LAKE THIBADEAU N.W.R.

Fresno Reservoir

Havre

Chinook

BLACK COULEE N.W.R.

Frenchman

Milk

HEWITT LAKE N.W.R.

Malta

BOWDOIN N.W.R.

Scobey

Plentywood

MEDICINE LAKE N.W.R.

FORT PECK INDIAN RESERVATION

Largest embankment dam in the U.S.

Glasgow

Wolf Point

FT. PECK DAM

FORT UNION TRADING POST N.H.S.

Missouri

LEWIS AND CLARK NAT. FOR.

NEZ PERCE N.H.P. (BEAR PAW BATTLEFIELD)

ROCKY BOYS I.R.

FORT BELKNAP INDIAN RESERVATION

UPPER MISSOURI RIVER BREAKS N.M.

Missouri

UPPER MISSOURI N.W.&S.R.

UL BEND N.W.R.

Fort Peck Lake

CHARLES M. RUSSELL NATIONAL WILDLIFE REFUGE

Fort Benton

BENTON LAKE N.W.R.

Great Falls

Sun

LEWIS

AND CLARK

Lewistown

Jordan

Circle

Redwater

Sidney

Glendive

MAKOSHIKA STATE PARK

Wibaux

Terry

NORTH DAKOTA

Missouri

Yellowstone

HELENA

GRANT-KOHRS RANCH N.H.S.

Deer Lodge

Helena

Canyon Ferry L.

Townsend

NATIONAL FOREST

WAR HORSE N.W.R.

LAKE MASON N.W.R.

Harlowton

Roundup

Musselshell

Miles City

Powder

Baker

SOUTH DAKOTA

Missouri

Jefferson

Butte

Belgrade

Bozeman

GALLATIN

HAILSTONE N.W.R.

HALFBREED LAKE N.W.R.

POMPEYS PILLAR N.M.

Big Timber

Livingston

Columbus

Laurel

Billings

Hardin

Crow Agency

Yellowstone

Forsyth

Bighorn

Colstrip

Tongue

CUSTER NATIONAL FOREST

Broadus

Powder

Little Missouri

DEERLODGE

Virginia City

Dillon

Madison

Gallatin

NATIONAL

Highest point in Montana

CUSTER

Clarks Fork

LITTLE BIGHORN BATTLEFIELD N.M.

NORTHERN CHEYENNE I.R.

CROW INDIAN RESERVATION

Red Rock

RED ROCK LAKES N.W.R.

West Yellowstone

Absaroka Range

FOREST

Granite Peak 12,799 ft 3,901 m

Red Lodge

NATIONAL

BIGHORN CANYON N.R.A.

Bighorn Mountains

Continental Divide

YELLOWSTONE NATIONAL PARK

MAP KEY

⭐ State capital

●●● City

✛ Mountain peak

⋯⋯ State or national boundary

)(Pass

⌐ Dam

⎯⎯ National Wild & Scenic River

⋯⋯ Continental divide

▢ Indian Reservation

▢ State Park unit

▢ National Park Service unit

▢ National Forest

▢ National Wildlife Refuge

WYOMING

0 ___ 50 miles

0 ___ 50 kilometers

Albers Conic Equal-Area Projection

ECONOMIC CORNERSTONE

Percentage of total farm receipts, 2017 data

Cattle & calves 42.1%

Other 11.0%

Hogs 1.5%

Sugar beets 1.6%

Barley 4.9%

Lentils & dried beans 5.2%

Hay 10.6%

Wheat 23.1%

Agriculture, especially cattle and grain, is important in Montana's economy, adding more than $3.5 billion to the state income each year.

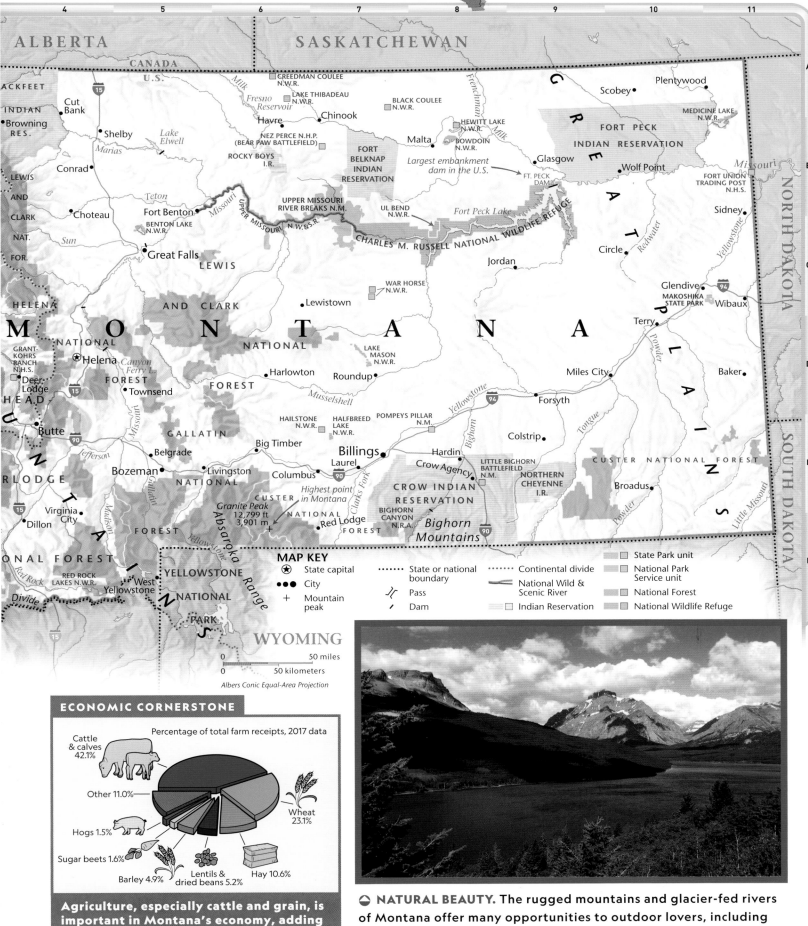

NATURAL BEAUTY. The rugged mountains and glacier-fed rivers of Montana offer many opportunities to outdoor lovers, including hiking and backpacking as well as fishing in summer, skiing in winter, and year-round wildlife viewing.

THE SILVER STATE:
NEVADA

THE BASICS

Statehood
October 31, 1864; 36th state

Total area (land and water)
110,572 sq mi (286,380 sq km)

Land area
109,781 sq mi (284,332 sq km)

Population
3,034,392

Capital
Carson City
Population 55,414

Largest city
Las Vegas
Population 644,644

Racial/ethnic groups
74.6% white; 9.8% African American; 8.8% Asian; 1.7% Native American; 28.8% Hispanic (any race)

Foreign born
19.5%

Urban population
94.2%

Population density
27.6 per sq mi (10.7 per sq km)

GEO WHIZ

The Applegate Trail, named for two brothers, offered a shorter alternative to the Oregon Trail.

Highway 375 is named Extraterrestrial Highway because of all the reported extraterrestrial sightings.

MOUNTAIN BLUEBIRD
SAGEBRUSH

Nevada

Nevada's earliest inhabitants were ancestors of today's Native Americans. Around 2,000 years ago, they began establishing permanent dwellings of clay and stone perched atop rocky ledges in what today is the state of Nevada. This was what Spanish explorers saw when they arrived in 1776. In years that followed, many expeditions passing through the area faced challenges of a difficult environment and Native Americans protecting their land. In the mid-1800s gold and silver were discovered. In 1861 the Nevada Territory was created, and three years later statehood was granted. Today, the Nevada landscape is dotted with ghost towns—places once prosperous but now abandoned except for curious tourists. Mining is now overshadowed by other economic activities. Casinos, modern hotels, and lavish entertainment attract thousands of visitors each year. Hoover Dam, on the Colorado River, supplies power to much of Nevada, as well as Arizona and California. But limited water promises to be a challenge to Nevada's future growth.

⬤ **TURNING BACK TIME.** The Luxor, re-creating a scene from ancient Egypt, is one of the many hotel-casinos that attract thousands of tourists to the four-mile (6-km) section of Las Vegas known as the Strip.

⬤ **DESERT BEAUTY.** A beavertail cactus thrives in the dry environment of Valley of Fire State Park. The park, Nevada's oldest, gets its name from red sandstone formations visible in the distance.

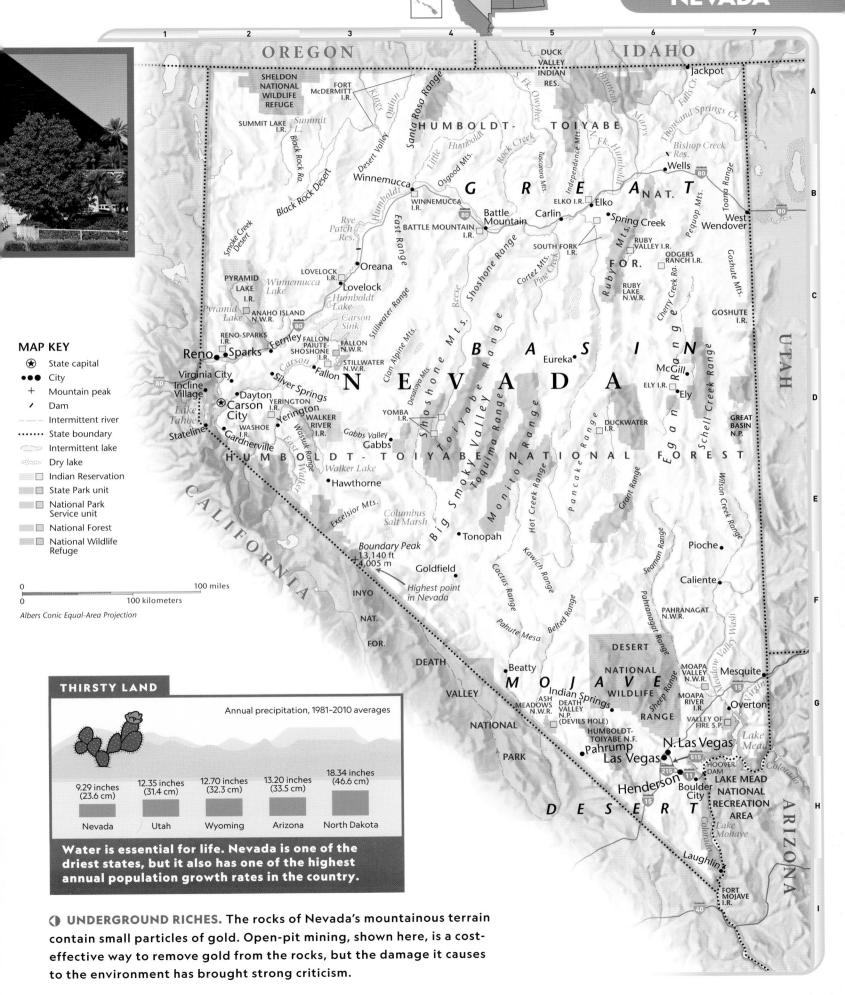

MAP KEY
- ⍟ State capital
- ●●● City
- + Mountain peak
- ⌐ Dam
- – – Intermittent river
- ····· State boundary
- ◯ Intermittent lake
- ⫶ Dry lake
- ☐ Indian Reservation
- ☐ State Park unit
- ☐ National Park Service unit
- ☐ National Forest
- ☐ National Wildlife Refuge

0 — 100 miles
0 — 100 kilometers
Albers Conic Equal-Area Projection

OREGON

IDAHO

UTAH

CALIFORNIA

ARIZONA

G R E A T   N A T.

FOR.

N E V A D A

B A S I N

HUMBOLDT-TOIYABE

HUMBOLDT-TOIYABE NATIONAL FOREST

Boundary Peak
13,140 ft
4,005 m
Highest point in Nevada

DEATH VALLEY NATIONAL PARK

MOJAVE

DESERT

INYO NAT. FOR.

THIRSTY LAND

Annual precipitation, 1981–2010 averages

9.29 inches (23.6 cm)	12.35 inches (31.4 cm)	12.70 inches (32.3 cm)	13.20 inches (33.5 cm)	18.34 inches (46.6 cm)
Nevada	Utah	Wyoming	Arizona	North Dakota

Water is essential for life. Nevada is one of the driest states, but it also has one of the highest annual population growth rates in the country.

◖ **UNDERGROUND RICHES.** The rocks of Nevada's mountainous terrain contain small particles of gold. Open-pit mining, shown here, is a cost-effective way to remove gold from the rocks, but the damage it causes to the environment has brought strong criticism.

STATE OF OREGON
1859

THE BASICS

Statehood
February 14, 1859; 33rd state

Total area (land and water)
98,379 sq mi (254,799 sq km)

Land area
95,988 sq mi (248,608 sq km)

Population
4,190,713

Capital
Salem
Population 173,442

Largest city
Portland
Population 653,115

Racial/ethnic groups
87.1% white; 2.2% African
American; 4.7% Asian;
1.8% Native American;
13.1% Hispanic (any race)

Foreign born
9.9%

Urban population
81.0%

Population density
43.7 per sq mi (16.9 per sq km)

GEO WHIZ

To recover wetlands and save
two endangered fish species,
100 tons (90 t) of explosives
were used to blast through
levees so that water from the
Williamson River could again
flow into Upper Klamath Lake.

Crater Lake (1,932 ft/589 m)
is the deepest in the United
States. It fills a depression
created when an eruption
caused the top of a mountain
to collapse. Wizard Island, at
the center of the lake, is the
top of the volcano.

Mount Hood, a dormant
volcano near Portland, is
Oregon's highest peak,
rising 11,239 feet (3,426 m).
Its last major eruption was in
the 1790s, a few years before
the Lewis and Clark expedition
reached the region.

OREGON GRAPE
WESTERN MEADOWLARK

Oregon

Long before the Oregon Trail brought settlers from the eastern United States, Native Americans fished and hunted in Oregon's coastal waters and forested valleys. Spanish explorers sailed along Oregon's coast in 1543, and in the 18th century fur traders from Europe set up forts in the region. In the mid-1800s settlers began farming the rich soil of the Willamette Valley. Oregon achieved statehood in 1859, and by 1883 railroads linked Oregon to the East, and Portland had become an important shipping center. Today, forestry, fishing, and agriculture make up a significant part of the state economy, but Oregon is diversifying into manufacturing and high-tech industries. Dams on the Columbia River generate inexpensive electricity to support energy-hungry industries, such as aluminum production. Computers, electronics, and research-based industries are expanding. Snowcapped volcanoes, old-growth forests, and a rocky coastline help make tourism an important growth industry.

◖ TOWER OF HISTORY.
The 125-foot (38-m)
Astoria Column, built
in 1926 near the mouth
of the Columbia River,
is decorated with
historic scenes of
exploration and settle-
ment along the Pacific
Northwest coast.

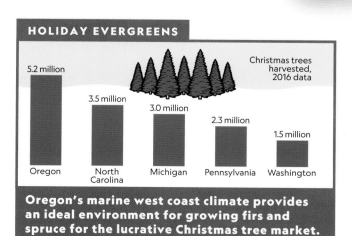

HOLIDAY EVERGREENS

Christmas trees
harvested,
2016 data

5.2 million — Oregon
3.5 million — North Carolina
3.0 million — Michigan
2.3 million — Pennsylvania
1.5 million — Washington

**Oregon's marine west coast climate provides
an ideal environment for growing firs and
spruce for the lucrative Christmas tree market.**

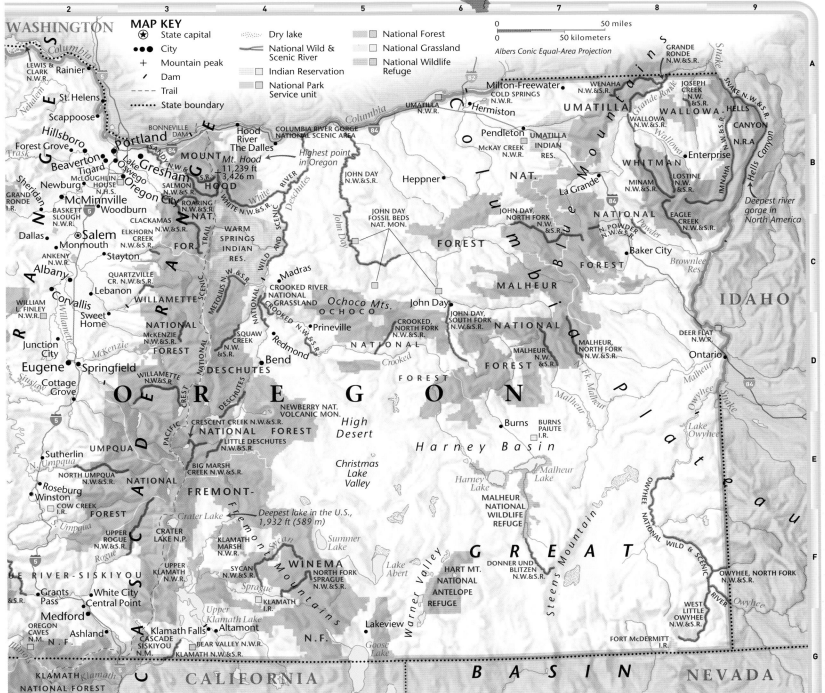

MAP KEY

★ State capital
●●● City
+ Mountain peak
⌐ Dam
- - - Trail
······· State boundary

Dry lake
National Wild & Scenic River
Indian Reservation
National Park Service unit

National Forest
National Grassland
National Wildlife Refuge

0   50 miles
0   50 kilometers
Albers Conic Equal-Area Projection

WASHINGTON

LEWIS & CLARK N.W.R.
Rainier
St. Helens
Scappoose
Hillsboro
Forest Grove
Portland
Beaverton
Tigard
Lake Oswego
Gresham
Newburg
McLOUGHLIN HOUSE N.H.S.
Oregon City
McMinnville
Woodburn
GRAND RONDE I.R.
Sheridan
Dallas
Salem
Monmouth
Stayton
ANKENY N.W.R.
Albany
Corvallis
WILLIAM L. FINLEY N.W.R.
Lebanon
Sweet Home
Junction City
Eugene
Springfield
Cottage Grove
Sutherlin
Roseburg
Winston
COW CREEK I.R.
Grants Pass
White City
Central Point
Medford
OREGON CAVES N.M.
Ashland

BONNEVILLE DAM
Hood River
The Dalles
MOUNT HOOD
Mt. Hood 11,239 ft 3,426 m
MOUNT HOOD N.F.
SALMON N.W.&S.R.
ROARING
CLACKAMAS
ELKHORN CREEK N.W.&S.R.
WARM SPRINGS INDIAN RES.
QUARTZVILLE CR. N.W.&S.R.
WILLAMETTE NATIONAL FOREST
McKENZIE N.W.&S.R.
SQUAW CREEK N.W.&S.R.
DESCHUTES
Bend
Redmond
NEWBERRY NAT. VOLCANIC MON.
CRESCENT CREEK N.W.&S.R.
NATIONAL FOREST
LITTLE DESCHUTES N.W.&S.R.
BIG MARSH CREEK N.W.&S.R.
UMPQUA
NORTH UMPQUA N.W.&S.R.
NATIONAL FOREST
FREMONT-
Crater Lake
CRATER LAKE N.P.
UPPER ROGUE N.W.&S.R.
KLAMATH MARSH N.W.R.
UPPER KLAMATH N.W.R.
SYCAN N.W.&S.R.
WINEMA
Klamath Falls
Altamont
Upper Klamath Lake
KLAMATH I.R.
BEAR VALLEY N.W.R.
KLAMATH N.W.&S.R.
CASCADE SISKIYOU N.M.
N.F.

COLUMBIA RIVER GORGE NATIONAL SCENIC AREA
Highest point in Oregon
WHITE N.W.&S.R.
White River
Deschutes
JOHN DAY N.W.&S.R.
Madras
CROOKED RIVER NATIONAL GRASSLAND
CROOKED N.W.&S.R.
Prineville
Ochoco Mts.
OCHOCO
NATIONAL
Crooked
High Desert
Christmas Lake Valley
Summer Lake
Lake Abert
Sycan
NORTH FORK SPRAGUE N.W.&S.R.
Sprague
Goose Lake

Columbia
Hermiston
Pendleton
McKAY CREEK N.W.R.
Heppner
JOHN DAY, NORTH FORK N.W.&S.R.
JOHN DAY FOSSIL BEDS NAT. MON.
John Day
CROOKED, NORTH FORK N.W.&S.R.
JOHN DAY, SOUTH FORK N.W.&S.R.
MALHEUR
NATIONAL
FOREST
Burns
BURNS PAIUTE I.R.
Harney Basin
Harney Lake
Malheur Lake
MALHEUR NATIONAL WILDLIFE REFUGE
HART MT. NATIONAL ANTELOPE REFUGE
Lakeview
DONNER UND BLITZEN N.W.&S.R.
Steens Mountain
Warner Valley

Milton-Freewater
COLD SPRINGS N.W.R.
UMATILLA N.W.R.
UMATILLA INDIAN RES.
WENAHA N.W.&S.R.
La Grande
N. POWDER N.W.&S.R.
JOHN DAY, NORTH FORK N.W.&S.R.
Baker City
Brownlee Res.
MALHEUR N.W. &S.R.
MALHEUR, NORTH FORK N.W.&S.R.
N. Fk. Malheur
Malheur
Burns

GRANDE RONDE N.W.&S.R.
UMATILLA NAT.
WALLOWA-
WHITMAN
Enterprise
WALLOWA N.W.&S.R.
WALLOWA-WHITMAN
MINAM N.W.&S.R.
LOSTINE N.W.&S.R.
EAGLE CREEK N.W.&S.R.
Deepest river gorge in North America
HELLS CANYON N.R.A.
JOSEPH CREEK N.W. &S.R.
SNAKE N.W. &S.R.
Hells Canyon
Snake
Imnaha
Powder
NATIONAL

IDAHO
DEER FLAT N.W.R.
Ontario
Lake Owyhee
OWYHEE NATIONAL WILD & SCENIC R.
OWYHEE, NORTH FORK N.W.&S.R.
WEST LITTLE OWYHEE N.W.&S.R.
FORT McDERMITT I.R.
Owyhee

Columbia Plateau

O R E G O N

GREAT

CALIFORNIA
BASIN
NEVADA
KLAMATH NATIONAL FOREST

Deepest lake in the U.S., 1,932 ft (589 m)

C A S C A D E   R A N G E

C O A S T   R A N G E

CHANGING LANDSCAPE.
Oregon's Pacific coast is a lesson on erosion and deposition. Rocky outcrops called sea stacks are leftovers of a former coastline that has been eroded by waves. The sandy beach is a result of eroded material being deposited along the shore.

THE BASICS

Statehood
January 4, 1896; 45th state

Total area (land and water)
84,897 sq mi (219,882 sq km)

Land area
82,170 sq mi (212,818 sq km)

Population
3,161,105

Capital
Salt Lake City
Population 200,591

Largest city
Salt Lake City
Population 200,591

Racial/ethnic groups
90.9% white; 1.4% African American; 2.6% Asian; 1.5% Native American; 14.0% Hispanic (any race)

Foreign born
8.2%

Urban population
90.6%

Population density
38.5 per sq mi (14.9 per sq km)

GEO WHIZ

A giant duck-billed dinosaur is among the many kinds of dinosaur fossils that have been found in the Grand Staircase–Escalante National Monument. Scientists think the plant-eater had 300 teeth and was at least 30 feet (9 m) long.

Great Salt Lake is the largest natural lake west of the Mississippi River. As a result of high levels of evaporation, the lake contains about 4.5 billion tons (4 billion t) of salt.

Utah

For thousands of years, present-day Utah was populated by Native Americans living in small hunter-gatherer groups, including the Ute for whom the state is named. Spanish explorers passed through Utah in 1776, and in the early 19th century trappers came from the East searching for beavers. In 1847 the arrival of Mormons marked the beginning of widespread settlement of the territory. They established farms and introduced irrigation. Discovery of precious metals in the 1860s brought miners to the territory. Today, 63 percent of Utah's land is managed by the federal government for military and defense industries and as national parks. As a result, the government is a leading employer in the state. Another important force in Utah is the Church of Jesus Christ of Latter-day Saints (Mormons), which has influenced culture and politics in the state for more than a century. Salt Lake City is the world headquarters of the church.

⬭ **MONUMENT TO FAITH.** Completed in 1893, the Salt Lake Temple is where Mormons gather to participate in religious ceremonies. Members regard their temples as Earth's most sacred places.

SEGO LILY

CALIFORNIA GULL

SPREADING THE FAITH

Mormon Church membership, 2018 data

Utah	2,090,402
California	767,301
Idaho	450,347
Arizona	428,069
Texas	353,317

From a colony of believers who settled in Utah's Salt Lake basin in the 1840s, followers of the Mormon faith have expanded into nearby states.

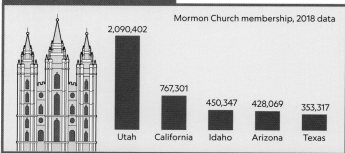

◑ **NATURE'S HANDIWORK.** Arches National Park includes more than 2,000 arches carved by forces of water and ice, extreme temperatures, and the shifting of underground salt beds over a period of 100 million years. Delicate Arch stands on the edge of a canyon, with the snowcapped La Sal Mountains in the distance.

THE BEEHIVE STATE:
UTAH

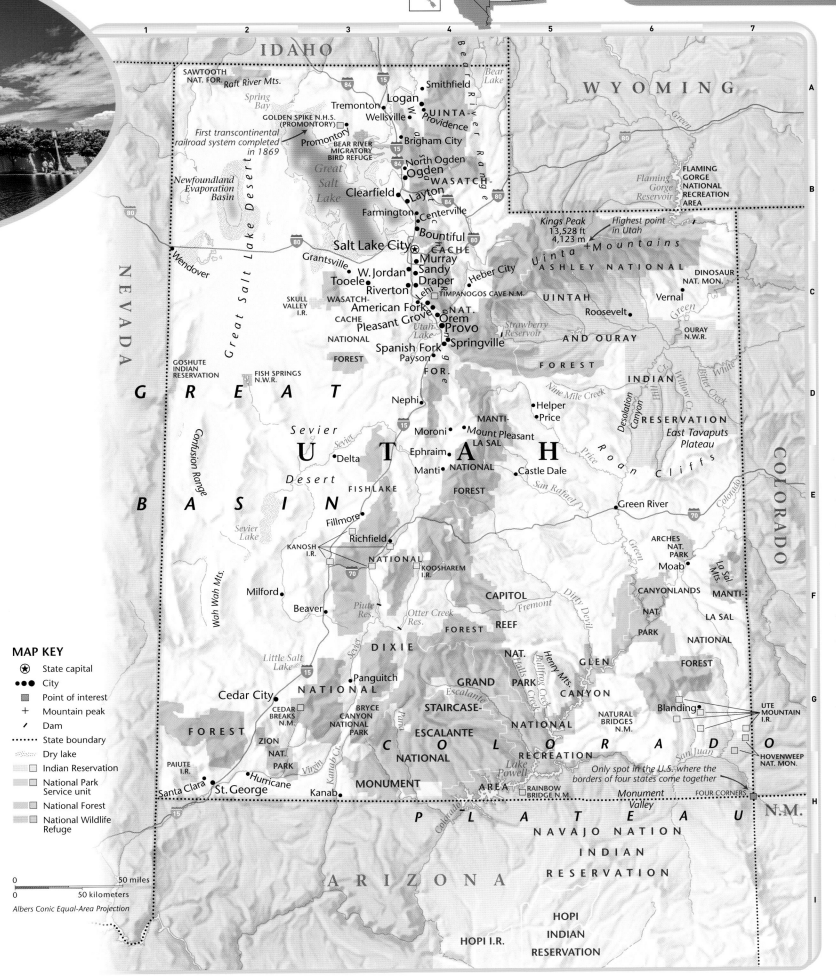

THE BASICS

Statehood
November 11, 1889; 42nd state

Total area (land and water)
71,298 sq mi (184,661 sq km)

Land area
66,456 sq mi (172,119 sq km)

Population
7,535,591

Capital
Olympia
Population 52,555

Largest city
Seattle
Population 744,955

Racial/ethnic groups
79.5% white; 4.2% African American; 8.9% Asian; 1.9% Native American; 12.7% Hispanic (any race)

Foreign born
13.8%

Urban population
84.1%

Population density
113.4 per sq mi (43.8 per sq km)

GEO WHIZ

The Olympic Peninsula is among the world's rainiest places, and its Hoh Rainforest is one of the world's few temperate rainforests.

Mount St. Helens, the most active volcano in the lower 48 states, is close to Seattle and to Portland, in Oregon. The eruption in May 1980 reduced its elevation by 1,314 feet (401 m) and caused the largest landslide in recorded history.

Orcas, also known as killer whales, are the world's largest dolphins. The fewer than 80 living in the waters of Puget Sound have been placed on the government's Endangered Species List.

AMERICAN GOLDFINCH
COAST RHODODENDRON

Washington

Long before Europeans explored along the coast of the Pacific Northwest, Native Americans inhabited the area, living mainly off abundant seafood found in coastal waters and rivers. In the late 18th century Spanish sailors and then British explorers, including Captain James Cook, visited the region. Under treaties with Spain (1819) and Britain (1846), the United States gained control of the land, and in 1853 the Washington Territory was formally separated from the Oregon Territory. Settlers soon based their livelihood on fishing, farming, and lumbering. Washington became the 42nd state in 1889. The 20th century was a time of growth and development for the state. Seattle became a major Pacific seaport. The Grand Coulee Dam, completed in 1941, provided the region with inexpensive electricity. Today, industry, led by Boeing and Microsoft, is a mainstay of the economy. Washington leads the country in production of apples and sweet cherries, and the state is the headquarters of the Starbucks chain of coffee shops.

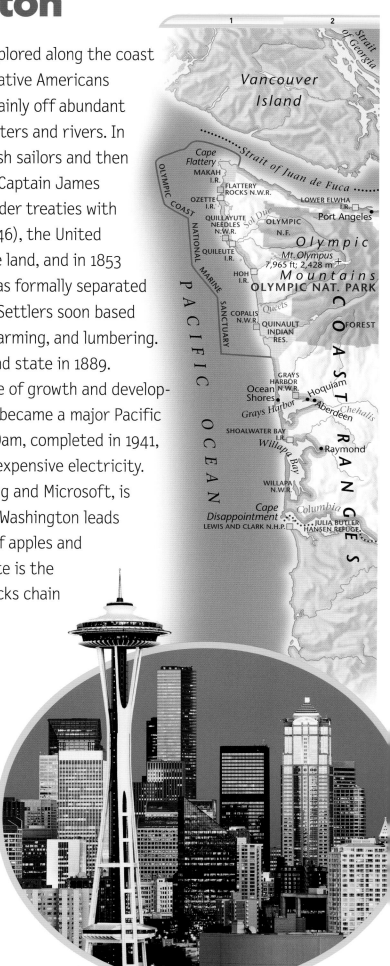

PACIFIC GATEWAY. Seattle, easily recognized by its distinctive Space Needle tower, is a major West Coast port and home to the North Pacific fishing fleet.

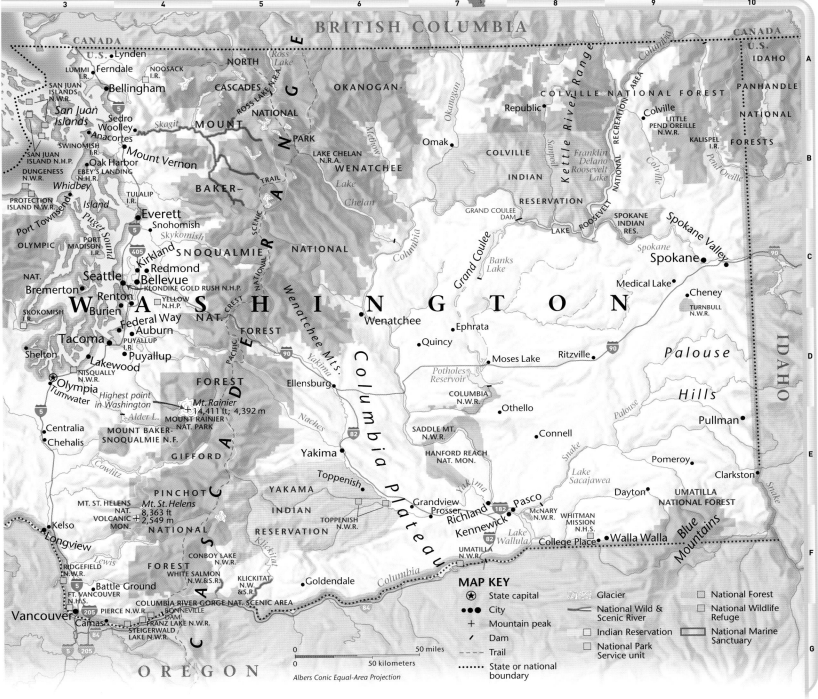

BRITISH COLUMBIA

CANADA
U.S.

CANADA
U.S.
IDAHO

Lynden
Ferndale
LUMMI I.R.
NOOSACK I.R.
NORTH
CASCADES
Ross Lake
Ross Lake N.R.A.
Bellingham
SAN JUAN ISLANDS N.W.R.
San Juan Islands
NATIONAL
Sedro Woolley
Skagit
MOUNT
PARK
Anacortes
SWINOMISH I.R.
SAN JUAN ISLAND N.H.P.
Oak Harbor
EBEY'S LANDING N.H.R.
Mount Vernon
BAKER-
RANGE
TRAIL
OKANOGAN-
Okanogan
Omak
COLVILLE NATIONAL FOREST
Republic
Kettle River Range
Colville
LITTLE PEND OREILLE N.W.R.
KALISPEL I.R.
PANHANDLE
NATIONAL
FORESTS
DUNGENESS N.W.R.
Whidbey
LAKE CHELAN N.R.A.
WENATCHEE
Methow
COLVILLE
INDIAN
Sanpoil
Columbia
PROTECTION ISLAND N.W.R.
Port Townsend
Island
TULALIP I.R.
Lake Chelan
Franklin Delano Roosevelt Lake
Pend Oreille
Port
Everett
Skykomish
NATIONAL
RESERVATION
GRAND COULEE DAM
LAKE ROOSEVELT NATIONAL RECREATION AREA
SPOKANE INDIAN RES.
Spokane Valley
OLYMPIC
PORT MADISON I.R.
Snohomish
SNOQUALMIE
Spokane
90
MOUNT
Kirkland
Puget Sound
Redmond
Grand Coulee
Banks Lake
Spokane
Spokane
NAT.
Seattle
Bellevue
Medical Lake
Cheney
Bremerton
Renton
KLONDIKE GOLD RUSH N.H.P.
TURNBULL N.W.R.
SKOKOMISH I.R.
Burien
YELLOW N.H.P.
W A S H I N G T O N
Federal Way
Wenatchee
Ephrata
Palouse
Shelton
Tacoma
Auburn
NAT.
Quincy
Moses Lake
Ritzville
90
Hills
PUYALLUP I.R.
Puyallup
FOREST
82
Lakewood
NISQUALLY N.W.R.
Olympia
Tumwater
FOREST
Highest point in Washington
Mt. Rainier
14,411 ft; 4,392 m
Wenatchee Mts.
Yakima
Ellensburg
COLUMBIA N.W.R.
Othello
Pullman
Centralia
Alder L.
MOUNT RAINIER NAT. PARK
Naches
Potholes Reservoir
Connell
Pomeroy
Chehalis
MOUNT BAKER-SNOQUALMIE N.F.
Cowlitz
GIFFORD
SADDLE MT. N.W.R.
Snake
Clarkston
MT. ST. HELENS NAT. VOLCANIC MON.
Mt. St. Helens
8,363 ft; 2,549 m
PINCHOT
Yakima
82
HANFORD REACH NAT. MON.
Lake Sacajawea
Dayton
UMATILLA NATIONAL FOREST
Kelso
YAKAMA
Toppenish
Grandview
Richland
Pasco
McNARY N.W.R.
WHITMAN MISSION N.H.S.
Longview
NATIONAL
INDIAN
Prosser
182
Kennewick
Walla Walla
RIDGEFIELD N.W.R.
Lewis
FOREST
RESERVATION
TOPPENISH N.W.R.
Klickitat
82
Lake Wallula
College Place
Blue Mountains
Battle Ground
CONBOY LAKE N.W.R.
UMATILLA N.W.R.
FT. VANCOUVER N.H.S.
WHITE SALMON N.W.&S.R.
KLICKITAT N.W.&S.R.
Goldendale
COLUMBIA RIVER GORGE NAT. SCENIC AREA
PIERCE N.W.R.
Vancouver
Camas
205
BONNEVILLE DAM
FRANZ LAKE N.W.R.
STEIGERWALD LAKE N.W.R.
Columbia
84
5
205
O R E G O N

IDAHO

MAP KEY

⬤ State capital	Glacier
●●● City	National Wild & Scenic River
+ Mountain peak	Indian Reservation
⚓ Dam	National Park Service unit
--- Trail	⬤⬤⬤ State or national boundary
▢ National Forest	
▢ National Wildlife Refuge	
▢ National Marine Sanctuary	

0   50 miles
0   50 kilometers
Albers Conic Equal-Area Projection

⬤ **HARVEST TIME.** Once a semiarid grassland, the Palouse Hills north of the Snake River in eastern Washington is now a major wheat-producing area.

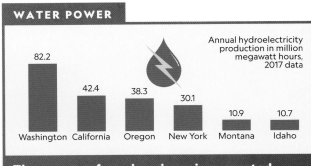

WATER POWER

Annual hydroelectricity production in million megawatt hours, 2017 data

Washington	California	Oregon	New York	Montana	Idaho
82.2	42.4	38.3	30.1	10.9	10.7

The energy of roaring rivers is converted into inexpensive electricity to light homes and power industries in Washington and other states.

Wyoming

When Europeans arrived in the 18th century in what would become Wyoming, various groups of Native Americans were already there, following herds of deer and bison across the plains. In the early 19th century fur traders moved into the area, and settlers followed later along the Oregon Trail. Laramie and many other towns developed around army forts built to protect wagon trains traveling through the territory. Today, fewer than 600,000 people live in all of Wyoming. The state's economy is based on agriculture—mainly grain and livestock production—and mining, especially energy resources. Wyoming has some of the world's largest surface coal mines as well as large deposits of petroleum and natural gas. The environment is also a major resource. Yellowstone, established in 1872, was the world's first national park.

THE BASICS

Statehood
July 10, 1890; 44th state

Total area
(land and water)
97,813 sq mi
(253,335 sq km)

Land area
97,093 sq mi (251,470 sq km)

Population
577,737

Capital
Cheyenne
Population 63,957

Largest city
Cheyenne
Population 63,957

Racial/ethnic groups
92.8% white; 1.3% African American; 1.0% Asian; 2.7% Native American; 10% Hispanic (any race)

Foreign born
3.6%

Urban population
64.8%

Population density
6.0 per sq mi (2.3 per sq km)

GEO WHIZ

The successful reintroduction of wolves into Yellowstone National Park has become a model for saving other species of endangered carnivores.

Devils Tower in northeast Wyoming was the first U.S. national monument.

○ **WANT TO RACE?** Unique to the High Plains of the West, the pronghorn can sprint up to 60 miles an hour (97 km/h).

WESTERN MEADOWLARK
INDIAN PAINTBRUSH

◐ **DRAMATIC LANDSCAPE.** Rising more than 13,000 feet (3,900 m), the Tetons, one of the youngest western mountain ranges, tower over a barn on the valley floor.

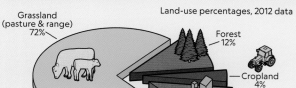

HOME ON THE RANGE

Grassland (pasture & range) 72%

Land-use percentages, 2012 data

Forest 12%

Cropland 4%

Urban & special use areas 12%

Almost three-quarters of Wyoming's land is in pasture. Cattle account for more than 60 percent of the state's agriculture income.

MONTANA

SOUTH DAKOTA

NEBRASKA

COLORADO

Absaroka Range

Lamar

CLARKS FORK YELLOWSTONE
N.W.&S.R.

SHOSHONE

Powell

Lovell

BIGHORN
CANYON

N.R.A.

*Bighorn
Lake*

Bighorn

N. Fork

Shoshone

Cody

BUFFALO BILL S.P.

*Buffalo Bill
Reservoir*

Greybull

S. Fork

YELLOWSTONE

NATIONAL

Greybull

Gooseberry Creek

Worland

Nowood

BIGHORN

NATIONAL

FOREST

Bighorn Mountains

Sheridan

I-90

*Lake
De Smet*

Buffalo

Clear Creek

Crazy Woman Creek

Powder

Little Powder

THUNDER

Gillette

I-90

GREAT

DEVILS
TOWER
N.M.

BLACK

Sundance

KEYHOLE
RESERVOIR S.P.

*Keyhole
Reservoir*

HILLS

NAT.

FOR.

Belle Fourche

BASIN

Newcastle

Black Hills

GER-

NATIONAL

FOREST

Owl Creek

Thermopolis

WIND RIVER

Wind

*Boysen
Reservoir*

Wright

NATIONAL

Cheyenne

Yellowstone

Highest point
in Wyoming

Gannett Peak
13,804 ft
4,207 m

Wind River Range

INDIAN

*Ocean
Lake*

RESERVATION

Riverton

W Y O M I N G

GRASSLAND

I-25

ON

FOREST

Pinedale

*New
Fork*

SHOSHONE

Lander

NATIONAL

FOREST

Wind

South
Pass
7,660 ft
2,335 m

Sweetwater

PATHFINDER
N.W.R.

*Pathfinder
Reservoir*

Continental Divide

Casper

Glenrock

North Platte

Douglas

M O U N T A I N S

Lusk

Niobrara

GLENDO
RESERVOIR S.P.

*Glendo
Reservoir*

Guernsey

North Platte

FT. LARAMIE
N.H.S.

Torrington

Big Sandy

*Big Sandy
Reservoir*

SEEDSKADEE
N.W.R.

Great Divide Basin

Blacks Fork

Green

Green
River

Rock Springs

Continental

FLAMING
GORGE
NATIONAL
RECREATION
AREA

*Flaming
Gorge
Reservoir*

Continental

Divide

SEMINOE
RESERVOIR S.P.

*Seminoe
Reservoir*

Rawlins

I-80

Hanna

*Medicine
Bow*

Medicine Bow

S. Fork Powder

Laramie Mountains

Medicine Bow Mountains

Saratoga

North Platte

ROUTT

BAMFORTH
N.W.R.

*Wheatland
Reservoir*

Wheatland

Laramie

MEDICINE BOW–

Chugwater Creek

Bear Creek

I-25

Horse Creek

Lodgepole Creek

*Lake
Hattie*

Laramie

MORTENSON
LAKE
N.W.R.

HUTTON
LAKE
N.W.R.

Cheyenne

I-80

NATIONAL FOREST

P L A I N S

0   50 miles

0   50 kilometers

Albers Conic Equal-Area Projection

MAP KEY

⊛ State capital

•• City

◼ Point of interest

+ Mountain peak

)⟋ Pass

⟋ Dam

••••••• State boundary

········ Continental Divide

∼∼ National Wild &
Scenic River

▦ Indian Reservation

▦ State Park unit

▦ National Park
Service unit

▤ National Forest

☐ National Grassland

▦ National Wildlife
Refuge

◐ **POWERFUL PLUMBING.**

**Steam and water from
Old Faithful Geyser, in
Yellowstone National Park,
erupt more than 100 feet
(30 m) into the air.**

POLITICAL MAP

U.S. Territories

ACROSS TWO SEAS

Listed below are the five largest* of the fourteen U.S. territories, along with their flags and key information. Two of these territories are in the Caribbean Sea, and three are in the Pacific Ocean.

U.S. CARIBBEAN TERRITORIES

PUERTO RICO

Total area: 5,325 sq mi (13,791 sq km)
Land area: 3,424 sq mi (8,868 sq km)
Population: 3,294,626
Capital: San Juan
Languages: Spanish, English

U.S. VIRGIN ISLANDS

Total area: 733 sq mi (1,898 sq km)
Land area: 134 sq mi (348 sq km)
Population: 106,977
Capital: Charlotte Amalie
Languages: English, Spanish or Spanish Creole, French or French Creole

U.S. PACIFIC TERRITORIES

AMERICAN SAMOA

Total area: 581 sq mi (1,505 sq km)
Land area: 76 sq mi (198 sq km)
Population: 50,826
Capital: Pago Pago
Language: Samoan, English

NORTHERN MARIANA ISLANDS

Total area: 1,976 sq mi (5,117 sq km)
Land area: 182 sq mi (472 sq km)
Population: 51,994
Capital: Saipan (Capital Hill)
Languages: Philippine languages, Chamorro, English

GUAM

Total area: 571 sq mi (1,478 sq km)
Land area: 210 sq mi (543 sq km)
Population: 167,772
Capital: Hagåtña (Agana)
Languages: English, Filipino, Chamorro

OTHER U.S. TERRITORIES

Baker Island, Howland Island, Jarvis Island, Johnston Atoll, Kingman Reef, Midway Islands, Navassa Island, Palmyra Atoll, Wake Island

*Close-up views of the five largest territories are highlighted in enlarged inset maps labeled with a letter. You can see where each territory is by looking for its corresponding letter on the main map.

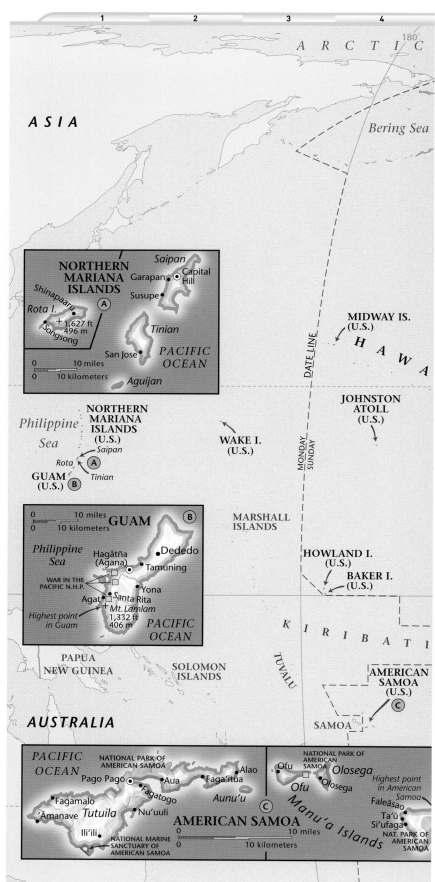

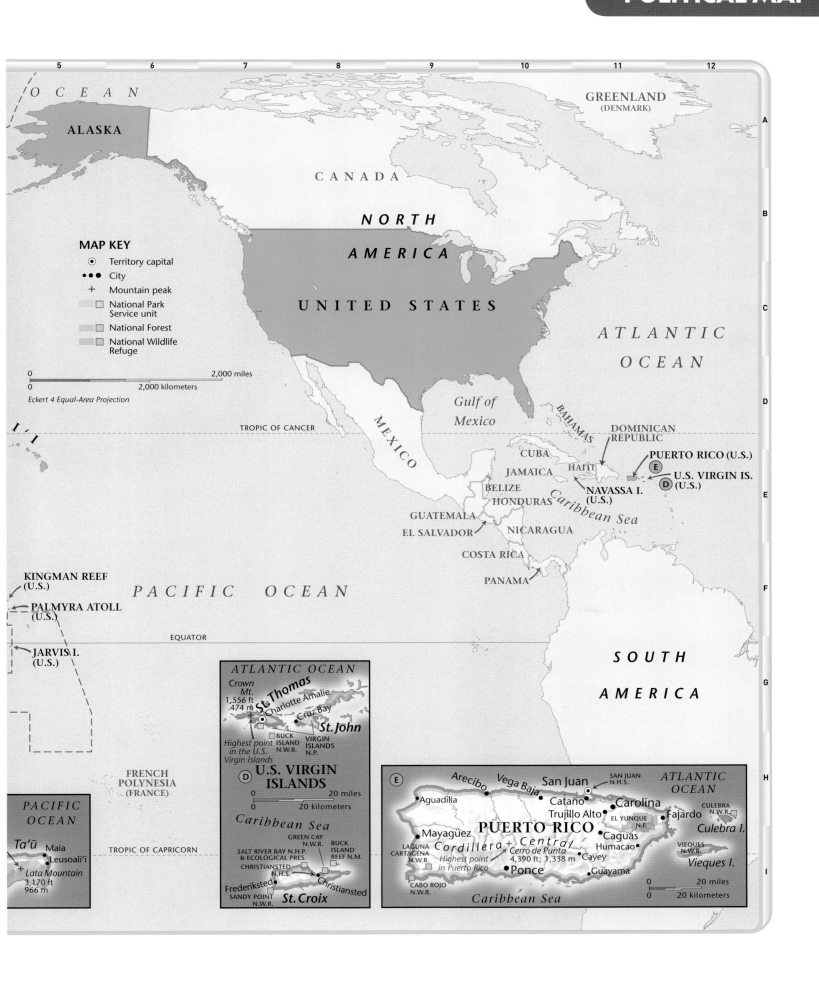

OCEAN

GREENLAND
(DENMARK)

ALASKA

CANADA

NORTH

AMERICA

MAP KEY

⊙ Territory capital
••• City
+ Mountain peak
▢ National Park Service unit
▢ National Forest
▢ National Wildlife Refuge

UNITED STATES

ATLANTIC

OCEAN

0   2,000 miles
0   2,000 kilometers

Eckert 4 Equal-Area Projection

TROPIC OF CANCER

Gulf of
Mexico

BAHAMAS

DOMINICAN
REPUBLIC

MEXICO

CUBA

PUERTO RICO (U.S.)
Ⓔ

HAITI

JAMAICA

U.S. VIRGIN IS.
Ⓓ (U.S.)

BELIZE

NAVASSA I.
(U.S.)

HONDURAS

Caribbean Sea

GUATEMALA

EL SALVADOR

NICARAGUA

COSTA RICA

KINGMAN REEF
(U.S.)

PACIFIC OCEAN

PANAMA

PALMYRA ATOLL
(U.S.)

EQUATOR

JARVIS I.
(U.S.)

SOUTH

AMERICA

ATLANTIC OCEAN

Crown
Mt.
1,556 ft
474 m

St. Thomas

Charlotte Amalie

Cruz Bay

St. John

BUCK
ISLAND
N.W.R.

VIRGIN
ISLANDS
N.P.

Highest point
in the U.S.
Virgin Islands

FRENCH
POLYNESIA
(FRANCE)

Ⓓ U.S. VIRGIN
ISLANDS

0   20 miles
0   20 kilometers

PACIFIC
OCEAN

Caribbean Sea

GREEN CAY
N.W.R.

BUCK
ISLAND
REEF N.M.

Ta'ū

Maia

SALT RIVER BAY N.H.P.
& ECOLOGICAL PRES.

Leusoali'i

CHRISTIANSTED
N.H.S.

TROPIC OF CAPRICORN

+ Lata Mountain
3,170 ft
966 m

Frederiksted

SANDY POINT
N.W.R.

Christiansted

St. Croix

Ⓔ

Arecibo

Vega Baja

San Juan

SAN JUAN
N.H.S.

ATLANTIC
OCEAN

Aguadilla

Cataño

Carolina

CULEBRA
N.W.R.

Trujillo Alto

EL YUNQUE
N.F.

Fajardo

Mayagüez

PUERTO RICO

Caguas

Culebra I.

LAGUNA
CARTAGENA
N.W.R.

Cordillera + Central

Cerro de Punta
4,390 ft; 1,338 m

Humacao

VIEQUES
N.W.R.

Highest point
in Puerto Rico

Cayey

Guayama

Vieques I.

CABO ROJO
N.W.R.

Ponce

0   20 miles
0   20 kilometers

Caribbean Sea

ABOUT THE
TERRITORIES

U.S. Territories

ISLANDS IN THE FAMILY

◗ **PRESERVING TRADITION.** Dancers from American Samoa, dressed in traditional costumes, prepare to perform in the Pacific Arts Festival.

Fourteen territories and commonwealths scattered across the Pacific and Caribbean came under U.S. influence after wars or various international agreements. Although they are neither states nor independent countries, the U.S. government provides economic and military aid. Puerto Rico's 3.3 million residents give it a population greater than that of 21 U.S. states. Many tourists seeking sunny beaches visit the U.S. Virgin Islands, purchased from Denmark for $25 million in 1917. American Samoa, Guam, and the Northern Mariana Islands in the Pacific have sizable populations, but several tiny atolls have no civilian residents and are administered by U.S. military or government departments.

◗ **RELIC OF THE PAST.** Sugar mill ruins on St. John, in the U.S. Virgin Islands, recall a way of life that dominated the Caribbean in the 18th and 19th centuries, when plantations used slave labor to grow sugarcane.

WHERE THE PICTURES ARE

— Managaha I.
  p. 157

— Brown tree snake
  p. 157

Aerial of San Juan
  pp. 156-157

Sugar mill
  p. 156

— Festival dancers
  pp. 156-157

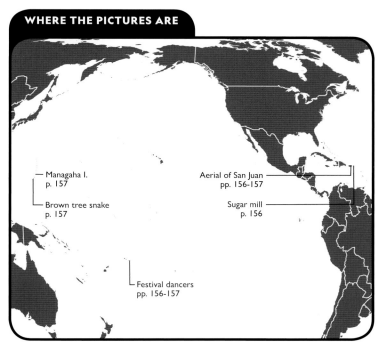

◐ **PACIFIC JEWEL.** Managaha Island sits in the blue-green waters of a lagoon along Saipan's western coast. Portions of the reef around it are dying due to overfishing, warming ocean water, and pollution. The lagoon holds wrecks from battles fought in Northern Mariana waters during World War II.

◐ **ATLANTIC PLAYGROUND.** Modern hotels, catering to more than four million tourists annually, rise above surf and sandy beaches in San Juan, Puerto Rico. The city was founded by the Spanish in 1521.

◑ **STOWAWAY.** The brown tree snake probably arrived in Guam in the 1950s. Since then, it has reduced the island's bird populations and causes power outages when it climbs electric poles.

U.S. FACTS & FIGURES

THE BASICS

Founding
1776

Total area (land and water)
3,796,742 sq mi (9,833,517 sq km)

Land area
3,531,905 sq mi (9,147,593 sq km)

Population
327,167,434

Capital
Washington, D.C.
Population 702,455

Largest city
New York
Population 8,398,748

Racial/ethnic groups
76.6% white; 13.4% African American; 5.8% Asian; 1.3% Native American; 18.1% Hispanic origin (any race)

Foreign born
13.4%

Urban population
80.7%

Population density
92.6 per sq mi (35.8 per sq km)

Language
No official national language; language spoken at home: English 78.2%; Spanish 13.4%

Economy
Agriculture: 0.9%; Industry: 19.1%; Services: 80.0%

BALD EAGLE,
NATIONAL SYMBOL

TOP STATES

Listed below are major producers of selected agriculture products, fish and seafood, and minerals.

AGRICULTURE PRODUCTS

Top 10 Agriculture Producing States (based on cash receipts, 2017)

1. California
2. Iowa
3. Texas
4. Nebraska
5. Minnesota
6. Illinois
7. Kansas
8. North Carolina
9. Wisconsin
10. Indiana

Leading Agriculture Products and Top Producers (based on cash receipts, 2017)

Cattle and calves: Nebraska, Texas, Kansas, Iowa, Colorado

Corn: Iowa, Illinois, Nebraska, Minnesota, Indiana

Soybeans: Illinois, Iowa, Minnesota, Indiana, Nebraska

Milk/dairy products: California, Wisconsin, New York, Idaho, Texas

Broilers: Georgia, Arkansas, North Carolina, Alabama, Mississippi

Hogs: Iowa, Minnesota, North Carolina, Illinois, Indiana

Wheat: North Dakota, Kansas, Montana, Washington, Minnesota

Chicken eggs: Iowa, Georgia, Indiana, Arkansas, Ohio

Cotton lint: Texas, Georgia, California, Mississippi, Arkansas

Grapes: California, Washington, Oregon, New York, Texas

FISH AND SEAFOOD

Volume of wild catch (2017): 9.9 billion lb (4.5 billion kg)
Volume of farmed catch (2016): 633.5 million lb (287.4 million kg)

Top 5 States in Fish and Seafood (based on value of commercial landings, 2017)

1. Alaska
2. Massachusetts
3. Maine
4. Louisiana
5. Washington

MINERALS

Leading Fossil Fuels and Top Producers

Petroleum: Texas, North Dakota, Alaska, California, New Mexico (2017)

Natural gas: Texas, Pennsylvania, Alaska, Oklahoma, Louisiana (2018)

Coal: Wyoming, West Virginia, Pennsylvania, Illinois, Kentucky (2017)

Top 10 Nonfuel Mineral Producing States (based on production value, 2017)

1. Nevada
2. Arizona
3. Texas
4. Alaska
5. California
6. Minnesota
7. Florida
8. Utah
9. Missouri
10. Michigan

Leading Nonfuel Minerals (based on production value, 2017)

1. Crushed stone
2. Gold
3. Cement
4. Copper
5. Sand/gravel
6. Iron ore
7. Lime
8. Zinc
9. Phosphate rock
10. Salt
11. Soda ash
12. Clay

EXTREMES

Strongest Surface Wind in U.S.
231 miles an hour (372 km/h), Mount Washington, New Hampshire, April 12, 1934

World's Tallest Living Tree
Hyperion; a coast redwood in Redwood National Park, California, 380.2 ft (115.9 m) high

World's Largest Gorge
Grand Canyon, Arizona: 277 mi (446 km) long, along the river, 600 ft to 18 mi (183 m to 29 km) wide, 1 mile (1.6 km) deep

Highest Recorded Air Temperature in the World
134°F (56.7°C), Death Valley, California, July 10, 1913

Lowest Recorded Air Temperature in U.S.
Minus 80°F (-62°C), at Prospect Creek, Alaska, January 23, 1971

Highest Point in U.S.
Denali (Mount McKinley), Alaska, 20,310 ft (6,190 m)

Lowest Point in U.S.
Death Valley, California: 282 feet (86 m) below sea level

Longest River System in U.S.
Mississippi-Missouri: 3,710 mi (5,971 km)

Rainiest Spot in U.S.
Waiʻaleʻale (mountain), Hawaiʻi: average annual rainfall 460 in (1,168 cm)

METROPOLITAN AREAS*
(with more than 5 million people)

1. New York, pop. 19,979,477
2. Los Angeles, pop. 13,291,486
3. Chicago, pop. 9,498,716
4. Dallas–Fort Worth, pop. 7,539,711
5. Houston, pop. 6,997,384
6. Washington, D.C., pop. 6,249,950
7. Miami, pop. 6,198,782
8. Philadelphia, pop. 6,096,372
9. Atlanta, pop. 5,949,951

* A metropolitan area is a city and its surrounding suburban areas.

GLOSSARY

atoll a circular coral reef enclosing a tropical lagoon

arid climate type of dry climate in which annual precipitation is generally less than 10 inches (25 cm)

biomass total weight of all organisms found in a given area; organic matter used as fuel

bituminous coal a soft form of coal used in industries and power plants

bog a poorly drained area with wet, spongy ground

broadleaf forest trees with wide leaves that are shed during the winter season

canal an artificial waterway that is used by ships or to carry water for irrigation

center-pivot irrigation an irrigation system that rotates around a piped water source at its middle, often resulting in circular field patterns

city proper an incorporated urban place with boundaries and central government

continental climate temperature extremes with long cold winters and heavy snowfall

continental divide an elevated area that separates rivers flowing toward opposite sides of a continent

Creole a modified form of a language, such as French or Spanish, used for communication between two groups; spoken in some Caribbean islands

delta lowland formed by silt, sand, and gravel deposited by a river at its mouth

desert vegetation plants such as cactus and dry shrubs that have adapted to conditions of low, often irregular precipitation

estuary area near a river's mouth where freshwater and saltwater are mixed by ocean tides

fork place in a river where the stream divides

Fortune 500 company one of the top 500 U.S. companies ranked by revenue

fossil remains of or an impression left by the remains of plants or animals preserved in rock

geothermal energy a clean, renewable form of energy provided by heat from Earth's interior

grassland areas with medium to short grasses; found where precipitation is not sufficient to support tree growth

gross domestic product (GDP) the total value of goods and services produced in a country in a year

highland climate a type of climate found in association with high mountains where elevation affects temperature and precipitation

hundredweight in the U.S., a commercial unit of measure equal to 100 pounds

ice age a very long period of cold climate when glaciers often cover large areas of land

intermittent river/lake a stream or lake that contains water only part of the time, usually after heavy rainfall or snowmelt

Latin America cultural region made up of Mexico and the countries of Central America, the Caribbean, and South America

levee an embankment, usually made of earth or concrete, built to prevent a river from overflowing

lignite low-grade coal used mainly to produce heat in thermal-electric generators

marine west coast climate type of mild climate found on the mid-latitude west coast of continents poleward of the Mediterranean climate

Mediterranean climate type of mild climate found on the mid-latitude west coast of continents

mesa a high, extensive, flat-topped hill; an eroded remnant of a plateau

metropolitan area a city and its surrounding suburbs or communities

mild climate a type of climate that has moderate temperatures with distinct seasons and ample precipitation

pinnacle a tall pillar of rock standing alone or on a summit

plain a large area of relatively flat land that is often covered with grasses

population density the average number of people living on each square mile (sq km) of a specific land area

rangeland areas of grass prairie that are used for grazing livestock

reactor a device that uses controlled nuclear fission to divide an atomic nucleus to generate power

Richter scale ranking of the power of an earthquake; the higher the number, the stronger the quake

Rust Belt a region made up of northeastern and midwestern states that have experienced a decline in heavy industry and an out-migration of population

scale on a map, a means of explaining the relationship between distances on the map and actual distances on Earth's surface

stalactite column of limestone hanging from the ceiling of a cave that forms as underground water drips down and evaporates, leaving dissolved minerals behind

stalagmite column of limestone that forms on the floor of a cave when underground water drips down and evaporates, leaving dissolved minerals behind

staple main item in an economy; also, main food for domestic consumption

subtropical climate type of mild climate found in the southeastern areas of continents

Sunbelt a region made up of southern and western states that are experiencing major in-migration of population and rapid economic growth

tectonic plate one of several thick slabs of Earth's crust that, according to geologic theory, move slowly over the semi-molten rock below

temperate rainforest forests in the coastal Pacific Northwest region of the U.S. with heavy rainfall and mild temperatures

territory land that is under the jurisdiction of a country but that is not a state or a province of that country

tropical zone the area bounded by the Tropic of Cancer and the Tropic of Capricorn, where it is usually warm year-round

tundra vegetation plants, often stunted in size, that have adapted to a cold, short growing season; found in polar regions and at high elevations

urban area associated with a town or city in which most people are engaged in nonagricultural employment

volcanic pipe a vertical opening beneath a volcano through which molten rock has passed

wetland land that is either covered with or saturated by water; includes swamps, marshes, and bogs

POSTAL ABBREVIATIONS

AK- Alaska	DE- Delaware	KY- Kentucky	MS- Mississippi	OH- Ohio	UT- Utah
AL- Alabama	FL- Florida	LA- Louisiana	MT- Montana	OK- Oklahoma	VA- Virginia
AR- Arkansas	GA- Georgia	MA- Massachusetts	NC- North Carolina	OR- Oregon	VI- U.S. Virgin Islands
AS- American Samoa	GU- Guam	MD- Maryland	ND- North Dakota	PA- Pennsylvania	VT- Vermont
AZ- Arizona	HI- Hawai'i	ME- Maine	NE- Nebraska	PR- Puerto Rico	WA- Washington
CA- California	IA- Iowa	MI- Michigan	NH- New Hampshire	RI- Rhode Island	WI- Wisconsin
CO- Colorado	ID- Idaho	MN- Minnesota	NJ- New Jersey	SC- South Carolina	WV- West Virginia
CT- Connecticut	IL- Illinois	MO- Missouri	NM- New Mexico	SD- South Dakota	WY- Wyoming
DC- District of Columbia	IN- Indiana	MP- Northern Mariana Islands	NV- Nevada	TN- Tennessee	
	KS- Kansas		NY- New York	TX- Texas	

MAP ABBREVIATIONS

°E .... degrees East	ME. .... Maine	OREG. .... Oregon
°N .... degrees North	mi .... miles	p., pp. .... page, pages
°S .... degrees South	MICH. .... Michigan	PA. .... Pennsylvania
°W .... degrees West	MINN. .... Minnesota	Pen. .... Peninsula
°C .... degrees Celsius	MISS. .... Mississippi	Pk. .... Peak
°F .... degrees Fahrenheit	MO. .... Missouri	Pres. .... Preserve
ALA. .... Alabama	MONT. .... Montana	Pt. .... Point
ARIZ. .... Arizona	Mt., Mts. .... Mount, Mountain, Mountains	R. .... River
ARK. .... Arkansas	N. .... North	Ra. .... Range
Br. .... Branch	Nat. .... National	Res. .... Reservoir
CALIF. .... California	NAT. MEM. .... National Memorial	RES. .... Reservation
COLO. .... Colorado	NAT. MON., N.M. .... National Monument	R.I. .... Rhode Island
CONN. .... Connecticut	NAT. RES. .... National Reserve	S. .... South
Cr. .... Creek	N.B. .... National Battlefield	S.C. .... South Carolina
D.C. .... District of Columbia	N.B.P. .... National Battlefield Park	S. DAK. .... South Dakota
DEL. .... Delaware	N.B.S. .... National Battlefield Site	S.H.P. .... State Historical Park
E. .... East	N.C. .... North Carolina	S.H.S. .... State Historical Site
Fk. .... Fork	N. DAK. .... North Dakota	S.P. .... State Park
FLA. .... Florida	NEBR. .... Nebraska	Sprs. .... Springs
ft .... feet	NEV. .... Nevada	sq km .... square kilometers
Ft. .... Fort	N.F. .... National Forest	sq mi .... square miles
GA. .... Georgia	N.G. .... National Grassland	St., Ste. .... Saint, Sainte
GDP .... Gross Domestic Product	N.H. .... New Hampshire	Str., Strs. .... Strait, Straits
I., Is. .... Island, Islands	N.H.A. .... National Historical Area	TENN. .... Tennessee
ILL. .... Illinois	N.H.P. .... National Historical Park	TVA .... Tennessee Valley Authority
IND. .... Indiana	N.H.S. .... National Historical Site	U.S. .... United States
INDIAN RES., I.R. .... Indian Reservation	N.J. .... New Jersey	VA. .... Virginia
KANS. .... Kansas	N. MEX. .... New Mexico	VT. .... Vermont
km .... kilometers	N.M.P. .... National Military Park	W. .... West
KY. .... Kentucky	N.P. .... National Park	WASH. .... Washington
L. .... Lake	N.R.A. .... National Recreation Area	WIS. .... Wisconsin
LA. .... Louisiana	N.W.R. .... National Wildlife Refuge	W. VA. .... West Virginia
m .... meters	N.W.&S.R. .... National Wild & Scenic River	WYO. .... Wyoming
MASS. .... Massachusetts	N.Y. .... New York	
MD. .... Maryland	OKLA. .... Oklahoma	

OUTSIDE WEBSITES

The following websites will provide additional valuable information about topics included in this atlas. Other sites can be found by putting topics of interest into your favorite search engine.*

Natural Environment:
Biomes: www.blueplanetbiomes.org
Climate: www.eoearth.org
Climate change: climate.gov/news-features/understanding-climate/global-climate-indicators

Climate:
www.noaa.gov/climate
www.world-climates.com
www.cpc.ncep.noaa.gov

Natural Hazards:
General: www.usgs.gov/mission-areas/natural-hazards
Droughts: droughtmonitor.unl.edu
Earthquakes: earthquake.usgs.gov
Hurricanes: www.nhc.noaa.gov
Tornadoes: www.tornadoproject.com
Tsunamis: www.tsunami.noaa.gov
Volcanoes: www.geo.mtu.edu/volcanoes
Wildfires: www.nifc.gov and www.fs.fed.us/managing-land/fire

Population:
Cities: www.city-data.com
Foreign-born: www.census.gov/topics/population/foreign-born.html
Population clock: www.census.gov/popclock
Population mobility: www.census.gov/data/tables/time-series/demo/geographic-mobility/historic.html
States: www.census.gov/quickfacts/fact/table/US/PST045218

Energy:
www.eia.gov/energyexplained/?page=us_energy_home
www.nrdc.org/issues/increase-renewable-energy

Native American Facts and Resources:
www.native-languages.org/kids.htm

Projections:
gisgeography.com/map-projections

U.S. Territories:
www.cia.gov/library/publications/resources/the-world-factbook/index.html

Check with an adult before going on the internet.

PLACE-NAME INDEX
Abbeville – Benton, AR

Map references are in bold-face (**59**) type. Letters and numbers following in lightface (G6) locate the place-names using the map grid. (Refer to page 7 for more details.)

A

Abbeville, AL **59** G6
Abbeville, LA **69** G4
Abbeville, SC **74** C2
Aberdeen, MD **37** A8
Aberdeen, MS **71** C5
Aberdeen, SD **109** B8
Aberdeen, WA **150** D2
Abert, Lake, OR **147** F5
Abilene, KS **95** C7
Abilene, TX **125** D5
Abingdon, VA **78** E3
Abraham Lincoln Birthplace National Historic Site, KY **67** D6
Absaroka Range, MT, WY **153** A3
Absecon, NJ **43** H3
Acadia N.P., ME **35** G6
Ada, OK **123** D9
Adak Island, AK **133** H8
Adams, MA **38** A1
Adamsville, RI **49** E7
Adel, GA **65** H4
Adirondack Mountains, NY **45** B7
Adirondack Park, NY **45** C7
Admiralty Island Nat. Mon., AK **133** F10
Adrian, MI **97** I7
Afognak Island, AK **133** F6
Afton, WY **152** E1
Agana see Hagåtña, GU **154** F1
Agat, GU **154** G1
Agate Fossil Beds Nat. Mon., NE **102** B1
ʻAmanave, AS **154** I1
Amarillo, TX **125** B3
Amchitka Island, AK **133** H7
American Falls, ID **141** H4
American Falls Reservoir, ID **141** H4
American N.W.&S.R., CA **135** D3
American Samoa (territory), US **154** G4
American, North Fork N.W.&S.R., CA **135** C4
Americus, GA **65** F3
Ames, IA **93** D5
Amesbury, MA **39** A7
Amherst, MA **39** C3
Amherst, NY **44** D2
Amistad N.R.A., TX **125** F4
Amistad Reservoir, TX **125** F4
Amite, LA **69** F7
Amlia Island, AK **133** H9
Ammonoosuc (river), NH **41** D3
Amory, MS **71** C5
Amsterdam, NY **45** D8
Anaconda, MT **142** D3
Anacortes, WA **151** B3
Anadarko, OK **123** D7
Anamosa, IA **93** C9
Anchorage, AK **133** E6
Andalusia, AL **59** G4
Anderson, IN **91** D4
Anderson, SC **74** C2
Anderson Ranch Reservoir, ID **141** G2
Andersonville National Historic Site, GA **65** F3
Andreafsky N.W.&S.R., AK **133** D4
Andreanof Islands, AK **133** H8
Andrew Johnson National Historic Site, TN **77** B10
Andrews, TX **125** D3
Androscoggin (river), ME, NH **41** C4
Angola, IN **91** A5
Aniak, AK **133** E4
Aniakchak N.W.&S.R., AK **133** G4
Aniakchak Nat. Mon. and Preserve, AK **133** G4
Ankeny, IA **93** D5
Ann Arbor, MI **97** H7
Ann, Cape, MA **39** A8
Anna, IL **89** I4
Anna, Lake, VA **79** C9

Agawam, MA **39** D3
Agua Fria (river), AZ **119** E4
Agua Fria Nat. Mon., AZ **119** E4
Aguadilla, PR **155** H9
Aguijan (island), MP **154** D1
Ahoskie, NC **73** B9
Aiken, SC **75** E4
Ainsworth, NE **103** B5
Aitkin, MN **99** D4
Ajo, AZ **119** G3
Akron, CO **137** B8
Akron, OH **107** C7
Alabama (river), AL **59** F3
Alabaster, AL **59** D3
Alagnak N.W.&S.R., AK **133** F5
Alamogordo, NM **121** G5
Alamosa, CO **137** F4
Alamosa, CO **137** F4
Alao, AS **154** H2
Alapaha (river), GA **65** H4
Alaska Highway, AK **133** E8
Alaska Peninsula, AK **132** G3
Alaska Range, AK **133** E6
Alaska, Gulf of, AK **133** G7
Alatna N.W.&S.R., AK **133** B6
Albany, GA **65** G3
Albany, KY **67** E7
Albany, NY **45** E8
Albany, OR **147** C2
Albemarle, NC **73** C5
Albemarle Sound, NC **73** B10
Albert Lea, MN **99** H4
Albertville, AL **59** B4
Albion, MI **97** H6
Albion, NE **103** C7
Albuquerque, NM **121** D4
Alburg, VT **51** A1
Alcoa, TN **77** C8
Alder Lake, WA **151** E4
ʻAlenuihaha Channel, HI **139** D7
Aleutian Islands, AK **133** G6
Aleutian World War II National Historic Area, AK **132** H2
Alexander Archipelago, AK **133** F9
Alexander City, AL **59** D5
Alexandria, IN **91** D4
Alexandria, LA **69** D4
Alexandria, MN **99** E2
Alexandria, SD **109** E9
Alexandria, VA **79** B10
Algoma, WI **111** E7
Algona, IA **93** B4

Alibates Flint Quarries Nat. Mon., TX **125** B4
Alice, TX **125** H6
Aliceville, AL **59** D1
Aliquippa, PA **46** D1
Allagash (river), ME **35** B4
Allagash, ME **35** A4
Allagash Lake, ME **35** C4
Allagash Wilderness Waterway, ME **35** C4
Allatoona Lake, GA **65** C2
Allegheny (river), PA **46** D2
Allegheny Mountains, **26** G2
Allegheny N.W.&S.R., PA **47** B3
Allegheny Portage Railroad National Historic Site, PA **47** D4
Allegheny Reservoir, PA **47** A3
Allendale, SC **75** F4
Allenton, RI **49** E4
Allentown, PA **47** D9
Alliance, NE **102** B2
Alliance, OH **107** C7
Alligator (river), NC **73** B10
Alma, MI **97** G6
Alma, NE **103** E6
Alpena, MI **97** E7
Alpine, TX **124** F2
Altamaha (river), GA **65** G6
Altamont, OR **147** G3
Altavista, VA **79** E7
Alton, IL **89** F3
Alton Bay, NH **41** G4
Altoona, PA **47** D4
Altoona, WI **111** D3
Alturas, CA **135** A4
Altus, OK **123** E6
Altus, Lake, OK **123** D6
Alva, OK **123** A7
Amana Colonies (site), IA **93** D8

Annapolis, MD **37** C8
Anniston, AL **59** C5
Ansonia, CT **31** D3
Anthony, KS **95** E6
Anthony, NM **121** H4
Anthony, RI **49** D4
Antietam N.B., MD **37** B5
Antigo, WI **111** D5
Antlers, OK **123** E11
Antrim, NH **41** H2
Apache-Sitgreaves National Forests, AZ, NM **119** E7
Apalachicola (river), FL **63** B3
Apishapa (river), CO **137** F7
Apostle Islands, WI **111** A4
Apostle Islands National Lakeshore, WI **111** A3
Appalachian Mountains, **54** C5
Appalachian National Scenic Trail, **45** G7
Appalachian Plateau, **26** F2
Apple (river), WI **111** D2
Appleton, WI **111** E6
Appomattox, VA **79** D7
Appomattox (river), VA **79** D8
Appomattox Court House N.H.P., VA **79** D7
Arapaho N.R.A., CO **137** B5
Arbuckle Mountains, OK **123** E8
Arcadia, FL **63** F7
Archbald, PA **47** B9
Arches N.P., UT **149** E6
Arco, ID **141** G4
Ardmore, OK **123** E9
Arecibo, PR **155** H10
Arena, Point, CA **135** D1
Arikaree (river), CO **137** C8
Arkabutla Lake, MS **71** A3
Arkadelphia, AR **61** E3
Arkansas (river), **54** C1
Arkansas City, KS **95** F7
Arkansas Post National Memorial, AR **61** E6
Arlington, TX **125** D7
Arlington, VA **79** B10
Arlington, VT **51** H2
Arlington Heights, IL **89** B5
Armour, SD **109** E8
Aroostook (river), ME **35** C5
Arroyo del Macho (river), NM **121** F5
Artesia, NM **121** G6
Arvada, CO **137** C5
Arvon, Mount, MI **97** C3
Asbury Park, NJ **43** E5
Ash Lawn-Highland (site), VA **79** C8
Ashaway, RI **49** F2
Ashdown, AR **61** F1
Asheboro, NC **73** B6
Asheville, NC **72** C2
Ashland, KY **67** B10
Ashland, ME **35** B5
Ashland, NE **103** D9
Ashland, NH **41** F3
Ashland, OH **107** C5
Ashland, OR **147** G2
Ashland, VA **79** D9
Ashland, WI **111** A3
Ashley, ND **105** F7
Ashtabula, OH **107** A7
Ashtabula, Lake, ND **105** D9
Ashton, RI **49** A4
Ashuelot (river), NH **41** I1
Ashwaubenon, WI **111** E7
Aspen, CO **137** D3
Assateague Island, MD **37** F11
Assateague Island National Seashore, MD, VA **37** F11
Assawoman Canal, DE **33** I7
Assawompset Pond, MA **39** D8
Astoria, OR **146** A1
Atascadero, CA **135** G3
Atchafalaya (river), LA **69** F5
Atchafalaya Bay, LA **69** H5
Atchison, KS **95** B9
Athens, AL **59** A3
Athens, GA **65** C4
Athens, OH **107** F5
Athens, TN **77** C8
Athol, MA **39** B4
Atka Island, AK **133** H9
Atkinson, NE **103** B6
Atkinson, NH **41** I4
Atlanta, GA **65** C2
Atlantic, IA **93** E3
Atlantic City, NJ **43** H4

Atlantic City Expressway, NJ **43** G2
Atmore, AL **59** H2
Atoka, OK **123** E10
Attleboro, MA **39** D6
Atwood Lake, OH **107** C7
Au Sable (river), MI **97** E6
Au Sable N.W.&S.R., MI **97** E7
Aua, AS **154** I2
Aubrey Cliffs, AZ **119** B3
Auburn, AL **59** E5
Auburn, IN **91** B5
Auburn, MA **39** C5
Auburn, ME **35** G3
Auburn, NE **103** D9
Auburn, NY **45** D5
Auburn, WA **151** D4
Audubon Lake, ND **105** C5
Auglaize (river), OH **107** B2
Augusta, GA **65** D6
Augusta, KS **95** E7
Augusta, ME **35** G3
Aunuʻu (island), AS **154** I2
Aurora, CO **137** C6
Aurora, IL **89** B5
Aurora, MO **101** F3
Aurora, NE **103** D7
Austin, MN **99** H5
Austin, RI **49** E3
Austin, TX **125** F6
Austintown, OH **107** B8
Ava, MO **101** F4
Avery Island, LA **69** G4
Azishcohos Lake, ME **35** E2
Aztec, NM **121** A2
Aztec Ruins Nat. Mon., NM **121** A2

B

B. Everett Jordan Lake, NC **73** B6
Backbone Mountain, MD **36** B1
Bad (river), SD **109** D4
Bad Axe, MI **97** F8
Badlands (region), ND **104** E2
Badlands N.P., SD **108** E2
Bainbridge, GA **65** H2
Baker, MT **143** D11
Baker (river), NH **41** F2
Baker City, OR **147** C8
Baker Island (territory), US **154** F4
Bakersfield, CA **135** G5
Bald Knob, AR **61** C5
Baldwin, MS **71** B5
Baltic, CT **31** C7
Baltimore, MD **37** B7
Bamberg, SC **75** E5
Bandelier Nat. Mon., NM **121** C4
Bangor, ME **35** F5
Bangor, PA **47** E9
Banks Lake, WA **151** C7
Bannock Range, ID **141** H5
Bantam Lake, CT **31** B3
Bar Harbor, ME **35** G6
Baraboo, WI **111** F5
Baranof Island, AK **133** G10
Barataria Bay, LA **69** H8
Barberton, OH **107** C6
Bardstown, KY **67** C6
Barkhamsted Reservoir, CT **31** A4
Barkley, Lake, KY, TN **66** E3
Barnegat Bay, NJ **43** F5
Barnstable, MA **39** E9
Barnwell, SC **75** E4
Barre, VT **51** D3
Barren (river), KY **67** D5
Barren River Lake, KY **67** E5
Barrington, RI **49** C5
Barrow, AK **133** A5
Barrow, Point, AK **133** A5
Barstow, CA **135** G6
Bartholomew, Bayou (river), LA **69** B4
Bartlesville, OK **123** A10
Bartlett, TN **76** C1
Barton, VT **51** B4
Bastrop, LA **69** A5
Batavia, NY **44** D3
Batesburg-Leesville, SC **75** D4
Batesville, AR **61** B5
Batesville, MS **71** B3
Bath, ME **35** H3
Bath, NY **45** E4
Baton Rouge, LA **69** F6

Batten Kill (river), VT **51** H1
Battle Creek, ID **141** I1
Battle Creek, MI **97** H5
Battle Ground, WA **151** F3
Battle Mountain, NV **145** B4
Baudette, MN **99** A3
Baxter Springs, KS **95** E10
Bay City, MI **97** G7
Bay City, TX **125** G8
Bay Minette, AL **59** H2
Bay St. Louis, MS **71** I4
Bayard, NM **121** G2
Bayonet Point, FL **63** D6
Bayonne, NJ **43** C5
Bayou Bartholomew (river), AR **61** E5
Bayou La Batre, AL **59** I1
Baytown, TX **125** F8
Beach, ND **104** D1
Beach Haven, NJ **43** G4
Beacon, NY **45** G8
Bear, DE **33** A5
Bear (river), ID, WY **141** I5
Bear Creek, AL **59** B2
Bear Creek, CO, KS **137** F8
Bear Creek N.W.&S.R., MI **97** F5
Bear Lake, ID, UT **149** A5
Bear River Migratory Bird Refuge, UT **149** B3
Bear River Range, ID **141** I6
Bearcamp (river), NH **41** F4
Beardstown, IL **89** D3
Beatrice, NE **103** E9
Beatty, NV **145** D5
Beaufort, SC **75** G6
Beaufort Sea, AK **133** A7
Beaumont, TX **125** F9
Beaver, OK **122** A4
Beaver, UT **149** F3
Beaver (river), OK **122** A4
Beaver (river), PA **46** C1
Beaver Creek, KS **94** B1
Beaver Creek, ND **105** F6
Beaver Creek N.W.&S.R., AK **133** C7
Beaver Dam, WI **111** G6
Beaver Falls, PA **46** D1
Beaver Island, MI **97** D5
Beaver Lake, AR **61** A2
Beaverton, OR **147** B2
Becharof Lake, AK **133** F5
Beckley, WV **81** G4
Bedford, IN **91** G3
Bedford, PA **47** E4
Bedford, VA **79** D6
Beebe, AR **61** C5
Beech Grove, IN **91** E4
Beeville, TX **125** G6
Bel Air, MD **37** A8
Belcourt, ND **105** A6
Belding, MI **97** G5
Belen, NM **121** D4
Belfast, ME **35** G4
Belgrade, MT **143** E5
Bella Vista, AR **61** A1
Bellaire, OH **107** E8
Belle Fourche, SD **108** C1
Belle Fourche (river), SD, WY **108** C2
Belle Glade, FL **63** F9
Bellefontaine, OH **107** D3
Bellefonte, DE **33** A5
Belleville, IL **89** G3
Belleville, KS **95** A6
Bellevue, NE **103** C9
Bellevue, OH **107** B4
Bellevue, WA **151** C4
Bellingham, MA **39** D6
Bellingham, WA **151** A3
Bellows Falls, VT **51** H4
Belmar, NJ **43** E5
Beloit, KS **95** B6
Beloit, WI **111** H6
Belpre, OH **107** F6
Belted Range, NV **145** F5
Belton, MO **101** C9
Belton, SC **74** C2
Belton, TX **125** E7
Belvidere, IL **89** A4
Bemidji, MN **99** C3
Bend, OR **147** D4
Bennettsville, SC **75** B8
Bennington, VT **51** I1
Benson, AZ **119** H6
Benson, MN **99** F2
Benton, AR **61** D4

Benton, IL 89 H4
Benton Harbor, MI 97 H4
Bentonville, AR 61 A1
Bent's Old Fort National Historic Site, CO 137 E7
Berea, KY 67 D8
Beresford, SD 109 F10
Bering Sea, AK 132 F2
Bering Strait, AK 132 C2
Berkeley, CA 135 E2
Berkeley (site), VA 79 D10
Berkeley Heights, NJ 43 C4
Berkshires, The, (hills), MA 38 C1
Berlin, MD 37 E11
Berlin, NH 41 C4
Berlin Lake, OH 107 C7
Bernalillo, NM 121 C4
Bernardsville, NJ 43 C3
Berryville, AR 61 A2
Bessemer, AL 59 D3
Bethany, MO 101 A3
Bethany, OK 123 C8
Bethany Beach, DE 33 I7
Bethel, AK 133 E4
Bethel, CT 31 D2
Bethel, ME 35 G2
Bethesda, MD 37 C6
Bethlehem, CT 31 C3
Bethlehem, PA 47 D9
Bettendorf, IA 93 D10
Beulah, ND 105 D4
Beverly, MA 39 B8
Biddeford, ME 35 H2
Big Bend N.P., TX 125 F3
Big Black (river), MS 71 E2
Big Blue (river), KS, NE 95 A7
Big Blue (river), IN 91 E4
Big Canyon (river), TX 125 F3
Big Coal (river), WV 81 G3
Big Cypress National Preserve, FL 63 G8
Big Cypress Swamp, FL 63 G8
Big Darby Creek, OH 107 D3
Big Darby Creek National Scenic River, OH 107 E4
Big Eau Pleine Reservoir, WI 111 D4
Big Fork (river), MN 99 B4
Big Hole N.B., MT 142 E3
Big Lake, ME 35 E6
Big Lost (river), ID 141 G4
Big Marsh Creek N.W.&S.R., OR 147 E3
Big Muddy (river), IL 89 H4
Big Nemaha (river), NE 103 E9
Big Piney (river), MO 101 F5
Big Piney Creek, AR 61 C3
Big Piney Creek N.W.&S.R., AR 61 B3
Big Raccoon Creek, IN 91 E2
Big Rapids, MI 97 G5
Big Sandy (river), AZ 119 D3
Big Sandy (river), KY, WV 80 F1
Big Sandy (river), WY 153 F3
Big Sandy Creek, CO 137 D7
Big Sioux (river), IA, SD 92 B1
Big Smoky Valley, NV 145 E4
Big South Fork National River and Recreation Area, KY, TN 77 A7
Big Spring, TX 125 D4
Big Stone Gap, VA 78 E2
Big Stone Lake, MN, SD 99 F1
Big Sunflower (river), MS 71 C2
Big Sur N.W.&S.R., CA 135 F3
Big Thicket National Preserve, TX 125 E9
Big Timber, MT 143 E6
Big Wood (river), ID 141 H3
Bighorn (river), MT, WY 128 C6
Bighorn Canyon N.R.A., MT, WY 143 F8
Bighorn Lake, WY 153 A5
Bighorn Mountains, MT, WY 153 A5
Bill Williams (river), AZ 119 E2
Billings, MT 143 E7
Biloxi, MS 71 I5
Biltmore House (site), NC 72 C2
Bingham, ME 35 E3
Binghamton, NY 45 F6
Birch Creek N.W.&S.R., AK 133 C7
Birmingham, AL 59 C3
Bisbee, AZ 119 H7
Biscayne Bay, FL 63 H9
Biscayne N.P., FL 63 H9
Bishop, CA 135 E5
Bishop Creek Reservoir, NV 145 B6
Bismarck, ND 105 E5
Bison, SD 109 B3
Bistineau, Lake, LA 68 B2
Bitter Creek, UT 149 D7
Bitterroot Range, ID, MT 141 B1
Bixby, OK 123 C10
Black (river), VT 51 G3
Black (river), AR, MO 61 B6
Black (river), AZ 119 F7
Black (river), MI 97 G8
Black (river), NY 45 C6
Black (river), SC 75 E8
Black (river), WI 111 E3
Black Belt (region), AL 59 E2
Black Canyon of the Gunnison N.P., CO 137 D2
Black Creek, MS 71 H5
Black Creek N.W.&S.R., MS 71 H4
Black Hawk, SD 108 D2
Black Hills, SD 108 D1
Black Hills, WY 153 B10
Black Mesa (peak), OK 122 A1
Black Mesa, AZ 119 B6
Black Mountain, KY 67 E10
Black Mountain, NC 72 C3
Black Mountains, AZ 119 C2
Black N.W.&S.R., MI 97 C1
Black Range, NM 121 G2
Black River Falls, WI 111 E3
Black Rock Desert, NV 145 B2
Black Rock Range, NV 145 A2
Black Warrior (river), AL 59 E2
Blackfoot, ID 141 H5
Blackfoot Mountains, ID 141 H5
Blackfoot Reservoir, ID 141 H5
Blacks Fork (river), WY 152 G2
Blacksburg, VA 79 E5
Blackstone, VA 79 E9
Blackstone (river), MA, RI 49 A4
Blackwater (river), MO 101 C3
Blackwell, OK 123 A8
Blades, DE 33 H5
Blair, NE 103 C9
Blakely, GA 65 G1
Blanchard, IA 93 F3
Blanchard (river), OH 107 C2
Blanco, Cape, OR 146 F1
Blanding, UT 149 G6
Block Island, RI 49 H3, I3
Block Island Sound, NY 45 G11
Bloodsworth Island, MD 37 F9
Bloomfield, CT 31 B5
Bloomfield, IA 93 F7
Bloomfield, NM 121 A2
Blooming Grove, OH 107 C4
Bloomington, IL 89 D4
Bloomington, IN 91 F3
Bloomington, MN 99 F4
Bloomsburg, PA 47 C7
Blue (river), CO 137 C4
Blue (river), IN 91 H3
Blue (river), OK 123 E10
Blue Earth (river), MN 99 H4
Blue Hill Bay, ME 35 G5
Blue Mesa Reservoir, CO 137 E3
Blue Mountain, NH 41 B3
Blue Mountain, PA 47 D7
Blue Mountains, OR 147 C7
Blue Ridge, GA, NC, VA 54 C5
Blue Ridge Parkway, VA 79 F5
Blue Springs, MO 101 C2
Bluefield, VA 78 E4
Bluefield, WV 81 H3
Bluegrass Parkway, KY 67 C6
Bluegrass Region, KY 67 B7
Bluestone (river), WV 81 H3
Bluestone Lake, WV 81 H4
Bluestone National Scenic River, WV 81 H4
Blythe, CA 135 H8
Blytheville, AR 61 B8
Boaz, AL 59 B4
Boca Raton, FL 63 G9
Bogalusa, LA 69 E8
Bogue Chitto (river), LA, MS 69 E8
Bois Blanc Island, MI 97 D6
Bois Brule (river), WI 111 B3
Bois de Sioux (river), MN 99 E1
Boise, ID 141 G1
Boise City, OK 122 A2
Bolivar, MO 101 E3
Bolivar, TN 76 C2
Bombay Hook Island, DE 33 D5
Bomoseen, Lake, VT 51 F1
Bonne Springs, KS 95 B10
Bonners Ferry, ID 141 A1
Bonneville Dam, OR, WA 147 B3
Booker T. Washington Nat. Mon., VA 79 E6
Boone, IA 93 C5
Boone, NC 72 B3
Boone (river), IA 93 B5
Booneville, AR 61 C2
Booneville, MS 71 A5
Boonsboro, MD 37 A5
Boonville, IN 91 I2
Boonville, MO 101 C4
Boothbay Harbor, ME 35 H4
Borah Peak, ID 141 G3
Borger, TX 125 B4
Borgne, Lake, LA 69 G8
Bossier City, LA 68 B1
Boston, MA 39 C7
Boston Harbor Islands N.R.A., MA 39 C7
Boston Mountains, AR 61 B2
Boston N.H.P., MA 39 B7
Bottineau, ND 105 A5
Boulder, CO 137 B5
Boulder City, NV 145 H6
Boundary Peak, NV 145 E3
Boundary Waters Canoe Area Wilderness, MN 99 B5
Bountiful, UT 149 B4
Bow Lake (lake), NH 41 H4
Bowers Beach, DE 33 F6
Bowie, MD 37 C7
Bowling Green, KY 67 E5
Bowling Green, OH 107 B3
Bowman, ND 104 F2
Boyer (river), IA 93 D3
Boyne City, MI 97 E6
Boysen Reservoir, WY 153 D5
Bozeman, MT 143 E5
Bradenton, FL 63 E6
Bradford, PA 47 A4
Bradford, RI 49 F2
Bradford, VT 51 E4
Brady, TX 125 E5
Brainerd, MN 99 D4
Brandenburg, KY 67 C5
Brandon, MS 71 F3
Brandon, VT 51 E2
Brandywine, DE 33 A5
Brandywine Creek, DE 33 A5
Branford, CT 31 E4
Branson, MO 101 F3
Brantley Lake, NM 121 G7
Brasstown Bald (peak), GA 65 A3
Brattleboro, VT 51 I3
Brazil, IN 91 F2
Brazos (river), TX 125 C5
Breaks Interstate Park, KY 67 D11
Breaux Bridge, LA 69 F4
Breckenridge, TX 125 D5
Bremerton, WA 151 C3
Brenham, TX 125 F7
Brentwood, NY 45 H9
Brentwood, TN 77 B5
Breton Islands, LA 69 H10
Breton Sound, LA 69 H9
Brevard, NC 72 C2
Brewer, ME 35 F5
Brewton, AL 59 H3
Brices Cross Roads National Battlefield Site, MS 71 B5
Bridgeport, CT 31 E3
Bridgeport, NE 102 C2
Bridgeport, WV 81 D5
Bridgeton, NJ 43 H1
Bridgeville, DE 33 H5
Bridgewater, MA 39 D7
Bridgewater, VA 79 C7
Bridgton, ME 35 G2
Brigantine, NJ 43 H4
Brigham City, UT 149 A4
Brighton, CO 137 B6
Brinkley, AR 61 D6
Bristol, NH 41 F3
Bristol, RI 49 D6
Bristol, TN 77 A11
Bristol, VA 78 F3
Bristol, VT 51 D2
Bristol Bay, AK 133 F4
Bristow, OK 123 C10
Britton, SD 109 A8
Britton Hill (peak), FL 62 A2
Broad (river), GA 65 C5
Broad (river), NC, SC 75 A4
Broad Brook, CT 31 A5
Broadkill Beach, DE 33 G7
Broadus, MT 143 E10
Brockton, MA 39 D7
Broken Arrow, OK 123 B10
Broken Bow, NE 103 C5
Broken Bow, OK 123 E12
Broken Bow Lake, OK 123 E12
Bromley Mountain, VT 51 G2
Brookfield, MO 101 B4
Brookfield, WI 111 G7
Brookhaven, MS 71 G2
Brookings, OR 146 G1
Brookings, SD 109 D10
Brookline, MA 39 C7
Brooklyn, CT 31 B8
Brooklyn Park, MN 99 F4
Brooks Range, AK 133 B4
Brookside, DE 33 B4
Brookville Lake, IN 91 F5
Brown v. Board of Education N.H.S., KS 95 C8
Brownfield, TX 125 D3
Browning, MT 142 B3
Brownlee Reservoir, ID, OR 141 F1
Browns Mills, NJ 43 F3
Brownsville, TN 76 C2
Brownsville, TX 125 I7
Brownville Junction, ME 35 E4
Brownwood, TX 125 E5
Brule (river), MI, WI 111 B6
Bruneau (river), ID, NV 141 H2
Bruneau, East Fork (river), ID 141 I2
Brunswick, GA 65 H7
Brunswick, MD 37 B5
Brunswick, ME 35 H3
Brunswick, OH 107 B6
Brush, CO 137 B7
Bryan, OH 107 B2
Bryan, TX 125 E7
Bryant, AR 61 D4
Bryant Creek, MO 101 F4
Bryce Canyon N.P., UT 149 G3
Buck Creek, OK 123 D5
Buck Island Reef Nat. Mon., VI 155 I8
Buckeye Lake, OH 107 E5
Buckhannon, WV 81 D5
Buckner Creek, KS 95 D3
Bucksport, ME 35 F5
Bucktown, MD 37 E9
Bucyrus, OH 107 C4
Budd Lake, NJ 43 B3
Buena Vista, VA 79 D7
Buffalo, NY 44 D2
Buffalo, OK 123 A5
Buffalo, SD 108 A2
Buffalo (river), TN 77 C4
Buffalo, WY 153 B7
Buffalo (river), AR 61 B2
Buffalo Bill Reservoir, WY 153 B4
Buffalo National River, AR 61 B3
Buffalo N.W.&S.R., AR 61 B2
Buhl, ID 141 I3
Bull Shoals Lake, AR, MO 61 A3
Bullfrog Creek, UT 149 G5
Bullhead City, AZ 119 D2
Bunkie, LA 69 E4
Burien, WA 151 C4
Burkburnett, TX 125 C6
Burke, SD 109 F7
Burley, ID 141 I5
Burlington, CO 137 C9
Burlington, IA 93 F9
Burlington, KS 95 D9
Burlington, NC 73 B6
Burlington, NJ 43 E2
Burlington, VT 51 C1
Burlington, WI 111 H6
Burns, OR 147 E6
Burt Lake, MI 97 D6
Burton, MI 97 G7
Burton, SC 75 G6
Burwell, NE 103 C6
Butler, MO 101 D2
Butler, PA 46 C2
Butte, MT 143 E4
Buzzards Bay, MA 39 E8

C

C.J. Strike Reservoir, ID 141 H1
C.W. McConaughy, Lake, NE 103 C3
Caballo Reservoir, NM 121 G3
Cabinet Mountains, ID, MT 142 A1
Cabot, AR 61 D5
Cabot, Mount, NH 41 C4
Cabrillo Nat. Mon., CA 135 I5
Cacapon (river), WV 81 D8
Cache (river), AR 61 C6
Cache La Poudre N.W.&S.R., CO 137 A5
Cactus Range, NV 145 F4
Caddo Lake, LA 68 A1
Cadillac, MI 97 F5
Cadillac Mountain, ME 35 G6
Caesar Creek Lake, OH 107 F2
Cagles Mill Lake, IN 91 F2
Caguas, PR 155 I11
Cahaba (river), AL 59 E3
Cairo, GA 65 H3
Cairo, IL 89 I4
Calais, ME 35 E7
Calamus (river), NE 103 B5
Calamus Reservoir, NE 103 B6
Calcasieu (river), LA 69 F3
Calcasieu Lake, LA 68 G2
Caldwell, ID 141 G1
Caldwell, NJ 43 C4
Caledonia, MN 99 H6
Calexico, CA 135 I7
Calhoun, GA 65 B2
Caliente, NV 145 F7
California, MO 101 D4
California, Gulf of, 114 F1
Caloosahatchee (river), FL 63 F8
Calvert City, KY 66 E2
Camas, WA 151 G3
Cambridge, MA 39 B7
Cambridge, MD 37 D9
Cambridge, NE 103 E5
Cambridge, OH 107 E6
Camden, AR 61 F3
Camden, DE 33 E5
Camden, ME 35 G4
Camden, NJ 43 F2
Camden, SC 75 C6
Camels Hump (peak), VT 51 C2
Cameron, MO 101 B2
Camilla, GA 65 H3
Camp Verde, AZ 119 D5
Campbell Hill (peak), OH 107 D3
Campbellsville, KY 67 D6
Canaan, CT 31 A2
Canaan, NH 41 F2
Canaan, VT 51 A6
Canadian (river), NM, OK, TX 116 C6
Canadian, North (river), OK 123 B6
Canandaigua, NY 45 D4
Canaveral National Seashore, FL 63 C8
Canaveral, Cape, FL 63 D9
Candlewood, Lake, CT 31 D2
Cando, ND 105 B7
Cane River Creole N.H.P. and Heritage Area, LA 68 D2
Caney (river), KS, OK 123 A10
Caney Fork (river), TN 77 C6
Cannonball (river), ND 105 E3
Cañon City, CO 137 E5
Cañon Largo (river), NM 121 B3
Canoochee (river), GA 65 F6
Canterbury, NH 41 G3
Canton, IL 89 D3
Canton, MO 101 A5
Canton, MS 71 E3
Canton, OH 107 C7
Canton, SD 109 E10
Canyon, TX 125 B3
Canyon Creek, ID 141 H1
Canyon de Chelly Nat. Mon., AZ 119 B7
Canyon Ferry Lake, MT 143 D5
Canyonlands N.P., UT 149 F6
Canyons of the Ancients Nat. Mon., CO 136 F1
Cap Rock Escarpment, TX 125 D4
Cape Charles, VA 79 D11
Cape Cod Bay, MA 39 D9

Cape Cod Canal, MA 39 D8
Cape Cod National Seashore, MA 39 D10
Cape Coral, FL 63 G7
Cape Elizabeth, ME 35 H3
Cape Fear (river), NC 73 D7
Cape Girardeau, MO 101 E8
Cape Hatteras National Seashore, NC 73 C11
Cape Island, SC 75 F8
Cape Krusenstern Nat. Mon., AK 133 B4
Cape Lookout National Seashore, NC 73 D10
Cape May, NJ 43 I2
Cape May Canal, NJ 43 I2
Cape May Court House, NJ 43 I3
Capitol Hill, MP 154 C2
Capitol Reef N.P., UT 149 F5
Captain Cook, HI 139 F8
Capulin Volcano Nat. Mon., NM 121 A7
Carbondale, CO 137 C3
Carbondale, IL 89 H4
Carbondale, PA 47 B9
Caribou, ME 35 B6
Caribou Range, ID 141 G6
Carl Sandburg Home National Historic Site, NC 72 C3
Carlin, NV 145 B5
Carlinville, IL 89 F3
Carlisle, PA 47 E6
Carlsbad, NM 121 G7
Carlsbad Caverns N.P., NM 121 H6
Carlyle Lake, IL 89 G4
Carmel, IN 91 E4
Carmi, IL 89 H5
Caro, MI 97 G7
Carolina, PR 155 H11
Carolina, RI 49 F3
Carp N.W.&S.R., MI 97 D5
Carrington, ND 105 D7
Carrizo Creek, NM 121 B7
Carrizo Plain Nat. Mon., CA 135 G4
Carrizo Springs, TX 125 G5
Carrizozo, NM 121 F5
Carroll, IA 93 C3
Carrollton, GA 65 D1
Carson (river), NV 145 D2
Carson City, NV 145 D2
Carson Sink (river), NV 145 C3
Carthage, IL 89 D2
Carthage, MO 101 F2
Carthage, MS 71 E4
Caruthersville, MO 101 G8
Cary, NC 73 B7
Casa Grande, AZ 119 F5
Casa Grande Ruins Nat. Mon., AZ 119 F5
Cascade, ID 141 F1
Cascade Range, 128 C2
Cascade Siskiyou Nat. Mon., OR 147 G3
Cascade, Lake, ID 141 F1
Casco Bay, ME 35 H3
Casper, WY 153 D7
Cass (river), MI 97 G7
Casselman (river), PA 47 F3
Casselton, ND 105 D9
Castillo de San Marcos Nat. Mon., FL 63 B8
Castine, ME 35 G5
Castle Dale, UT 149 E5
Castle Rock, CO 137 C6
Castle Rock Lake, WI 111 F5
Castleton, VT 51 F2
Catahoula Lake, LA 69 D4
Catalina, AZ 119 G6
Cataño, PR 155 H11
Catawba (river), NC, SC 75 B5
Cathedral Bluffs, CO 136 B1
Catoctin Mountain Park, MD 37 A5
Catonsville, MD 37 B7
Catskill, NY 45 E8
Catskill Mountains, NY 45 F8
Catskill Park, NY 45 F7
Cattaraugus Creek, NY 44 E2
Cavalier, ND 105 A9
Cave City, KY 67 D6
Cave Run Lake, KY 67 C9
Cayce, SC 75 D5
Cayey, PR 155 I11
Cayuga Lake, NY 45 E5
Cecil M. Harden Lake, IN 91 E2
Cedar (river), IA 93 A6
Cedar (river), MI 97 D3
Cedar (river), NE 103 C6
Cedar Bluff Reservoir, KS 95 C3
Cedar Breaks Nat. Mon., UT 149 G2
Cedar City, UT 149 G2
Cedar Creek, IN 91 B5
Cedar Creek, ND 104 E2
Cedar Creek Reservoir, ID 141 I2
Cedar Falls, IA 93 C7
Cedar Rapids, IA 93 D8
Celina, OH 107 D2
Centennial Mountains, ID 141 F5
Center, ND 105 D4
Center Hill Lake, TN 77 B6
Center Ossipee, NH 41 F4
Center Point, AL 59 C3
Center Sandwich, NH 41 F4
Centereach, NY 45 H9
Centerville, IA 93 F6
Centerville, OH 107 E2
Centerville, UT 149 B4
Central City, IA 93 C8
Central City, NE 103 C7
Central Falls, RI 49 B5
Central Lowland (plain), 84 E5
Central Point, OR 147 F2
Centralia, IL 89 G4
Centralia, MO 101 C5
Centralia, WA 151 E3
Centreville, MS 71 H1
Cerro de Punta (mountains), PR 155 I10
Chaco Culture N.H.P., NM 121 B2
Chacuaco Canyon, CO 137 F7
Chadron, NE 102 A2
Challis, ID 141 F3
Chalmette, LA 69 G8
Chama, NM 121 A4
Chamberlain, SD 109 D7
Chamberlain Lake, ME 35 C4
Chambersburg, PA 47 E5
Champaign, IL 89 E5
Champlain, Lake, NY, VT 45 B9
Chandeleur Islands, LA 69 G10
Chandeleur Sound, LA 69 G10
Chandler, AZ 119 F5
Channel Islands, CA 135 H3
Channel Islands N.P., CA 135 H3
Channel Islands National Marine Sanctuary, CA 135 H4
Chanute, KS 95 E9
Chaparral, NM 121 H4
Chapel Hill, NC 73 B6
Chappaquiddick Island, MA 39 F9
Chariton, IA 93 E6
Chariton (river), IA, MO 101 B4
Charles (river), MA 39 C6
Charles City, IA 93 B7
Charles Mound, IL 89 A3
Charles Pinckney National Historic Site, SC 75 F8
Charles Town, WV 81 D10
Charleston, IL 89 F5
Charleston, MO 101 F8
Charleston, SC 75 G7
Charleston, WV 81 F3
Charlestown, IN 91 H4
Charlestown, NH 41 G1
Charlestown, RI 49 G3
Charley N.W.&S.R., AK 133 C7
Charlotte, MI 97 H6
Charlotte, NC 73 C4
Charlotte Amalie, VI 155 G7
Charlotte Harbor, FL 63 F7
Charlottesville, VA 79 C8
Chatham, MA 39 E10
Chattahoochee (river), AL, GA 54 D5
Chattahoochee River N.R.A., GA 65 C2
Chattanooga, TN 77 D6
Chattooga (river), SC 74 B1
Chattooga N.W.&S.R., GA, NC, SC 65 A4
Chautauqua Lake, NY 44 E1
Cheaha Mountain, AL 59 C5
Cheat (river), WV 81 C6
Cheat Mountain, WV 81 F6
Cheboygan, MI 97 D6
Checotah, OK 123 C11
Cheektowaga, NY 44 D2
Cheesequake, NJ 43 D4
Chehalis, WA 151 E3
Chehalis (river), WA 150 D2
Chelan, Lake, WA 151 B6
Chelmsford, MA 39 B6
Chemung (river), NY 45 E4
Cheney, WA 151 C9
Cheney Reservoir, KS 95 D6
Chepachet, RI 49 B3
Cheraw, SC 75 B7
Cherokee, IA 92 B2
Cherokee Lake, TN 77 A9
Cherokee Village, AR 61 A5
Cherokees, Lake O' the, OK 123 A11
Cherry Creek, SD 109 C3
Cherry Creek Range, NV 145 C6
Cherry Hill, NJ 43 F2
Chesapeake, VA 79 E11
Chesapeake and Delaware Canal, DE, MD 33 C4
Chesapeake and Ohio Canal, MD 36 A2
Chesapeake and Ohio Canal N.H.P., MD 37 B5
Chesapeake Bay, MD, VA 26 H4
Chesapeake Bay Bridge see William Preston Lane Jr. Memorial Bridge, MD 37 C8
Chesapeake Bay Bridge-Tunnel, VA 79 E11
Chesapeake Beach, MD 37 D8
Cheshire, CT 31 D4
Cheshire Reservoir, MA 38 B1
Chester, IL 89 H3
Chester, PA 47 F9
Chester, SC 75 B5
Chester, VA 79 D9
Chester, VT 51 G3
Chester, WV 81 A5
Chester (bay), MD 37 C8
Chesterfield, CT 31 D7
Chestertown, MD 37 B9
Chesuncook Lake, ME 35 D4
Cheswold, DE 33 E5
Chetco (river), OR 146 G1
Chetco N.W.&S.R., OR 146 G1
Chevelon Creek, AZ 119 D6
Cheyenne, WY 153 G9
Cheyenne (river), SD, WY 109 C3
Cheyenne Bottoms (lake), KS 95 C5
Cheyenne Wells, CO 137 D9
Chicago, IL 89 B6
Chichagof Island, AK 133 F9
Chickamauga and Chattanooga N.M.P., GA, TN 65 A1
Chickamauga Lake, TN 77 C7
Chickasaw N.R.A., OK 123 E9
Chickasawhay (river), MS 71 G5
Chickasha, OK 123 D8
Chico, CA 135 C3
Chicopee, MA 39 C3
Chikaskia (river), OK 123 A8
Childress, TX 125 C5
Chilikadrotna N.W.&S.R., AK 133 E5
Chillicothe, IL 89 C3
Chillicothe, MO 101 B3
Chillicothe, OH 107 F4
Chimayo, NM 121 B5
Chimney Rock National Historic Site, NE 102 C1
Chincoteague, VA 79 C12
Chincoteague Bay, MD 37 F11
Chinle, AZ 119 B7
Chinle Wash (river), AZ 119 A7
Chino Valley, AZ 119 D4
Chinook, MT 143 B7
Chippewa (river), MN 99 E2
Chippewa (river), WI 111 C3
Chippewa Falls, WI 111 D3
Chippewa, Lake, WI 111 B3
Chiputneticook Lakes, ME 35 D6
Chiricahua Nat. Mon., AZ 119 H7
Chisholm, MN 99 C5
Chittenden Reservoir, VT 51 E2
Choctawhatchee (river), AL, FL 62 B2
Choptank (bay), MD 37 D8
Choptank (river), MD 37 D9
Choteau, MT 143 B4
Chowan (river), NC 73 A9
Christiansburg, VA 79 E5
Christiansted, VI 155 I8
Christiansted National Historic Site, VI 155 I7
Christina (river), DE 33 B4
Christmas Lake Valley, OR 147 E5
Chubbuck, ID 141 H5
Chugach Mountains, AK 133 E7
Chukchi Sea, AK 132 A3
Chula Vista, CA 135 I6
Church Hill, TN 77 A10
Churchill Lake, ME 35 C4
Cicero, IL 89 B5
Cimarron (river), CO, KS, OK 123 B7
Cimarron Turnpike, OK 123 B9
Cimarron, North Fork (river), CO, KS 94 E1
Cincinnati, OH 107 G1
Cinnaminson, NJ 43 F2
Circle, MT 143 C10
Circleville, OH 107 F4
Citronelle, AL 59 H1
City of Rocks National Reserve, ID 141 I4
Clackamas N.W.&S.R., OR 147 C3
Clan Alpine Mountains, NV 145 D3
Clanton, AL 59 E3
Clara Barton National Historic Site, MD 37 C6
Claremont, NH 41 G1
Claremore, OK 123 B10
Clarinda, IA 93 F3
Clarion, PA 47 C3
Clarion (river), PA 47 C3
Clarion N.W.&S.R., PA 47 C3
Clark, SD 109 C9
Clark Fork (river), MT 142 B1
Clarks Fork (river), MT 143 E7
Clarks Fork Yellowstone N.W.&S.R., WY 153 A3
Clarksburg, WV 81 D5
Clarksdale, MS 71 B2
Clarkston, WA 151 E10
Clarksville, AR 61 C2
Clarksville, TN 77 A4
Clay Center, KS 95 B7
Claymont, DE 33 A6
Clayton, DE 33 D4
Clayton, NM 121 B8
Clear Creek, AZ 119 D5
Clear Creek, WY 153 A7
Clear Lake, CA 135 C2
Clear Lake, IA 93 A5
Clear Lake, SD 109 C10
Clearfield, PA 47 C4
Clearfield, UT 149 B3
Clearwater, FL 63 E6
Clearwater, SC 75 E3
Clearwater (river), ID 141 D1
Clearwater, Middle Fork N.W.&S.R., ID 141 D2
Clearwater Mountains, ID 141 D2
Clearwater, North Fork (river), ID 141 D2
Clearwater, South Fork (river), ID 141 E2
Clemson, SC 74 B2
Cleveland, MS 71 C2
Cleveland, OH 107 B6
Cleveland, TN 77 D7
Clifton, AZ 119 F7
Clifton, NJ 43 B4
Clifton Forge, VA 79 D6
Clinch (river), TN, VA 77 A9
Clinch Mountain, VA 78 E3
Clingmans Dome (peak), TN 77 C9
Clinton, AR 61 B4
Clinton, CT 31 E5
Clinton, IA 93 D10
Clinton, IL 89 E4
Clinton, IN 91 E2
Clinton, MO 101 D3
Clinton, MS 71 E2
Clinton, NC 73 C7
Clinton, OK 123 C6
Clinton, SC 75 C3
Clinton, TN 77 B8
Cloquet, MN 99 D5
Clovis, NM 121 E8
Clyde (river), VT 51 A5
Coast Mountains, AK 133 E10
Coast Ranges, CA 135 B2
Coast Ranges, 128 B2
Coastal Plain, 54 E2
Coatesville, PA 47 E8
Cobble Mountain Reservoir, MA 38 C2
Cobleskill, NY 45 E7
Cocheco (river), NH 41 G5
Cochetopa Hills, CO 137 E4
Cockeysville, MD 37 A7
Coconino Plateau, AZ 119 C4
Cod, Cape, MA 39 E9
Cody, WY 153 B4
Coeur d'Alene, ID 141 B1
Coeur d'Alene (river), ID 141 C1
Coeur d'Alene Lake, ID 141 C1
Coffeyville, KS 95 F9
Cohansey (river), NJ 43 H1
Colby, KS 94 B2
Colchester, CT 31 C6
Cold Spring, MN 99 F3
Coldwater, MI 97 I6
Coldwater (river), MS 71 B2
Colebrook, NH 41 B3
Coleman, OK 123 E10
Coleman, TX 125 E5
College, AK 133 C7
College Place, WA 151 F8
College Station, TX 125 E7
Collierville, TN 76 D1
Collins, MS 71 G4
Collinsville, CT 31 B4
Collinsville, VA 79 E6
Colonial Beach, VA 79 C10
Colonial N.H.P., VA 79 D10
Colorado (river), 128 H4
Colorado City, AZ 119 A3
Colorado Nat. Mon., CO 136 D1
Colorado Plateau, AZ 114 B2
Colorado Springs, CO 137 D6
Colstrip, MT 143 E9
Columbia, MD 37 B7
Columbia, MO 101 C4
Columbia, MS 71 G3
Columbia, PA 47 E7
Columbia, SC 75 D5
Columbia, TN 77 C4
Columbia (river), OR, WA 147 A2
Columbia City, IN 91 B5
Columbia Falls, MT 142 B2
Columbia Plateau, OR 128 B3
Columbia River Gorge National Scenic Area, OR, WA 151 F4
Columbus, GA 65 F1
Columbus, IN 91 F4
Columbus, KS 95 E10
Columbus, MS 71 C5
Columbus, MT 143 E7
Columbus, NE 103 C8
Columbus, OH 107 E4
Columbus Salt Marsh (river), NV 145 E3
Colville, WA 151 B9
Colville (river), AK 133 B5
Colville (river), WA 151 B9
Combahee (river), SC 75 G6
Compensating Reservoir, CT 31 B4
Conanicut Island, RI 49 E5
Conchas (river), NM 121 C6
Conchas Lake, NM 121 C7
Concord, MA 39 B6
Concord, NC 73 C5
Concord, NH 41 H3
Concord (river), MA 39 B6
Concordia, KS 95 B6
Conecuh (river), AL 59 G4
Conejos (river), CO 137 G4
Conemaugh (river), PA 47 D3
Confusion Range, UT 149 D1
Congamond Lakes, CT 31 A4
Congaree (river), SC 75 D5
Congaree N.P., SC 75 D5
Conneaut, OH 107 A8
Connecticut (river), CT, MA, NH, VT 26 D6
Connell, WA 151 E8
Connellsville, PA 46 E2
Connersville, IN 91 E5
Conrad, MT 143 B4
Conroe, TX 125 F8

Continental Divide, CO, ID, MT, NM, WY 141 E4
Contoocook, NH 41 H3
Contoocook (river), NH 41 H3
Conway, AR 61 C4
Conway, NH 41 E4
Conway, SC 75 D9
Conway Lake, NH 41 E4
Cook Inlet, AK 133 E6
Cookeville, TN 77 B6
Coolidge, AZ 119 F5
Coon Rapids, MN 99 F4
Cooper (river), SC 75 F7
Cooperstown, ND 105 D8
Cooperstown, NY 45 E7
Coos (river), OR 146 E1
Coos Bay, OR 146 E1
Coosa (river), AL, GA 59 D4
Coosawattee (river), GA 65 B2
Coosawhatchie (river), SC 75 F5
Copper (river), AK 133 E7
Copperas Cove, TX 125 E6
Coquille, OR 146 E1
Coral Springs, FL 63 G9
Coralville, IA 93 D8
Coram, NY 45 H9
Corbin, KY 67 E8
Cordele, GA 65 F3
Cordell Bank National Marine Sanctuary, CA 135 D1
Cordillera Central (mountains), PR 155 I9
Cordova, AK 133 E7
Core Sound, NC 73 D10
Corinth, MS 71 A5
Corning, AR 61 A7
Corning, NY 45 F4
Coronado Nat. Mon., AZ 119 H6
Corpus Christi, TX 125 H7
Corpus Christi Bay, TX 114 G8
Corrumpa Creek, NM 121 A7
Corry, PA 46 A2
Corsicana, TX 125 D7
Cortez, CO 136 F1
Cortez Mountains, NV 145 C5
Cortland, NY 45 E5
Corvallis, OR 147 C2
Corydon, IN 91 H4
Coshocton, OH 107 D6
Cossatot (river), AR 61 E1
Cossatot N.W.&S.R., AR 61 E1
Coteau des Prairies, SD 109 A9
Cottage Grove, OR 147 D2
Cottonwood, AZ 119 D4
Coudersport, PA 47 B5
Council Bluffs, IA 92 E2
Council Grove, KS 95 C8
Coventry, CT 31 B6
Coventry Center, RI 49 D3
Covington, GA 65 D3
Covington, KY 67 A8
Covington, LA 69 F8
Covington, VA 79 D6
Cowlitz (river), WA 151 E3
Cowpasture (river), VA 79 C6
Cowpens N.B., SC 75 A4
Cozad, NE 103 D5
Craig, CO 137 B2
Crane Creek Reservoir, ID 141 F1
Cranston, RI 49 C4
Crater Lake, OR 147 F3
Crater Lake N.P., OR 147 F3
Craters of the Moon Nat. Mon. and Preserve, ID 141 H4
Crawford, NE 102 A1
Crawfordsville, IN 91 D2
Crazy Horse Memorial, SD 108 D1
Crescent City, CA 135 A1
Crescent Creek N.W.&S.R., OR 147 E3
Cresco, IA 93 A7
Creston, IA 93 E4
Crestview, FL 62 A2
Crestwood Village, NJ 43 F4
Crete, NE 103 D8
Crisfield, MD 37 F9
Crooked (river), OR 147 D5
Crooked N.W.&S.R., OR 147 C4
Crooked, North Fork N.W.&S.R., OR 147 D5
Crookston, MN 99 C1
Crosby, ND 104 A2
Crossett, AR 61 G5
Crossville, TN 77 B7
Crow Agency, MT 143 E8
Crow Creek, CO 137 B6
Crow Creek, SD 109 D7
Crow Wing (river), MN 99 D3
Crow, North Fork (river), MN 99 E3
Crow, South Fork (river), MN 99 F3
Crowley, LA 69 G4
Crowleys Ridge, AR 61 C7
Crown Mountain, VI 155 G7
Crown Point, IN 91 B2
Crownpoint, NM 121 C2
Cruz Bay, VI 155 G8
Crystal Lake, NH 41 G4
Crystal Springs, MS 71 F2
Cuivre (river), MO 101 C6
Culebra Island, PR 155 I12
Culebra Range, CO 137 G5
Cullman, AL 59 B3
Culpeper, VA 79 B8
Cumberland, KY 67 E10
Cumberland, MD 36 A2
Cumberland (river), KY, TN 54 C4
Cumberland Gap, KY, VA 67 E9
Cumberland Gap N.H.P., KY, TN, VA 67 E9
Cumberland Hill, RI 49 A4
Cumberland Island, GA 65 H7
Cumberland Island National Seashore, GA 65 H7
Cumberland, Lake, KY 67 E7
Cumberland Mountains, KY 67 E9
Cumberland Plateau, 54 C5
Curecanti N.R.A., CO 137 E3
Current (river), MO 101 E5
Currituck Sound, NC 73 A10
Cushing, OK 123 C9
Custer, SD 108 D1
Cut Bank, MT 143 A4
Cuyahoga (river), OH 107 B7
Cuyahoga Falls, OH 107 B6
Cuyahoga Valley N.P., OH 107 B6
Cynthiana, KY 67 B8
Cypress Swamp, DE 33 I6

D

Dagsboro, DE 33 I6
Dahlonega, GA 65 B3
Dale City, VA 79 B9
Dale Hollow Lake, KY,TN 77 A7
Daleville, AL 59 G5
Dallas, OR 147 C2
Dallas, TX 125 D7
Dalles, The, OR 147 B4
Dalton, GA 65 B2
Dalton, MA 38 B1
Dan (river), NC, VA 73 A6
Danbury, CT 31 D2
Danforth, ME 35 D6
Danielson, CT 31 B8
Dannemora, NY 45 A8
Dansville, NY 44 E3
Danvers, MA 39 B7
Danville, IL 89 E6
Danville, KY 67 D7
Danville, VA 79 F7
Daphne, AL 59 I1
D'Arbonne, Bayou (river), LA 69 B3
Dardanelle, AR 61 C3
Dardanelle, Lake, AR 61 C2
Darien, CT 31 F2
Darling, Lake, ND 105 B4
Darlington, SC 75 C7
Daufuskie Island, SC 75 H5
Dauphin Island, AL 59 I1
Davenport, IA 93 D9
David Berger National Memorial, OH 107 B6
David City, NE 103 C8
Davis Mountains, TX 124 F2
Davis, Mount, PA 47 F3
Dawson, GA 65 G2
Dayton, NV 145 D2
Dayton, OH 107 E2
Dayton, TN 77 C7
Dayton, WA 151 E9
Dayton Aviation Heritage N.H.P., OH 107 E2
Daytona Beach, FL 63 C8
Dayville, CT 31 B8
De Gray Lake, AR 61 E3
De Land, FL 63 C8
De Pere, WI 111 E7
De Queen, AR 61 E1
De Quincy, LA 68 F2
De Ridder, LA 68 E2
De Smet, SD 109 C9
De Soto, MO 101 D6
De Soto National Memorial, FL 63 E6
De Witt, AR 61 E6
De Witt, IA 93 D9
Dead (river), ME 35 E3
Deadwood, SD 108 C1
Deadwood Reservoir, ID 141 F2
Deale, MD 37 D8
Dearborn, MI 97 H7
Death Valley, CA 135 F6
Death Valley N.P., CA, NV 135 E6
Decatur, AL 59 B3
Decatur, IL 89 E4
Decatur, IN 91 C6
Decorah, IA 93 A8
Dededo, GU 154 F2
Deep (river), NC 73 C6
Deep Creek Lake, MD 36 A1
Deep Fork (river), OK 123 C9
Deep River, CT 31 D6
Deepwater Point, DE 33 E6
Deer Creek, OH 107 F4
Deer Creek, MS 71 E2
Deer Creek Lake, OH 107 F4
Deer Isle, ME 35 G5
Deer Lodge, MT 143 D4
Deerfield, MA 39 B3
Deerfield (river), MA 38 B2
Defiance, OH 107 B2
DeKalb, IL 89 B4
Del Rio, TX 125 G4
Delano, CA 135 F4
Delaware, OH 107 D4
Delaware (river), DE, NJ, PA 24 F4
Delaware and Raritan Canal, NJ 43 E3
Delaware Bay, DE, NJ 24 G4
Delaware City, DE 33 B5
Delaware, East Branch (river), NY 45 F7
Delaware Lake, OH 107 D4
Delaware Memorial Bridge, DE 33 B5
Delaware Water Gap N.R.A., NJ, PA 43 B2
Delaware, West Branch (river), NY 45 F7
Delmar, DE 33 I5
Delmarva Peninsula, DE, MD, VA 26 H4
Delphos, OH 107 C2
Delray Beach, FL 63 G9
Delta, CO 137 D2
Delta, UT 149 E3
Delta N.W.&S.R., AK 133 D7
Deltona, FL 63 D8
Deming, NM 121 H2
Demopolis, AL 59 E2
Denali (peak) see McKinley, Mount, AK 133 D6
Denali N.P. and Preserve, AK 133 D6
Denham Springs, LA 69 F6
Denison, IA 93 C3
Denison, TX 125 C7
Dennis, MA 39 E10
Denton, MD 37 C9
Denton, TX 125 C7
Denver, CO 137 C6
Derby, KS 95 E7
Derby Center, VT 51 A4
Derby Line, VT 51 A4
Dermott, AR 61 F6
Derry, NH 41 I4
Des Lacs (river), ND 105 B4
Des Moines, IA 93 D5
Des Moines (river), IA, MN 93 B4
Des Plaines (river), IL 89 B5
Desatoya Mountains, NV 145 D4
Deschutes (river), OR 147 B4
Deschutes N.W.&S.R., OR 147 D4
Desert National Wildlife Range, NV 145 F6
Desert Valley, NV 145 B3
Desolation Canyon, UT 149 D6
Detroit, MI 97 H8
Detroit (river), MI 97 H8
Detroit Lakes, MN 99 D2
Devils Lake, ND 105 B7
Devils Postpile Nat. Mon., CA 135 E5
Devils Tower Nat. Mon., WY 153 A9
Dewey Beach, DE 33 H7
Dexter, ME 35 E4
Dexter, MO 101 F7
Dickinson, ND 104 D2
Dickson, TN 77 B4
Dillingham, AK 133 F4
Dillon, MT 143 F4
Dillon, SC 75 C8
Dinosaur Nat. Mon., CO, UT 136 A1
Dirty Devil (river), UT 149 F5
Disappointment, Cape, WA 150 E1
Dismal (river), NE 103 C4
Dixon, IL 89 B3
Dixon Entrance (strait), AK 133 H10
Dodge City, KS 95 D3
Dodgeville, WI 111 G4
Dolan Springs, AZ 119 C2
Dolores, CO 136 E1
Donaldsonville, LA 69 G6
Donner Und Blitzen N.W.&S.R., OR 147 F7
Door Peninsula, WI 111 E7
Dothan, AL 59 G5
Double Trouble, NJ 43 F4
Douglas, AZ 119 H7
Douglas, GA 65 G5
Douglas, WY 153 E8
Douglas Lake, TN 77 B9
Dover, DE 33 E5
Dover, NH 41 H5
Dover, NJ 43 B3
Dover, OH 107 D6
Dover-Foxcroft, ME 35 E4
Dowagiac, MI 97 I5
Doylestown, PA 47 E10
Dracut, MA 39 A6
Drayton, ND 105 A9
Drift Prairie, ND 105 B7
Driskill Mountain, LA 69 B3
Drummond Island, MI 97 D7
Dry Cimarron (river), NM 121 A7
Dry Lake, ND 105 B7
Dry Tortugas N.P., FL 63 I6
Du Bay, Lake, WI 111 D5
Du Bois, PA 47 C4
Du Quoin, IL 89 H4
Dublin, GA 65 E5
Dublin, OH 107 E4
Dubuque, IA 93 C9
Duck (river), TN 77 C4
Dulce, NM 121 A3
Duluth, MN 99 D5
Dumas, AR 61 F6
Dumas, TX 125 A3
Dunbar, WV 81 F3
Duncan, OK 123 E8
Dundalk, MD 37 B8
Dunkirk, NY 44 E1
Dunmore, Lake, VT 51 E2
Dunmore, PA 47 B9
Dunn, NC 73 C7
Dupree, SD 109 B4
Durango, CO 137 G2
Durant, OK 123 F10
Durham, CT 31 D5
Durham, NC 73 B7
Durham, NH 41 H5
Dutch Harbor, AK 132 H2
Dworshak Reservoir, ID 141 C2
Dyersburg, TN 76 B1
Dyersville, IA 93 C9

E

Eagan, MN 99 F5
Eagar, AZ 119 E7
Eagle Creek, KY 67 B7
Eagle Creek N.W.&S.R., OR 147 C8
Eagle Lake, CA 135 B4
Eagle Lake, ME 35 B5
Eagle Lake, ME 35 C4
Eagle Mountain, MN 99 B7
Eagle Pass, TX 125 G4
Eagle River, WI 111 C5
Earle, AR 61 C7
Easley, SC 74 B2
East Brunswick, NJ 43 D4
East Chicago, IN 91 A2
East Derry, NH 41 I4
East Falmouth, MA 39 E9
East Grand Forks, MN 99 B1
East Greenwich, RI 49 D4
East Hampton, CT 31 C6
East Hartford, CT 31 B5
East Hartland, CT 31 A4
East Haven, CT 31 E4
East Lansing, MI 97 H6
East Liverpool, OH 107 C8
East Millinocket, ME 35 D5
East Mountain, VT 51 B5
East Okoboji Lake, IA 93 A3
East Point, GA 65 C2
East Providence, RI 49 B5
East Range, NV 145 B3
East Ridge, TN 77 D7
East River, CT 31 E5
East St. Louis, IL 89 G3
East Tavaputs Plateau, UT 149 D6
Eastern Bay, MD 37 C8
Easthampton, MA 38 C2
Eastman, GA 65 F4
Easton, MD 37 D9
Easton, PA 47 D9
Eastport, ME 35 F7
Eatonton, GA 65 D4
Eatontown, NJ 43 D5
Eau Claire, WI 111 D3
Ebey's Landing National Historical Reserve, WA 151 B3
Eden, NC 73 A6
Edenton, NC 73 B9
Edgartown, MA 39 F9
Edgefield, SC 75 D3
Edgemont, SD 108 E1
Edgewood, MD 37 B8
Edison, NJ 43 D4
Edison National Historic Site, NJ 43 C4
Edisto (river), SC 75 F6
Edisto Island, SC 75 G6
Edisto, North Fork (river), SC 75 E5
Edisto, South Fork (river), SC 75 E4
Edmond, OK 123 C8
Edwards Plateau, TX 125 E5
Edwardsville, IL 89 G3
Eel (river), CA 135 B1
Eel (river), IN 91 B4
Eel (river), IN 91 F2
Eel N.W.&S.R., CA 135 B1
Effigy Mounds Nat. Mon., IA 93 A8
Effingham, IL 89 F5
Egan Range, NV 145 E6
Egg Harbor City, NJ 43 G3
Eisenhower National Historic Site, PA 47 F6
El Campo, TX 125 G7
El Centro, CA 135 I7
El Dorado, AR 61 G4
El Dorado, KS 95 D7
El Dorado Lake, KS 95 D7
El Malpais Nat. Mon., NM 121 D2
El Morro Nat. Mon., NM 121 D2
El Paso, TX 124 D1
El Reno, OK 123 C7
Elbert, Mount, CO 137 D4
Elberton, GA 65 C5
Eldon, MO 101 D4
Eldora, IA 93 C6
Eleanor Roosevelt National Historic Site, NY 45 F8
Elephant Butte Reservoir, NM 123 F3
Eleven Point (river), MO 101 F5
Eleven Point N.W.&S.R., MO 101 F6
Elgin, IL 89 B5
Elizabeth, NJ 43 C4
Elizabeth City, NC 73 A10
Elizabeth Islands, MA 39 F7
Elizabethton, TN 77 B11
Elizabethtown, KY 67 C6
Elizabethtown, PA 47 E7
Elk (river), KS 95 E8
Elk (river), WV 81 F5
Elk City Lake, KS 95 E9
Elk City, OK 123 C6
Elk N.W.&S.R., OR 146 F1
Elk Point, SD 109 F10
Elkhart, IN 91 A4
Elkhart, KS 94 F1
Elkhead Mountains, CO 137 A2
Elkhorn (river), NE 103 B7
Elkhorn Creek N.W.&S.R., OR 147 C3

Elkins, WV **81** E6
Elko, NV **145** B5
Elkton, MD **37** A9
Ellendale, DE **33** G6
Ellendale, ND **105** F8
Ellensburg, WA **151** D6
Ellicott City, MD **37** B7
Ellington, CT **31** A6
Ellis (river), NH **41** D4
Ellis Island, NY, NJ **45** H8
Ellisville, MS **71** G4
Ellsworth, KS **95** C5
Ellsworth, ME **35** F5
Elmira, NY **45** F4
Eloy, AZ **119** G5
Elsmere, DE **33** A5
Elwell, Lake, MT **143** B5
Elwood, IN **91** D4
Ely, MN **99** C6
Ely, NV **145** D6
Elyria, OH **107** B5
Embarras (river), IL **89** F5
Emmetsburg, IA **93** A4
Emmett, ID **141** G1
Emmonak, AK **132** D3
Emporia, KS **95** C8
Emporia, VA **79** E9
Emporium, PA **47** B5
Endicott, NY **45** F5
Endwell, NY **45** F6
Enfield, CT **31** A5
Enfield, NH **41** F2
England, AR **61** D5
Englewood, OH **107** E2
Enid, OK **123** B8
Enid Lake, MS **71** B3
Enosburg Falls, VT **51** A3
Enterprise, AL **59** G5
Enterprise, OR **147** B8
Ephraim, UT **149** E4
Ephrata, PA **47** E8
Ephrata, WA **151** D7
Equinox, Mount, VT **51** H2
Erie, Lake, **84** E9
Erie Canal, NY **44** D2
Erie, PA **46** A2
Erling, Lake, AR **61** G2
Erwin, TN **77** B10
Escalante (river), UT **149** G4
Escanaba, MI **97** D4
Escondido, CA **135** I6
Esmond, RI **49** B4
Espanola, NM **121** B4
Essex, CT **31** D6
Essex, MD **37** B8
Essex Junction, VT **51** C2
Estancia, NM **121** D4
Estes Park, CO **137** B5
Estherville, IA **93** A3
Etowah (river), GA **65** B1
Euclid, OH **107** A6
Eudora, AR **61** G6
Eufaula, AL **59** F6
Eufaula Lake, OK **123** D11
Eugene, OR **147** D2
Eugene O'Neill National Historic Site, CA **135** E2
Eunice, LA **69** F4
Eunice, NM **121** G8
Eureka, CA **135** B1
Eureka, KS **95** D8
Eureka, MT **142** A2
Eureka, NV **145** D5
Eureka, SD **109** A6
Eureka Springs, AR **61** A2
Evangeline, LA **69** F3
Evans, GA **65** D6
Evanston, IL **89** B6
Evanston, WY **152** G1
Evansville, IN **91** I1
Everett, WA **151** C4
Everglades, The, FL **63** H8
Everglades N.P., FL **63** H9
Evergreen, AL **59** G3
Ewing, NJ **43** E3
Excelsior Mountains, NV **145** E3
Exeter, NH **41** H5
Exeter, RI **49** E4

F

Fabens, TX **124** E1
Fabius, Middle (river), MO **101** A4
Fabius, South (river), MO **101** B5
Faga'itua, AS **154** H2
Fagamalo, AS **154** I1
Fagatele Bay National Marine Sanctuary, AS **154** I1
Fagatogo, AS **154** I1
Fair Haven, VT **51** F1
Fairbanks, AK **133** D7
Fairborn, OH **107** E2
Fairbury, NE **103** E8
Fairfield, CT **31** E2
Fairfield, IA **93** E8
Fairfield, IL **89** G5
Fairfield, OH **107** F1
Fairfield, VT **51** B3
Fairfield Bay, AR **61** B4
Fairhaven, MA **39** E8
Fairhope, AL **59** I1
Fairmont, MN **99** H3
Fairmont, WV **81** C5
Fairmount, NY **45** D5
Fairview, KY **67** E4
Fairview, OK **123** B7
Fajardo, PR **155** H12
Falcon Reservoir, TX **125** H5
Faleāsao, AS **154** I4
Falfurrias, TX **125** H6
Fall (river), KS **95** D8
Fall Line (escarpment), NJ, PA **26** G4
Fall River, MA **39** E7
Fallon, NV **145** D3
Falls City, NE **103** E10
Falls Creek, NV **145** A6
Falls Lake, NC **73** B7
Falmouth, MA **39** F8
Falmouth, ME **35** H3
Fargo, ND **105** D10
Faribault, MN **99** G4
Farmington, ME **35** F3
Farmington, MO **101** E7
Farmington, NH **41** G5
Farmington, NM **121** A2
Farmington, UT **149** B4
Farmington (river), CT **31** B4
Farmington N.W.&S.R., CT **31** A3
Farmington, East Branch (river), CT **31** A4
Farmington, West Branch (river), CT, MA **31** A3
Farmville, VA **79** D8
Farragut, TN **77** B8
Father Marquette National Memorial, MI **97** D6
Faulkton, SD **109** B7
Fayette, AL **59** C2
Fayetteville, AR **61** B1
Fayetteville, NC **73** C7
Fayetteville, TN **77** D5
Fayetteville, WV **81** G4
Fear, Cape, NC **73** E8
Feather, Middle Fork N.W.&S.R., CA **135** C3
Federal Way, WA **151** D4
Federalsburg, MD **37** D9
Felton, DE **33** F5
Fenwick Island, DE **33** I7
Fergus Falls, MN **99** D2
Ferguson, MO **101** C7
Fernandina Beach, FL **63** A8
Ferndale, WA **151** A3
Fernley, NV **145** C2
Ferriday, LA **69** D5
Festus, MO **101** D7
Fillmore, UT **149** E3
Findlay, OH **107** C3
Finger Lakes, NY **45** E4
Fire Island National Seashore, NY **45** H9
First Connecticut Lake, NH **41** A4
First Ladies National Historic Site, OH **107** C7
Fish (river), ME **35** B5
Fish Creek, WV **81** C4
Fishing Bay, MD **37** E9
Fitchburg, MA **39** B5
Fitzgerald, GA **65** G4
Flagstaff, AZ **119** C5
Flagstaff Lake, ME **35** E2
Flambeau (river), WI **111** C3
Flaming Gorge N.R.A., WY **153** G3
Flaming Gorge Reservoir, UT, WY **153** G3
Flandreau, SD **109** D10
Flat River Reservoir, RI **49** D3
Flathead (river), MT **142** C2
Flathead Lake, MT **142** B3
Flathead N.W.&S.R., MT **142** B3
Flathead, South Fork (river), MT **142** B3
Flatrock (river), IN **91** F4
Flattery, Cape, WA **150** B1
Flatwoods, KY **67** B10
Flemington, NJ **43** D2
Flint, MI **97** G7
Flint (river), GA **65** E2
Flint (river), MI **97** G7
Flint Hills, KS **95** E7
Flora, IL **89** G5
Florence, AL **59** A2
Florence, AZ **119** F5
Florence, CO **137** E5
Florence, KY **67** A7
Florence, OR **146** D1
Florence, SC **75** C8
Florida Bay, FL **63** H9
Florida Keys (islands), FL **63** I8
Florida Keys National Marine Sanctuary, FL **63** I7
Florida, Straits of, FL **63** I9
Florida's Turnpike, FL **63** E8
Florissant, MO **101** C7
Florissant Fossil Beds Nat. Mon., CO **137** D5
Floyd (river), IA **92** B2
Foley, AL **59** I2
Follansbee, WV **81** A5
Folsom, CA **135** D3
Fond du Lac, WI **111** F6
Fontana Lake, NC **72** C1
Fontenelle Reservoir, WY **152** F2
Ford (river), MI **97** C3
Fordyce, AR **61** F4
Forest, MS **71** E4
Forest Acres, SC **75** D5
Forest City, IA **93** A5
Forest City, NC **72** C3
Forest Grove, OR **147** B2
Forrest City, AR **61** D7
Forsyth, MT **143** D9
Fort Atkinson, WI **111** G6
Fort Benton, MT **143** B5
Fort Bowie National Historic Site, AZ **119** G7
Fort Bragg, CA **135** C1
Fort Caroline National Memorial, FL **63** B8
Fort Clatsop National Memorial, OR **146** A1
Fort Collins, CO **137** B5
Fort Davis National Historic Site, TX **124** E2
Fort Defiance, AZ **119** C7
Fort Dodge, IA **93** C4
Fort Donelson N.B., TN **76** A3
Fort Fairfield, ME **35** B6
Fort Foote Park, MD **37** D6
Fort Frederica Nat. Mon., GA **65** H7
Fort Gibson Lake, OK **123** C11
Fort Kent, ME **35** A5
Fort Knox (site), KY **67** C6
Fort Laramie National Historic Site, WY **153** F9
Fort Larned National Historic Site, KS **95** D4
Fort Lauderdale, FL **63** G9
Fort Lee, NJ **43** C5
Fort Loudoun Lake, TN **77** B8
Fort Madison, IA **93** F8
Fort Matanzas Nat. Mon., FL **63** B8
Fort McHenry Nat. Mon. and Historic Shrine, MD **37** B8
Fort Mill, SC **75** A5
Fort Morgan, CO **137** B7
Fort Myers, FL **63** F7
Fort Necessity N.B., PA **46** F2
Fort Payne, AL **59** B5
Fort Peck Dam, MT **143** B9
Fort Peck Lake, MT **143** B8
Fort Pickens, FL **62** B1
Fort Pierce, FL **63** E9
Fort Pierre, SD **109** D5
Fort Pulaski Nat. Mon., GA **65** F8
Fort Raleigh National Historic Site, NC **73** B10
Fort Scott, KS **95** D10
Fort Scott National Historic Site, KS **95** D10
Fort Smith, AR **61** C1
Fort Smith National Historic Site, AR **61** B1
Fort Stanwix Nat. Mon., NY **45** C6
Fort Stockton, TX **125** E3
Fort Sumner, NM **121** D7
Fort Sumter Nat. Mon., SC **75** G7
Fort Thompson, SD **109** D6
Fort Ticonderoga, NY **45** C9
Fort Union Nat. Mon., NM **121** B6
Fort Union Trading Post National Historic Site, MT, ND **143** B11
Fort Vancouver National Historic Site, WA **151** F3
Fort Walton Beach, FL **62** B2
Fort Washington Park, MD **37** D6
Fort Wayne, IN **91** B5
Fort Worth, TX **125** D7
Fort Yates, ND **105** F5
Fort Yukon, AK **133** C7
Fortymile N.W.&S.R., AK **133** D8
Fossil Butte Nat. Mon., WY **152** F2
Foster Center, RI **49** C2
Foster Creek, SD **109** C8
Fostoria, OH **107** B3
Fountain, CO **137** D6
Four Corners (site), AZ, CO, NM, UT **119** A7
Four Mountains, Islands of, AK **132** H1
Fox, IL, WI **89** B5
Framingham, MA **39** C6
Francis Case, Lake, SD **109** E7
Francis, Lake, NH **41** B4
Franconia, NH **41** D3
Frankford, DE **33** I7
Frankfort, IN **91** D3
Frankfort, KY **67** B7
Franklin, IN **91** F4
Franklin, KY **67** E5
Franklin, LA **69** G5
Franklin, MA **39** D6
Franklin, NC **72** C1
Franklin, NH **41** G3
Franklin, NJ **43** B3
Franklin, TN **77** B5
Franklin, VA **79** E10
Franklin Delano Roosevelt Lake, WA **151** B9
Frederica, DE **33** F5
Frederick, MD **37** B5
Frederick, OK **123** E6
Fredericksburg, VA **79** C9
Fredericksburg and Spotsylvania County Battlefields Memorial N.M.P., VA **79** C9
Fredericktown, MO **101** E7
Frederiksted, VI **155** I7
Fredonia, KS **95** E8
Fredonia, NY **44** E1
Freehold, NJ **43** E4
Freeman, Lake, IN **91** C3
Freeman, SD **109** E9
Freeport, IL **89** A3
Freeport, TX **125** G8
Freeport, NY **45** H9
Fremont, MI **97** G5
Fremont, NE **103** C9
Fremont, OH **107** B4
Fremont (river), UT **149** F5
French Broad (river), TN **77** B10
Frenchman (river), MT **143** A8
Frenchman Creek, CO, NE **103** E4
Frenchville, ME **35** A5
Fresno, CA **135** F4
Friendship Hill National Historic Site, PA **46** F2
Frio (river), TX **125** G6
Frissell, Mount, CT **31** A2
Front Range, CO,WY **128** D7
Front Royal, VA **79** B8
Frostburg, MD **36** A2
Fruitland, MD **37** E10
Fryeburg, ME **35** G2
Fullerton, NE **103** C7
Fulton, KY **66** E1
Fulton, MO **101** C5
Fulton, MS **71** B5
Fulton, NY **45** D5
Fundy, Bay of, **26** C9

G

Gabbs, NV **145** D3
Gabbs Valley, NV **145** D3
Gadsden, AL **59** C4
Gaffney, SC **75** A4
Gahanna, OH **107** E4
Gaillard, Lake, CT **31** D4
Gainesville, FL **63** C7
Gainesville, GA **65** B3
Gaithersburg, MD **37** C6
Galax, VA **79** F5
Galena, AK **133** C5
Galena, IL **89** A2
Galesburg, IL **89** C2
Galilee, RI **49** G4
Galion, OH **107** C4
Gallatin, MO **101** B3
Gallatin, TN **77** B5
Gallatin (river), MT **143** E5
Gallinas (river), NM **121** C6
Gallipolis, OH **107** G5
Gallo Arroyo (river), NM **121** E5
Gallup, NM **121** C1
Galveston, TX **125** F9
Galveston Bay, TX **114** F9
Gannett Peak, WY **153** D3
Gantt, SC **74** B2
Garapan, MP **154** C2
Garden City, KS **94** D2
Garden City, SC **75** E9
Garden Peninsula, MI **97** D4
Garden State Parkway, NJ **43** G4
Gardiner, ME **35** G3
Gardner, MA **39** B4
Gardner Lake, CT **31** C6
Gardner Pinnacles, HI **139** F3
Gardnerville, NV **145** D2
Gareloi Island, AK **133** H8
Garland, TX **125** D7
Garner, NC **73** B7
Garnett, KS **95** D9
Garrison, ND **105** C4
Gary, IN **91** A2
Gas City, IN **91** D4
Gasconade (river), MO **101** F4
Gaston, Lake, NC, VA **73** A8
Gastonia, NC **73** C4
Gates, NY **44** D3
Gates of the Arctic N.P. and Preserve, AK **133** B6
Gatesville, TX **125** E6
Gateway N.R.A., NJ, NY **43** D5
Gatlinburg, TN **77** C9
Gauley (river), WV **81** F4
Gauley River N.R.A., WV **81** F4
Gay Head (point), MA **39** F8
Gaylord, MI **97** E6
Genesee (river), NY **44** E3
Geneseo, IL **89** C3
Geneseo, NY **44** E3
Geneva, AL **59** H5
Geneva, NE **103** D8
Geneva, NY **45** D4
Geneva, OH **107** A7
George, Lake, FL **63** C7
George, Lake, NY **45** C8
George Rogers Clark N.H.P., IN **91** G1
George Washington Birthplace Nat. Mon., VA **79** C10
George Washington Carver Nat. Mon., MO **101** F2
Georgetown, DE **33** H6
Georgetown, KY **67** C8
Georgetown, OH **107** G3
Georgetown, SC **75** E9
Georgetown, TX **125** F6
Georgia, Strait of, WA **150** A2
Gering, NE **102** B1
Germantown, MD **37** C6
Germantown, TN **76** D1
Gettysburg, PA **47** F6
Gettysburg, SD **109** B6
Gettysburg N.M.P., PA **47** F6
Gibbon, NE **103** D6
Gila (river), AZ **119** F7
Gila Bend, AZ **119** F4
Gila Cliff Dwellings Nat. Mon., NM **121** F2
Gilford Park, NJ **43** F5
Gillette, WY **153** B8
Glacier Bay N.P. and Preserve, AK **133** F9
Glacier N.P., MT **142** A3

Gladstone — Hood River

Gladstone, MI **97** D4
Glasgow, DE **33** B4
Glasgow, KY **67** E6
Glasgow, MT **143** B9
Glassboro, NJ **43** G2
Glastonbury, CT **31** B5
Glen Burnie, MD **37** C7
Glen Canyon Dam, AZ **119** A5
Glen Canyon N.R.A., AZ, UT **149** G5
Glen Ullin, ND **105** E4
Glendale, AZ **119** F4
Glendale, RI **49** A3
Glendive, MT **143** C10
Glendo Reservoir, WY **153** E9
Glenns Ferry, ID **141** H2
Glenrock, WY **153** D8
Glens Falls, NY **45** D8
Glenwood, IA **92** E2
Glenwood Springs, CO **137** C3
Globe, AZ **119** F6
Gloucester, MA **39** B8
Gloversville, NY **45** D8
Gold Beach, OR **146** F1
Golden Beach, MD **37** E7
Golden Gate N.R.A., CA **135** E1
Golden Spike National Historic Site, UT **149** A3
Goldendale, WA **151** F5
Goldfield, NV **145** F4
Goldsboro, NC **73** C8
Gonzales, LA **69** G6
Gooding, ID **141** H3
Goodland, KS **94** B1
Goodlettsville, TN **77** B5
Goose (river), ND **105** C9
Goose Creek, ID **141** I3
Goose Creek, SC **75** F7
Goose Lake, CA, OR **135** A4
Goose Point, DE **33** D6
Gordon, NE **103** A3
Gordon Creek, NE **103** B4
Gore Range, CO **137** B4
Gorham, NH **41** D4
Goshen, IN **91** A4
Goshute Mountains, NV **145** C7
Gothenburg, NE **103** D5
Gouverneur, NY **45** B6
Grafton, ND **105** B9
Grafton, WV **81** D6
Grambling, LA **69** B3
Granby, CT **31** A4
Grand (river), MI **97** G6
Grand (river), MO **101** A2
Grand (river), OH **107** A7
Grand (river), SD **109** A3
Grand Canyon, AZ **119** B3
Grand Canyon N.P., AZ **119** B3
Grand Canyon-Parashant Nat. Mon., AZ **119** B3
Grand Canyon Village, AZ **119** B4
Grand Coulee (valley), WA **151** C7
Grand Coulee Dam, WA **151** C8
Grand Detour, IL **89** B4
Grand Forks, ND **105** C10
Grand Haven, MI **97** G4
Grand Island, NE **103** D7
Grand Island N.R.A., MI **97** C4
Grand Isle, LA **69** I8
Grand Isle, VT **51** B1
Grand Junction, CO **136** D1
Grand Lake, LA **69** G3
Grand Lake, ME **35** D6
Grand Lake (St. Marys Lake), OH **107** D2
Grand Manan Channel, ME **35** F7
Grand Marais, MN **99** C7
Grand Mesa, CO **137** D2
Grand Portage Nat. Mon., MN **99** B8
Grand Rapids, MI **97** G5
Grand Rapids, MN **99** C4
Grand Staircase-Escalante Nat. Mon., UT **149** G4
Grand Teton N.P., WY **152** C2
Grand Traverse Bay, MI **97** D5
Grand Valley, CO **136** D1
Grand Wash Cliffs, AZ **119** B2
Grand, South (river), MO **101** D2
Grand, South Fork (river), SD **108** A2
Grande Ronde (river), OR **147** A8

Grande Ronde N.W.&S.R., OR **147** A8
Grandfather Mountain, NC **72** B3
Grandview, WA **151** E7
Grangeville, ID **141** D1
Granite City, IL **89** G3
Granite Peak, MT **143** E6
Graniteville, VT **51** D4
Grant, NE **103** D3
Grant Range, NV **145** E6
Grant-Kohrs Ranch National Historic Site, MT **143** D4
Grants, NM **121** D2
Grants Pass, OR **147** F2
Grantsville, UT **149** C3
Grasonville, MD **37** C8
Grasshopper Glacier (site), MT **143** F6
Grays Harbor, WA **150** D1
Grays Lake, ID **141** H6
Gray's Reef National Marine Sanctuary, GA **65** G8
Great Barrington, MA **38** C1
Great Basin, NV **145** B5
Great Basin N.P., NV **145** D7
Great Bay, NH **41** H5
Great Bay, NJ **43** G4
Great Bend, KS **95** C5
Great Dismal Swamp, NC, VA **54** B8
Great Divide Basin, WY **153** F5
Great Egg Harbor (river), NJ **43** G3
Great Egg Harbor N.W.&S.R., NJ **43** G3
Great Falls, MT **143** C5
Great Miami (river), OH **107** D2
Great Pee Dee (river), NC, SC **54** C6
Great Plains, **84** A1
Great Plains Reservoirs, CO **137** E8
Great Pond, ME **35** F3
Great Quittacus Pond, MA **39** E4
Great Sacandaga Lake, NY **45** D8
Great Salt Lake, UT **149** B3
Great Salt Lake Desert, UT **149** C2
Great Salt Plains Lake, OK **123** B7
Great Sand Dunes N.P. and Preserve, CO **137** F5
Great Smoky Mountains, NC, TN **72** C1
Great Smoky Mountains N.P., NC, TN **72** B1
Great Swamp, RI **49** F3
Greece, NY **44** D3
Greeley, CO **137** B6
Green (river), CO, UT, WY **128** F6
Green Bay, WI **111** E7
Green Bay (bay), WI **111** D7
Green Mountains, VT **51** H2
Green River, UT **149** E6
Green River, WY **153** G3
Green River Lake, KY **67** D7
Green Swamp, NC **73** E7
Green Valley, AZ **119** H6
Greenbelt Park, MD **37** C7
Greenbrier, AR **61** C4
Greenbrier (river), WV **81** G5
Greencastle, IN **91** E2
Greeneville, TN **77** B10
Greenfield, IN **91** E4
Greenfield, MA **39** B3
Greenfield, OH **107** F3
Greensboro, NC **73** B6
Greensburg, IN **91** F5
Greensburg, KS **95** E4
Greensburg, PA **47** E3
Greenville, AL **59** F3
Greenville, DE **33** A5
Greenville, ME **35** E4
Greenville, MI **97** G5
Greenville, MS **71** D1
Greenville, NC **73** C8
Greenville, NH **41** I3
Greenville, OH **107** D1
Greenville, PA **46** B1
Greenville, RI **49** B3
Greenville, SC **74** B2
Greenway (site), VA **79** D10
Greenwich, CT **31** F1

Greenwood, AR **61** C1
Greenwood, DE **33** G5
Greenwood, IN **91** E4
Greenwood, MS **71** C3
Greenwood, SC **75** C3
Greer, SC **75** B3
Greers Ferry Lake, AR **61** C4
Greeson, Lake, AR **61** E2
Gregory, SD **109** E6
Grenada, MS **71** C3
Grenada Lake, MS **71** C3
Gresham, OR **147** B3
Greybull, WY **153** B5
Greybull (river), WY **153** B4
Greylock, Mount, MA **38** A1
Greys (river), WY **152** D2
Griffin, GA **65** D3
Grinnell, IA **93** D6
Gros Ventre (river), WY **152** C2
Groton, SD **109** B8
Groton, CT **31** D7
Grove, OK **123** B12
Grove City, PA **46** C2
Groveton, NH **41** C3
Guadalupe (river), TX **125** F7
Guadalupe Mountains, NM **121** G6
Guadalupe Mountains N.P., TX **124** E1
Guadalupe Peak, TX **124** E2
Guam (territory), US **154** E1
Guayama, PR **155** I11
Guernsey, WY **153** E9
Guilford, CT **31** E5
Guilford, ME **35** E4
Guilford Courthouse N.M.P., NC **73** B6
Gulf Islands National Seashore, FL, MS **62** B1
Gulf of the Farallones National Marine Sanctuary, CA **135** E2
Gulf Shores, AL **59** I2
Gulfport, MS **71** I4
Gulkana N.W.&S.R., AK **133** D7
Gunnison, CO **137** E3
Guntersville, AL **59** B4
Guntersville Lake, AL **59** B4
Gurdon, AR **61** F3
Guthrie, OK **123** C8
Guyandotte (river), WV **80** G2
Guymon, OK **122** A3

H

Hackensack, NJ **43** B5
Hackettstown, NJ **43** C3
Haddam, CT **31** D5
Haddonfield, NJ **43** F2
Hagåtña (Agana), GU **154** F1
Hagerman, NM **121** F6
Hagerman Fossil Beds Nat. Mon., ID **141** H2
Hagerstown, MD **37** A5
Hailey, ID **141** G3
Haines, AK **133** F9
Haines City, FL **63** E7
Hal Rogers Parkway, KY **67** D8
Haleakala N.P., HI **139** D8
Hallock, MN **99** A1
Halls Creek, UT **149** G5
Hamburg, AR **61** G5
Hamburg, NY **44** E2
Hamden, CT **31** D4
Hamilton, AL **59** B1
Hamilton, MT **142** D1
Hamilton, OH **107** F1
Hamilton, RI **49** E4
Hammonasset (river), CT **31** D5
Hammond, IN **91** A1
Hammond, LA **69** F3
Hammonton, NJ **43** G3
Hampton, IA **93** B6
Hampton, NH **41** H5
Hampton, SC **75** F5
Hampton, VA **79** E11
Hampton National Historic Site, MD **37** B7
Hams Fork (river), WY **152** F2
Hanahan, SC **75** F7
Hanama'ulu, HI **138** A2
Hancock, MD **37** A4
Hanford, CA **135** F4
Hanford Reach Nat. Mon., WA **151** E7
Hankinson, ND **105** F10
Hanna, WY **153** F7
Hannibal, MO **101** B5

Hanover, NH **41** F2
Hanover, PA **47** F7
Harbeson, DE **33** H6
Harbor Beach, MI **97** F8
Hardin, MT **143** E8
Harding, Lake, GA **65** E1
Hardinsburg, KY **67** C5
Hardwick, VT **51** C4
Harlan, IA **93** D3
Harlan County Lake, NE **103** E6
Harlingen, TX **125** I7
Harlowton, MT **143** D6
Harmony, RI **49** B3
Harney Basin, OR **147** E6
Harney Lake, OR **147** E6
Harney Peak, SD **108** D2
Harpers Ferry N.H.P., WV **81** D10
Harriman, TN **77** B8
Harriman Reservoir, VT **51** I2
Harrington, DE **33** F5
Harris, RI **49** C4
Harrisburg, IL **89** H5
Harrisburg, PA **47** E7
Harrison, AR **61** A3
Harrison, TN **77** D7
Harrisonburg, VA **79** C7
Harrisonville, MO **101** D2
Harrisville, RI **49** A3
Harrodsburg, KY **67** C7
Harry S. Truman National Historic Site, MO **101** C2
Harry S. Truman Reservoir, MO **101** D3
Hart Mountain National Antelope Refuge, OR **147** F6
Hartford, CT **31** B5
Hartford City, IN **91** D5
Hartington, NE **103** A8
Hartland, ME **35** F4
Hartland, VT **51** F4
Hartselle, AL **59** B3
Hartsville, SC **75** C7
Hartwell, GA **65** B4
Hartwell Lake, GA, SC **74** C1
Harvard, IL **89** A4
Harvey, ND **105** C6
Harwinton, CT **31** B3
Hastings, MI **97** H5
Hastings, NE **103** D7
Hatchie (river), TN **76** C2
Hatteras, Cape, NC **73** C11
Hatteras Island, NC **73** B11
Hattiesburg, MS **71** G4
Hau'ula, HI **139** B4
Havasu, Lake, AZ, CA **119** D2
Havelock, NC **73** D9
Haverhill, MA **39** A7
Haverhill, NH **41** E2
Haverhill-Bath Bridge, NH **41** D2
Havre, MT **143** B6
Havre de Grace, MD **37** A9
Haw (river), NC **73** B6
Hawai'i (island), HI **139** E9
Hawai'i Volcanoes N.P., HI **139** F9
Hawaiian Islands Humpback Whale National Marine Sanctuary, HI **139** D5
Hawkeye Point (peak), IA **92** A2
Hawthorne, NV **145** E3
Hayden, ID **141** B1
Hays, KS **95** C4
Hayward, CA **135** E2
Hayward, WI **111** B3
Hazard, KY **67** D10
Hazardville, CT **31** A5
Hazen, ND **105** D4
Hazlehurst, GA **65** G5
Hazlehurst, MS **71** F2
Hazleton, PA **47** C8
H.E. Bailey Turnpike, OK **123** D7
Heart (river), ND **105** E4
Heavener, OK **123** D12
Heber City, UT **149** C4
Heber Springs, AR **61** C5
Hebron, NE **103** E8
Helena, AR **61** D7
Helena, MT **143** D4
Hells Canyon, ID **141** E1
Hells Canyon N.R.A., ID, OR **147** A9
Helper, UT **149** D5
Henderson, KY **66** C3

Henderson, NC **73** B7
Henderson, NV **145** H6
Henderson, TN **76** C2
Henderson, TX **125** D8
Hendersonville, NC **72** C2
Hendersonville, TN **77** B5
Henlopen, Cape, DE **33** G7
Hennepin Canal, IL **89** C3
Henniker, NH **41** H3
Henry Mountains, UT **149** G5
Henryetta, OK **123** C10
Henrys Lake, ID **141** F6
Heppner, OR **147** B6
Herbert Hoover National Historic Site, IA **93** D8
Hereford, CO **137** A6
Hereford, TX **125** A3
Hermann, MO **101** C5
Hermiston, OR **147** A6
Hermitage, The, (site), TN **77** B5
Hershey, PA **47** E7
Hesperia, CA **135** H6
Hesston, KS **95** D6
Hettinger, ND **105** F3
Hialeah, FL **63** G9
Hiawatha, KS **95** A9
Hibbing, MN **99** C5
Hickory, NC **73** B4
High Bridge, NJ **43** C2
High Desert, OR **147** E5
High Plains, **128** D7
High Point, NC **73** B5
High Point (peak), NJ **43** A3
Highland Lake, NH **41** H2
Highland Lakes, NJ **43** A4
Highmore, SD **109** C6
Hightstown, NJ **43** E3
Hill Country (region), TX **125** H5
Hill Creek, UT **149** D6
Hillsboro, KS **95** D7
Hillsboro, ND **105** D10
Hillsboro, NH **41** H2
Hillsboro, OH **107** F3
Hillsboro, OR **147** B2
Hillsdale, MI **97** I6
Hillsdale Lake, KS **95** C10
Hilo, HI **139** F9
Hilton Head Island (island), SC **75** H6
Hilton Head Island, SC **75** H6
Hinesville, GA **65** G7
Hinsdale, NH **41** I1
Hinton, WV **81** G4
Hiwassee (river), TN **77** D8
Hiwassee Lake, NC **72** C1
Hobart, OK **123** D6
Hobbs, NM **121** G8
Hockanum (river), CT **31** B5
Hockessin, DE **33** A4
Hocking (river), OH **107** F6
Hoisington, KS **95** C5
Holbrook, AZ **119** D6
Holdenville, OK **123** D10
Holdrege, NE **103** D6
Holland, MI **97** H5
Hollandale, MS **71** D2
Hollidaysburg, PA **47** D4
Hollis, OK **123** D5
Holly Springs, MS **71** A4
Hollywood, FL **63** G9
Holston (river), TN, VA **77** A10
Holston, North Fork (river), VA **78** F3
Holston, South Fork (river), VA **78** F3
Holt Creek, NE **103** B6
Holton, KS **95** B9
Holualoa, HI **139** F8
Holyoke, CO **137** A9
Holyoke, MA **39** C3
Home of Franklin D. Roosevelt National Historic Site, NY **45** F8
Homer, AK **133** F6
Homer, LA **69** A3
Homestead, FL **63** H9
Homestead Nat. Mon. of America, NE **103** E8
Homewood, AL **59** D3
Homochitto (river), MS **71** G1
Homosassa Springs, FL **63** D6
Hondo, Rio (river), NM **121** F6
Honey Lake, CA **135** B4
Honolulu, HI **139** C4
Hood, Mount, OR **147** B4
Hood River, OR **147** B4

Hooper Bay, AK **132** E3
Hoopeston, IL **89** D6
Hoosic (river), MA **38** A1
Hoover, AL **59** D3
Hoover Dam, AZ, NV **119** B1
Hopatcong, Lake, NJ **43** B3
Hopatcong, NJ **43** B3
Hope, AR **61** F2
Hope, RI **49** C3
Hope Mills, NC **73** C7
Hope Valley, RI **49** E2
Hopewell, VA **79** D10
Hopewell Culture N.H.P., OH **107** F4
Hopewell Furnace National Historic Site, PA **47** E8
Hopkinsville, KY **66** E3
Hoquiam, WA **150** D2
Horn Lake, MS **71** A3
Hornell, NY **44** E3
Horse Creek, WY **153** G9
Horsehead Lake, ND **105** D6
Horseheads, NY **45** F4
Horsepasture N.W.&S.R., NC **72** C2
Horseshoe Bend, AR **61** A5
Horseshoe Bend N.M.P., AL **59** D5
Hot Creek Range, NV **145** E5
Hot Springs, AR **61** E3
Hot Springs, SD **108** E2
Hot Springs N.P., AR **61** D3
Houghton, MI **97** B2
Houghton Lake, MI **97** F6
Houlton, ME **35** C6
Houma, LA **69** H7
Housatonic (river), CT, MA **31** D3
Houston, DE **33** F5
Houston, MS **71** C4
Houston, TX **125** F8
Hovenweep Nat. Mon., CO **136** F1
Howard, SD **109** D9
Howland, ME **35** E5
Howland Island (territory), US **154** F3
Hubbard Lake, MI **97** E7
Hubbell Trading Post National Historic Site, AZ **119** C7
Huber Heights, OH **107** E2
Hudson (river), NJ, NY **45** C8
Hudson, Lake, OK **123** B11
Hudson, NY **45** E8
Hudson, WI **111** D1
Huerfano (river), CO **137** F5
Hueytown, AL **59** D3
Hugh Butler Lake, NE **103** D4
Hugo, OK **123** E11
Hugo Lake, OK **123** E11
Hugoton, KS **94** E2
Humacao, PR **155** I11
Humboldt, IA **93** B4
Humboldt, TN **76** B2
Humboldt (river), NV **145** B3
Humboldt Lake, NV **145** C3
Humboldt, North Fork (river), NV **145** A5
Humphreys Peak, AZ **119** C5
Huntingburg, IN **91** H2
Huntingdon, PA **47** D5
Huntington, IN **91** C5
Huntington, WV **80** F1
Huntington, NY **45** H9
Huntington Lake, IN **91** C5
Huntsville, AL **59** A4
Huntsville, TX **125** E8
Hurley, WI **111** B4
Hurlock, MD **37** D9
Huron, Lake, **84** C8
Huron, SD **109** D8
Hurricane, UT **149** H2
Hurricane, WV **80** F2
Hurricane Creek N.W.&S.R., AR **61** B3
Hutchinson, KS **95** D6
Hutchinson, MN **99** F3
Hyannis, MA **39** E9
Hyattsville, MD **37** C7

I

Idabel, OK **123** F12
Idaho Falls, ID **141** G5
Iditarod National Historic Trail, AK **133** E5
Iliamna Lake, AK **133** F5
Ili'ili, AS **154** I1
Ilion, NY **45** D7
Illinois (river), IL **89** E2
Illinois (river), OK **123** B12
Illinois (river), OR **146** G1
Illinois N.W.&S.R., OR **146** F1
Immokalee, FL **63** G8
Imnaha N.W.&S.R., OR **147** B9
Imperial, NE **103** D3
Imperial Valley, CA **135** I7
Independence, IA **93** C8
Independence, KS **95** E9
Independence, MO **101** C2
Independence Mountains, NV **145** B5
Indian (river), FL **63** E9
Indian Head, MD **37** D6
Indian Lake, OH **107** D3
Indian Nation Turnpike, OK **123** D10
Indian N.W.&S.R., MI **97** C4
Indian River Bay, DE **33** I7
Indian River Inlet, DE **33** H8
Indian Springs, NV **145** G6
Indiana, PA **47** D3
Indiana Dunes National Lakeshore, IN **91** A2
Indianapolis, IN **91** E4
Indianola, IA **93** E5
Indianola, MS **71** D2
International Falls, MN **99** B4
Intracoastal Waterway, AL, FL, LA, NC, SC **59** I2
Iola, KS **95** D9
Ionia, MI **97** G6
Iowa (river), IA **93** B5
Iowa City, IA **93** D8
Iowa Falls, IA **93** C6
Ipswich, MA **39** A8
Ipswich, SD **109** B7
Irmo, SC **75** D5
Iron Mountain, MI **97** D3
Irondequoit, NY **44** D4
Ironton, OH **107** H5
Ironwood, MI **97** C1
Ironwood Forest Nat. Mon., AZ **119** G5
Iroquois (river), IL, IN **89** C5
Irving, TX **125** D7
Irvington, NJ **43** C4
Ishpeming, MI **97** C3
Island Falls, ME **35** C5
Island Park, RI **49** D6
Island Park Reservoir, ID **141** F6
Island Pond, VT **51** B5
Isle au Haut, ME **35** G5
Isle Royale, MI **97** A2
Isle Royale N.P., MI **97** A2
Isles of Shoals, ME, NH **35** I2
Itasca, Lake, MN **99** C3
Ithaca, NY **45** E5
Iuka, MS **71** A6
Ivishak N.W.&S.R., AK **133** B7

J

J. Percy Priest Lake, TN **77** B5
J. Strom Thurmond Reservoir, GA, SC **65** C5
Jack Lee, Lake, AR **61** G4
Jackman, ME **35** D3
Jackpot, NV **145** A6
Jacks Fork (river), MO **101** F5
Jackson, AL **59** G2
Jackson, KY **67** D9
Jackson, MI **97** H6
Jackson, MO **101** E7
Jackson, MS **71** F3
Jackson, OH **107** G5
Jackson, TN **76** C2
Jackson, WY **152** C2
Jackson Lake, WY **152** C2
Jacksonville, AL **59** C5
Jacksonville, AR **61** D5
Jacksonville, FL **63** B7
Jacksonville, IL **89** E3
Jacksonville, NC **73** D8
Jacksonville Beach, FL **63** B8
Jaffrey, NH **41** I2
James (river), ND, SD **84** C3
James (river), VA **79** D8
James A. Garfield National Historic Site, OH **107** A7
Jamestown, ND **105** D8
Jamestown, NY **44** F2
Jamestown, RI **49** E5
Jamestown, VA **79** D10
Jamestown Reservoir, ND **105** D8
Janesville, WI **111** H6
Jarbidge (river), ID **141** I2
Jarvis Island (territory), US **155** G5
Jasper, AL **59** C2
Jasper, IN **91** H2
Jay Peak, VT **51** A3
Jeanerette, LA **69** G5
Jeannette, PA **46** E2
Jefferson, IA **93** D4
Jefferson (river), MT **143** E4
Jefferson City, MO **101** D5
Jefferson City, TN **77** B9
Jeffersontown, KY **67** B6
Jeffersonville, IN **91** H4
Jekyll Island, GA **65** H7
Jemez, E. Fork N.W.&S.R., NM **121** C4
Jenks, OK **123** B10
Jennings, LA **69** G3
Jericho, VT **51** C2
Jerimoth Hill (peak), RI **49** B2
Jerome, ID **141** H3
Jersey City, NJ **43** C5
Jersey Shore, PA **47** C6
Jerseyville, IL **89** F2
Jerusalem, RI **49** G4
Jesse James Farm and Museum, MO **101** B2
Jesup, GA **65** G6
Jewel Cave Nat. Mon., SD **108** E1
Jewett City, CT **31** C8
Jimmy Carter National Historic Site, GA **65** F2
John D. Rockefeller, Jr. Memorial Parkway, WY **152** B2
John Day, North Fork N.W.&S.R., OR **147** C7
John Day, OR **147** C6
John Day, South Fork N.W.&S.R., OR **147** D6
John Day (river), OR **147** C5
John Day Fossil Beds Nat. Mon., OR **147** C5
John Day N.W.&S.R., OR **147** B5
John Day, South Fork N.W.&S.R., OR **147** D6
John F. Kennedy Space Center (site), FL **63** D9
John H. Kerr Reservoir, NC, VA **79** E8
John Martin Reservoir, CO **137** E8
John Muir N.H.S., CA **135** D2
John N.W.&S.R., AK **133** B6
John Redmond Reservoir, KS **95** D9
Johnson, VT **51** B3
Johnson City, TN **77** B10
Johnston, RI **49** B4
Johnston Atoll (territory), US **154** E4
Johnstown, PA **47** E3
Johnstown Flood National Memorial, PA **47** D4
Joliet, IL **89** C5
Jonesboro, AR **61** B7
Jonesboro, LA **69** C3
Jonesport, ME **35** F6
Joplin, MO **101** F2
Jordan, MT **143** C9
Jordan Creek, ID **141** H1
Joseph Creek N.W.&S.R., OR **147** A8
Joshua Tree N.P., CA **135** H7
Juan de Fuca, Strait of, WA **150** B1
Julia Butler Hansen Refuge, WA **150** E2
Jump (river), WI **111** C3
Junction City, KS **95** B7
Junction City, OR **147** D2
Juneau, AK **133** F10
Juniata (river), PA **47** D6
Jupiter, FL **63** F9

K

Ka'ena Point, HI **139** B4
Kadoka, SD **109** D4
Kaho'olawe (island), HI **139** D7
Kahuku Point, HI **139** B4
Kahului, HI **139** C7
Kaibab Plateau, AZ **119** B4
Kailua, HI **139** B5
Kailua-Kona, HI **139** F8
Kaiwi Channel, HI **139** C5
Kalae (South Cape), HI **139** G8
Kalaheo, HI **138** A2
Kalamazoo, MI **97** H5
Kalamazoo (river), MI **97** H5
Kalaoa, HI **139** F8
Kalaupapa, HI **139** C6
Kalaupapa N.H.P., HI **139** C6
Kalispell, MT **142** B2
Kalkaska, MI **97** E5
Kaloko-Honokohau N.H.P., HI **139** F8
Kamiah, ID **141** D2
Kamuela see Waimea, HI **139** E8
Kanab, UT **149** H3
Kanab Creek, AZ, UT **119** B4
Kanawha (river), WV **81** F3
Kane'ohe, HI **139** B5
Kankakee, IL **89** C5
Kankakee (river), IL, IN **89** C5
Kannapolis, NC **73** C5
Kanopolis Lake, KS **95** C6
Kansas (river), KS **95** B9
Kansas City, KS **95** B10
Kansas City, MO **101** C2
Kapa'a, HI **138** A2
Kapa'au, HI **139** E8
Kaskaskia (river), IL **89** F4
Kaskaskia Island, IL **89** H3
Katahdin, Mount, ME **35** D5
Katmai N.P. and Preserve, AK **133** F5
Kaua'i (island), HI **138** A2
Kaukauna, WI **111** E6
Kaulakahi Channel, HI **138** A1
Kaunakakai, HI **139** C6
Kaw Lake, OK **123** A9
Kawich Range, NV **145** E5
Kayenta, AZ **119** B6
Keahole Point, HI **139** F8
Keansburg, NJ **43** D4
Kearney, NE **103** D6
Keene, NH **41** H2
Kekaha, HI **138** A1
Kelleys Island, OH **107** B5
Kellogg, ID **141** C1
Kelso, WA **151** F3
Kemmerer, WY **152** F2
Kenai, AK **133** E6
Kenai Fjords N.P., AK **133** F6
Kenai Peninsula, AK **133** E6
Kendall, FL **63** H9
Kendall Park, NJ **43** D3
Kendallville, IN **91** B5
Kenmare, ND **105** A3
Kennebec, SD **109** D6
Kennebec (river), ME **35** G3
Kennebunk, ME **35** I2
Kenner, LA **69** G7
Kennesaw Mountain National Battlefield Park, GA **65** C2
Kennett, MO **101** G7
Kennett Square, PA **47** F9
Kennewick, WA **151** F7
Kenosha, WI **111** H7
Kenova, WV **80** F1
Kent, CT **31** B2
Kent, OH **107** B7
Kent Island, MD **37** C8
Kenton, OH **107** C3
Kentucky (river), KY **67** B7
Kentucky Lake, KY **66** E2
Kentucky, Middle Fork (river), KY **67** D9
Kentucky, North Fork (river), KY **67** C9
Kentucky, South Fork (river), KY **67** D9
Kentwood, MI **97** G5
Keokuk, IA **93** F8
Keowee, Lake, SC **74** B2
Kern N.W.&S.R., CA **135** G5
Kernersville, NC **73** B5
Kerrville, TX **125** F5
Ketchikan, AK **133** G11
Ketchum, ID **141** G3
Kettering, OH **107** E2
Kettle River Range, WA **151** B8
Keuka Lake, NY **45** E4
Kewanee, IL **89** C3
Keweenaw N.H.P., MI **97** B2
Keweenaw Peninsula, MI **97** B3
Key Largo, FL **63** H9
Key West, FL **63** I7
Keya Paha (river), NE, SD **103** A5
Keyhole Reservoir, WY **153** B9
Keyser, WV **81** C8
Keystone Lake, OK **123** B10
Kiamichi (river), OK **123** E11
Kickapoo (river), WI **111** G3
Kihei, HI **139** D7
Kilauea Crater (site), HI **139** F9
Killeen, TX **125** E6
Killik (river), AK **133** B6
Killington Peak, VT **51** F3
Kimball, NE **102** C1
Kinderhook, NY **45** E8
Kingfield, ME **35** F3
Kingfisher, OK **123** C8
Kingman, AZ **119** D2
Kingman, KS **95** E6
Kingman Reef (territory), US **155** F5
Kings (river), NV **145** A3
Kings Canyon N.P., CA **135** E5
Kings Mountain, NC **73** C4
Kings Mountain N.M.P., SC **75** A4
Kings Peak, UT **149** B5
Kings N.W.&S.R., CA **135** F5
Kingsland, GA **65** H7
Kingsport, TN **77** A10
Kingston, NH **41** H5
Kingston, NY **45** F8
Kingston, PA **47** C8
Kingston, RI **49** F4
Kingstree, SC **75** E7
Kingsville, TX **125** H6
Kingwood, WV **81** C6
Kinsley, KS **95** D4
Kinston, NC **73** C8
Kiowa, CO **137** C6
Kirkland, WA **151** C4
Kirksville, MO **101** A4
Kirkwood, MO **101** D7
Kirwin Reservoir, KS **95** A4
Kiska Island, AK **133** H7
Kissimmee, FL **63** D8
Kissimmee (river), FL **63** E8
Kitt Peak National Observatory, AZ **119** H5
Kittanning, PA **47** D3
Kittatinny Mountains, NJ **43** B2
Kittery, ME **35** I2
Kitts Hummock, DE **33** E6
Kitty Hawk, NC **73** B10
Klamath (river), CA, OR **128** D2
Klamath Falls, OR **147** G3
Klamath N.W.&S.R., CA, OR **135** A1
Klickitat (river), WA **151** F5
Klickitat N.W.&S.R., WA **151** F5
Klondike Gold Rush N.H.P., AK **133** E9
Knife (river), ND **105** D3
Knife River Indian Villages National Historic Site, ND **105** D4
Knoxville, IA **93** E6
Knoxville, TN **77** B8
Kobuk N.W.&S.R., AK **133** C5
Kobuk Valley N.P., AK **133** B5
Kodiak, AK **133** G6
Kodiak Island, AK **133** G6
Kokomo, IN **91** D4
Koocanusa, Lake, MT **142** A2
Kootenai (river), ID, MT **141** A1
Kosciusko, MS **71** D4
Kotzebue, AK **133** B4
Koyukuk (river), AK **133** C5
Koyukuk, North Fork N.W.&S.R., AK **133** B6
Kumukahi, Cape, HI **139** F10
Kure Atoll, HI **138** E1
Kuskokwim (river), AK **133** C6
Kuskokwim Mountains, AK **133** E4
Kuskokwim, North Fork (river), AK **133** D5

L

La Crescent, MN **99** H6
La Crosse, WI **111** F3
La Follette, TN **77** B8
La Grande, OR **147** B7
La Grange, GA **65** E1
La Grange, KY **67** B6
La Junta, CO **137** F7
La Moine (river), IL **89** D2
La Perouse Pinnacle (island), HI **139** F3
La Plata, MD **37** E7
La Salle, IL **89** C4

BACK OF THE BOOK

La'ie – Marion, IL

La'ie, HI **139** B4
Laconia, NH **41** G4
Ladder Creek, KS **94** C2
Ladson, SC **75** F7
Ladysmith, WI **111** C3
Lafayette, CO **137** B5
LaFayette, GA **65** B1
Lafayette, IN **91** D2
Lafayette, LA **69** G4
Lafayette, Mount, NH **41** D3
Lafourche, Bayou (river), LA **69** H7
Lahaina, HI **139** C7
La'ie, HI **139** B4
Lake Andes, SD **109** F8
Lake Charles, LA **68** G2
Lake City, FL **63** B6
Lake City, SC **75** D8
Lake Clark N.P. and Preserve, AK **133** E5
Lake Erie Beach, NY **44** E2
Lake Geneva, WI **111** H6
Lake Havasu City, AZ **119** D2
Lake Mead N.R.A., AZ, NV **119** C2
Lake Meredith N.R.A., TX **125** A4
Lake Placid, NY **45** B8
Lake Providence, LA **69** A6
Lake Roosevelt N.R.A., WA **151** C8
Lake Village, AR **61** G6
Lakehurst, NJ **43** F4
Lakeland, FL **63** E7
Lakeview, OR **147** G5
Lakeville, CT **31** A2
Lakeville, MN **99** G4
Lakewood, NJ **43** E4
Lakewood, WA **151** D3
Lakin, KS **94** D2
Lamar, CO **137** E9
Lambertville, MI **97** I7
Lambertville, NJ **43** D2
Lamesa, TX **125** D3
Lamlam, Mount, GU **154** G1
Lamoille (river), VT **51** B2
LaMoure, ND **105** E8
Lamprey (river), NH **41** H4
Lamprey N.W.&S.R., NH **41** H5
Lāna'i (island), HI **139** D6
Lāna'i City, HI **139** D6
Lancaster, CA **135** G5
Lancaster, NH **41** C3
Lancaster, OH **107** E5
Lancaster, PA **47** E8
Lancaster, SC **75** B6
Lancaster, WI **111** G4
Land Between the Lakes N.R.A., KY, TN **66** E3
Land O'Lakes, WI **111** B5
Lander, WY **153** D4
Lanett, AL **59** E6
Langdon, ND **105** A8
L'Anguille (river), AR **61** C6
L'Anse, MI **97** C2
Lansing, KS **95** B10
Lansing, MI **97** H6
LaPorte, IN **91** A3
Laramie, WY **153** G8
Laramie (river), CO, WY **153** F9
Laramie Mountains, CO, WY **153** E8
Laredo, TX **125** H5
Larimore, ND **105** C9
Larned, KS **95** D4
Larose, LA **69** H7
Las Animas, CO **137** E8
Las Cruces, NM **121** G4
Las Vegas, NM **121** C5
Las Vegas, NV **145** G6
Lassen Volcanic N.P., CA **135** B3
Last Chance, CO **137** C7
Lata Mountain, AS **155** I5
Laughlin, NV **145** I6
Laurel, DE **33** I5
Laurel, MS **71** G4
Laurel, MT **143** E7
Laurens, SC **75** C3
Laurinburg, NC **73** D6
Laurium, MI **97** B2
Lava Beds Nat. Mon., CA **135** A3
Lawrence, IN **91** E4
Lawrence, KS **95** B9
Lawrence, MA **39** A7
Lawrenceburg, IN **91** F6
Lawrenceburg, KY **67** C7
Lawrenceburg, TN **77** C4
Lawrenceville, IL **89** G6
Lawton, OK **123** E7
Laysan Island, HI **138** E2
Layton, UT **149** B4
Le Mars, IA **92** B2
Lead, SD **108** C1
Leadville, CO **137** D4
Leaf (river), MS **71** G5
Leavenworth, KS **95** B10
Lebanon, IN **91** D3
Lebanon, KS **95** A5
Lebanon, KY **67** D7
Lebanon, MO **101** E4
Lebanon, NH **41** F2
Lebanon, OH **107** F2
Lebanon, OR **147** C2
Lebanon, PA **47** E7
Lebanon, TN **77** B5
Lebanon, VA **78** E3
Lee, MA **38** C1
Leech Lake, MN **99** D3
Lee's Summit, MO **101** C2
Leesburg, FL **63** D7
Leesburg, VA **79** A9
Leesville, LA **68** E2
Leesville Lake, OH **107** D7
Lehi, UT **149** C4
Lehigh (river), PA **47** C8
Lehua Island, HI **138** A1
Leitchfield, KY **67** D5
Leland, MS **71** D2
Lemhi (river), ID **141** F4
Lemhi Pass, MT **142** F3
Lemhi Range, ID **141** F3
Lemmon, SD **109** A3
Lemon, Lake, IN **91** F3
Lennox, SD **109** E10
Lenoir, NC **73** B4
Lenoir City, TN **77** B8
Lenox, MA **38** B1
Leola, SD **109** A7
Leominster, MA **39** B5
Leon (river), TX **125** E6
Leusoali'i, AS **155** I5
Levelland, TX **125** C3
Levisa Fork (river), KY **67** C10
Levittown, NY **45** H9
Levittown, PA **47** E10
Lewes, DE **33** G7
Lewes and Rehoboth Canal, DE **33** G7
Lewis (river), WA **151** F3
Lewis and Clark Lake, NE, SD **109** F9
Lewis Smith Lake, AL **59** B3
Lewisburg, PA **47** C7
Lewisburg, TN **77** C5
Lewisburg, WV **81** G5
Lewiston, ID **141** D1
Lewiston, ME **35** G3
Lewistown, MT **143** C6
Lewistown, PA **47** D6
Lexington, KY **67** C8
Lexington, MA **39** B7
Lexington, NC **73** B5
Lexington, NE **103** D5
Lexington, TN **76** C3
Lexington, VA **79** D7
Lexington Park, MD **37** E8
Libby, MT **142** B1
Liberal, KS **94** F2
Liberty, MO **101** C2
Licking (river), KY **67** A8
Licking (river), OH **107** E5
Licking, North Fork (river), KY **67** B8
Licking, South Fork (river), KY **67** B8
Lihu'e, HI **138** A2
Lillinonah, Lake, CT **31** D2
Lima, OH **107** C2
Limestone, ME **35** B6
Limon, CO **137** D7
Lincoln, DE **33** G6
Lincoln, IL **89** E4
Lincoln, ME **35** E5
Lincoln, NE **103** D9
Lincoln, NH **41** E3
Lincoln Boyhood National Memorial, IN **91** H2
Lincoln City, OR **146** C1
Lincoln Home National Historic Site, IL **89** E3
Lincolnton, NC **73** C4
Lindenwold, NJ **43** F2
Lindsborg, KS **95** C6
Linton, IN **91** G2
Linton, ND **105** F6
Lisbon, ND **105** E9
Lisbon, NH **41** D2
Lisbon Falls, ME **35** G3
Lisianski Island, HI **138** E2
Liston Point, DE **33** C5
Litchfield, CT **31** B3
Litchfield, IL **89** F3
Litchfield, MN **99** F3
Little (river), AR, OK **61** F1
Little (river), KY **66** E3
Little (river), LA **69** D4
Little (river), OK **123** D9
Little Beaver Creek National Scenic River, OH **107** C8
Little Bighorn Battlefield Nat. Mon., MT **143** E8
Little Blue (river), KS, NE **95** A7
Little Colorado (river), AZ **119** D7
Little Compton, RI **49** E6
Little Darby Creek, OH **107** E3
Little Deschutes N.W.&S.R., OR **147** E4
Little Diomede Island, AK **132** C3
Little Egg Harbor, NJ **43** G4
Little Falls, MN **99** E3
Little Falls, NY **45** D7
Little Humboldt (river), NV **145** B4
Little Kanawha (river), WV **81** D3
Little Lost (river), ID **141** F4
Little Miami (river), OH **107** F2
Little Miami, East Fork (river), OH **107** G2
Little Miami National Scenic River, OH **107** F2
Little Missouri, MT **143** F11
Little Missouri (river), AR, ND, SD **84** C1
Little Missouri N.W.&S.R., AR **61** E2
Little Muddy (river), ND **104** B2
Little Pee Dee (river), NC, SC **75** D9
Little Powder (river), WY **153** B8
Little Red (river), AR **61** C5
Little River Canyon National Preserve, AL **59** B5
Little Rock, AR **61** D4
Little Rock Central High School National Historic Site, AR **61** D5
Little Sac (river), MO **101** E3
Little Salt Lake (dry lake), UT 151 G2
Little Sandy (river), KY **67** B10
Little Sioux (river), IA **92** C2
Little Snake (river), CO **137** A2
Little Tallahatchie (river), MS **71** B4
Little Wabash (river), IL **89** G5
Little White (river), SD **109** F4
Little Wood (river), ID **141** H3
Littleton, CO **137** C6
Littleton, ME **35** C6
Littleton, NH **41** D3
Live Oak, FL **63** B6
Livingston, AL **59** E1
Livingston, MT **143** E5
Livingston, Lake, TX **114** E9
Livonia, MI **97** H7
Llano (river), TX **125** E5
Llano Estacado (plain), NM, TX **114** D5
Lochsa (river), ID **141** D2
Lock Haven, PA **47** C6
Lockport, NY **44** D2
Locust Creek, MO **101** A4
Locust Fork (river), AL **59** C3
Lodgepole Creek, NE, WY **102** C1
Lodi, CA **135** D3
Logan, OH **107** F5
Logan, UT **149** A4
Logan, WV **80** G2
Logan Creek, NE **103** B8
Logansport, IN **91** C3
Lolo Pass, MT **142** D2
Lompoc, CA **135** G4
London, KY **67** D8
Londonderry, NH **41** I4
Lone Grove, OK **123** E8
Long Bay, NC, SC **73** E7
Long Beach, CA **135** H5
Long Beach, MS **71** I4
Long Beach, NY **45** H9
Long Beach Island, NJ **43** G5
Long Branch, NJ **43** D5
Long Island, NY **45** H9
Long Island Sound, NY **45** G9
Long Lake (lake), ME **35** A5
Long Lake (lake), ME **35** B4
Long Lake, ND **105** E6
Long Pond, MA **39** E7
Long Prairie, MN **99** E3
Long Trail, VT **51** D2
Longfellow Mountains, ME **35** F2
Longmont, CO **137** B5
Longview, TX **125** D8
Longview, WA **151** F3
Lonsdale, RI **49** B5
Looking Glass (river), MI **97** G6
Lookout, Cape, NC **73** D10
Lookout Pass, ID **141** C2
Lookout, Point, MD **37** F8
Lorain, OH **107** B5
Lordsburg, NM **121** G1
Loris, SC **75** D9
Los Alamos, NM **121** C4
Los Angeles, CA **135** H5
Los Lunas, NM **121** D4
Los Pinos (river), CO **137** F2
Lost River Range, ID **141** F3
Lostine N.W.&S.R., OR **147** B8
Loudonville, OH **107** C5
Louie B. Nunn Parkway, KY **67** E6
Louisiana, MO **101** B6
Louisville, CO **137** B5
Louisville, KY **67** B6
Louisville, MS **71** D4
Loup (river), NE **103** C7
Loup, Middle (river), NE **103** C5
Loup, North (river), NE **103** B5
Loup, South (river), NE **103** C5
Loveland, CO **137** B5
Lovell, WY **153** A5
Lovelock, NV **145** C3
Loving, NM **121** G7
Lovington, NM **121** G8
Lowell, IN **91** B2
Lowell, Lake, ID **141** G1
Lowell, MA **39** A6
Lowell N.H.P., MA **39** A6
Lower Bay, NJ **43** D5
Lower Peninsula, MI **97** F5
Lower Red Lake, MN **99** B3
Lowville, NY **45** C6
Loxahatchee N.W.&S.R., FL **63** F10
Lubbock, TX **125** C4
Lucedale, MS **71** H5
Ludington, MI **97** F4
Ludlow, MA **39** C3
Ludlow, VT **51** G3
Lufkin, TX **125** E8
Lumber (river), NC **73** D6
Lumber N.W.&S.R., NC **73** D6
Lumberton, NC **73** D7
Luray, VA **79** B8
Lusk, WY **153** D10
Luverne, MN **99** H2
Lyman, WY **152** G2
Lynchburg, TN **77** C5
Lynchburg, VA **79** D7
Lynches (river), SC **75** D8
Lynden, WA **151** A3
Lyndon B. Johnson N.H.P., TX **125** F6
Lyndonville, VT **51** C5
Lynn, MA **39** B7
Lyons, KS **95** D5

M

Machias, ME **35** F7
Machias (river), ME **35** F6
Machiasport, ME **35** F7
Mackinac Island, MI **97** D6
Mackinac, Straits of, MI **97** D5
Mackinaw (river), IL **89** D4
Macomb, IL **89** D2
Macon, Bayou (river), LA **69** B5
Macon, GA **65** E3
Macon, MO **101** B4
Macoupin Creek, IL **89** F2
Mad (river), VT **51** D3
Madawaska, ME **35** A5
Madeline Island, WI **111** A4
Madill, OK **123** E9
Madison, AL **59** A3
Madison, CT **31** E5
Madison, IN **91** G5
Madison, ME **35** F3
Madison, MN **99** F2
Madison, NE **103** C8
Madison, SD **109** D9
Madison, WI **111** G5
Madison, WV **80** G2
Madison (river), WY **152** A1
Madison (river), MT **143** E4
Madison Heights, VA **79** D7
Madisonville, KY **66** D3
Madras, OR **147** C4
Magazine Mountain (peak), AR **61** C2
Magee, MS **71** F3
Maggie L. Walker National Historic Site, VA **79** D9
Magic Reservoir, ID **141** H3
Magnolia, AR **61** G3
Mahoning (river), OH **107** B8
Maia, AS **155** I5
Maine, Gulf of, ME **35** H5
Makawao, HI **139** C7
Malad City, ID **141** I4
Malden, MA **39** B7
Malden, MO **101** G7
Malheur (river), OR **147** D8
Malheur Lake, OR **147** E7
Malheur, North Fork (river), OR **147** D7
Malheur, North Fork N.W.&S.R., OR **147** D7
Malone, NY **45** A8
Malta, MT **143** B8
Malvern, AR **61** E3
Mammoth Cave N.P., KY **67** D5
Manalapan (river), NJ **43** D4
Manasquan, NJ **43** E5
Manassas, VA **79** B9
Manassas National Battlefield Park, VA **79** B9
Manchester, CT **31** B5
Manchester, IA **93** C8
Manchester, MD **37** A7
Manchester, NH **41** H4
Manchester, OH **107** G3
Manchester, TN **77** C6
Manchester Center, VT **51** H2
Mancos (river), CO **136** G1
Mandan, ND **105** E5
Mandeville, LA **69** F8
Mangum, OK **123** D6
Manhattan, KS **95** B7
Manila, AR **61** B8
Manistee, MI **97** F4
Manistee (river), MI **97** F5
Manistee N.W.&S.R., MI **97** F5
Manistique, MI **97** D4
Manitou Islands, MI **97** E4
Manitou Passage, MI **97** E5
Manitowoc, WI **111** E7
Mankato, MN **99** G4
Manning, SC **75** D7
Mannington, WV **81** C5
Mansfield, LA **68** C1
Mansfield, Mount, VT **51** C2
Mansfield, OH **107** C5
Mansfield, PA **47** B6
Mansfield Hollow Lake, CT **31** B7
Manti, UT **149** E4
Manu'a Islands, AS **154** I3
Manville, RI **49** A4
Many, LA **68** D2
Manzanar National Historic Site, CA **135** F5
Maple (river), ND **105** E9
Maple (river), ND **105** F8
Maquoketa, IA **93** C9
Maquoketa (river), IA **93** C9
Marais des Cygnes (river), KS, MO **95** C10
Marathon, FL **63** I8
Marble Canyon, AZ **119** B5
Marblehead, MA **39** B8
Marcy, Mount, NY **45** B8
Marfa, TX **124** F2
Marianna, AR **61** D7
Marianna, FL **63** A3
Marias (river), MT **143** B4
Marietta, GA **65** C2
Marietta, OH **107** F7
Marinette, WI **111** D7
Marion, AL **59** E2
Marion, IA **93** C8
Marion, IL **89** H4

Marion, IN **91** C4
Marion, KY **66** D3
Marion, OH **107** D4
Marion, SC **75** C8
Marion, VA **78** E4
Marion Lake, KS **95** C7
Marion, Lake, SC **75** E6
Mark Twain Lake, MO **101** B5
Marked Tree, AR **61** C7
Marksville, LA **69** E4
Marlborough, CT **31** C6
Marlborough, MA **39** C6
Marlow, OK **123** E8
Maro Reef, HI **138** F2
Marquette, MI **97** C3
Mars Hill, ME **35** B6
Marsh Island, LA **69** H4
Marshall, MI **97** H6
Marshall, MN **99** G2
Marshall, MO **101** C4
Marshall, TX **125** D9
Marshallton, DE **33** B4
Marshalltown, IA **93** C6
Marsh-Billings-Rockefeller N.H.P., VT **51** F3
Marshfield, WI **111** D4
Marshyhope Creek, DE, MD **35** G4
Martha's Vineyard (island), MA **39** F8
Martin, Lake, AL **59** E5
Martin, SD **109** E4
Martin, TN **76** B2
Martin Luther King, Jr. National Historic Site, GA **65** C2
Martin Van Buren National Historic Site, NY **45** E8
Martins Ferry, OH **107** D8
Martinsburg, WV **81** C9
Martinsville, IN **91** F3
Martinsville, VA **79** E6
Marydel, DE **33** E4
Marys (river), NV **145** A6
Marysville, KS **95** A7
Marysville, OH **107** D3
Maryville, MO **101** A2
Maryville, TN **77** C8
Mascoma Lake, NH **41** F2
Mason, MI **97** H6
Mason, OH **107** F2
Mason City, IA **93** A6
Massabesic Lake, NH **41** H4
Massachusetts Bay, MA **39** B8
Massena, NY **45** A7
Massillon, OH **107** C6
Matagorda Bay, TX **114** F8
Matanuska (river), AK **133** E6
Mattawamkeag (river), ME **35** D6
Matthews, NC **73** C4
Mattoon, IL **89** F5
Maui (island), HI **139** C7
Mauldin, SC **75** B3
Maumee, OH **107** B3
Maumee (river), IN, OH **91** B6
Maumee Bay, OH **107** A3
Maumelle, AR **61** D4
Mauna Kea (peak), HI **139** E9
Mauna Loa (peak), HI **139** F9
Maurepas, Lake, LA **69** F7
Maurice (river), NJ **43** G2
Maurice N.W.&S.R., NJ **43** H2
May, Cape, NJ **43** I2
Mayagüez, PR **155** I9
Mayfield, KY **66** E2
Mayfield Creek, KY **66** E1
Mays Landing, NJ **43** H3
Maysville, KY **67** B9
Mayville, ND **105** C9
McAlester, OK **123** D10
McAllen, TX **125** I6
McCall, ID **141** F1
McCandless, PA **46** D2
McComb, MS **71** G2
McCook, NE **103** E4
McGee Creek Lake, OK **123** E10
McGehee, AR **61** F6
McGill, NV **145** D6
McIntosh, SD **109** A4
McKee Creek, IL **89** E2
McKeesport, PA **46** D2
McKenzie, TN **76** B3
McKenzie (river), OR **147** D2
McKenzie N.W.&S.R., OR **147** D3
McKinley, Mount (Denali), AK **133** D6
McLean, VA **79** A9
McLoughlin House National Historic Site, OR **147** B2
McMinnville, OR **147** B2
McMinnville, TN **77** C6
McPherson, KS **95** C6
Mead, Lake, AZ, NV **119** B2
Meade, KS **95** E3
Meade (river), AK **133** A5
Meadow Valley Wash (river), NV **145** G7
Meadville, PA **46** B2
Mechanicsburg, PA **47** E6
Mechanicsville, VA **79** D9
Medford, MA **39** B7
Medford, OR **147** G2
Medford, WI **111** D4
Medical Lake, WA **151** C9
Medicine Bow (river), WY **153** F7
Medicine Bow Mountains, CO **137** A4
Medicine Lodge, KS **95** E5
Medicine Lodge (river), KS **95** E4
Medina, NY **44** D3
Medina, OH **107** B6
Medora, ND **104** D2
Meeker, CO **137** B2
Meherrin (river), VA **79** E8
Melbourne, FL **63** D9
Melozitna (river), AK **133** C5
Memphis, TN **76** C1
Memphremagog, Lake, VT **51** A4
Mena, AR **61** D1
Menahga, MN **99** D3
Menasha, WI **111** E6
Mendota, IL **89** B4
Mendota, Lake, WI **111** G5
Menlo Park, NJ **43** D4
Menominee, MI **97** E3
Menominee (river), MI, WI **97** D3
Menomonee Falls, WI **111** G7
Menomonie, WI **111** D2
Mentor, OH **107** A7
Mequon, WI **111** G7
Merced, CA **135** E4
Merced N.W.&S.R., CA **135** E4
Mercersburg, PA **47** F5
Mercerville, NJ **43** E3
Meredith, Lake, CO **137** E7
Meredith, NH **41** F3
Meriden, CT **31** C4
Meridian, MS **71** E5
Merrill, WI **111** D5
Merrillville, IN **91** A2
Merrimack, NH **41** I3
Merrimack (river), MA, NH **39** A7
Merritt Island, FL **63** D9
Merrymeeting Lake, NH **41** G4
Mesa, AZ **119** F5
Mesa de Maya, CO **137** G7
Mesa Verde N.P., CO **136** G1
Mesabi Range, MN **99** C4
Mesquite, NV **145** G7
Metairie, LA **69** G8
Meteor Crater, AZ **119** D5
Methow (river), WA **151** B6
Methuen, MA **39** A7
Metolius N.W.&S.R., OR **147** D3
Metropolis, IL **89** I4
Mettawee (river), VT **51** G1
Mexico, Gulf of, **54** G3
Mexico, ME **35** F2
Mexico, MO **101** C5
Miami, FL **63** G9
Miami, OK **123** A11
Miami Beach, FL **63** G9
Miami Canal, FL **63** F9
Michigan City, IN **91** A2
Michigan, Lake, **84** D7
Middleboro, MA **39** D8
Middlebury, VT **51** E2
Middlesboro, KY **67** E9
Middleton, WI **111** G5
Middletown, CT **31** C5
Middletown, DE **33** C4
Middletown, NY **45** G8
Middletown, OH **107** F2
Middletown, RI **49** E5
Midland, MI **97** G6
Midland, TX **125** D3
Midway, DE **33** H7
Midway Islands (territory), US **154** D4
Milaca, MN **99** E4
Milan, NM **121** D2
Milan, TN **76** B2
Milbank, SD **109** B10
Miles City, MT **143** D10
Milford, CT **31** E3
Milford, DE **33** G6
Milford, MA **39** C6
Milford, NE **103** D8
Milford, NH **41** I3
Milford, UT **149** F2
Milford Lake, KS **95** B7
Mililani Town, HI **139** B4
Milk (river), MT **143** B8
Mill Creek, IN **91** F3
Millbrook, AL **59** E4
Millcreek, PA **46** A2
Mille Lacs Lake, MN **99** D4
Milledgeville, GA **65** D4
Millen, GA **65** E6
Miller, SD **109** C7
Millers (river), MA **39** A4
Millington, TN **76** C1
Millinocket, ME **35** D5
Millsboro, DE **33** I6
Millville, NJ **43** H2
Millwood Lake, AR **61** F2
Milo, ME **35** E4
Milton, DE **33** G6
Milton, MA **39** C7
Milton, NH **41** G5
Milton, VT **51** B2
Milton, Lake, OH **107** C7
Milton-Freewater, OR **147** A7
Milwaukee, WI **111** G7
Milwaukee (river), WI **111** F6
Minam N.W.&S.R., OR **147** B8
Minden, LA **68** B2
Minden, NE **103** D6
Mineral Wells, TX **125** D6
Minidoka Internment Camp Nat. Mon., ID **141** H3
Minneapolis, KS **95** B6
Minneapolis, MN **99** F4
Minnesota (river), MN **99** F2
Minot, ND **105** B4
Minute Man N.H.P., MA **39** B6
Minuteman Missile National Historic Site, SD **109** D3
Mio, MI **97** E6
Mishawaka, IN **91** A4
Mission, TX **125** I6
Mission Viejo, CA **135** H6
Missisquoi (river), VT **51** A2
Mississinewa (river), IN **91** D5
Mississinewa Lake, IN **91** C4
Mississippi (river), **54** B2
Mississippi National River and N.R.A., MN **99** F4
Mississippi Petrified Forest, MS **71** E2
Mississippi River Delta, LA **69** I10
Mississippi Sound, AL, MS **71** I5
Missoula, MT **142** C3
Missouri (river), **84** F5
Missouri National Recreational River, NE, SD **103** A7
Missouri N.W.&S.R., MT **143** B6
Misty Fiords Nat. Mon., AK **133** G11
Mitchell, SD **109** E8
Mitchell, Mount, NC **72** B3
Moab, UT **149** F6
Moberly, MO **101** B4
Mobile, AL **59** H1
Mobile (river), AL **59** H1
Mobile Bay, AL **59** I1
Mobridge, SD **109** B5
Modesto, CA **135** E3
Mogollon Rim, AZ **119** E6
Mohave, Lake, AZ, NV **119** C1
Mohawk (river), NY **45** D7
Mohican (river), OH **107** D5
Mojave Desert, CA, NV **128** F4
Mojave National Preserve, CA **135** G7
Moline, IL **89** C2
Moloka'i (island), HI **139** C6
Monadnock Mountain, NH **41** I2
Monahans, TX **125** E3
Moncks Corner, SC **75** F7
Monessen, PA **46** E2
Monett, MO **101** F3
Monhegan Island, ME **35** H4
Monitor Range, NV **145** E4
Monmouth, IL **89** C2
Monmouth, OR **147** C2
Mono Lake, CA **135** D5
Monocacy (river), MD **37** A6
Monocacy N.B., MD **37** B6
Monomoy Island, MA **39** E10
Monona, WI **111** G5
Monongahela (river), PA, WV **26** G1
Monroe, GA **65** C3
Monroe, LA **69** B4
Monroe, MI **97** I7
Monroe, NC **73** C5
Monroe, WI **111** H5
Monroe Lake, IN **91** G3
Monroeville, AL **59** G2
Montauk Point, NY **45** G11
Monte Vista, CO **137** F4
Monterey, CA **135** F2
Monterey Bay, CA **135** F2
Monterey Bay National Marine Sanctuary, CA **135** E2
Montevallo, AL **59** D3
Montevideo, MN **99** F2
Montezuma Castle Nat. Mon., AZ **119** D5
Montgomery, AL **59** E4
Montgomery, WV **81** F3
Montgomery Village, MD **37** B6
Monticello, AR **61** F5
Monticello, IA **93** C9
Monticello, IN **91** C3
Monticello, NY **45** F7
Monticello (site), VA **79** C8
Montpelier, ID **141** I6
Montpelier (site), VA **79** C8
Montpelier, VT **51** D3
Montrose, CO **137** E2
Monument Valley, AZ, UT **149** H6
Moodus, CT **31** D6
Moore, OK **123** D8
Moore Reservoir, NH, VT **51** C5
Moorefield, WV **81** D8
Moores Creek N.B., NC **73** D8
Moorhead, MN **99** D1
Moose (river), ME **35** D2
Moose (river), VT **51** C5
Moosehead Lake, ME **35** D4
Mooselookmeguntic Lake, ME **35** F2
Moosup, CT **31** B8
Moosup (river), RI **49** C2
Mora, MN **99** E4
Mora (river), NM **121** C6
Moreau (river), SD **109** B4
Morehead, KY **67** B9
Morehead City, NC **73** D9
Morgan City, LA **69** H6
Morgan Horse Farm (site), VT **51** D1
Morganfield, KY **66** C3
Morganton, NC **72** B3
Morgantown, WV **81** C6
Moriarty, NM **121** D4
Mormon Reservoir, ID **141** H3
Moroni, UT **149** D4
Morrilton, AR **61** C4
Morris, IL **89** C5
Morris, MN **99** E2
Morristown N.H.P., NJ **43** C3
Morristown, NJ **43** C3
Morristown, TN **77** B9
Morrisville, VT **51** B3
Morton, IL **89** D4
Moscow, ID **141** C1
Moses Lake, WA **151** D7
Mosquito Creek Lake, OH **107** B8
Moss Point, MS **71** I5
Mott, ND **105** E3
Moultrie, GA **65** H3
Moultrie, Lake, SC **75** E7
Moundsville, WV **81** B4
Mount Airy, NC **73** A5
Mount Desert Island, ME **35** G6
Mount Holly, NJ **43** F3
Mount Hope Bay, RI **49** D6
Mount Pleasant, IA **93** E8
Mount Pleasant, UT **149** D4
Mount Rainier N.P., WA **151** E4
Mount Rushmore Nat. Mon., SD **108** D2
Mount St. Helens National Volcanic Monument, WA **151** E4
Mount Vernon, IN **91** I1
Mount Vernon, KY **67** D8
Mount Vernon, WA **151** B4
Mount Vernon (site), VA **79** B10
Mountain Fork (river), OK **123** E12
Mountain Grove, MO **101** F5
Mountain Home, AR **61** A4
Mountain Home, ID **141** H2
Mountain Parkway, KY **67** C9
Mountain View, AR **61** B5
Mountain View, HI **139** F9
Mountain Village, AK **132** D3
Mountainair, NM **121** D4
Mouse (river) see Souris, ND **105** B5
Mt. Carmel, IL **89** G5
Mt. Carmel, PA **47** D7
Mt. Pleasant, MI **97** G6
Mt. Pleasant, SC **75** G7
Mt. Pleasant, TX **125** C8
Mt. Sterling, KY **67** C8
Mt. Vernon, IL **89** G4
Mt. Vernon, OH **107** D5
Mud Lake, ID **141** G5
Mud Lake, MN **99** B2
Muddy Boggy Creek, OK **123** E10
Muir Woods Nat. Mon., CA **135** D2
Mulberry (river), AR **61** B2
Mulberry Fork (river), AL **59** B3
Mulberry N.W.&S.R., AR **61** B2
Mulchatna N.W.&S.R., AK **133** E5
Mullen, NE **103** B4
Mullens, WV **81** H3
Mullett Lake, MI **97** D6
Mullica (river), NJ **43** G3
Mullins, SC **75** C9
Mulvane, KS **95** E7
Muncie, IN **91** D5
Munising, MI **97** C4
Murdo, SD **109** D5
Murfreesboro, AR **61** E2
Murfreesboro, TN **77** B5
Murphysboro, IL **89** H4
Murray, KY **66** E2
Murray, Lake, SC **75** C4
Murray, UT **149** C4
Muscatatuck (river), IN **91** G4
Muscatine, IA **93** E9
Muscle Shoals, AL **59** A2
Musconetcong (river), NJ **43** C2
Muscongus Bay, ME **35** H4
Muskegon, MI **97** G4
Muskegon (river), MI **97** G5
Muskingum (river), OH **107** E6
Muskogee, OK **123** C11
Muskogee Turnpike, OK **123** C11
Musselshell (river), MT **143** D7
Myrtle Beach, SC **75** D9
Mystic, CT **31** D8
Mystic Island, NJ **43** G4
Mystic Seaport (site), CT **31** D8

N

Naches (river), WA **151** E5
Nacogdoches, TX **125** E9
Naknek, AK **133** F5
Namakan Lake, MN **99** B5
Namekagon (river), WI **111** B2
Nampa, ID **141** G1
Nanticoke (river), DE, MD **37** E9
Nantucket, MA **39** F10
Nantucket Island, MA **39** F10
Nantucket Sound, MA **39** F9
Napa, CA **135** D2
Napatree Point, RI **49** G1
Naperville, IL **89** B5
Naples, FL **63** G7
Napoleon, ND **105** E6
Napoleon, OH **107** B2
Nappanee, IN **91** B4
Narragansett Bay, RI **49** E5
Narragansett Pier, RI **49** F4
Nashua, NH **41** I4
Nashua (river), MA **39** B5
Nashville, AR **61** F2
Nashville, IL **89** G4
Nashville, TN **77** B5
Natchaug (river), CT **31** B7
Natchez, MS **71** G1

Natchez N.H.P. — Paris, AR

Natchez N.H.P., MS **71** F1
Natchez Trace Parkway, AL, MS **71** D4
Natchitoches, LA **68** C2
National Park of American Samoa, AS **154** I4
Natural Bridges Nat. Mon., UT **149** G6
Naugatuck, CT **31** D3
Naugatuck (river), CT **31** D3
Nauvoo, IL **89** D1
Navajo, NM **121** B1
Navajo Nat. Mon., AZ **119** B6
Navajo Reservoir, NM **121** A3
Navassa Island (territory), US **155** E11
Nazareth, PA **47** D9
Near Islands, AK **133** G5
Nebraska City, NE **103** D9
Neches (river), TX **125** E8
Necker Island, HI **139** F4
Needles, CA **135** G8
Neenah, WI **111** E6
Nehalem (river), OR **147** A2
Neligh, NE **103** B7
Nelson Island, AK **132** E3
Nelsonville, OH **107** F5
Neosho, MO **101** F2
Neosho (river), KS, OK **84** G4
Nepaug Reservoir, CT **31** B4
Nephi, UT **149** D4
Neptune, NJ **43** E5
Ness City, KS **95** C3
Neuse (river), NC **73** C8
Nevada, IA **93** D5
Nevada, MO **101** E2
New (river), VA **78** F4
New, South Fork (river), NC **73** A4
New Albany, IN **91** H4
New Albany, MS **71** B4
New Bedford, MA **39** E7
New Bedford Whaling N.H.P., MA **39** E7
New Bern, NC **73** C9
New Braunfels, TX **125** F6
New Brunswick, NJ **43** D4
New Canaan, CT **31** E1
New Castle, DE **33** B5
New Castle, IN **91** E5
New Castle, PA **46** C1
New City, NY **45** G8
New Echota State Historic Site, GA **65** B2
New Fairfield, CT **31** D2
New Hampton, IA **93** B7
New Harmony State Historic Site, IN **91** H1
New Hartford, CT **31** B4
New Haven, CT **31** D4
New Iberia, LA **69** G5
New Ipswich, NH **41** I3
New Jersey Turnpike, NJ **43** E3
New Lexington, OH **107** E5
New London, CT **31** D7
New London, NH **41** G2
New London, WI **111** E6
New Madrid, MO **101** F8
New Martinsville, WV **81** C4
New Milford, CT **31** C2
New N.W.&S.R., NC **73** A4
New Orleans, LA **69** G8
New Paltz, NY **45** F8
New Philadelphia, OH **107** D6
New Richmond, WI **111** D1
New River Gorge Bridge, WV **81** F4
New River Gorge National River, WV **81** G4
New Rochelle, NY **45** H8
New Rockford, ND **105** C7
New Salem, ND **105** E4
New Smyrna Beach, FL **63** C8
New Town, ND **105** C3
New Ulm, MN **99** G3
New York, NY **45** H8
New York State Thruway, NY **45** D4
Newark, DE **33** B4
Newark, NJ **43** C4
Newark, OH **107** E5
Newberry, SC **75** C4
Newberry National Volcanic Monument, OR **147** D4
Newburg, OR **147** B2
Newburgh, NY **45** G8
Newbury, VT **51** D5
Newburyport, MA **39** A8
Newcastle, WY **153** C10
Newfound Lake, NH **41** F3
Newfoundland Evaporation Basin (dry lake), UT **149** B2
Newington, CT **31** C5
Newmarket, NH **41** H5
Newnan, GA **65** D2
Newport, AR **61** B6
Newport, DE **33** B5
Newport, KY **67** A8
Newport, ME **35** F4
Newport, NH **41** G2
Newport, OR **146** C1
Newport, RI **49** F5
Newport, TN **77** B9
Newport, VT **51** A4
Newport News, VA **79** E11
Newton, IA **93** D6
Newton, KS **95** D7
Newton, MS **71** F4
Newton, NC **73** B4
Newton, NJ **43** B3
Newtown, CT **31** D2
Nez Perce N.H.P., ID **141** D1
Nez Perce Pass, MT **142** E2
Ni'ihau (island), HI **138** B1
Niagara, WI **111** C7
Niagara Falls, NY **44** D2
Niagara Falls (waterfall), NY **26** D2
Niagara River, NY **44** D2
Niangua (river), MO **101** E4
Niantic, CT **31** D7
Niceville, FL **62** A2
Nicodemus National Historic Site, KS **95** B4
Nihoa (island), HI **139** F4
Niles, MI **97** I4
Niles, OH **107** B8
Nine Mile Creek, UT **149** D5
Nine-Mile Prairie, NE **103** D8
Ninety Six National Historic Site, SC **75** C3
Ninigret Pond, RI **49** G3
Niobrara (river), NE, WY **103** A4
Niobrara National Scenic River, NE **103** A5
Niskayuna, NY **45** E8
Nitro, WV **80** F2
Noatak National Preserve, AK **133** B5
Noatak N.W.&S.R., AK **133** B4
Noblesville, IN **91** D4
Nocona, TX **125** C6
Nodaway, East (river), IA **93** E3
Nogales, AZ **119** H6
Nolichucky (river), TN **77** B10
Nolin River Lake, KY **67** D5
Nomans Land (island), MA **39** F8
Nome, AK **132** C3
Nonquit Pond, RI **49** E6
Norfolk, CT **31** A3
Norfolk, NE **103** B8
Norfolk, VA **79** E11
Norfork Lake, AR **61** A5
Normal, IL **89** D4
Norman, OK **123** D8
Norman, Lake, NC **73** B4
Norris Lake, TN **77** B8
Norristown, PA **47** E9
North Adams, MA **38** A1
North Attleboro, MA **39** D6
North Augusta, SC **75** E3
North Bend, OH **107** F1
North Bend, OR **146** E1
North Bennington, VT **51** I1
North Branford, CT **31** D4
North Canton, OH **107** C7
North Cascades N.P., WA **151** A5
North Charleston, SC **75** F7
North Conway, NH **41** E4
North Fork Sprague N.W.&S.R., OR **147** F4
North Grosvenor Dale, CT **31** A8
North Haven, CT **31** D4
North Hero, VT **51** B1
North Hero Island, VT **51** A1
North Island, SC **75** E9
North Las Vegas, NV **145** G6
North Little Rock, AR **61** D4
North Manchester, IN **91** B4
North Myrtle Beach, SC **75** D10
North Ogden, UT **149** B4
North Olmsted, OH **107** B6
North Platte, NE **103** D4
North Pole, AK **133** D7
North Powder N.W.&S.R., OR **147** C7
North Providence, RI **49** B4
North Scituate, RI **49** B3
North Sioux City, SD **109** F10
North Slope, AK **133** B5
North Springfield, VT **51** G3
North Sterling Reservoir, CO **137** A8
North Stratford, NH **41** C3
North Sylamore Creek N.W.&S.R., AR **61** B4
North Troy, VT **51** A4
North Umpqua N.W.&S.R., OR **147** E2
North Vernon, IN **91** G5
North Walpole, NH **41** H1
North Wildwood, NJ **43** I3
Northampton, MA **39** C3
Northern Mariana Islands (territory), US **154** E1
Northfield, MN **99** G5
Northfield, NH **41** G3
Northfield, VT **51** D3
Northwestern Hawaiian Islands, HI **138** E1
Northwood, ND **105** C9
Norton, KS **95** A3
Norton, VA **78** E2
Norton Sound, AK **133** D4
Norwalk, CT **31** F2
Norwalk, OH **107** B5
Norway, ME **35** G2
Norwich, CT **31** C7
Norwich, NY **45** E6
Norwich, VT **51** F4
Norwood, MA **39** C7
Norwood, OH **107** F2
Nottoway (river), VA **79** E10
Nowitna N.W.&S.R., AK **133** D6
Nowood (river), WY **153** B5
Noxontown Pond, DE **33** C4
Noxubee (river), MS **71** D5
Nubanusit Lake, NH **41** H2
Nueces (river), TX **125** G6
Nunivak Island, AK **132** E3
Nu'uuli, AS **154** I1

O

Oahe, Lake, ND, SD **109** B6
O'ahu (island), HI **139** B5
Oak Bluffs, MA **39** F9
Oak Harbor, WA **151** B3
Oak Hill, WV **81** G4
Oak Orchard, DE **33** H7
Oak Ridge, TN **77** B8
Oakdale, LA **69** E3
Oakes, ND **105** F8
Oakland, CA **135** E2
Oakland, MD **36** B1
Oakland, ME **35** F3
Oakley, KS **94** B2
Oakville, CT **31** C3
Obed (river), TN **77** B7
Obed N.W.&S.R., TN **77** B7
Oberlin, KS **95** A3
Obion (river), TN **76** B1
Ocala, FL **63** C7
Ocean City, MD **37** E11
Ocean City, NJ **43** H3
Ocean Lake, WY **153** D4
Ocean Pines, MD **37** E11
Ocean Shores, WA **150** D1
Ocean Springs, MS **71** I5
Ocean View, DE **33** I7
Oceanside, CA **135** I6
Ochlockonee (river), FL, GA **63** B4
Ochoco Mountains, OR **147** C5
Ocmulgee (river), GA **65** G4
Ocmulgee Nat. Mon., GA **65** E4
Oconee (river), GA **65** F5
Oconee, Lake, GA **65** D4
Oconto, WI **111** D7
Oconto (river), WI **111** D7
Ocracoke Island, NC **73** C10
Odessa, DE **33** C4
Odessa, TX **125** E3
Oelwein, IA **93** B8
Ofu, AS **154** H3
Ofu (island), AS **154** I3
Ogallala, NE **103** D3
Ogden, UT **149** B4
Ogdensburg, NY **45** A6
Ogeechee (river), GA **65** E6
Ogunquit, ME **35** I2
Ohio (river), **84** G7
Ohoopee (river), GA **65** F6
Oil City, PA **46** B2
Okanogan (river), WA **151** B7
Okatibbee Lake, MS **71** E5
Okeechobee, Lake, FL **63** F8
Okefenokee Swamp, GA **65** H5
Oklahoma City, OK **123** C8
Okmulgee, OK **123** C10
Okobojo Creek, SD **109** C5
Okolona, MS **71** C5
Olathe, KS **95** C10
Old Faithful (site), WY **152** B2
Old Hickory Lake, TN **77** B5
Old Oraibi (site), AZ **119** C6
Old Orchard Beach, ME **35** H2
Old Saybrook, CT **31** E6
Old Town, ME **35** F5
Olean, NY **44** F3
Olentangy (river), OH **107** D4
Oliver, Lake, GA **65** E1
Olivia, MN **99** G3
Olney, IL **89** G5
Olosega, AS **154** H3
Olosega (island), AS **154** H3
Olympia, WA **151** D3
Olympic Coast National Marine Sanctuary, WA **150** B1
Olympic Mountains, WA **150** C2
Olympic N.P., WA **150** C2
Olympus, Mount, WA **150** C2
Omaha, NE **103** C9
Omak, WA **151** B7
Onalaska, WI **111** F3
Onancock, VA **79** D12
Onawa, IA **92** C2
One Hundred and Two (river), MO **101** A2
Oneida, NY **45** D6
Oneida Lake, NY **45** D6
O'Neill, NE **103** B6
Oneonta, NY **45** E7
Onida, SD **109** C6
Onslow Bay, NC **73** D9
Ontario, Lake, **26** D2
Ontario, OR **147** D9
Ontonagon N.W.&S.R., MI **97** B2
Oologah Lake, OK **123** B10
Oostanaula (river), GA **65** B1
Opelika, AL **59** E5
Opelousas, LA **69** F4
Opp, AL **59** G4
Optima Lake, OK **122** B4
Orange, CT **31** E3
Orange, MA **39** B3
Orange, VA **79** C8
Orange City, IA **92** B2
Orangeburg, SC **75** E5
Orchard City, CO **137** D2
Ord, NE **103** C6
Ordway, CO **137** E7
Oreana, NV **145** C3
Oregon, OH **107** A3
Oregon Caves Nat. Mon., OR **147** G2
Oregon City, OR **147** B3
Oregon Dunes N.R.A., OR **146** D1
Orem, UT **149** C4
Orford, NH **41** E2
Organ Pipe Cactus Nat. Mon., AZ **119** G3
Orlando, FL **63** D8
Orleans, MA **39** E10
Orleans, VT **51** B4
Oro Valley, AZ **119** G6
Orofino, ID **141** D1
Orono, ME **35** F5
Oroville Dam, CA **135** C3
Orrville, OH **107** C6
Ortonville, MN **99** F1
Osage, IA **93** A6
Osage (river), MO **101** E3
Osage City, KS **95** C8
Osage Fork (river), MO **101** E4
Osawatomie, KS **95** C10
Osceola, AR **61** B8
Osceola, IA **93** E5
Osgood Mountains, NV **145** B4
Oshkosh, WI **111** F6
Oskaloosa, IA **93** E7
Ossabaw Island, GA **65** G7
Ossabaw Sound, GA **65** G7
Ossipee Lake, NH **41** F4
Oswego, NY **45** C5
Oswego (river), NY **45** D5
Othello, WA **151** E7
Otis Reservoir, MA **38** C1
Ottawa, IL **89** C4
Ottawa, KS **95** C9
Otter Creek (river), VT **51** E1
Otter Creek Reservior, UT **149** F4
Otter Tail (river), MN **99** E1
Otter Tail Lake, MN **99** D2
Ottumwa, IA **93** E7
Ouachita (river), AR, LA **54** D2
Ouachita, Lake, AR **61** D3
Ouachita Mountains, AR, OK **61** D1
Outer Banks (islands), NC **73** C10
Overland Park, KS **95** B10
Overton, NV **145** G7
Owasso, OK **123** B10
Owatonna, MN **99** G4
Owensboro, KY **67** C4
Owl Creek, WY **153** C4
Owosso, MI **97** G6
Owyhee (river), OR **147** D8
Owyhee, Lake, OR **147** E8
Owyhee Mountains, ID **141** H1
Owyhee, North Fork N.W.&S.R., OR **147** F9
Owyhee N.W.&S.R., OR **147** E8
Owyhee, South Fork (river), ID, NV **141** I1
Oxford, MA **39** C5
Oxford, MS **71** B4
Oxford, NC **73** B7
Oxford, OH **107** F1
Oxnard, CA **135** H4
Oxon Cove Park and Oxon Hill Farm, MD **37** D6
Ozark, AL **59** G5
Ozark, AR **61** C2
Ozark National Scenic Riverways, MO **101** F6
Ozark Plateau, **84** G5
Ozarks, Lake of the, MO **101** D4
Ozona, TX **125** E4

P

Pachaug Pond, CT **31** C8
Pacific Crest National Scenic Trail, CA **135** G5
Paden City, WV **81** C4
Padre Island, TX **114** G8
Padre Island National Seashore, TX **125** H7
Paducah, KY **66** D2
Page, AZ **119** A5
Pago Pago, AS **154** I1
Pagosa Springs, CO **137** G3
Pahala, HI **139** F9
Pahranagat Range, NV **145** F6
Pahrump, NV **145** G5
Pahute Mesa, NV **145** F4
Painesville, OH **107** A7
Paint Creek, OH **107** F3
Paint N.W.&S.R., MI **97** C2
Painted Desert, AZ **119** B5
Palatka, FL **63** C7
Palestine, TX **125** E8
Palisades Reservoir, ID **141** H6
Palm Bay, FL **63** E9
Palm Coast, FL **63** C8
Palm Springs, CA **135** H7
Palmer, AK **133** E6
Palmer (river), RI **49** C5
Palmyra Atoll (territory), US **155** F5
Palo Alto, CA **135** E2
Palo Alto Battlefield National Historical Site, TX **125** I7
Palouse (river), WA **151** E9
Palouse Hills, WA **151** D9
Pamlico (river), NC **73** C9
Pamlico Sound, NC **73** C10
Pampa, TX **125** B4
Pana, IL **89** F4
Panama City, FL **63** B3
Pancake Range, NV **145** E5
Panguitch, UT **149** G3
Panorama Point (peak), NE **102** C1
Paola, KS **95** C10
Papillion, NE **103** C9
Paragould, AR **61** B7
Paramus, NJ **43** B5
Paria (river), AZ **119** A4
Paris, AR **61** C2

Paris, IL **89** E6
Paris, KY **67** B8
Paris, TN **76** B3
Paris, TX **125** C8
Park (river), ND **105** B9
Park Falls, WI **111** C4
Park Hills, MO **101** E6
Park Range, CO **137** A3
Park Rapids, MN **99** D3
Park River, ND **105** B9
Parker, AZ **119** E2
Parker, SD **109** E9
Parkersburg, WV **81** D3
Parkston, SD **109** E8
Parkville, MD **37** B8
Parma, OH **107** B6
Parris Island, SC **75** H6
Parsippany, NJ **43** C4
Parsons, KS **95** E9
Pasadena, CA **135** H5
Pascagoula, MS **71** I5
Pascagoula (river), MS **71** H5
Pasco, WA **151** F8
Pascoag, RI **49** A2
Pascoag Lake, RI **49** A2
Paso Robles, CA **135** G3
Passaic, NJ **43** C5
Passaic (river), NJ **43** C4
Passamaquoddy Bay, ME **35** E7
Passumpsic (river), VT **51** C5
Paterson, NJ **43** B4
Pathfinder Reservoir, WY **153** E6
Patoka (river), IN **91** H2
Patoka Lake, IN **91** H3
Patten, ME **35** C5
Patuxent (bay), MD **37** E7
Patuxent (river), MD **37** B6
Pauls Valley, OK **123** D9
Paulsboro, NJ **43** F1
Pawcatuck, CT **31** D8
Pawcatuck (river), CT, RI **31** D8
Pawhuska, OK **123** A10
Pawnee (river), KS **95** D3
Pawtucket, RI **49** B5
Pawtucket Reservoir, RI **49** A5
Pawtuxet (river), RI **49** C4
Payette, ID **141** G1
Payette (river), ID **141** G1
Payette, North Fork (river), ID **141** G1
Payette, South Fork (river), ID **141** G2
Payson, AZ **119** E5
Payson, UT **149** D4
Pea (river), AL **59** G4
Pea Patch Island, DE **33** B5
Pea Ridge N.M.P., AR **61** A1
Peabody, MA **39** B7
Peace (river), FL **63** F7
Peachtree City, GA **65** D2
Peaked Mountain, ME **35** B5
Pearl, MS **71** E3
Pearl (river), LA, MS **69** F9
Pearl and Hermes Atoll, HI **138** E1
Pearl City, HI **139** B4
Pearl Harbor, HI **139** C4
Pearsall, TX **125** G5
Pease (river), TX **125** C5
Pecatonica (river), WI **111** H4
Pecos, TX **124** E2
Pecos (river), NM, TX **114** E6
Pecos N.H.P., NM **121** C5
Pecos N.W.&S.R., NM **121** C5
Peekskill, NY **45** G8
Pekin, IL **89** D3
Pelican Rapids, MN **99** D2
Pell City, AL **59** C4
Pella, IA **93** E6
Pembina, ND **105** A9
Pembina (river), ND **105** A8
Pemigewasset (river), NH **41** E3
Peñasco, Rio (river), NM **121** G6
Pend Oreille (river), WA **151** B10
Pend Oreille, Lake, ID **141** B1
Pender, NE **103** B8
Pendleton, OR **147** B7
Penn Hills, PA **46** D2
Penn Yan, NY **45** E4
Penns Grove, NJ **43** G1
Pennsauken, NJ **43** F2
Pennsville, NJ **43** G1
Pennsylvania Turnpike, PA **47** E3
Pennyrile Parkway, KY **66** D3
Penobscot (river), ME **35** E5
Penobscot Bay, ME **35** G5
Penobscot, East Branch (river), ME **35** C5
Penobscot, West Branch (river), ME **35** D3
Pensacola, FL **62** B1
Peoria, IL **89** D3
Pepin, Lake, MN **99** G5
Pepin, WI **111** E2
Pequop Mountains, NV **145** B6
Perdido (river), AL, FL **59** H2
Pere Marquette N.W.&S.R., MI **97** F4
Perham, MN **99** D2
Perry, FL **63** B5
Perry, GA **65** F3
Perry, IA **93** D4
Perry, OK **123** B8
Perry Hall, MD **37** B8
Perry Lake, KS **95** B9
Perry's Victory and International Peace Memorial, OH **107** A4
Perrysburg, OH **107** B3
Perryton, TX **125** A4
Perryville, MO **101** E7
Perth Amboy, NJ **43** D4
Peru, IL **89** C4
Peru, IN **91** C4
Peshtigo (river), WI **111** C6
Petal, MS **71** G4
Petenwell Lake, WI **111** E5
Peterborough, NH **41** I2
Petersburg, AK **133** F10
Petersburg, VA **79** D9
Petersburg, WV **81** D7
Petersburg N.B., VA **79** E9
Petoskey, MI **97** D6
Petrified Forest N.P., AZ **119** D7
Petroglyph Nat. Mon., NM **121** D4
Phenix City, AL **59** E6
Philadelphia, MS **71** E4
Philadelphia, PA **47** E10
Philip, SD **109** D4
Philippi, WV **81** D6
Phillipsburg, KS **95** A4
Phillipsburg, NJ **43** C2
Phoenix, AZ **119** F4
Picayune, MS **71** I3
Pickwick Lake, AL, MS, TN **59** A1
Pictured Rocks National Lakeshore, MI **97** C4
Piedmont, AL **59** C5
Piedmont (region), **54** D5
Piedmont Lake, OH **107** D7
Piedra (river), CO **137** F3
Pierre, SD **109** D5
Pigeon (river), IN **91** A5
Pigeon (river), MI **97** D6
Pigeon (river), MN **99** B8
Pikes Peak, CO **137** D5
Pikeville, KY **67** D11
Pine (river), WI **111** C6
Pine Barrens (region), NJ **43** G3
Pine Bluff, AR **61** E5
Pine City, MN **99** E5
Pine Creek, NV **145** C5
Pine Creek, PA **47** B6
Pine Creek Gorge, PA **47** B6
Pine Hill, NJ **43** F2
Pine Mountain, KY **67** E9
Pine N.W.&S.R., MI **97** F5
Pine Ridge, NE **102** A2
Pine Ridge, SD **109** F3
Pinedale, WY **153** D3
Pinehurst, NC **73** C6
Pinelands National Reserve, NJ **43** F4
Pinetop-Lakeside, AZ **119** E7
Pineville, LA **69** D4
Pinnacles N.P., CA **135** F3
Pioche, NV **145** E7
Pioneer Valley, MA **39** B3
Pipe Spring Nat. Mon., AZ **119** A4
Pipestem Creek, ND **105** D7
Pipestone, MN **99** G2
Pipestone Nat. Mon., MN **99** G1
Piqua, OH **107** D2
Piscataqua (river), NH **41** H5
Piscataquis (river), ME **35** E4
Piscataway, NJ **43** D4
Piscataway Park, MD **37** D6
Pit (river), CA **135** B3
Pittsburg, KS **95** E10
Pittsburgh, PA **46** D2
Pittsfield, IL **89** E2
Pittsfield, MA **38** B1
Pittsfield, ME **35** F4
Pittsfield, NH **41** G4
Pittsford, VT **51** F2
Piute Reservior, UT **149** F3
Plainfield, CT **31** C8
Plainfield, IN **91** E3
Plainfield, NJ **43** C4
Plainfield, VT **51** D4
Plains, GA **65** F2
Plainview, TX **125** C4
Plainville, CT **31** C4
Plainville, KS **95** B4
Plaistow, NH **41** I5
Plankinton, SD **109** E8
Plano, TX **125** D7
Plaquemine, LA **69** F6
Platte (river), NE **103** D9
Platte, SD **109** E7
Platte, North (river), CO, NE, WY **128** D8
Platte, South (river), CO, NE **128** E8
Platteville, WI **111** H4
Plattsburgh, NY **45** A8
Plattsmouth, NE **103** D9
Playas Lake, NM **121** H2
Pleasant Grove, UT **149** C4
Pleasant Prairie, WI **111** H7
Pleasantville, NJ **43** H3
Pleasure Ridge Park, KY **67** C6
Plentywood, MT **143** A11
Plover, WI **111** E5
Plum, PA **46** D2
Plymouth, IN **91** B3
Plymouth, MA **39** D8
Plymouth, MN **99** F4
Plymouth, VT **51** F3
Pocahontas, AR **61** A6
Pocatello, ID **141** H5
Pocomoke (river), MD **37** F10
Pocomoke City, MD **37** F10
Pocono Mountains, PA **47** C9
Pocotopaug Lake, CT **31** C5
Poinsett, Lake, SD **109** C9
Point Hope, AK **133** B4
Point Judith, RI **49** G4
Point Judith Pond, RI **49** F4
Point Pleasant, NJ **43** E5
Point Pleasant, OH **107** G2
Point Pleasant, WV **80** E2
Point Reyes National Seashore, CA **135** D2
Polacca, AZ **119** C6
Polson, MT **142** C3
Pomeroy, WA **151** E9
Pompeys Pillar Nat. Mon., MT **143** E8
Ponaganset (river), RI **49** B2
Ponaganset Reservoir, RI **49** B2
Ponca City, OK **123** A9
Ponce, PR **155** I10
Pond (river), KY **67** D4
Pontchartrain, Lake, LA **69** G8
Pontiac, IL **89** C4
Pontiac, MI **97** H7
Pontoosuc Lake, MA **38** B1
Pontotoc, MS **71** B4
Poplar Bluff, MO **101** F7
Poplarville, MS **71** H4
Popple (river), WI **111** C6
Poquonock Bridge, CT **31** D7
Poquoson, VA **79** E11
Porcupine (river), AK **133** B8
Port Allen, LA **69** F6
Port Angeles, WA **150** B2
Port Arthur, TX **125** F9
Port Charlotte, FL **63** F7
Port Clinton, OH **107** B4
Port Huron, MI **97** G8
Port Jervis, NY **45** G7
Port Lavaca, TX **125** G7
Port Penn, DE **33** C5
Port Royal, SC **75** H6
Port Royal Sound (river), SC **75** H6
Port St. Lucie, FL **63** F9
Port Sulphur, LA **69** H8
Port Townsend, WA **151** B3
Port Washington, WI **111** G7
Portage, IN **91** A2
Portage, MI **97** H5
Portage, WI **111** F5
Portage (river), OH **107** B3
Portal, ND **105** A3
Portales, NM **121** E8
Portland, CT **31** C5
Portland, IN **91** D6
Portland, ME **35** H3
Portland, OR **147** B2
Portland, TN **77** A5
Portland, TX **125** H7
Portneuf Range, ID **141** H5
Portsmouth, NH **41** H5
Portsmouth, OH **107** G4
Portsmouth, RI **49** E6
Portsmouth, VA **79** E11
Post Falls, ID **141** B1
Poteau, OK **123** D12
Potholes Reservoir, WA **151** D7
Potlatch (river), ID **141** D1
Potomac, MD **37** C6
Potomac (river), MD, VA, WV **37** E7
Potomac, North Branch (river), MD, WV **36** B2
Potomac, South Branch (river), WV **36** B2
Potsdam, NY **45** A7
Pottstown, PA **47** E9
Pottsville, PA **47** D8
Poughkeepsie, NY **45** F8
Poultney, VT **51** F1
Poultney (river), VT **51** F1
Poverty Point Nat. Mon., LA **69** B5
Powder (river), MT, WY **128** C7
Powder (river), OR **147** C8
Powder, South Fork (river), WY **153** D6
Powder Wash, CO **137** A2
Powell, WY **153** A4
Powell (river), TN, VA **77** A9
Powell, Lake, UT **149** H5
Pownal Center, VT **51** I1
Poygan, Lake, WI **111** E6
Prairie Dog Creek, KS **95** A3
Prairie du Chien, WI **111** G3
Pratt, KS **95** E5
Prattville, AL **59** E4
Prescott, AR **61** F3
Prescott, AZ **119** D4
Prescott Valley, AZ **119** D4
Presidential Range, NH **41** D4
Presidio, TX **124** F2
Presque Isle, ME **35** B6
Presque Isle N.W.&S.R., MI **97** C1
Preston, ID **141** I5
Preston, MN **99** H6
Prestonsburg, KY **67** C10
Pribilof Islands, AK **132** F2
Price (river), UT **149** E5
Price, UT **149** D5
Prichard, AL **59** H1
Priest (river), ID **141** B1
Priest Lake, ID **141** A1
Prince Frederick, MD **37** E7
Prince of Wales Island, AK **133** G10
Prince of Wales, Cape, AK **132** C2
Prince William Forest Park, VA **79** B9
Prince William Sound, AK **133** E7
Princeton, IN **91** H1
Princeton, KY **66** D3
Princeton, ME **35** E6
Princeton, NJ **43** D3
Princeton, WV **81** H4
Princeville, HI **138** A2
Prineville, OR **147** D4
Proctor, MN **99** D5
Proctor, VT **51** F2
Promontory, UT **149** A3
Prospect, CT **31** C4
Prosser, WA **151** F7
Providence, RI **49** B5
Providence, UT **149** A4
Providence (river), RI **49** C5
Provincetown, MA **39** D10
Provo, UT **149** C4
Prudence Island, RI **49** D5
Prudhoe Bay, AK **133** A6
Pryor Creek, OK **123** B11
Pueblo, CO **137** E6
Pueblo Bonito (site), NM **121** B2
Puerco (river), AZ **119** D7
Puerco, Rio (river), NM **121** D3
Puerto Rico (territory), US **155** E11
Puget Sound, WA **151** C3
Pukalani, HI **139** C7
Pulaski, TN **77** C4
Pulaski, VA **79** E5
Pullman, WA **151** E10
Pumpkin Creek, NE **102** C1
Punkin Center, CO **137** D7
Punta Gorda, FL **63** F7
Punxsutawney, PA **47** C3
Purcell, OK **123** D8
Purchase Parkway, KY **66** E1
Purgatoire (river), CO **137** G7
Putnam, CT **31** A8
Putney, VT **51** H3
Pu'uhonua O Honaunau N.H.P., HI **139** F8
Pu'ukohola Heiau National Historic Site, HI **139** E8
Pu'uwai, HI **138** A1
Puyallup, WA **151** D4
Pymatuning Reservoir, PA, OH **46** B1
Pyramid Lake (river), NV **145** C2

Q

Quabbin Reservoir, MA **39** B4
Quaddick Reservoir, CT **31** A8
Quaker Hill, CT **31** D7
Quakertown, PA **47** D9
Quartzsite, AZ **119** E2
Quartzville Creek N.W.&S.R., OR **147** C3
Queen (river), RI **49** E3
Queets (river), WA **150** C1
Questa, NM **121** A5
Quincy, IL **89** E1
Quincy, MA **39** C7
Quincy, WA **151** D7
Quinebaug (river), CT **31** C7
Quinn (river), NV **145** A3
Quinnipiac (river), CT **31** D4
Quinsigamond, Lake, MA **39** C5
Quitman, GA **65** H4
Quitman, MS **71** F5
Quonochontaug, RI **49** G2
Quonochontaug Pond, RI **49** G2

R

Rabun Gap, GA **65** A4
Raccoon (river), IA **93** C4
Raccoon Creek, OH **107** G5
Racine, WI **111** H7
Radcliff, KY **67** C6
Radford, VA **79** E5
Raft River Mountains, UT **149** A2
Rahway, NJ **43** C4
Rainbow Bridge Nat. Mon., UT **149** H5
Rainier, Mount, WA **151** D4
Rainier, OR **147** A2
Rainy (river), MN **99** B4
Rainy Lake, MN **99** A4
Raisin (river), MI **97** H6
Raleigh, NC **73** B7
Raleigh Bay, NC **73** D10
Rampart Range, CO **137** D5
Ramsey, NJ **43** B4
Randolph, MA **39** C7
Randolph, VT **51** E3
Randolph Center, VT **51** E3
Rangeley, ME **35** E2
Rangeley Lake, ME **35** F2
Rangely, CO **136** B1
Rantoul, IL **89** D5
Rapid City, SD **108** D2
Rapid N.W.&S.R., ID **141** E1
Rappahannock (river), VA **79** C10
Raquette (river), NY **45** B7
Raritan (river), NJ **43** D4
Rat Islands, AK **133** H7
Rathbun Lake, IA **93** F6
Raton, NM **121** A6
Ravenna, NE **103** D6
Ravenswood, WV **81** E3
Rawlins, WY **153** F6
Raymond, NH **41** H4
Raymond, WA **150** E2
Rayne, LA **69** G4
Raystown Lake, PA **47** E5
Rayville, LA **69** B5
Reading, PA **47** E8
Red (river), **114** C7

Red, Elm Fork (river) — Seneca, SC

Red, Elm Fork (river), OK **123** D5
Red, North Fork (river), OK **123** D5
Red, North Fork (river), TX **125** B4
Red, Prairie Dog Town Fork (river), OK, TX **123** E5
Red, Salt Fork (river), OK, TX **123** D5
Red Bank, NJ **43** D5
Red Bank, TN **77** D7
Red Bay, AL **59** B1
Red Bluff Lake, TX **114** E5
Red Bud, IL **89** G3
Red Cedar (river), WI **111** D2
Red Cloud, NE **103** E7
Red Hills, KS **95** E3
Red Lake, AZ **119** C2
Red Lake, MN **99** C3
Red Lake (river), MN **99** B2
Red Lion, PA **47** E7
Red Lodge, MT **143** F7
Red N.W.&S.R., KY **67** C9
Red Oak, IA **93** E3
Red River of the North (river), MN, ND **84** A3
Red Rock, Lake, IA **93** E6
Red Rock Creek, OK **123** B8
Red Willow Creek, NE **103** D4
Red Wing, MN **99** G5
Redding, CA **135** B2
Redfield, SD **109** C8
Redmond, OR **147** D4
Redmond, WA **151** C4
Redwood Falls, MN **99** G3
Redwood N.P., CA **135** A1
Reedsburg, WI **111** F4
Reedsport, OR **146** D1
Reedy Island, DE **33** C5
Reelfoot Lake, TN **76** B2
Reese (river), NV **145** C4
Rehoboth Bay, DE **33** H7
Rehoboth Beach, DE **33** H7
Reidsville, NC **73** A6
Reisterstown, MD **37** B7
Rend Lake, IL **89** H4
Reno, NV **145** D2
Rensselaer, IN **91** C2
Renton, WA **151** C4
Republic, MO **101** F3
Republic, WA **151** A8
Republican (river), KS, NE **84** F2
Republican, South Fork (river), KS, CO **94** A1
Reserve, NM **121** F1
Reston, VA **79** B9
Rexburg, ID **141** G5
Reynoldsburg, OH **107** E4
Rhinelander, WI **111** C5
Rhode Island (island), RI **49** E6
Rhode Island Sound, RI **49** G4
Rice City, RI **49** D2
Rice Lake, WI **111** C2
Richard B. Russell Lake, GA, SC **65** C5
Richardson lakes, ME **35** F2
Richfield, UT **149** E3
Richford, VT **51** A3
Richland, WA **151** E7
Richland Center, WI **111** G4
Richland Creek N.W.&S.R., AR **61** B3
Richlands, VA **78** E3
Richmond, IN **91** E6
Richmond, MO **101** C3
Richmond, VA **79** D9
Richmond, VT **51** C2
Richmond N.B. Park, VA **79** D9
Richwood, WV **81** F5
Ridgecrest, CA **135** G6
Ridgefield, CT **31** E2
Ridgeland, MS **71** E3
Ridgewood, NJ **43** B5
Ridgway, PA **47** B4
Rifle, CO **137** C2
Rifle (river), MI **97** F7
Rigby, ID **141** G5
Riggins, ID **141** E1
Ringwood, NJ **43** B4
Rio Chama N.W.&S.R., NM **121** B4
Rio Grande (river), CO, NM, TX **114** G7
Rio Grande City, TX **125** I6
Rio Grande N.W.&S.R., NM **121** A5
Rio Grande Wild and Scenic River, TX **125** F3
Rio Rancho, NM **121** D4
Ripley, MS **71** A4
Ripley, TN **76** C1
Ripley, WV **81** E3
Ripon, WI **111** F6
Ritzville, WA **151** D8
River Falls, WI **111** D1
Riverside, CA **135** H6
Riverton, UT **149** C4
Riverton, WY **153** D5
Roan Cliffs, UT **149** E6
Roan Mountain, TN **77** B11
Roan Plateau, CO **136** C1
Roanoke, AL **59** D5
Roanoke, VA **79** D6
Roanoke (river), NC, VA **54** C7
Roanoke (Staunton) (river), VA **79** E7
Roanoke Island, NC **73** B10
Roanoke Rapids, NC **73** A8
Roaring N.W.&S.R., OR **147** B3
Robert South Kerr Lake, OK **123** D12
Robinson, IL **89** F6
Robstown, TX **125** H6
Rochester, IN **91** B4
Rochester, MN **99** G5
Rochester, NH **41** G5
Rochester, NY **45** D4
Rock (river), IL, WI **89** B3
Rock Creek, NV **145** B5
Rock Hill, SC **75** B5
Rock Island, IL **89** C2
Rock Springs, WY **153** G3
Rockcastle (river), KY **67** D8
Rockford, IL **89** A4
Rockingham, NC **73** D6
Rockland, MA **39** C8
Rockland, ME **35** G4
Rockport, ME **35** G4
Rockport, TX **125** H7
Rockville, MD **37** C6
Rocky Ford, CO **137** E7
Rocky Mount, NC **73** B8
Rocky Mount, VA **79** E6
Rocky Mountain N.P., CO **137** B5
Rocky Mountains, **128** A4
Rogers, AR **61** A1
Rogers City, MI **97** D7
Rogers, Mount, VA **78** F4
Rogue (river), OR **147** F2
Rolla, MO **101** E5
Rolla, ND **105** A6
Rolling Fork (river), KY **67** D6
Rome, GA **65** B1
Rome, NY **45** D6
Romney, WV **81** D8
Roosevelt, UT **149** C6
Root (river), MN **99** H6
Roseau, MN **99** A2
Roseau (river), MN **99** A2
Rosebud, SD **109** E5
Roseburg, OR **147** E2
Rosepine, LA **68** E2
Ross Barnett Reservoir, MS **71** E3
Ross Lake, WA **151** A5
Ross Lake N.R.A., WA **151** A5
Roswell, GA **65** C2
Roswell, NM **121** F6
Rota Island, MP **154** D1
Rough (river), KY **67** D4
Rough River Lake, KY **67** C5
Round Rock, TX **125** F6
Round Valley Reservoir, NJ **43** C3
Roundup, MT **143** D7
Roxboro, NC **73** A7
Ruby Mountains, NV **145** C6
Rugby, ND **105** B6
Ruidoso, NM **121** F5
Ruleville, MS **71** C2
Rum (river), MN **99** E4
Rumford, ME **35** F2
Rupert, ID **141** I4
Rush Creek, CO **137** D8
Rushville, IN **91** E5
Rushville, NE **102** A2
Russell, KS **95** C5
Russell Cave Nat. Mon., AL **59** A5
Russellville, AL **59** B2
Russellville, AR **61** C3
Ruston, LA **69** B3
Rutland, VT **51** F2
Rye, NH **41** H5
Rye Patch Reservoir, NV **145** B3

S

Sabine (river), LA, TX **54** E2
Sabine Lake, LA **68** G1
Sable, Cape, FL **63** H8
Sac (river), MO **101** E3
Sacajawea, Lake, WA **151** E8
Saco, ME **35** H2
Saco (river), ME, NH **35** H2
Sacramento, CA **135** D3
Sacramento (river), CA **135** B2
Sacramento Mountains, NM **121** F5
Safford, AZ **119** F7
Sag Harbor, NY **45** G10
Sagamore Hill National Historic Site, NY **45** H9
Sagavanirktok (river), AK **133** B6
Saginaw, MI **97** G7
Saginaw Bay, MI **97** F7
Saguache Creek, CO **137** E3
Saguaro N.P., AZ **119** G5
Saint Albans, VT **51** B2
Saint John (river), ME **35** B4
Saint John, Baker Branch (river), ME **35** C3
Saint John, Northwest Branch (river), ME **35** B3
Saint John, Southwest Branch (river), ME **35** C3
Sainte Genevieve, MO **101** D7
Saint-Gaudens National Historic Site, NH **41** G1
Saipan (island), MP **154** C2
Sakakawea, Lake, ND **105** C3
Sakonnet Point, RI **49** F6
Sakonnet River, RI **49** E6
Salamanca, NY **44** F2
Salamonie (river), IN **91** C5
Salamonie Lake, IN **91** C4
Salem, IL **89** G4
Salem, IN **91** G4
Salem, MA **39** B8
Salem, MO **101** E5
Salem, NH **41** I4
Salem, NJ **43** G1
Salem, OH **107** C7
Salem, OR **147** C2
Salem, SD **109** E9
Salem, VA **79** D6
Salem, WV **81** D5
Salem (river), NJ **43** G1
Salem Maritime National Historic Site, MA **39** B8
Salida, CO **137** E4
Salina, KS **95** C6
Salinas, CA **135** F3
Salinas Pueblo Missions Nat. Mon., NM **121** E4
Saline (river), KS **95** C6
Saline (river), AR **61** E4
Saline (river), IL **89** H5
Saline Bayou (river), LA **69** B3
Saline Bayou N.W.&S.R., LA **69** C3
Salisbury, MD **37** E10
Salisbury, NC **73** B5
Salish Mountains, MT **142** A2
Sallisaw, OK **123** C12
Salmon, ID **141** E3
Salmon (river), CT **31** C6
Salmon (river), ID **141** F3
Salmon, Middle Fork (river), ID **141** F3
Salmon, Middle Fork N.W.&S.R., ID **141** E3
Salmon Falls (river), ME, NH **35** I2
Salmon Falls Creek Reservoir, ID **141** I3
Salmon N.W.&S.R., AK **133** B4
Salmon N.W.&S.R., ID **141** E2
Salmon N.W.&S.R., OR **147** B3
Salmon River Mountains, ID **141** F2
Salmon, South Fork (river), ID **141** F2
Salt (river), AZ **119** E6
Salt (river), KY **67** C6
Salt (river), MO **101** B5
Salt Creek (river), IN **91** G3
Salt Creek, IL **89** E4
Salt Fork Lake, OH **107** D7
Salt Lake City, UT **149** C4
Salt River Bay N.H.P. and Ecological Preserve, VI **155** I8
Salton Sea (lake), CA **135** I7
Saluda (river), SC **75** C4
Salvador, Lake, LA **69** H7
Sam Rayburn Reservoir, TX **125** E9
San Andres Mountains, NM **121** F5
San Angelo, TX **125** E4
San Antonio, TX **125** F6
San Antonio (river), TX **125** G6
San Antonio Missions N.H.P., TX **125** G6
San Bernardino, CA **135** H6
San Blas, Cape, FL **54** F5
San Carlos, AZ **119** F6
San Carlos Reservoir, AZ **119** F6
San Clemente (island), CA **135** I5
San Diego, CA **135** I6
San Francisco, CA **135** E2
San Francisco (river), NM **121** F1
San Francisco Maritime N.H.P., CA **135** E1
San Joaquin (river), CA **135** E4
San Jose, CA **135** E3
San Jose, MP **154** D1
San Jose, Rio (river), NM **121** D2
San Juan, PR **155** H11
San Juan (river), CO, NM, UT **114** B3
San Juan Island N.H.P., WA **151** B3
San Juan Islands, WA **151** B3
San Juan Mountains, CO **137** F2
San Juan National Historic Site, PR **155** H11
San Luis, AZ **119** G1
San Luis Creek, CO **137** E4
San Luis Lake, CO **137** F5
San Luis Obispo, CA **135** G3
San Luis Valley, CO **137** F4
San Manuel, AZ **119** G6
San Marcos, TX **125** F6
San Miguel (river), CO **136** E1
San Pedro (river), AZ **119** G6
San Rafael, CA **135** D2
San Rafael (river), UT **149** E5
Sanak Island, AK **132** H3
Sanbornville, NH **41** F5
Sand Arroyo (river), CO **137** F9
Sand Creek, IN **91** F4
Sand Creek, SD **109** D8
Sand Hills, NE **103** B3
Sand Springs, OK **123** B10
Sandersville, GA **65** E5
Sandpoint, ID **141** B1
Sandstone, MN **99** E5
Sandusky, MI **97** G8
Sandusky, OH **107** B4
Sandusky (river), OH **107** C4
Sandusky Bay, OH **107** B4
Sandwich, IL **89** B4
Sandwich, MA **39** E9
Sandy, UT **149** C4
Sandy Hook (point), NJ **43** D5
Sandy Hook Bay, NJ **43** D5
Sandy N.W.&S.R., OR **147** B3
Sandy Point, RI **49** H3
Sandy Springs, GA **65** C2
Sanford, FL **63** D8
Sanford, ME **35** I2
Sanford, NC **73** C6
Sangamon (river), IL **89** E4
Sangre de Cristo Mountains, CO, NM **128** F7
Sanibel Island, FL **63** G7
Sanpoil (river), WA **151** B8
Santa Ana, CA **135** H5
Santa Barbara, CA **135** H4
Santa Catalina (island), CA **135** I5
Santa Clara, UT **149** H2
Santa Claus, IN **91** H2
Santa Cruz, CA **135** E2
Santa Cruz (island), CA **135** H4
Santa Cruz (river), AZ **119** G5
Santa Fe, NM **121** C5
Santa Maria, CA **135** G4
Santa Monica, CA **135** H5
Santa Monica Mountains N.R.A., CA **135** H5
Santa Rita, GU **154** G1
Santa Rosa, CA **135** D2
Santa Rosa (island), CA **135** H3
Santa Rosa, NM **121** D6
Santa Rosa and San Jacinto Mountains Nat. Mon., CA **135** H7
Santa Rosa Lake, NM **121** D6
Santa Rosa Range, NV **145** A4
Santee (river), SC **75** E8
Santee Dam, SC **75** E7
Sapelo Island, GA **65** G7
Sapelo Sound, GA **65** G7
Sappa Creek, KS **94** A2
Sapulpa, OK **123** B10
Saraland, AL **59** H1
Saranac Lake, NY **45** B8
Sarasota, FL **63** F6
Saratoga, WY **153** G7
Saratoga N.H.P., NY **45** D8
Saratoga Springs, NY **45** D8
Sardis Lake, MS **71** B3
Sardis Lake, OK **123** D11
Sassafras (bay), MD **37** B9
Sassafras Mountain, SC **74** A2
Satilla (river), GA **65** H5
Saugatuck Reservoir, CT **31** E2
Saugus Iron Works National Historic Site, MA **39** B7
Sauk Centre, MN **99** E3
Sault Sainte Marie, MI **97** C6
Saunderstown, RI **49** E4
Savanna, IL **89** B3
Savannah, GA **65** F7
Savannah, MO **101** B2
Savannah, TN **76** C3
Savannah (river), GA, SC **54** D6
Sawtooth N.R.A., ID **141** G3
Sawtooth Range, ID **141** F2
Saylesville, RI **49** B5
Sayre, OK **123** D5
Sayre, PA **47** A7
Sayreville, NJ **43** D4
Scantic (river), CT **31** B5
Scappoose, OR **147** B2
Scarborough, ME **35** H2
Schaumburg, IL **89** B5
Schell Creek Range, NV **145** D6
Schenectady, NY **45** D8
Schuyler, NE **103** C8
Schuylkill (river), PA **47** D8
Scioto (river), OH **107** C3
Scituate Reservoir, RI **49** C3
Scobey, MT **143** A10
Scott City, KS **94** C2
Scotts Bluff Nat. Mon., NE **102** C1
Scottsbluff, NE **102** B1
Scottsboro, AL **59** A4
Scottsburg, IN **91** G4
Scottsdale, AZ **119** F4
Scranton, PA **47** B9
Sea Islands, GA, SC **54** E6
Sea Isle City, NJ **43** I3
Seaford, DE **33** H5
Seaman Range, NV **145** F6
Searcy, AR **61** C5
Searsport, ME **35** F5
Seaside, OR **146** A1
Seaside Heights, NJ **43** F5
Seattle, WA **151** C4
Sebago Lake, ME **35** H2
Sebec Lake, ME **35** E4
Sebring, FL **63** E8
Second Lake, NH **41** A4
Sedalia, MO **101** D3
Sedona, AZ **119** D5
Sedro Woolley, WA **151** B4
Seekonk, MA **39** E6
Seekonk (river), RI **49** B5
Seguam Island, AK **133** H10
Selawik N.W.&S.R., AK **133** C5
Selby, SD **109** B6
Selbyville, DE **33** I7
Seligman, AZ **119** C3
Selinsgrove, PA **47** D7
Selkirk Mountains, ID **141** B1
Sells, AZ **119** H5
Selma, AL **59** E3
Selway (river), ID **141** D2
Seminoe Reservoir, WY **153** F7
Seminole, Lake, FL, GA **65** I2
Seminole, OK **123** D9
Semisopochnoi Island, AK **133** H7
Senatobia, MS **71** B3
Seneca, KS **95** A8
Seneca, SC **74** B1

Seneca Falls, NY 45 D4
Seneca Lake, NY 45 E4
Senecaville Lake, OH 107 E7
Sequatchie (river), TN 77 C7
Sequoia N.P., CA 135 F5
Sespe Creek N.W.&S.R., CA 135 H5
Severn (river), MD 37 C7
Severna Park, MD 37 C8
Sevier (river), UT 149 G3
Sevier Desert, UT 149 D3
Sevier Lake (dry lake), UT 149 E2
Sevierville, TN 77 B9
Seward, AK 133 F6
Seward, NE 103 D8
Seward Peninsula, AK 133 C4
Seymour, CT 31 D3
Seymour, IN 91 G4
Seymour, MO 101 F4
Seymour Lake, VT 51 A5
Shafer, Lake, IN 91 C3
Shaker Heights, OH 107 B6
Shamokin, PA 47 D7
Shannock, RI 49 F3
Sharon, CT 31 B2
Sharon, PA 46 C1
Sharpe, Lake, SD 109 D6
Sharpsburg, MD 37 B4
Shasta, Mount, CA 135 A2
Shasta Lake, CA 135 B3
Shawano, WI 111 D6
Shawnee, OK 123 D9
Shawneetown, IL 89 H5
Sheboygan, WI 111 F7
Sheenjek N.W.&S.R., AK 133 B7
Sheep Range, NV 145 G6
Shelburne, VT 51 C1
Shelburne Falls, MA 38 B2
Shelby, MS 71 C2
Shelby, MT 143 B4
Shelby, OH 107 C5
Shelbyville, IN 91 F4
Shelbyville, KY 67 B7
Shelbyville, TN 77 C5
Shelbyville, Lake, IL 89 F4
Sheldon, IA 92 A2
Shell Creek, NE 103 C7
Shell Rock (river), IA 93 B6
Shelley, ID 141 H5
Shelton, CT 31 E3
Shelton, WA 151 D3
Shenandoah, IA 93 F3
Shenandoah (river), VA 79 A8
Shenandoah Mountain, VA 79 C7
Shenandoah N.P., VA 79 B8
Shenipsit Lake, CT 31 B6
Shepaug (river), CT 31 C2
Sheridan, AR 61 E4
Sheridan, OR 147 B2
Sheridan, WY 153 A6
Sherman, TX 125 C7
Sherman Mills, ME 35 D5
Shetucket (river), CT 31 C7
Sheyenne (river), ND 105 C6
Shiloh N.M.P., TN 76 C3
Shinapaaru, MP 154 D1
Shinnston, WV 81 D5
Ship Bottom, NJ 43 G4
Ship Rock (peak), NM 121 A1
Shippensburg, PA 47 E6
Shiprock, NM 121 A2
Shoshone, ID 141 H3
Shoshone (river), WY 153 B4
Shoshone, North Fork (river), WY 153 B3
Shoshone, South Fork (river), WY 153 B3
Shoshone Mountains, NV 145 D4
Shoshone Range, NV 145 C4
Show Low, AZ 119 E6
Shreveport, LA 68 B1
Shrewsbury, MA 39 C5
Sidney, MT 143 B11
Sidney, NE 102 C2
Sidney, NY 45 E6
Sidney, OH 107 D2
Sidney Lanier, Lake, GA 65 B3
Sierra Nevada, CA 135 C3
Sierra Vista, AZ 119 H6
Sikeston, MO 101 F8
Silicon Valley, CA 135 E2
Siloam Springs, AR 61 A1
Silver City, NM 121 G2
Silver Lake, MA 39 D8
Silver Spring, MD 37 C6
Silver Springs, NV 145 D2
Simi Valley, CA 135 H5
Simpsonville, SC 75 B3
Simsbury, CT 31 B4
Sinclair, Lake, GA 65 D4
Sioux Center, IA 92 A2
Sioux City, IA 92 C1
Sioux Falls, SD 109 E10
Sipsey (river), AL 59 D1
Sipsey Fork N.W.&S.R., AL 59 B2
Sisquoc N.W.&S.R., CA 135 G4
Sisseton, SD 109 A9
Sissonville, WV 81 E3
Sitka, AK 133 F10
Sitka N.H.P., AK 133 G10
Si'ufaga, AS 154 I4
Siuslaw (river), OR 147 D2
Skagit (river), WA 151 B4
Skagway, AK 133 E10
Skiatook Lake, OK 123 B10
Skillet Fork (river), IL 89 G4
Skowhegan, ME 35 F3
Skykomish (river), WA 151 C4
Skyline Drive, VA 79 C8
Slatersville, RI 49 A3
Slaughter Beach, DE 33 G6
Slayton, MN 99 G2
Sleeping Bear Dunes National Lakeshore, MI 97 E5
Slide Mountain, NY 45 F8
Slidell, LA 69 F8
Smackover, AR 61 G4
Smith Canyon, CO 137 F8
Smith Island, MD 37 F9
Smith Mountain Lake, VA 79 E6
Smith, North Fork N.W.&S.R., OR 146 G1
Smith N.W.&S.R., CA 135 A1
Smithfield, NC 73 C7
Smithfield, UT 149 A4
Smithfield, VA 79 E10
Smoke Creek Desert, NV 145 C2
Smoky Hill (river), KS 94 C1
Smoky Hills, KS 95 B4
Smoky Mountains, ID 141 G3
Smyrna, DE 33 D5
Smyrna, GA 65 C2
Smyrna, TN 77 B5
Smyrna (river), DE 33 D5
Snake (river), ID, OR, WA, WY 128 B3
Snake N.W.&S.R., ID, OR 141 D1
Snake River Plain, ID 141 H4
Snohomish, WA 151 C4
Snow Hill, MD 37 F10
Snow, Mount, VT 51 H2
Snowflake, AZ 119 D6
Snyder, TX 125 D4
Socastee, SC 75 D9
Socorro, NM 121 E3
Soda Springs, ID 141 H6
Soddy-Daisy, TN 77 C7
Sol Duc (river), WA 150 C1
Soledad, CA 135 F3
Solomon (river), KS 95 B6
Solomon, North Fork (river), KS 95 B3
Solomon, South Fork (river), KS 95 B4
Solomons, MD 37 E8
Somers Point, NJ 43 H3
Somerset, KY 67 D8
Somerset, MA 39 E7
Somerset, PA 47 E3
Somerset Reservoir, VT 51 H2
Somersworth, NH 41 G5
Somerville, NJ 43 D3
Songsong, MP 154 D1
Sonora, TX 125 F4
Sonoran Desert, AZ, CA 119 F3
Sooner Lake, OK 123 B9
Souhegan (river), NH 41 I3
Souris (Mouse) (river), ND 105 B5
South (river), NC 73 D7
South Bass Island, OH 107 A4
South Bend, IN 91 A3
South Berwick, ME 35 I2
South Boston, VA 79 E7
South Burlington, VT 51 C2
South Charleston, WV 81 F3
South Hadley, MA 39 C3
South Haven, MI 97 H4
South Hero Island, VT 51 B1
South Hill, VA 79 E8
South Lake Tahoe, CA 135 D4
South Milwaukee, WI 111 G7
South Paris, ME 35 G2
South Pass, WY 153 E4
South Point; see Kalae, HI 139 G8
South Point, OH 107 H5
South Portland, ME 35 H3
South Sioux City, NE 103 B9
South Yarmouth, MA 39 E10
Southampton, NY 45 G10
Southaven, MS 71 A3
Southbridge, MA 39 D4
Southbury, CT 31 D3
Southern Pines, NC 73 C6
Southington, CT 31 C4
Southport, NC 73 E8
Southwest Harbor, ME 35 G5
Spanish Fork, UT 149 C4
Sparks, NV 145 D2
Sparta, NJ 43 B3
Sparta, TN 77 B6
Sparta, WI 111 F3
Spartanburg, SC 75 B3
Spearfish, SD 108 C1
Spencer, IA 93 A3
Spencer, MA 39 C4
Spencer, WV 81 E3
Spirit Lake, IA 93 A3
Spokane, WA 151 C9
Spokane (river), ID, WA 151 C9
Spokane Valley, WA 151 C10
Spoon (river), IL 89 D3
Spooner, WI 111 C2
Sprague (river), OR 147 F4
Spring (river), AR 61 A6
Spring Bay (dry lake), UT 149 A2
Spring Creek, NV 145 B6
Spring Hill, FL 63 D6
Spring Hill, TN 77 C5
Spring Lake, NC 73 C7
Spring Valley, NY 45 G8
Springdale, AR 61 A1
Springer, NM 121 B6
Springer Mountain, GA 65 B3
Springfield, CO 137 F9
Springfield, IL 89 E3
Springfield, MA 39 C3
Springfield, MO 101 F3
Springfield, OH 107 E3
Springfield, OR 147 D2
Springfield, TN 77 A5
Springfield, VT 51 G3
Springfield Armory National Historic Site, MA 39 D3
Springhill, LA 68 A2
Springvale, ME 35 H2
Springville, UT 149 C4
Spruce Knob (peak), WV 81 E7
Spruce Knob-Seneca Rocks N.R.A., WV 81 E7
Squam Lake, NH 41 F3
Squapan Lake, ME 35 C5
Square Lake, ME 35 A5
Squaw Creek N.W.&S.R., OR 147 D4
St. Albans, WV 80 F2
St. Andrew Sound, GA 65 H7
St. Anthony, ID 141 G5
St. Augustine, FL 63 B8
St. Catherine, Lake, VT 51 G1
St. Catherines Island, GA 65 G7
St. Catherines Sound, GA 65 G7
St. Charles, MD 37 D7
St. Charles, MO 101 C6
St. Charles (river), CO 137 E6
St. Clair, Lake, MI 97 H8
St. Clair, MI 97 H8
St. Clair Shores, MI 97 H8
St. Cloud, MN 99 E4
St. Croix (island), VI 155 I7
St. Croix (river), ME 35 D7
St. Croix (river), MN, WI 99 E5
St. Croix Falls, WI 111 C1
St. Croix Island International Historic Site, ME 35 E7
St. Croix N.W.&S.R., MN, WI 111 D1
St. Croix National Scenic Riverway, MN, WI 111 B2
St. Elias, Mount, AK 133 E8
St. Elias Mountains, AK 133 E8
St. Francis (river), ME 35 A4
St. Francis (river), AR, MO 61 A7
St. Francis, ME 35 A4
St. George, UT 149 H2
St. Georges, DE 33 C4
St. Helena Island, SC 75 H6
St. Helena Sound, SC 75 G6
St. Helens, Mount, WA 151 F4
St. Helens, OR 147 A2
St. Ignace, MI 97 D6
St. James, MN 99 G3
St. James, MO 101 D5
St. Joe (river), ID 141 C1
St. Joe N.W.&S.R., ID 141 C2
St. John (island), VI 155 G8
St. Johns, AZ 119 D7
St. Johns, MI 97 G6
St. Johns (river), FL 63 D8
St. Johnsbury, VT 51 C5
St. Jones (river), DE 33 E5
St. Joseph, MI 97 I4
St. Joseph, MO 101 B2
St. Joseph (river), IN, MI 91 A4
St. Joseph (river), IN, OH 91 B5
St. Lawrence (river), NY 45 A6
St. Lawrence Island, AK 132 D2
St. Louis, MO 101 D7
St. Louis (river), MN 99 D5
St. Lucie Canal, FL 63 F9
St. Maries, ID 141 C1
St. Maries (river), ID 141 C1
St. Marys, GA 65 I7
St. Marys, OH 107 D2
St. Marys, PA 47 B4
St. Marys, WV 81 D4
St. Marys (river), FL 63 B7
St. Marys (river), IN, OH 91 C5
St. Marys (river), MI 97 C6
St. Marys City, MD 37 F8
St. Marys Lake see Grand Lake, OH 107 D2
St. Matthew Island, AK 132 E1
St. Michaels, MD 37 D8
St. Paul, AK 132 F1
St. Paul, MN 99 F5
St. Paul, NE 103 C7
St. Paul's Church National Historic Site, NY 45 H8
St. Peter, MN 99 G4
St. Peters, MO 101 C6
St. Petersburg, FL 63 E6
St. Simons Island, GA 65 H7
St. Thomas (island), VI 155 G7
Stafford, CT 31 A6
Stafford Pond, RI 49 D6
Staffordville Reservoir, CT 31 A6
Stamford, CT 31 F1
Stamps, AR 61 G2
Stanley, ND 105 B3
Starkville, MS 71 C5
State College, PA 47 D5
Stateline, NV 145 D1
Staten Island, NY 45 H8
Statesboro, GA 65 F6
Statesville, NC 73 B4
Statue of Liberty Nat. Mon., NY 45 H8
Staunton (river); see Roanoke, VA 79 E7
Staunton, VA 79 C7
Stayton, OR 147 C2
Steamboat Springs, CO 137 B3
Steamtown National Historic Site, PA 47 B9
Steele, ND 105 E6
Steens Mountain, OR 147 F7
Stellwagen Bank National Marine Sanctuary, MA 39 B9
Stephenville, TX 125 D6
Sterling, CO 137 A8
Sterling, IL 89 B3
Steubenville, OH 107 D8
Stevens Point, WI 111 E5
Stillwater, MN 99 F5
Stillwater, OK 123 B9
Stillwater (river), OH 107 D1
Stillwater Range, NV 145 C3
Stilwell, OK 123 C12
Stockbridge, MA 38 C1
Stockton, CA 135 D3
Stockton Lake, MO 101 E3
Stone Mountain (site), GA 65 C3
Stones River N.B., TN 77 B5
Stonewall Jackson Lake, WV 81 D5
Stonington, ME 35 G5
Stony (river), AK 133 E5
Storm Lake, IA 93 B3
Storrs, CT 31 B6
Story City, IA 93 C5
Stoughton, MA 39 C7
Stoughton, WI 111 G5
Stowe, VT 51 C3
Stratford, CT 31 E3
Stratford Point, CT 31 E3
Stratton Mountain, VT 51 H2
Strawberry Reservoir, UT 149 C5
Streator, IL 89 C4
Strong (river), MS 71 F3
Strongsville, OH 107 B6
Stroudsburg, PA 47 C9
Stuarts Draft, VA 79 C7
Stump Lake, ND 105 C8
Sturbridge, MA 39 C4
Sturgeon Bay, WI 111 D8
Sturgeon N.W.&S.R., MI 97 D4
Sturgis, MI 97 I5
Sturgis, SD 108 C2
Stuttgart, AR 61 E5
Sudbury Reservoir, MA 39 C6
Sudbury, Assabet and Concord N.W.&S.R., MA 39 B6
Suffolk, VA 79 E11
Sugar (river), NH 41 G1
Sugar (river), WI 111 H5
Sugar Creek (creek), IN 91 E2
Sugar Creek (creek), IN 91 E4
Sugar Land, TX 125 F8
Sugarloaf Mountain, ME 35 E2
Suitland, MD 37 D7
Sullivan, MO 101 D6
Sullys Hill National Game Preserve, ND 105 C7
Sulphur, LA 68 G2
Sulphur, OK 123 E9
Sulphur Creek, SD 109 C3
Sulphur Springs, TX 125 C8
Summer Lake, OR 147 F5
Summersville, WV 81 F4
Summersville Lake, WV 81 F4
Summerville, SC 75 F7
Summit Lake, NV 145 A2
Sumner Lake, NM 121 D6
Sumter, SC 75 D6
Sun (river), MT 143 C4
Sun City, AZ 119 F4
Sun Prairie, WI 111 G5
Sunapee Lake, NH 41 G2
Sunapee, Mount, NH 41 G2
Sunbury, PA 49 C7
Suncook, NH 41 H4
Suncook (river), NH 41 H4
Suncook Lakes, NH 41 G4
Sundance, WY 153 B10
Sunflower, Mount, KS 94 B1
Sunland Park, NM 121 H4
Sunnyside, WA 151 E6
Sunnyvale, CA 135 E2
Sunset Crater Volcano Nat. Mon., AZ 119 C5
Superior, Lake, 84 B6
Superior, NE 103 E7
Superior, WI 111 A2
Surf City, NJ 43 G4
Surfside Beach, SC 75 E9
Surry Mountain Lake, NH 41 H1
Susanville, CA 135 B3
Susitna (river), AK 133 D6
Susquehanna (river), MD, NY, PA 37 A8
Susquehanna, West Branch (river), PA 47 C5
Susupe, MP 154 C2
Sutherlin, OR 147 E2
Sutton Lake, WV 81 E5
Suwannee (river), FL 63 C6
Swainsboro, GA 65 E5
Swanson Reservoir, NE 103 E4
Swanton, VT 51 A2
Sweet Home, OR 147 D2
Sweetwater, TN 77 C8
Sweetwater, TX 125 D4
Sweetwater (river), WY 153 E5
Sweetwater Lake, ND 105 B8
Swift (river), MA 39 C3
Sycamore, IL 89 B4
Sycan (river), OR 147 F4
Sycan N.W.&S.R., OR 147 F4
Sylacauga, AL 59 D4

Sylvania — Washburn, WI

Sylvania, OH **107** A3
Syracuse, NY **45** D5
Sysladobsis Lake, ME **35** E6

T

Table Rock Lake, MO **101** F3
Tacoma, WA **151** D3
Taconic Range, MA, NY, VT **45** F9
Tahlequah, OK **123** C11
Tahoe, Lake, CA, NV **135** C4
Tahquamenon (East Branch) N.W.&S.R., MI **97** C5
Taliesin (site), WI **111** G4
Talladega, AL **59** D4
Tallahala Creek, MS **71** G4
Tallahassee, FL **63** B4
Tallahatchie (river), MS **71** C3
Tallapoosa (river), AL **59** E4
Tallassee, AL **59** E5
Talleyville, DE **33** A5
Tallgrass Prairie National Preserve, KS **95** C7
Tallulah, LA **69** B6
Tamaqua, PA **47** D8
Tampa, FL **63** E6
Tampa Bay, FL **63** E6
Tampico, IL **89** B3
Tamuning, GU **154** F1
Tanaga Island, AK **133** H8
Tanana (river), AK **133** D7
Taneytown, MD **37** A6
Tangier Island, VA **79** C11
Tangier Sound, MD **37** F9
Tangipahoa (river), LA **69** E7
Taos, NM **121** B5
Tar (river), NC **73** B8
Tarboro, NC **73** B8
Tarpon Springs, FL **63** E6
Tarrytown, NY **45** G8
Ta'ü (island), AS **155** I5
Ta'ü, AS **154** I4
Taum Sauk Mountain, MO **101** E6
Taunton, MA **39** D7
Taunton (river), MA **39** E7
Tawas City, MI **97** F7
Taylors, SC **75** B3
Taylorville, IL **89** E4
Tazewell, VA **78** E4
Teche, Bayou (river), LA **69** G5
Tecumseh, MI **97** I7
Tecumseh, OK **123** D9
Tekamah, NE **103** C9
Tell City, IN **91** I3
Tellico Lake, TN **77** C8
Telluride, CO **137** F2
Telos Lake, ME **35** C4
Tempe, AZ **119** F4
Temperance, MI **97** I7
Temple, TX **125** E7
Ten Thousand Islands, FL **63** H8
Tenkiller Lake, OK **123** C11
Tennessee (river), AL, KY, MS, TN **54** C4
Tennessee-Tombigbee Waterway, MS **71** B5
Tensas (river), LA **69** C5
Terre Haute, IN **91** F2
Terrebonne Bay, LA **69** I7
Terry, MT **143** D10
Terryville, CT **31** C3
Teton (river), MT **143** B5
Texarkana, AR **61** F1
Texarkana, TX **125** C9
Texoma, Lake, OK **123** F9
Thames (river), CT **31** D7
Theodore Roosevelt Inaugural National Historic Site, NY **44** D1
Theodore Roosevelt Lake, AZ **119** E5
Theodore Roosevelt N.P. (Elkhorn Ranch Site), ND **104** D1
Theodore Roosevelt N.P. (South Unit), ND **104** D2
Thermopolis, WY **153** C5
Thibodaux, LA **69** G6
Thief River Falls, MN **99** B2
Third Lake, NH **41** A4
Thomas Stone National Historic Site, MD **37** D6
Thomaston, GA **65** E2
Thomaston, ME **35** G4
Thomasville, AL **59** F2

Thomasville, GA **65** H3
Thomasville, NC **73** B5
Thompson, CT **31** A8
Thompson (river), IA, MO **101** A3
Thompson Falls, MT **142** C1
Thomson, GA **65** D5
Thornton, CO **137** C6
Thousand Islands, NY **45** B5
Thousand Springs Creek, NV **145** A6
Three Mile Island, PA **47** E7
Three Rivers, MI **97** I5
Thunder Bay, MI **97** E7
Thunder Bay (river), MI **97** E6
Thunder Butte Creek (river), SD **109** B3
Thurmont, MD **37** A5
Ticonderoga, NY **45** C9
Tiffin, OH **107** B4
Tifton, GA **65** G4
Tillamook, OR **146** B1
Tillery, Lake, NC **73** C5
Tilton, NH **41** G3
Timbalier Bay, LA **69** I7
Timber Lake, SD **109** B4
Timberlake, VA **79** D7
Timms Hill (peak), WI **111** C4
Timpanogos Cave Nat. Mon., UT **149** C5
Tims Ford Lake, TN **77** C5
Timucuan Ecological and Historic Preserve, FL **63** A8
Tinayguk N.W.&S.R., AK **133** B6
Tinian (island), MP **154** D2
Tinton Falls, NJ **43** E5
Tioga, ND **104** B2
Tioga (river), PA **47** A6
Tiogue Lake, RI **49** D4
Tippecanoe (river), IN **91** B3
Tishomingo, OK **123** E9
Titusville, FL **63** D8
Titusville, PA **46** B2
Tiverton, RI **49** D6
Tlikakila N.W.&S.R., AK **133** E5
Toana Range, NV **145** B7
Toccoa, GA **65** B4
Toiyabe Range, NV **145** D4
Tok, AK **133** D8
Toledo, OH **107** A3
Toledo Bend Reservoir, LA, TX **68** D2
Tomah, WI **111** F4
Tomahawk, WI **111** C5
Tombigbee (river), MS **71** G6
Tombigbee (river), AL **59** G1
Tombstone, AZ **119** H7
Toms (river), NJ **43** E4
Toms River, NJ **43** F4
Tonawanda, NY **44** D2
Tongue (river), MT **143** E9
Tonopah, NV **145** E4
Tonto Nat. Mon., AZ **119** F5
Tooele, UT **149** C3
Topeka, KS **95** B9
Toppenish, WA **151** E6
Toquima Range, NV **145** E4
Toronto, OH **107** D8
Torrington, CT **31** B3
Torrington, WY **153** F10
Touro Synagogue National Historic Site, RI **49** F5
Towanda, PA **47** B7
Towner, ND **105** B5
Townsend, DE **33** D4
Townsend, MT **143** D5
Towson, MD **37** B7
Tradewater (river), KY **66** D3
Trans-Alaska Pipeline, AK **133** C6
Trask (river), OR **146** B1
Traverse City, MI **97** E5
Traverse, Lake, MN, SD **99** E1
Tremonton, UT **149** A3
Trenton, MO **101** B3
Trenton, NJ **43** E3
Trenton, TN **76** B2
Trinidad, CO **137** G6
Trinity (river), TX **125** E8
Trinity Islands, AK **133** G5
Trinity N.W.&S.R., CA **135** B2
Trinity Site, NM **121** F4
Trotwood, OH **107** E2
Troy, AL **59** F5
Troy, MI **97** H7
Troy, NH **41** I2
Troy, NY **45** E8

Troy, OH **107** E2
Trujillo Alto, PR **155** H11
Trumann, AR **61** B7
Trumbull, CT **31** E3
Truro, MA **39** D10
Truth or Consequences, NM **121** F3
Tschida, Lake, ND **105** E3
Tuba City, AZ **119** B5
Tuckahoe (river), NJ **43** H3
Tuckerman, AR **61** B6
Tucson, AZ **119** G6
Tucumcari, NM **121** C7
Tug Fork (river), KY, WV **67** C11
Tugaloo (river), GA, SC **65** B4
Tulare, CA **135** F4
Tularosa, NM **121** F5
Tulia, Lake, UT **149** C4
Tullahoma, TN **77** C5
Tulsa, OK **123** B10
Tumacacori N.H.P., AZ **119** H5
Tumwater, WA **151** D3
Tuolumne N.W.&S.R., CA **135** D4
Tupelo, MS **71** B5
Tupelo N.B., MS **71** B5
Turkey (river), IA **93** B8
Turlock, CA **135** E3
Turner Turnpike, OK **123** C9
Turners Falls, MA **39** B3
Turtle Mountains, ND **105** A6
Turtle-Flambeau Flowage, WI **111** B4
Tuscaloosa, AL **59** D2
Tuscarawas (river), OH **107** C6
Tuscarora Mountains, NV **145** B5
Tuscarora Mountain, PA **47** E5
Tuscola, IL **89** E5
Tuskegee, AL **59** E5
Tuskegee Institute National Historic Site, AL **59** F5
Tuttle Creek Lake, KS **95** B7
Tutuila (island), AS **154** I1
Tuxedo Park, NY **45** G8
Tuzigoot Nat. Mon., AZ **119** D4
Twin Falls, ID **141** I3
Twin Lakes, CT **31** A2
Two Butte Creek, CO **137** F9
Two Harbors, MN **99** D6
Two Rivers, WI **111** E7
Tybee Island, GA **65** F8
Tygart Lake, WV **81** D6
Tygart Valley (river), WV **81** E6
Tyler, TX **125** D8
Tyndall, SD **109** F9
Tyrone, PA **47** D4

U

Uhrichsville, OH **107** D7
Uinta Mountains, UT **149** C5
Ukiah, CA **135** C2
Ulysses, KS **94** C3
Ulysses S. Grant National Historic Site, MO **101** D7
Umbagog Lake, NH **41** B4
Umnak Island, AK **132** H1
Umpqua (river), OR **146** E1
Umpqua, North (river), OR **147** E2
Umpqua, South (river), OR **147** F2
Umsaskis Lake, ME **35** B4
Unalakleet, AK **133** D4
Unalakleet N.W.&S.R., AK **133** D4
Unalaska, AK **132** H2
Unalaska Island, AK **132** H2
Uncompahgre (river), CO **137** E2
Uncompahgre Plateau, CO **136** E1
Unimak Island, AK **132** G2
Union, MO **101** D6
Union, SC **75** B4
Union City, NJ **43** C5
Union City, TN **76** A2
Union Springs, AL **59** F5
Union Village, RI **49** A4
Uniontown, PA **46** E2
Unionville, CT **31** B4
University City, MO **101** D7
'Upolu Point, HI **139** D8
Upper Ammonoosuc (river), NH **41** C3
Upper Arlington, OH **107** E4
Upper Darby, PA **47** E9
Upper Delaware Scenic and

Recreational River, PA, NY **47** B10
Upper Iowa (river), IA **93** A7
Upper Klamath Lake, OR **147** G3
Upper Mississippi River National Wildlife and Fish Refuge, IA, IL, MN, WI **99** G6
Upper Missouri River Breaks Nat. Mon., MT **143** B7
Upper Peninsula, MI **97** C3
Upper Red Lake, MN **99** B3
Upper Rogue N.W.&S.R., OR **146** F1
Upper Sandusky, OH **107** C4
Urbana, IL **89** E5
Urbana, OH **107** D3
Urbandale, IA **93** D5
U.S. Military Academy, NY **45** G4
U.S. Virgin Islands (territory), US **155** E12
Utah Lake, UT **149** C4
Ute Creek, NM **121** B7
Utica, NY **45** D6
Utukok (river), AK **133** A4
Uvalde, TX **125** G5

V

Vail, CO **137** C4
Valdez, AK **133** E7
Valdosta, GA **65** H4
Valencia, NM **121** D4
Valentine, NE **103** A4
Vallejo, CA **135** D2
Valley, AL **59** E6
Valley City, ND **105** D8
Valley Falls, RI **49** B5
Valley Forge N.H.P., PA **47** E9
Valparaiso, IN **91** B2
Van Buren, AR **61** C1
Van Buren, ME **35** A6
Van Wert, OH **107** C2
Vanceburg, KY **67** B9
Vancouver, WA **151** G3
Vandalia, IL **89** F4
Vanderbilt Mansion National Historic Site, NY **45** F8
Vaughan, MS **71** E3
Vega Baja, PR **155** H10
Venice, FL **63** F6
Ventnor City, NJ **43** H4
Ventura, CA **135** H4
Verde (river), AZ **119** D4
Verde N.W.&S.R., AZ **119** E5
Verdigre Creek, NE **103** B7
Verdigris (river), KS, OK **123** A11
Vergennes, VT **51** D1
Vermilion (river), IL **89** C4
Vermilion (river), IL, IN **89** E6
Vermilion Cliffs Nat. Mon., AZ **119** A5
Vermilion Lake, MN **99** B5
Vermilion N.W.&S.R., IL **89** D5
Vermillion, SD **109** F10
Vermillion Creek, CO **136** A1
Vermillion, Middle Fork (river), IL **89** D5
Vernal, UT **149** C6
Vernon, CT **31** B6
Vernon, TX **125** C5
Vero Beach, FL **63** E9
Versailles, KY **67** C7
Vicksburg, MS **71** E2
Vicksburg N.M.P., MS **71** E2
Victoria, TX **125** G7
Vidalia, GA **65** F5
Vidalia, LA **69** D5
Vienna, WV **81** D3
Vieques Island, PR **155** I12
Villas, NJ **43** I2
Ville Platte, LA **69** F4
Vinalhaven, ME **35** G5
Vincennes, IN **91** G1
Vineland, NJ **43** G2
Vineyard Haven, MA **39** F8
Vineyard Sound, MA **39** F8
Vinita, OK **123** A11
Vinton, IA **93** C7
Virgin (river), AZ, NV, UT **145** G7
Virgin Islands N.P., VI **155** H8
Virginia, MN **99** C5
Virginia Beach, VA **79** E11
Virginia City, MT **143** E4

Virginia City, NV **145** D2
Viroqua, WI **111** F3
Visalia, CA **135** F4
Vivian, LA **68** A1
Volga, SD **109** D10
Voyageurs N.P., MN **99** B5

W

Wabash, IN **91** C4
Wabash (river), IL, IN **84** G7
Waccamaw (river), SC **75** E9
Waccamaw, Lake, NC **73** D7
Wachusett Reservoir, MA **39** B5
Waco, TX **125** E7
Waconda Lake, KS **95** B5
Wadena, MN **99** D3
Wagner, SD **109** F8
Wagoner, OK **123** C11
Wah Wah Mountains, UT **149** F2
Wahoo, NE **103** C9
Wahpeton, ND **105** E10
Wai'ale'ale (peak), HI **138** A2
Waialua, HI **139** B4
Waialua, HI **139** C6
Waikoloa, HI **139** E8
Wailuku, HI **139** C7
Waimea (Kamuela), HI **139** E8
Waipahu, HI **139** B4
Wake Island (territory), US **154** E2
WaKeeney, KS **95** B3
Wakefield, RI **49** F4
Walcott, Lake, ID **141** H4
Waldoboro, ME **35** G4
Waldorf, MD **37** D7
Waldron, AR **61** D1
Walhalla, ND **105** A9
Walker, East (river), NV **145** D2
Walker, MN **99** D3
Walker Lake, NV **145** E3
Walkersville, MD **37** B6
Wall, SD **109** D3
Walla Walla, WA **151** F9
Wallenpaupack, Lake, PA **47** B9
Wallingford, CT **31** D4
Wallingford, VT **51** G2
Wallkill (river), NJ **43** B3
Wallops Island, VA **79** C12
Wallowa (river), OR **147** B8
Wallowa N.W.& S.R., OR **147** B8
Wallula, Lake, WA **151** F8
Wallum Lake, RI **49** A2
Walnut (river), KS **95** E7
Walnut Canyon Nat. Mon., AZ **119** D5
Walnut Creek, KS **95** C4
Walnut Ridge, AR **61** B6
Walpole, NH **41** H1
Walsenburg, CO **137** F6
Walt Disney World, FL **63** D7
Walter F. George Reservoir, AL, GA **59** F6
Walterboro, SC **75** F6
Walters, OK **123** E7
Wamego, KS **95** B8
Wanaque, NJ **43** B4
Wanaque Reservoir, NJ **43** B4
Wapakoneta, OH **107** D2
Wapsipinicon (river), IA **93** A7
War in the Pacific N.H.P., GU **154** F1
Ware, MA **39** C4
Ware (river), MA **39** C4
Warner Robins, GA **65** E4
Warner Valley, OR **147** G5
Warren, AR **61** E5
Warren, MI **97** H8
Warren, MN **99** B1
Warren, NH **41** E4
Warren, OH **107** B8
Warren, PA **47** A3
Warren, RI **49** C5
Warrensburg, MO **101** C3
Warrensburg, NY **45** C8
Warrenton, VA **79** B9
Warrior, AL **59** C3
Warsaw, IN **91** B4
Warwick, RI **49** D5
Wasatch Range, UT **128** D5
Waseca, MN **99** G4
Washburn, ME **35** B6
Washburn, ND **105** D5
Washburn, WI **111** A3

Washington, GA **65** C5
Washington, IA **93** E8
Washington, IN **91** G2
Washington, KS **95** A7
Washington, MO **101** D6
Washington, NC **73** C9
Washington, NJ **43** C2
Washington, PA **46** E1
Washington Court House, OH **107** F3
Washington Island, WI **111** C8
Washington, Mount, NH **41** D4
Washita (river), OK **123** C6
Washita Battlefield National Historic Site, OK **123** C5
Wasilla, AK **133** E6
Wassuk Range, NV **145** D2
Watch Hill, RI **49** G1
Watchaug Pond, RI **49** F3
Water Valley, MS **71** B3
Waterbury, CT **31** C3
Waterbury, VT **51** C3
Wateree (river), SC **75** D6
Wateree Lake, SC **75** C6
Waterloo, IA **93** C7
Watertown, CT **31** C3
Watertown, NY **45** C4
Watertown, SD **109** C9
Watertown, WI **111** G6
Waterville, ME **35** F4
Watford City, ND **104** C2
Watkins Glen, NY **45** E4
Watonga, OK **123** C7
Watseka, IL **89** D6
Watts Bar Lake, TN **77** C7
Waubay Lake, SD **109** B9
Waukegan, IL **89** A5
Waukesha, WI **111** G6
Waukon, IA **93** A8
Waupaca, WI **111** E5
Waupun, WI **111** F6
Waurika Lake, OK **123** E7
Wausau, WI **111** D5
Wauseon, OH **107** B2
Wauwatosa, WI **111** G7
Waverly, IA **93** B7
Waverly, NE **103** D9
Waverly, OH **107** F4
Wawasee, Lake, IN **91** B4
Waycross, GA **65** H5
Wayne, NE **103** B8
Wayne, NJ **43** B4
Waynesboro, GA **65** D6
Waynesboro, MS **71** G5
Waynesboro, PA **47** F6
Waynesboro, VA **79** C7
Waynesburg, PA **46** E1
Waynesville, MO **101** E5
Waynesville, NC **72** C2
Weatherford, OK **123** C7
Webb City, MO **101** F2
Webster, MA **39** D5
Webster, SD **109** B9
Webster City, IA **93** C5
Weir Farm National Historic Site, CT **31** E2
Weirton, WV **81** A5
Weiser, ID **141** F1
Weiser (river), ID **141** F1
Weiss Lake, AL **59** B5
Welch, WV **81** H3
Weldon (river), MO **101** A3
Wellesley, MA **39** C6
Wellfleet, MA **39** D10
Wellington, KS **95** E6
Wells, ME **35** I2
Wells, NV **145** B6
Wells River, VT **51** D5
Wellsboro, PA **47** B6
Wellsburg, WV **81** B5
Wellston, OH **107** G5
Wellsville, NY **44** E4
Wellsville, UT **149** A4
Wellton, AZ **119** G2
Wenaha N.W.&S.R., OR **147** A8
Wenatchee, WA **151** D6
Wendover, UT **149** C1
Wentworth, Lake, NH **41** F4
Wessington Springs, SD **109** D8
West (river), VT **51** H3
West Allis, WI **111** G7
West Bend, WI **111** G7
West Chester, PA **47** E9
West Columbia, SC **75** D5
West Des Moines, IA **93** D5
West Fargo, ND **105** D10

West Frankfort, IL **89** H4
West Grand Lake, ME **35** E6
West Hartford, CT **31** B4
West Haven, CT **31** E4
West Helena, AR **61** D7
West Jordan, UT **149** C4
West Kingston, RI **49** F3
West Little Owyhee N.W.&S.R., OR **147** G8
West Memphis, AR **61** C8
West Milford, NJ **43** B4
West Monroe, LA **69** B4
West Okoboji Lake, IA **93** A3
West Palm Beach, FL **63** F9
West Plains, MO **101** F5
West Point, MS **71** C5
West Point, NE **103** B9
West Point, NY **45** G4
West Point, VA **79** D10
West Point Lake, AL, GA **65** D1
West Quoddy Head, ME **35** F8
West Rutland, VT **51** F2
West Seneca, NY **44** D2
West Warwick, RI **49** F4
West Wendover, NV **145** B7
West Yellowstone, MT **143** F5
Westbrook, CT **31** E4
Westbrook, ME **35** H2
Westerly, RI **49** G1
Western Kentucky Parkway, KY **67** D4
Westerville, OH **107** D4
Westfield, MA **38** C2
Westfield, Middle Branch (river), MA **38** B2
Westfield, NY **44** E1
Westfield (river), MA **38** C2
Westfield, West Branch (river), MA **38** C1
Westfield N.W.&S.R., MA **38** C2
Westminster, CO **137** C5
Westminster, MD **37** A6
Weston, WV **81** D5
Westport, CT **31** E2
Wet Mountains, CO **137** E5
Wethersfield, CT **31** B5
Wewoka, OK **123** D9
Weymouth, MA **39** C7
Wheatland, WY **153** F9
Wheaton, MN **99** E1
Wheeler Lake, AL **59** A3
Wheeler Peak, NM **121** B5
Wheelersburg, OH **107** G4
Wheeling, WV **81** B4
Whidbey Island, WA **151** B3
Whiskeytown-Shasta-Trinity N.R.A., CA **135** B2
White (river), CO, UT **149** D7
White (river), AR, MO **61** A2
White (river), AZ **119** E7
White (river), IN **91** D5
White (river), MI **97** G4
White (river), NE, SD **109** D5
White (river), OR **147** B4
White (river), VT **51** E3
White Butte (peak), ND **104** E2
White City, OR **147** F2
White, East Fork (river), IN **91** G3
White Earth (river), ND **105** B3
White Hall, IL **89** F2
White Horse, NJ **43** E3
White Lake, LA **69** H3
White Mountains, NH **41** E2
White N.W.&S.R., OR **147** B4
White Oak Lake, AR **61** F3
White Plains, NY **45** G8
White River, SD **109** D5
White River Junction, VT **51** F4
White River Plateau, CO **137** C2
White Rocks N.R.A., VT **51** G2
White Salmon N.W.&S.R., WA **151** F5
White Sands Nat. Mon., NM **121** G4
White Sulphur Springs, WV **81** G5
White Woman Creek, KS **94** C1

Whitefield, NH **41** D3
Whitefish, MT **142** B2
Whitefish Bay, MI **97** C6
Whitefish N.W.&S.R., MI **97** C4
Whiteriver, AZ **119** E7
Whiteville, NC **73** D7
Whitewater, WI **111** G6

Whitewater (river), IN **91** F6
Whitman, MA **39** D8
Whitman Mission National Historic Site, WA **151** F8
Whitney, Mount, CA **135** F5
Wibaux, MT **143** C11
Wichita, KS **95** E7
Wichita (river), TX **125** C6
Wichita Falls, TX **125** C6
Wichita Mountains, OK **123** D6
Wichita Mountains Wildlife Refuge, OK **123** D6
Wickenburg, AZ **119** E4
Wickford, RI **49** E4
Wiggins, MS **71** H4
Wilber, NE **103** D8
Wilburton, OK **123** D11
Wild Rice (river), MN **99** C1
Wild Rice (river), ND **105** F9
Wildcat Brook N.W.&S.R., NH **41** D4
Wildcat Creek, IN **91** D3
Wilder, VT **51** F4
Wildwood, NJ **43** I3
Wilkes-Barre, PA **47** C8
Will Rogers Turnpike, OK **123** B10
Willamette (river), OR **147** C2
Willamette N.W.&S.R., OR **147** D3
Willapa Bay, WA **150** E2
Willard, OH **107** C4
Willcox, AZ **119** G7
Willcox Playa (river), AZ **119** G7
William "Bill" Dannelly Reservoir, AL **59** F3
William H. Harsha Lake, OH **107** G2
William Howard Taft National Historic Site, OH **107** G2
William Preston Lane Jr. Memorial Bridge (Chesapeake Bay Bridge), MD **37** C8
Williams, AZ **119** C4
Williamsburg, KY **67** E8
Williamsburg, VA **79** D10
Williamson, WV **80** G2
Williamsport, MD **37** A4
Williamsport, PA **47** C7
Williamston, NC **73** B9
Williamstown, KY **67** B8
Williamstown, NJ **43** G2
Williamstown, WV **81** C3
Willimantic, CT **31** B7
Willimantic (river), CT **31** B7
Willimantic Reservoir, CT **31** B7
Willingboro, NJ **43** E2
Williston, ND **104** B2
Williston, SC **75** E4
Willmar, MN **99** F3
Willoughby, Lake, VT **51** B5
Willow Creek, UT **149** D6
Wills Creek, OH **107** E6
Wilmington, DE **33** A5
Wilmington, MA **39** B7
Wilmington, NC **73** D8
Wilmington, OH **107** F3
Wilson, NC **73** B8
Wilson Creek Range, NV **145** E7
Wilson Lake, AL **59** A2
Wilson Lake, KS **95** B5
Wilson's Creek N.B., MO **101** F3
Wilton, CT **31** E2
Wilton, ME **35** F3
Wilton, NH **41** I3
Winchendon, MA **39** A4
Winchester, IN **91** D6
Winchester, KY **67** C8
Winchester, NH **41** I1
Winchester, TN **77** D6
Winchester, VA **79** A8
Wind (river), WY **153** C5
Wind Cave N.P., SD **108** E2
Wind N.W.&S.R., AK **133** B7
Wind River Range, WY **153** C3
Windber, PA **47** E4
Windom, MN **99** H3
Window Rock, AZ **119** C7
Windsor, CT **31** B5
Windsor, VT **51** F4
Windsor Heights, IA **93** D4
Windsor Locks, CT **31** A5
Winfield, AL **59** C2

Winfield, KS **95** E7
Winnebag, Lake, WI **111** F6
Winnebago (river), IA **93** A6
Winnemucca, NV **145** B4
Winnemucca Lake, NV **145** C2
Winner, SD **109** E6
Winnfield, LA **69** C3
Winnibigoshish, Lake, MN **99** C3
Winnipesaukee, Lake, NH **41** F4
Winnisquam Lake, NH **41** G3
Winnsboro, LA **69** C5
Winnsboro, SC **75** C5
Winona, MN **99** G6
Winona, MS **71** C3
Winooski (river), VT **51** C2
Winooski, VT **51** C2
Winslow, AZ **119** D6
Winslow, ME **35** F4
Winsted, CT **31** A3
Winston, OR **147** E2
Winston-Salem, NC **73** B5
Winter Haven, FL **63** E7
Winterset, IA **93** E5
Winterthur Museum and Gardens, DE **33** A5
Winthrop, ME **35** G3
Wiscasset, ME **35** G3
Wisconsin (river), WI **111** E5
Wisconsin, Lake, WI **111** G5
Wisconsin Dells, WI **111** F5
Wisconsin Rapids, WI **111** E5
Wishek, ND **105** F6
Wissota, Lake, WI **111** D3
Withlacoochee (river), GA **65** H4
Woburn, MA **39** B7
Wolf (river), WI **111** D6
Wolf Creek, OK **123** B5
Wolf N.W.&S.R., WI **111** D6
Wolf Point, MT **143** B10
Wolf Trap N.P. for the Performing Arts, VA **79** B9
Wolfeboro, NH **41** F4
Women's Rights N.H.P., NY **45** D5
Wood (river), RI **49** F2
Woodall Mountain, MS **71** A6
Woodbine, NJ **43** H3
Woodbridge, VA **79** B9
Woodburn, OR **147** B2
Woodbury, NJ **43** F2
Woodland, ME **35** E7
Woodland Park, CO **137** D5
Woods Hole, MA **39** F8
Woods, Lake of the, MN **99** A3
Woodstock, VT **51** F3
Woodstown, NJ **43** G1
Woodsville, NH **41** E2
Woodward, OK **123** B6
Woonasquatucket (river), RI **49** B4
Woonasquatucket Reservoir, RI **49** B3
Woonsocket, RI **49** A4
Woonsocket, SD **109** D8
Wooster, OH **107** C6
Worcester, MA **39** C5
Worden Pond, RI **49** F3
Worland, WY **153** B5
World War II Valor in the Pacific, HI **139** C4
Worthington, MN **99** H2
Wounded Knee Massacre Site, SD **109** E3
Wrangell, AK **133** G11
Wrangell-St. Elias N.P. and Preserve, AK **133** E8
Wright, WY **153** C8
Wright Brothers National Memorial, NC **73** B10
Wrightsville Beach, NC **73** E8
Wupatki Nat. Mon., AZ **119** C5
Wyaconda (river), MO **101** A5
Wylie Lake, SC **75** A5
Wynne, AR **61** C7
Wyoming, RI **49** E2
Wyoming Range, WY **152** D2
Wytheville, VA **78** E4

X
Xenia, OH **107** E3

Y
Yadkin (river), NC **73** B4
Yakima, WA **151** E6
Yakima (river), WA **151** D6

Yalobusha (river), MS **71** C4
Yampa (river), CO **137** B2
Yankton, SD **109** F9
Yantic (river), CT **31** C7
Yarmouth, ME **35** H3
Yazoo (river), MS **71** E2
Yazoo City, MS **71** E2
Yellow (river), WI **111** D3
Yellow Dog N.W.&S.R., MI **97** C3
Yellowstone (river), MT, WY **143** C11
Yellowstone Lake, WY **152** A2
Yellowstone N.P., ID, MT, WY **152** A2
Yerington, NV **145** D2
Yoakum, TX **125** G7
Yocona (river), MS **71** B3
Yona, GU **154** F1
Yonkers, NY **45** G8
York, AL **59** E1
York, NE **103** D8
York, PA **47** E7
York, SC **75** A5
York (river), VA **79** D10
York Village, ME **35** I2
Yorktown, VA **79** D11
Yosemite N.P., CA **135** E4
Youghiogheny (river), PA **47** F3
Youngstown, OH **107** B8
Ypsilanti, MI **97** H7
Yreka, CA **135** A2
Yuba City, CA **135** C3
Yucca House Nat. Mon., CO **136** G3
Yukon, OK **123** C8
Yukon (river), AK **133** E4
Yukon Delta, AK **132** D3
Yukon-Charley Rivers National Preserve, AK **133** C8
Yuma, AZ **119** G2
Yuma, CO **137** B8
Yunaska Island, AK **133** G10

Z
Zachary, LA **69** F6
Zanesville, OH **107** E6
Zapata, TX **125** H5
Zeeland, MI **97** H5
Zion N.P., UT **149** G2
Zoar, Lake, CT **31** D3
Zuni, NM **121** D1
Zuni (river), AZ **119** D7

Previously released by the National Geographic Society as *National Geographic United States Atlas for Young Explorers.*
First edition copyright © 1999 National Geographic Society
Updated edition copyright © 2004 National Geographic Society
Third and Fourth editions copyright © 2008, 2012
National Geographic Society
Fifth edition released by National Geographic Partners, LLC, as *National Geographic Kids United States Atlas.* Fifth edition copyright © 2017 National Geographic Partners, LLC
Sixth edition copyright © 2020 National Geographic Partners, LLC

Since 1888, the National Geographic Society has funded more than 12,000 research, exploration, and preservation projects around the world. The Society receives funds from National Geographic Partners, LLC, funded in part by your purchase. A portion of the proceeds from this book supports this vital work. To learn more, visit natgeo.com/info.

For more information, visit nationalgeographic.com, call 1-877-873-6846, or write to the following address:

National Geographic Partners
1145 17th Street N.W.
Washington, DC 20036-4688 U.S.A.

Visit us online at nationalgeographic.com/books

For librarians and teachers: nationalgeographic.com/books/librarians-and-educators

More for kids from National Geographic: natgeokids.com

National Geographic Kids magazine inspires children to explore their world with fun yet educational articles on animals, science, nature, and more. Using fresh storytelling and amazing photography, *Nat Geo Kids* shows kids ages 6 to 14 the fascinating truth about the world—and why they should care. kids.nationalgeographic.com/subscribe

For rights or permissions inquiries, please contact National Geographic Books Subsidiary Rights: bookrights@natgeo.com

Designed by Kathryn Robbins

National Geographic supports K–12 educators with ELA Common Core Resources. Visit natgeoed.org/commoncore for more information.

The publisher would like to thank everyone who worked to make this book come together: Martha Sharma, geographer/writer/researcher; Suzanne Fonda, project manager; Angela Modany, associate editor; Rachel Kenny, designer; Hilary Andrews, associate photo editor; Mike McNey, map production; Maureen J. Flynn, map edit; Chris Philpotts, illustrator; Sally Abbey and Vivian Suchman, managing editors; Joan Gossett, production editorial manager; and Gus Tello and Anne LeongSon, design production assistants.

Trade paperback ISBN: 978-1-4263-3821-2
Trade Hardcover ISBN: 978-1-4263-3822-9
Reinforced library binding ISBN: 978-1-4263-3823-6

Printed in Hong Kong
20/PPHK/1

Photo Credits

Map Acknowledgments

There's always more ...
TO EXPLORE!

National Geographic Kids has the perfect atlas for kids of every age, from preschool through high school—all with the latest age-appropriate facts, maps, images, and more.

The atlas series is designed to grow as kids grow, adding more depth and relevant material at every level to help them stay curious about the world and to succeed at school and in life!

AGES 7-10

NATIONAL GEOGRAPHIC KiDS
BEGINNER'S
UNITED STATES ATLAS

AGES 11-14

NATIONAL GEOGRAPHIC KiDS
UNITED STATES ATLAS

It's your country. Learn it. Love it. Explore it.

PARENT'S CHOICE AWARD WINNER!

3 9082 14240 3180

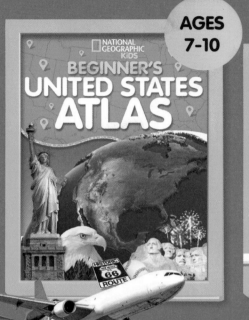

NATIONAL GEOGRAPHIC KiDS

AVAILABLE WHEREVER BOOKS ARE SOLD